GUIDE TO BETTER DUP

The *Guide To Better Acol Bridge* was written for _____ ___ are ambitious enough to improve their bidding skills beyond the ____ _____ f Acol bidding and wish to consolidate and advance your prowess, th _____ *r Acol Bridge.*

Once you start reaching the best contract regularly, yo _____ rer play does not let you down. The *Guide To Better Card Play* was ___ _____ _ls and defensive technique. It does not contain exotic and rare mat ____ _____ ____ you can give yourself the best chance to make the contracts you reach by pro _____ _ __nd foundation of fundamental declarer play. The other half dealing with defence covers the logic and methods needed to defeat contracts that can be beaten. Opening leads, signals and the later plays are all featured.

The *Guide To Better Duplicate Bridge* focuses on improving your tournament technique. Duplicate bridge requires special skills, both in the bidding and in the play. When playing pairs, it may not be enough to make your contract or to defeat their contract. Perhaps you need to make an overtrick, perhaps in defending it may be all right to allow their contract to make as long as you do not give declarer an undeserved overtrick. Your objective at matchpoints is to outscore the other pairs who will hold the same cards as your partnership. The *Guide To Better Duplicate Bridge* provides the bidding methods and strategy needed to do well at pairs, not only when the bidding involves only your side but also when both sides have entered the auction. Bidding today is far more competitive than it was only a decade ago and the player who is not familiar with the best methods will lag behind and not score as well as those who know their objectives and have the means to accomplish them.

Declarer play and defence may also have their own special requirements at duplicate. Each of the chapters includes material on declarer technique and defensive strategy appropriate to the pairs game. If you are used to playing rubber bridge, your thoughts are constantly on making your contract or defeating theirs. You may need to adjust your thinking to pairs strategy where your objectives are not always so clear. Nine tricks in 3NT will not be enough if the other declarers are scoring ten. Similarly, you cannot afford to let your opponents score eleven tricks in Four Spades if the other pairs are holding the contract to ten tricks.

This book is for you if you are serious about wanting to improve your duplicate skills. Naturally it will help if you have a partner as enthusiastic and ambitious as you are. If you and your partner adopt most of the bidding methods recommended in the *Guide To Better Duplicate Bridge* and you regularly follow the guide-lines for declarer play and defence geared towards matchpoint thinking, you should find that your scores will improve significantly. Winning is not everything but it still comes way ahead of losing. We all like to win, so follow the *Guide* and you should be a winner more often.

As time marches on, new methods appear. You will find some state-of-the-art bidding structures in the new appendices in this edition. For serious players, they are heartily recommended.

Ron Klinger first played for Australia in 1970 as a member of the team that won the Far East Open Teams Championship. Since then he has competed in the world championships in 1976, 1978, 1980, 1984, 1988, 1989, 1993 and 2000. He won the BOLS Brilliancy Prize as a player in 1976 and as a journalist in 1980. He won the Far East Open Pairs Championship in 1985 and 1987 and the South Pacific Zonal Teams Championship in 1993. In 1989 he was a member of the Australian team which reached the semi-finals of the Bermuda Bowl, the world teams championship. In addition to the many state and national titles to his credit, he is an Australian Grand Master and a World Bridge Federation World Master.

*He has written more than forty books, published locally and overseas, and has had books translated into several other languages. The **Guide To Better Card Play** won the Bridge Book of the Year Award in 1991, presented by the American Bridge Teachers Association. **Basic Bridge – The Guide To Good Acol Bidding & Play** is the standard textbook for those taking up the game. The **Guide To Better Duplicate Bridge** has been compiled from the many classes he has conducted on duplicate techniques.*

GUIDE TO BETTER DUPLICATE BRIDGE

Ron Klinger

CASSELL
IN ASSOCIATION WITH
PETER CRAWLEY

First published in Great Britain 1995
First paperback edition published 1996
This new edition first published 2002
in association with Peter Crawley
by Cassell
Wellington House, 125 Strand, London WC2R 0BB
a member of the Orion Publishing Group

A catalogue record for this book
is available from the British Library

ISBN 0-304-36320-0

Typeset by Modern Bridge Publications
P.O. Box 140, Northbridge NSW 1560, Australia

Printed in Finland by
WS Bookwell Ltd.

CONTENTS

INTRODUCTION

The *Guide* aims to improve your technique at tournament bridge. If some traditional methods have to be scrapped to achieve this, so be it. Out with the old, in with the new is not adopted for its own sake. Sticking with the old has no intrinsic merit either. What you need are methods which have a proven winning record and these are provided in the *Guide*.

If you are satisfied with the methods that you have been playing for the last 20-30 years, that is fine. Go right ahead. If you are prepared to admit that the tried and true are sometimes trying and not so true, you have the attitude to benefit from the *Guide*.

This *Guide To Better Duplicate Bridge* is for Acol players, but you can adopt and adapt many of the recommended methods no matter what system you play. Some of the material may be new to you but it is very likely that the *Guide* methods will be far more widespread in the coming years. Some will remember the sixties and seventies when negative doubles and transfers were the province of the expert pairs. Now they are part and parcel of the standard techniques of the competent club tournament player. Roman Key Card Blackwood, introduced only at the start of the eighties, has become the cornerstone of modern slam bidding.

The expert methods today, which will probably become routine in the years to come, are splinters, 2♣ puppet, Jacoby 2NT, Michaels cue-bids, Lebensohl, Rubinsohl and competitive doubles. A more contentious prediction is that multi-twos will spread through the bridge community as players realise that they can bid many more hands by starting with a multi. Just as transfers vastly expand your bidding capacity, so multi-openings do the same for weak hands which we would like to open but which do not meet the accepted criteria for one-openings.

Incorporate as much as you can but prefer to do it piecemeal. Too much too soon can overload your mind and your partnership. Cover an area with your partner(s) and cover it thoroughly. When you are confident you have mastered that area, move on to the next area.

The more modern and advanced approaches are included in the various chapters under 'Expert Methods' and in the Appendices. These are recommended for seasoned partnerships or very enthusiastic pairs.

Should you play 4-card or 5-card majors? The Acol system is based on 4-card majors. Despite what some bridge teachers and writers pontificate, the answer is that it matters very little whether you play fives or fours. The facts of life are that at international level about 2/3 of pairs play a system based on 5-card majors. The systems vary but they have in common that major suit openings at the one-level promise 5+ cards.

The reverse side of this coin is that 1/3 of pairs at top level play some 4-card major system. Do these pairs deliberately handicap themselves? Of course not. If you could prove that 5-card majors were superior, everyone would play them and every pair at the top would be playing 5-card majors. The fact that a significant minority of top class players play 4-card major methods is testimony that there is nothing fundamentally wrong with that approach.

You should play the methods with which you are comfortable. Given you are happy with 4-card Acol, stick with it. If you play it well, you will do well. No method will withstand poor application.

One area where 5-card majors tend to have an advantage is competitive bidding at the three-level. Knowing the number of trumps you and partner hold is an important factor in making sensible decisions at the three-level. Players who use 4-card majors and raise freely with 3-card support find much greater difficulty in determining whether the partnership holds seven, eight or nine trumps.

It is naturally important to read the text but do not omit the exercises and the sets of partnership hands for bidding practice. If you can arrange a group of four players, that is ideal for the bidding sets for four and for the 96 set play hands. You can sort out the cards for each player from the lists of hands at the back of the book and when the auction is over, consult the recommended bidding in the text or in the exercise answers also at the back of the book.

Standard terminology is used. LHO = left-hand opponent, RHO = right-hand opponent, advancer is the partner of the first defensive bidder (overcaller or takeout doubler). The + sign is used to mean 'or more', so that 16+ HCP = 16 high card points *or more*, 5+ suit = 5-card *or longer* suit. Bids in brackets are bids made by the opponents.

Above all, bridge is a game and is meant to be enjoyed. The best slogan for your partnership is *Cheerfulness in the face of adversity*. Keep your sense of perspective and play the game with a chuckle and a sense of humour. Above all, smile at partner, ruefully perhaps. If your partners do not have a smile, give them one of yours. Thus you can make sure that your game is always *happy bridging*.

Ron Klinger, 1995, 2002

FOR THE NEW TOURNAMENT PLAYER

HOW DUPLICATE BRIDGE IS PLAYED
(Skip this section if you are a regular duplicate player)

'Duplicate bridge' is the name given to organised bridge tournaments as opposed to social or rubber bridge which involves just four players. The main kinds of competitive bridge are pairs events and teams events.

Bridge is played internationally. In each odd-numbered year there are the Bermuda Bowl (World Open Teams) and the Venice Cup (World Women's Teams) in which 16 teams representing different geographical zones compete. Every four years in the 'Bridge Olympiad' a far greater number of teams compete. Regularly more than sixty countries have been represented at these Olympiads. In the other even-numbered years the World Bridge Federation conducts the World Pairs Championships (open pairs, women's pairs, mixed pairs) as well as the Rosenblum Cup (another World Open Teams). World Junior Championships (under-25) and World Senior Championships have been added recently.

Each country holds national championships and many tournaments of lower status. There are also tournaments to select the players who will represent their country.

Many clubs run an Individual Championship once a year. In pairs and teams events, you keep the same partner for each session and usually throughout the event. In an Individual each competitor changes partners after one, two or three deals. These events are not considered serious events since partnership understandings tend to be minimal. A polite nature and a calm temperament are the prerequisites to surviving an Individual.

Pairs events are more common than any other type of event. The advantage of duplicate is that the element of having good cards or bad cards is reduced to a minimum, since in general all players play exactly the same deals. Another advantage is that you can compete against the top players merely by playing in the same tournament. In few other sports could a novice compete against a world champion in a tournament. Duplicate also improves your game, since the hand records are available to check afterwards where you may have gone wrong.

There are some vital differences between duplicate and ordinary (rubber) bridge in regard to technicalities and strategy. Except at the first table, you will not shuffle and deal the cards. The cards come to you in a tray, called a 'board' and you must put the cards back in the correct slot after the deal has been played. The board is marked N, E, S and W, and must be placed properly on the table; the board also states which side is vulnerable and who is the dealer. During the play, the cards are not thrown into the middle of the table. The players keep their own cards in front of them, turning the card played face down after the trick is over. You are allowed to examine the trick just played only while your card remains face up. Tricks won are placed in front of you and perpendicular to the edge of the table ('pointing' towards partner). Tricks lost are placed in front of you and parallel to the edge of the table ('pointing' towards the opponents). After each deal is over, you still have your original thirteen cards in front of you and can see at a glance how many tricks have been won and how many lost.

Each board in tournament bridge is scored independently. In rubber bridge if you make a part-score you have an advantage for the next deal, but in tournament bridge you do not carry forward any scores. You enter the score for the hand played, and on the next board both sides start from zero again.

As each deal is totally unrelated to what happened on the previous deal, there are significant scoring differences at duplicate :
(1) Honours do not count (unless otherwise stated by the tournament rules).
(2) For bidding and making a part-score, add 50 to the trick total.
(3) For bidding and making a game not vulnerable, add 300 to the trick total.
(4) For bidding and making a game vulnerable, add 500 to the trick total.

The result you obtain on the board is entered on the 'travelling score sheet' at the back of the board. You may not look at that until the hand is over, since it contains a record of the hand and also how other pairs fared on the board.

Your score on each board is compared with the scores of every other pair that played the board. If you are North-South, your real opponents are all the other North-South pairs, not the particular East-West pair you play each time. On each board, a certain number of matchpoints is awarded. You receive 2 points for each pair whose score you beat, 1 point for each time you tie with the score of another pair and 0 for each pair whose score beats yours. If your score beats three other pairs, you receive 6 matchpoints. If your score is better than five pairs and ties with three others, you will score 13 matchpoints (5 x 2 plus 3).

The total number of matchpoints available on each deal is usually two less than the number of pairs who play the board. If 13 pairs play a board, the best score receives 24 matchpoints, a 'top', the next best score receives 22 and so on down to the worst score which receives 0, a 'bottom'. An average score would be 12 matchpoints. (Some countries score in single matchpoints, 1 point for beating another pair and ½ a point for each score with which you tie.)

The scoring is done once for the North-South pairs and then for the East-West pairs. Obviously, if a North-South pair scores a top, the corresponding East-West pair against whom they played the board gets a bottom. Each pair's points over all the boards are totalled and the pair with the highest number of points wins.

Tactics in pairs events differ from those in rubber bridge. Careful declarer play and defence are the order of the day. Every overtrick and every undertrick could be vital. They make the difference between good scores and bad scores. In rubber bridge, declarer's aim is almost always to make the contract and the defence's aim is to defeat it. At pairs the aim is to obtain the best possible score which may mean from declarer's viewpoint that making the contract is a secondary consideration while from the defenders' viewpoint, the possibility of giving away an overtrick in trying to defeat the contract may be unwarranted.

Being extremely competitive in the bidding is essential. Almost always force the opposition to the three-level on part-score deals. Be quick to re-open the bidding if they stop at a very low level in a suit. In pairs events, re-opening the bidding occurs ten times more often than at rubber bridge.

Minor suit contracts at the game zone should be avoided. Prefer 3NT to 5♣ or 5◇, even if 3NT is riskier, since making an overtrick in 3NT scores more than a minor suit game. On the other hand, it is not necessary to bid borderline games or close slams. The reward for success is not so great in pairs events as to justify 24 point games or 31 point slams. You should be in game or in slam if it has a 50% or better chance. If less, you will tend to score better by staying out of it.

Chapter 16 deals with the tactics that matter in teams events. Most of the time you will be competing in pairs events. What counts at duplicate pairs is how often a certain strategy will work for you, not the size of the result. If a certain action scores 50 extra points 8 times out of 10, but loses 500 twice, it is sensible at duplicate but ridiculous at rubber bridge.

Penalty doubles are far more frequent at pairs since players are anxious to improve their score. The rule about a two-trick safety margin is frequently disregarded since one down, doubled, vulnerable, may be a top-score while one down, undoubled, vulnerable, may be below average.

Safety plays which involve sacrificing a trick to ensure the contract almost never apply in pairs, unless the contract you have reached is an unbelievably good one. In an excellent contract, particularly one that has been doubled, play as safely as you can to make sure of your contract. Overtricks will not matter in such a case.

Much of the time your contract will be similar to that reached by most of the other pairs. On these deals you need to do better than the other declarers in the same contract. Adopt the line of play which will bring in the highest score most of the time. Failing in your contract may not matter. At pairs, each deal carries exactly the same number of matchpoints and each deal is worth about 4% of your maximum possible total. If you foul up one deal, say by losing 800, you can recover all the lost ground on another deal just by making one overtrick if that overtrick gives you a top board.

A most important point to remember is that a bidding system is not some secret between you and your partner. You and your partner are not allowed to have any secret understanding about your bids. That is against the Laws of the game. A bidding system is not a secret code. The opponents are entitled to know as much about what the bidding means as you or your partner. If they ask you what you understand by a certain bid of your partner's, you must tell them truthfully. Of course, partner's bid may be meaningless and if you cannot understand it, all you can do is to be honest and tell the opposition that you do not know what partner's bid means.

Similarly, if you do not understand the opposition's bidding, you are entitled to ask. When it is your turn to bid but before you make your bid, you ask the partner of the bidder 'Please explain the bidding.' You may ask during the auction or after the auction has ended, when it is your turn to play. Unless it affects your making a bid, prefer to wait until the auction is over. After all, the opposition might not understand their bidding either and when you ask, they may well realise their mistake.

If an irregularity occurs at the table, do not be dismayed if the Director is called. That is a normal part of the game and it is the Director's job to keep the tournament running smoothly and to sort out any irregularities.

CHAPTER 1
REVISE YOUR NO-TRUMP REBIDS

Standard Acol no-trump structure

12-14: Open 1NT.

15-16: Open 1-suit, rebid 1NT if available. If partner has responded at the two-level, rebid 2NT. With a choice of rebidding 1NT or rebidding in a suit below 1NT, choose the suit rebid.

17-18: Open 1-suit, rebid with a jump to 2NT or raise a 1NT response to 2NT.

19: Open 1-suit, rebid with a jump to 3NT.

After a two-level response, rebid 2NT with 15-17 and 3NT with 18-19.

20-22: Open 2NT.

23-up: Open 2♣ and rebid in no-trumps.

Problems with the jump-rebid of 2NT

As the jump to 2NT shows 17-18 points, it is not forcing. That leaves responder badly placed if wanting to play in a part-score other than 2NT.

WEST	W	E	EAST
♠ A 8 5	1♣	1♡	♠ 7 3
♡ A 9	2NT . . .		♡ K 7 6 4 2
◇ K 6 3			◇ Q 8 7 4 2
♣ A Q 7 6 2			♣ 8

Is there anyone who would pass 1♣ on the East cards? I hope not. What then after the 2NT rebid?

The best part-score for East-West is in diamonds, but 3◇ is forcing and might lead to a ridiculous 3NT. East's only weak options are to pass 2NT (which could work on a very lucky day but will usually be one down at least) or bid 3♡ (which will fail badly most days).

One measure of a system's efficiency is how many hands it can cope with effectively. The 2NT rebid falls down badly on this test. It is likely to pose an insoluble problem whenever responder has a weak, unbalanced hand without ambitions for game. How should these hands be bid?

WEST	W	E	EAST
♠ A K 5	1◇	1♡	♠ 7 3
♡ A 9 4	2NT . . .		♡ Q J 7 2
◇ K Q 6 3			◇ 2
♣ Q 6 2			♣ K 9 7 5 4 3

How can the partnership land in the sensible club part-score when a rebid of 3♣ is forcing? 3NT is likely to do badly on a 3-1 club break and even when clubs are 2-2, 3NT could still go down. Passing 2NT might work if clubs are 2-2, but then you could do better playing in 3♣ for +130 or +150. If clubs are 3-1, say South has A-J-x, then 2NT will bring no joy and yet 3♣ is still comfortable.

Even when a sign-off in 3♡ is indicated, you may be already too high.

WEST	W	E	EAST
♠ K Q 8	1♣	1♡	♠ J 7
♡ 10 9 3	2NT . . .		♡ Q J 8 6 4 2
◇ Q J 3			◇ 10 7 4
♣ A K Q 7			♣ J 3

In the real world, no East would pass 1♣, but it would come as no surprise to lose five tricks in 3♡ (and more in 2NT). To reach the three-level on these cards is living beyond our means, a concept with which we are all familiar.

Another problem is when responder has exactly a 5-card suit and lacks the values for game. Leave it in 2NT and you could be in the wrong part-score:

WEST	W	E	EAST
♠ A 8 5	1♣	1♡	♠ 7 3
♡ A 8 3	2NT . . .		♡ K 7 6 4 2
◇ Q J 3			◇ K 7 4
♣ A K 7 4			♣ 9 3 2

If East passes 2NT, there is every prospect of losing four spades, one diamond and one heart. With only seven obvious tricks, you need to develop at least one more, but even if hearts are 3-2, they may have their 6+ tricks before you have your eight.

Playing in hearts, you will succeed on the normal 3-2 trump break. If you do decide to remove 2NT to 3♡, a doubtful decision, you could find this :

WEST	W	E	EAST
♠ A 8 5	1♣	1♡	♠ 7 3
♡ 9 3	2NT . . .		♡ K 7 6 4 2
◇ A 10 3			◇ K 7 4
♣ A K Q 7 4			♣ 9 3 2

Now the 3-2 club break sees 2NT home while 3♡ could easily lose four trump tricks and a spade.

What should responder do over 2NT with a weak hand and support for opener's minor?

WEST	W	E	EAST
♠ A 7 2	1♣	1♠	♠ K 5 4 3
♡ A 9 5	2NT . . .		♡ 6 4
◇ K 9 3 2			◇ Q J 8 4
♣ K Q J			♣ 8 5 2

In 2NT, you would lose four hearts and two aces most of the time. In 3◇, if the diamonds are 3-2, you have nine easy tricks. It is true that if the hearts are 4-4, 2NT will make but the chance of a 4-4 break is only about 33%. Playing in 2NT brings a good board 1/3 of the time while playing in 3◇ achieves the better result 2/3 of the time. At pairs, frequency is the critical factor.

3♢ could be even more clearcut :

WEST	W	E	EAST
♠ A 7 2	1♣	1♠	♠ K Q 4 3
♡ A 9 5	2NT . . .		♡ 6
♢ K 8 6 3			♢ J 7 5 4 2
♣ K Q J			♣ 8 5 2

On a heart lead, 2NT is virtually hopeless while 3♢ should make easily, probably with an overtrick. 5♢ is not a good bet as it requires ace-doubleton in diamonds with South, about a 20% chance.

What's the problem, you ask? Why not just bid 3♢, to play, on the preceding two East hands? Quite right, but what should responder do then with a game-going hand with support for opener? If 3♢ is to play, what should responder do with 9-10 points and 4 spades - 5 diamonds or 5 spades - 4 diamonds? To bid 3♢ misses game. To bid 4♢ may bypass the better game contract and to bid 3♠ with five spades may also miss the best spot.

WEST	W	E	EAST
♠ A 7 2	1♣	1♠	♠ K Q 4 3
♡ A 9 5	2NT . . .		♡ 6
♢ K Q J			♢ 8 6 3
♣ K 8 6 3			♣ A 7 5 4 2

Most pairs would land in 3NT which requires the clubs to be 2-2 (assuming a heart lead and the normal 5-4 split). Yet if clubs are 2-2, about a 40% chance, you should be in 6♣. Despite the general advice against minor suit games, you will usually do better in 5♣ than in 3NT on these cards.

However, the two hands could be:

WEST	W	E	EAST
♠ A 7 2	1♣	1♠	♠ K Q 4 3
♡ K Q J	2NT . . .		♡ 6
♢ A 9 5			♢ 8 6 3
♣ K 8 6 3			♣ A 7 5 4 2

Now 3NT is much better than 5♣. On a diamond lead, 5♣ needs not only clubs 2-2 but also the spades 3-3. Total chance is about 15%. While a diamond lead may make 3NT awkward, a heart lead is far more likely. Now if clubs are 2-2 and spades 3-3, you have eleven tricks while you figure to make nine or ten tricks in 3NT even if clubs happen to be 3-1.

Responder cannot bid 3♣, droppable, but having to choose a rebid of 3NT or 4♣ makes bidding no better than a lottery. What you need is more room for investigation.

WEST	W	E	EAST
♠ 7 2	1♣	1♠	♠ K Q 6 4 3
♡ A 9 5	2NT . . .		♡ 6
♢ A K 2			♢ 8 6 3
♣ K Q J 6 3			♣ A 7 5 4

3NT could easily fail after a heart lead. 6♣ is a good slam, better than 50%, and even 4♠ is better than 3NT. Yet if West had more in hearts and less in clubs, then 3NT would be the place to be.

Problems with the jump-rebid to 3NT

The jump-rebid to 3NT to show exactly 19 points has a number of flaws. The most troublesome is locating the best game contract.

WEST	W	E	EAST
♠ A 8 5	1♣	1♠	♠ 9 7 4 3 2
♡ A J	3NT . . .		♡ 7 6 4
♢ K 9 3 2			♢ A 7 4
♣ A Q J 6			♣ K 8

If West does not rebid 3NT, either the shape or the strength will be distorted. If West does rebid 3NT, how does the partnership reach 4♠, which needs little more than the 3-2 spade break? 3NT has eight tricks and very little prospect of more before the opponents come to five tricks or more.

The 3NT rebid curbs or eliminates game exploration. It replaces partnership co-operation with hope and prayer. The problem can also affect two-suiters.

WEST	W	E	EAST
♠ A J	1♣	1♠	♠ 9 7 4 3 2
♡ A 9 5	3NT . . .		♡ K 7 6 4
♢ K 9 3			♢ Q 4
♣ A Q J 6 3			♣ K 8

It would be silly for East to bid on as 3NT is easily the best spot with 4♡ or 4♠ in jeopardy. Yet, if East does pass, what if the hands looked like this?

WEST	W	E	EAST
♠ K Q	1♣	1♠	♠ 9 7 4 3 2
♡ A 9 5 2	3NT . . .		♡ K 7 6 4
♢ K 9 3			♢ Q 4
♣ A Q J 6			♣ K 8

Here 3NT has excellent chances for failure and 4♡ needs little more than a 3-2 break. Even if you do happen to make 3NT, you will score more in 4♡.

The hands could also be :

WEST	W	E	EAST
♠ K Q 6	1♣	1♠	♠ 9 7 4 3 2
♡ A 9 5	3NT . . .		♡ K 7 6 4
♢ K 9 3			♢ Q 4
♣ A Q J 6			♣ K 8

Here the best spot is 4♠. 3NT might be defeated on a diamond lead and even if it makes via two spades (♠A onside), two hearts, one diamond and four clubs, you will score more in 4♠. If the ♠A is onside, a 3-2 spade break gives you eleven tricks. Even if the ♠A is with North, you will make 4♠ most of the time while 3NT will usually fail.

All of the foregoing is just to illustrate the problems presented by standard methods. The aim is to cause you dissatisfaction with your approach to handling relatively ordinary problems. If you are unhappy with this state of affairs, if you want something better, you should try the following approach. It will not solve every problem but for most hands, it will enable you to judge more accurately and replace guesswork with method.

Revised Acol no-trump structure

12-14: Open 1NT.

15-18: Open 1-suit, rebid 1NT if available. If partner has responded at the two-level, rebid 2NT. With a choice of rebidding 1NT or rebidding in a suit below 1NT, choose the suit rebid.

19-20: Open 1-suit, rebid with a jump to 2NT.

After a two-level response, rebid 2NT with 15-up and 3NT with 19-20.

21-22: Open 2NT.

23-up: Open 2♣ (or 2◇ Benjamin) and rebid in no-trumps.

The 2NT structure is covered in Chapter 5 and Benjamin Twos are in Chapters 9, 10 and 11.

Bidding after opener's 1NT rebid (15-18)

One approach has responder's suit rebid of 2◇, 2♡ or 2♠ not forcing and not encouraging, with all game invitations travelling via the 2♣ checkback rebid (see Chapter 2). A jump to the three-level is game-forcing and a new suit jump shows a 5-5 pattern. Rebid structures for responder's game-going hands after the 1NT rebid are in Chapter 2.

Some of the problem hands seen earlier can now be solved easily.

WEST	W	E	EAST
♠ A 8 5	1♣	1♡	♠ 7 3
♡ A 9	1NT	2◇	♡ K 7 6 4 2
◇ K 6 3	No		◇ Q 8 7 4 2
♣ A Q 7 6 2			♣ 8

2◇ is an excellent contract and even if West bid 2♡, the partnership is in the realm of the rational.

WEST	W	E	EAST
♠ K Q 8	1♣	1♡	♠ J 7
♡ 10 9 3	1NT	2♡	♡ Q J 8 6 4 2
◇ Q J 3	No		◇ 10 7 4
♣ A K Q 7			♣ J 3

You will be able to smile smugly as you make eight tricks and contemplate those poor devils in 3♡.

WEST	W	E	EAST
♠ A 7 2	1◇	1♠	♠ K 5 4 3
♡ A 9 5	1NT	2◇	♡ 6 4
◇ K 9 3 2	No		◇ Q J 8 4
♣ K Q J			♣ 8 5 2

East's 2◇ rebid just says, 'We are safer in 2◇ than in 1NT and I have no ambitions for game.'

WEST	W	E	EAST
♠ A 7 2	1◇	1♠	♠ K Q 4 3
♡ A 9 5	1NT	2◇	♡ 6
◇ K 8 6 3	No		◇ J 7 5 4 2
♣ K Q J			♣ 8 5 2

Again the partnership can land in a low, safe, sensible part-score. In this type of auction, opener should normally pass when responder reverts to opener's suit. Although the major suit scores more, most of the time you will achieve a better result by playing in the better trump fit.

Bidding after opener's jump rebid to 2NT

As this shows 19-20 points, it creates a game-forcing auction. It allows responder to suggest an alternative contract without bypassing 3NT.

WEST	W	E	EAST
♠ A 8 5	1♣	1♠	♠ 9 7 4 3 2
♡ A J	2NT	3♠	♡ 7 6 4
◇ K 9 3 2	4♠	No	◇ A 7 4
♣ A Q J 6			♣ K 8

West might bid 4♣ over 3♠ as a cue-bid to show spade support and the ♣A. East would sign off in 4♠.

WEST	W	E	EAST
♠ A J	1♣	1♠	♠ 9 7 4 3 2
♡ A 9 5	2NT	3♡	♡ K 7 6 4
◇ K 9 3	3NT	No	◇ Q 4
♣ A Q J 6 3			♣ K 8

Having shown both majors, East has no anxiety about passing 3NT.

WEST	W	E	EAST
♠ K Q	1♣	1♠	♠ 9 7 4 3 2
♡ A 9 5 2	2NT	3♡	♡ K 7 6 4
◇ K 9 3	4♡	No	◇ Q 4
♣ A Q J 6			♣ K 8

West might also bid 4♣ as a cue-bid supporting hearts (see Chapter 15). East would sign off in 4♡.

Opener's no-trump rebids are a two-level response

2NT = 15-up. This is forcing since responder should have around the 10-point mark. Responder may suggest a signoff by rebidding his suit, for example, 1♠ : 2♣, 2NT : 3♣. This suggests 8-9 HCP and a 6-card suit. Opener should pass with 15 points or a poor 16. With better, bid on.

4NT over 2NT = quantitative try for 6NT. To ask for aces, bid a new suit first and follow up with 4NT.

3NT rebid by opener = 19-20 *and denies a 5-card major.* This is important since otherwise the superior 5-3 major suit fit can be missed. What if opener has a 19-20 5-3-3-2 pattern with a 5-card major? The recommendation is to rebid 2NT to allow responder to show 3-card support.

WEST	W	E	EAST
♠ K Q 8 7 2	1♠	2♣	♠ J 4 3
♡ A 9 5	2NT	3♠	♡ 6 4
◇ K Q 3	4♡	4♠	◇ A J 4
♣ K Q	No		♣ A 9 5 4 2

4♡ is a cue-bid showing the maximum 2NT hand. With the weaker variety, opener would just rebid 4♠ and leave slam bidding to East.

If East bids 3NT over 2NT, opener with 19-20 points should rebid 4NT and leave further action to responder.

Opener's 3NT rebid after a one-level response

As the 3NT rebid is not needed for a balanced hand, what should this rebid mean? A sensible suggestion is to use it for a 19-20 point 4-4-4-1 with a singleton in responder's suit. The rest is up to responder.

EXERCISES USING THE REVISED NO-TRUMP STRUCTURE

A. The bidding has started 1◇ : 1♠, 1NT. What should responder rebid with each of these hands?

1.	♠ A 9 5 3 2	2.	♠ Q J 7 4 2	3.	♠ K J 10 5 2	4.	♠ K 8 6 3	5.	♠ 9 8 6 4 3 2
	♡ Q 7 5 3		♡ J 8 7 5 3		♡ 9 8		♡ 3		♡ 8 5 2
	◇ 8 5		◇ Q 5		◇ Q 4		◇ J 7 4 3		◇ A J 2
	♣ 7 4		♣ 7		♣ 7 6 3 2		♣ Q 8 5 2		♣ 9

B. The bidding has started 1♣ : 1♠, 2NT. What should responder rebid with these hands?

1.	♠ 9 8 6 4 3 2	2.	♠ A 10 8 4 2	3.	♠ J 8 7 4 3	4.	♠ A K 7 3 2	5.	♠ A J 6 4 3
	♡ 8 5 2		♡ K 8 7 3		♡ A Q 6		♡ J 10 2		♡ Q J 9 4 2
	◇ A J 2		◇ 9 7 5		◇ 6 5 2		◇ 3		◇ 4
	♣ 9		♣ 4		♣ 7 3		♣ K 8 6 3		♣ 10 6

C. The bidding has started 1♡ : 2♣. What should opener do next?

1.	♠ J 8 7 3	2.	♠ A Q 9	3.	♠ A K 9	4.	♠ A Q 5	5.	♠ K J 8 3
	♡ A J 7 3		♡ K Q 8 7 2		♡ K J 8 6		♡ K Q 8 4 3		♡ A K 5 4
	◇ A K Q		◇ K 4 2		◇ A Q 2		◇ A 7 2		◇ K 4 2
	♣ 8 2		♣ Q 7		♣ Q 8 3		♣ A 3		♣ A J

PARTNERSHIP BIDDING : How should the following hands be bid? West is the dealer each time.

SET 1 — WEST	SET 1 — EAST	SET 2 — WEST	SET 2 — EAST
1. ♠ J 9 3	1. ♠ 8 6	1. ♠ J 9 7 6 2	1. ♠ K Q 4
♡ K 7 5	♡ Q 9 8 4 2	♡ A 3	♡ Q J 7
◇ A K 7	◇ Q J 5 2	◇ 5 3	◇ A K J 2
♣ A Q 4 3	♣ J 8	♣ J 10 7 3	♣ K 9 8
2. ♠ J 9 8 4 3 2	2. ♠ A 6	2. ♠ A 9	2. ♠ J 10 7 3 2
♡ - - -	♡ K Q 8 4	♡ Q 7 5 2	♡ A J 6 4
◇ A 10 7 2	◇ K 6 4	◇ A 8 5	◇ 7 6
♣ 6 5 2	♣ K Q 9 3	♣ A K Q 2	♣ 8 3
3. ♠ 9	3. ♠ K J 8 7 3	3. ♠ A Q 7 3	3. ♠ K 9 2
♡ A Q 6 2	♡ 8 5 3	♡ A J 2	♡ K 8 5 3
◇ A J 5 3	◇ Q 7 6 2	◇ A 6 3	◇ J 4
♣ A 7 5 4	♣ 2	♣ K J 5	♣ A 8 7 2
4. ♠ K 9 6 3 2	4. ♠ 5 4	4. ♠ A Q 8 7 3	4. ♠ K 9 2
♡ 3	♡ K 6 5 2	♡ A J	♡ K 8 5 3
◇ Q 8 5 4	◇ A J 7 2	◇ A 6 3	◇ Q 4
♣ J 6 3	♣ A K Q	♣ K J 5	♣ Q 8 7 2
5. ♠ A 8 3	5. ♠ Q 9 7 6 2	5. ♠ A Q 8 7 3	5. ♠ K 4
♡ A 7 6	♡ K 8 4 2	♡ A Q	♡ K 10 2
◇ K Q 9 7	◇ 8 5	◇ A 6 3	◇ J 10 5
♣ K Q 6	♣ J 5	♣ K 9 5	♣ A Q 8 7 2
6. ♠ A K 3	6. ♠ Q 9 7 6 2	6. ♠ A K 9 3	6. ♠ Q J 7 2
♡ A 7	♡ K 8 4 2	♡ A Q 5 3	♡ 7 2
◇ 9 7 4 2	◇ J 5	◇ Q 6 4	◇ A 2
♣ A K 4 3	♣ 8 5	♣ A 7	♣ K 9 5 4 2

PLAY HANDS ON REVISED NO-TRUMP REBIDS FOR OPENER
(These hands can be made up by using pages 176-183)

Hand 1: Staying low — Opening lead — Trump management

Dealer North : Nil vulnerable

NORTH
- ♠ 10 9 5 4
- ♥ J 8 5
- ♦ 8 3
- ♣ A 10 5 2

WEST
- ♠ K 8 6 2
- ♥ 7 2
- ♦ A 9 6 2
- ♣ 9 6 4

EAST
- ♠ A Q
- ♥ A Q 10 6
- ♦ K J 7 5
- ♣ J 8 3

SOUTH
- ♠ J 7 3
- ♥ K 9 4 3
- ♦ Q 10 4
- ♣ K Q 7

WEST	NORTH	EAST	SOUTH
	No	1◇	No
1♠	No	1NT	No
2◇	No	No	No

Bidding: East's 1NT rebid shows 15-18 and West's return to 2◇ denies any interest in game. Note the superiority of this sequence to one which starts 1◇ : 1♠, 2NT.

North is much too weak to compete over 2◇ and South's shape is too flat to take action.

Lead: King of clubs. A trump lead is out and to lead from a single honour such as J-x-x or K-x-x-x is dangerous. Better to lead from two honours than from a single honour.

Recommended play: North signals encouragement and South continues with the queen of clubs and a third club. North should then switch to a low heart, dummy's weak suit. East should finesse the queen, not the 10, as dummy has only a doubleton. South wins and returns a heart, won by East.

Declarer continues with a diamond to the ace and a diamond back to the jack, the normal technique with eight trumps missing the queen. The finesse loses to South and declarer makes just eight tricks.

Notes: (1) On a heart lead, East can make 10 tricks. The heart loser has vanished and East would now cash the A-Q of spades, cross to the ace of diamonds and play the king of spades, discarding a club. Careful play by East from here on would hold the losers to three.

(2) A spade lead gives East an overtrick as East can discard a club loser on the king of spades, as above.

(3) After winning the third club North should not play the fourth club. East would ruff and discard a heart from dummy whether South overruffs or not. East can now score nine tricks.

Hand 2: Choosing the trump suit — Taking a discard

Dealer East : N-S vulnerable

NORTH
- ♠ J 7 4
- ♥ Q 10 5
- ♦ 10 6 3
- ♣ K Q 10 9

WEST
- ♠ K 10 5 3 2
- ♥ K 8 6 3
- ♦ 8 4
- ♣ 6 3

EAST
- ♠ A Q 6
- ♥ A 9 7 2
- ♦ K Q 5 2
- ♣ A 7

SOUTH
- ♠ 9 8
- ♥ J 4
- ♦ A J 9 7
- ♣ J 8 5 4 2

WEST	NORTH	EAST	SOUTH
		1◇	No
1♠	No	2NT	No
3♥	No	4♥	All pass

Bidding: With two 4-card suits, it is usually best to open with the cheaper suit. East's 'revised' 2NT shows 19-20 points balanced and is forcing to game. West bids 3♥, showing at least 5 spades and 4 hearts. East could support spades or hearts. In such cases, prefer the 4-4 fit to a 5-3 fit. The 4-4 fit will often score more tricks than a 5-3 or even a 5-4 fit and at pairs, just one overtrick can mean the difference between a good board and a poor one. East could bid 4♣ over 3♥ as a cue-bid to show heart support and the ♣A. West would then sign off in 4♥.

Lead: King of clubs. Clearly the most attractive choice.

Recommended play: Take the ace of clubs. Cash the ace of hearts and the king of hearts. Leave the remaining trump out and start on the spades : ♠A, ♠Q, spade to the king. On the fourth spade discard dummy's losing club as North ruffs. You lose just one heart and one diamond. 11 tricks = +450.

Notes: (1) West must not duck the first club. Then you make only ten tricks.

(2) If North had two spades or fewer, North could ruff sooner and cash a club but West still makes ten tricks.

(3) If East-West play in 4♠, there is no way to avoid losing a club, a diamond and a heart. In spades, ten tricks are the limit. In hearts, eleven tricks are possible with a slightly lucky layout.

(4) What would West do if the bidding were to start 1◇ : 1♠, 3NT? Pass is the logical move since there is no guarantee of an 8-card fit in either minor. 3NT is a silly contract and should fail on a club lead but even if 3NT happened to make, you score much better playing in 4♥.

Hand 3: Slam decision at pairs — Declarer technique in an inferior contract

Dealer South : E-W vulnerable

NORTH
♠ 8 4
♥ A 10 7 6
♦ Q J 5
♣ A K 7 6

WEST
♠ K 9 7 3 2
♥ 9 3 2
♦ 10 9 7
♣ Q 8

EAST
♠ 10 6 5
♥ J 4
♦ 6 4 2
♣ J 10 9 3 2

SOUTH
♠ A Q J
♥ K Q 8 5
♦ A K 8 3
♣ 5 4

WEST	NORTH	EAST	SOUTH
			1♦
No	1♥	No	2NT
No	3♣	No	4♥
No	4NT	No	5♥
No	5NT	No	6♥
No	No	No	

Bidding: South uses the 2NT game-force rebid to show the high card strength (19-20) and the balanced nature of the hand. South intends to revert to 4♥ if North bids 3NT. North might bid 6NT over 2NT but chooses 3♣ in case a club slam is possible. South's 4♥ shows 4-card support (3♥ would be 3-card preference). North checks on aces and kings and wrongly chooses 6♥ instead of 6NT. However, 6♥ is the contract to be played.

Lead: Jack of clubs. As it happens, a spade lead works better but the club lead is the normal choice.

Recommended play: North wins the lead and draws trumps. The diamonds are cashed and a spade is discarded from hand on the fourth diamond. Next comes the ace of spades followed by the queen of spades. If West plays low, discard a club. If West covers, North ruffs and dummy's ♠J is a winner. North-South thus make thirteen tricks for a probable top board.

Notes: (1) North should realise as soon as dummy appears that choosing 6♥ was a poor decision. With N-S holding 35 HCP, almost every pair will be in 6NT once a king is found to be missing.

If the king of spades is with East, everyone in 6NT will make 13 tricks via the repeated spade finesse. North cannot beat those pairs by taking the spade finesse the same way. Therefore North plays for the ♠K to be with West and takes the ruffing finesse line. If this works, North will outscore those in 6NT. If not, the score will hardly be worse. The trouble with obtaining a top this way is that it is unlikely to improve North's bidding.

(2) North could play to ruff two clubs in dummy to make 13 tricks but this may not succeed (and does not on the actual deal) and it will not help if the ♠K is with East. North should therefore play for West to hold the ♠K.

Hand 4: Trump management — Power of the 4-4 fit

Dealer West : Both vulnerable

NORTH
♠ A 7 5 3
♥ A 8 4 2
♦ K 3
♣ A K J

WEST
♠ K Q J
♥ Q J 7 3
♦ 10 5 2
♣ 8 6 4

EAST
♠ 10 9
♥ K 10 6
♦ Q J 7 4
♣ 7 5 3 2

SOUTH
♠ 8 6 4 2
♥ 9 5
♦ A 9 8 6
♣ Q 10 9

WEST	NORTH	EAST	SOUTH
No	1♥	No	1♠
No	2NT	No	3NT
No	4♠	All pass	

Bidding: South should not bypass the spade suit despite it's weakness. *Sic transit gloria mundane.* Note how convenient it is for North to use the jump to 2NT to create a game-force. This allows opener to describe strength and shape. The corollary is that when opener uses the game raise (4♠ here), this will not be a balanced hand. South innocently raises 2NT to 3NT and then opener reveals the concealed support. North could bid 4♣ over 3NT, a cue-bid with spade support. South would sign off in 4♠.

Lead: King of spades. The sequence lead is the safest and is attractive in reducing the North-South's ruffing potential.

Recommended play: South should duck the first spade and if West leads a second round, take the next spade. South continues with a diamond to the king, a diamond to the ace and a diamond ruff. The jack of clubs is led and overtaken by South's queen, followed by the fourth diamond, ruffed in dummy if West does not over-ruff first. Declarer scores ten tricks, losing just one heart and two trump tricks.

Notes: (1) On some other lead, best technique with such a trump combination is to duck the first round. On regaining the lead, cash ♠A and leave the top trump out. When West leads a trump, declarer adopts the same approach, ducking the first round. Winning the first spade is slightly risky but works on the actual deal.

(2) Playing ace and another spade would allow West to draw a third round of trumps and South would fail.

(3) Notice the power of the 4-4 fit in spades. There are only eight tricks in no-trumps but played in spades and with the spades 3-2, the 4-4 fit generates two extra tricks.

CHAPTER 2

BIDDING AFTER OPENER'S 1NT REBID

After the bidding has started, 1X : 1Y, 1NT (the recommended range for opener is 15-18 points) responder will have one of three objectives, to sign off in a part-score, to invite game or to insist on game.

Standard part-score sign off

Responder may pass 1NT. Without excellent shape, hands below 8 HCP should usually sign off. Responder's rebid of 2♢, 2♡ or 2♠ over 1NT indicates no desire for game unless the rebid is in a suit higher-ranking than the suit originally bid by responder. If responder repeats his own suit, opener should pass. If responder reverts to opener's suit (other than 2♣), opener should pass.

WEST	EAST	
1♣	1♡	A new suit lower-ranking than
1NT	2♢ . . .	responder's first suit asks opener to give a preference.

Opener should usually choose the suit where greater length is held. With 2-card major support and 3-card minor support, it is reasonable to revert to the major. With support for the major and a good fit in both of responder's suits, opener may raise the major to the three-level if opener is maximum.

WEST	W	E	EAST
♠Q J 8	1♢	1♠	♠K 9 7 5 2
♡A K 4	1NT	2♡	♡J 10 8 5 3
♢A 8 7 2	?		♢J 5
♣A 8 3			♣7

Opener has two honours in each of responder's suits and has aces in responder's short suits. With an absolutely maximum 1NT rebid, opener should bid 3♠, not 2♠, and responder should bid game. Give West ♢K-x-x-x and ♣K-J-x and 2♠ is plenty.

For responder's sign off in clubs, see later.

Game invitation using 2♣ 'checkback'

With 8-9 HCP, responder is worth an invitation to game. With good shape, 7 HCP will do.

All game invitations travel through a 2♣ rebid by responder. The 2♣ checkback is artificial and asks opener to indicate hand strength.

Opener can reveal three hand strengths:

2♢ = absolutely minimum. 15 HCP or very poor 16.
2♡ / 2♠ / 2NT = 16 HCP or a particularly bad 17.
3-level bids = 17-18, game-forcing.

What makes for a bad 16 or 17? The 4-3-3-3 pattern is a poor feature. Suits with unsupported jacks or queens should also be downgraded.

When choosing 2♡/2♠/2NT or a three-level rebid, bid the cheapest suitable feature. Bypassing a suit denies a relevant holding in that suit. Bidding an 'impossible' suit shows a strong stopper in that suit.

WEST	EAST	
1♣	1♡	2♢ = absolutely minimum, 2♡ = 3-card support, 2♠ = a strong spade stopper but denies three hearts. 2NT denies three hearts.
1NT	2♣	
?		

The three-level bids = 17-18 points, 3♣ = five clubs, 3♢ = four diamonds, 3♡ = 3-card heart support, 3♠ shows strong spades (and suggests worry about diamonds) and denies three hearts, while 3NT denies three hearts, either 3-2-4-4 or 3-2-3-5, but opener judges the long suit(s) do not merit showing, given responder has only 8-9 points. There is no need to tell the opposition too much unless it is necessary for finding the best contract. Thus, the rebids of 3♣ or 3♢ would indicate concern about 3NT as the right spot. 3♣ or 3♢ does not deny three hearts. Responder should rebid a five-card major.

WEST	W	E	EAST
♠A 6 4	1♣	1♡	♠Q 5
♡Q J 8	1NT	2♣	♡K 9 7 5 2
♢K Q 3	2♢	2♡	♢J 5 2
♣K 8 7 2	No		♣Q 6 4

2♢ = absolutely minimum 1NT rebid.

WEST	W	E	EAST
♠A K 4	1♣	1♡	♠Q 5
♡Q J 8	1NT	2♣	♡K 9 7 5 2
♢K Q 3	3♡	4♡	♢J 5 2
♣K 8 7 2	No		♣Q 6 4

3♡ = 17-18 points with three hearts.

WEST	EAST	
1♢	1♠	2♢ = absolutely minimum, 2♡ = four hearts, 2♠ = three spades and denies four hearts. 2NT denies 3 spades and also denies 4 hearts.
1NT	2♣	
?		

The 2♢ rebid does not show five diamonds. It is wholly artificial and just shows minimum points. Over 2♢, responder can pass, bid 2♡ / 2♠, natural, or bid 2NT without four hearts or five spades.

If opener rebids at the three-level (17-18), 3♣ = four clubs, perhaps 4-4, perhaps 5-4 in the minors. 3♢ = five diamonds and may yet have three spades. 3♡ = four hearts and may still have three spades. 3♠ = three spades and denies four hearts, while 3NT denies three spades and denies four hearts.

Over 3♣, 3♢ or 3♡, responder should bid 3♠ with a 5-card suit. Opener may have 3-card support.

WEST	W	E	EAST
♠J 6 4	1♢	1♠	♠K Q 10 5 3
♡Q 8	1NT	2♣	♡K 9
♢A Q J 7 3	3♢	3♠	♢5 2
♣A K J	4♠	No	♣7 6 4 2

3♢ = 17-18 points with five diamonds

Responder's game-forcing rebids

A new suit rebid at the two-level in a higher-ranking suit

WEST	EAST	
1◇	1♡	East's 2♠ is a game-force and shows 4 spades and 4+ hearts.
1NT	2♠ . . .	Further bidding is natural.

WEST	EAST	
1♣	1◇	2♡ = game-force with 4 hearts and 4+ diamonds. Responder is
1NT	2♡ . . .	worried about no-trumps.

A jump rebid to the three-level
(a) In a new suit

If the second suit is spades, hearts or diamonds, this promises five cards in the second suit. If the second suit is clubs, 4+ clubs are promised.

Opener should support one of responder's suits if possible. Otherwise bid 3NT with both of the other suits securely stopped.

WEST	EAST	
1◇	1♠	East has 5+ spades and 5 hearts and enough for game. East may
1NT	3♡ . . .	have ambitions for slam.

If opener wishes to support spades, 3♠ is strong support and 4♠ is weaker support. To support hearts, 4♡ is the weaker version and a cue-bid of 4♣ or 4◇ is a strong raise in hearts.

(b) In responder's original suit

This shows a 6-card suit and suggests slam possibilities. With a 6-card major, responder could rebid at game-level.

WEST	EAST	
1◇	1♠	3♠ is game-forcing with 6+
1NT	3♠ . . .	spades.

If opener is among those who might rebid 1NT with a singleton in responder's suit, opener now bids 3NT to show a singleton spade. Otherwise, 3NT = a rag doubleton in responder's suit. With better support, raise the major to the four-level as a weak raise and bid a new suit as a cue-bid with a strong raise.

(c) In opener's minor suit

The jump rebid in opener's minor suit shows 4+ support but perhaps only a 4-card major.

WEST	EAST	
1◇	1♡	East's 3◇ is forcing to game and shows 4+ diamonds. East may
1NT	3◇ . . .	have 4 hearts or 5 hearts.

Opener's first priority is to show 3-card support for the hearts with 3♡. If responder does not wish to play in hearts, responder can now rebid 3NT or revert to opener's minor.

With only a doubleton in hearts, opener may bid 3NT with strength in the unbid suits, make a stopper bid in one of the unbid suits or pursue a slam in diamonds with a cue-bid of 4♣ or a raise to 4◇. In the auction above, a bid of 3♠ shows a stopper in spades and concern about clubs for 3NT.

(d) When the opening bid is 1♡

WEST	EAST	
1♡	1♠	East's 3♡ is a game-force with three hearts. Responder may
1NT	3♡ . . .	have four or five spades.

With 4 hearts, opener bids 3♠ with 3-card support, 3NT otherwise. With 5 hearts, opener bids 4♡ if weak or, if possible, cue-bids 4♣/4◇ when maximum.

Responder's 2NT rebid

Since all invitational hands travel via 2♣, responder does not need a 2NT rebid as an invitation. The 2NT rebid demands that opener bids 3♣, a 'puppet' bid. Responder may then—

(a) Pass. *This is the weak sign-off in clubs.*

(b) Bid a new suit. This shows a 5-4 pattern whereas the immediate jump to the three-level shows a 5-5 pattern. The ability to show the extra length in the second suit is a valuable feature.

(c) Rebid in responder's original suit. This shows exactly a 5-card suit while the immediate jump rebid of responder's suit shows a 6+ suit.

(d) Rebid in opener's suit.

This shows 5+ diamonds if the opening was 1◇ and 4+ hearts if the opening bid was 1♡. There is nothing comparable if the opening bid was 1♣ : use the jump rebid to 3♣. In the case of the 3♡ rebid, responder has slam ambitions since a 4♡ rebid would have been chosen otherwise.

(e) Rebid 3NT

This sequence is used to show a void or singleton in opener's suit with a 5-4-4-0 pattern or a 4-4-4-1 if that is possible. Clearly responder is worried whether opener's suit is adequate for a 3NT contract.

Examples

This comes from Chapter 1, page 9:

WEST	W	E	EAST
♠A K 5	1◇	1♡	♠7 3
♡A 9 4	1NT	2NT	♡Q J 7 2
◇K Q 6 3	3♣	No	◇2
♣Q 6 2			♣K 9 7 5 4 3

The loss of playing 2♣ is illusory. The opponents would not have sold out to 2♣. This is similar:

WEST	W	E	EAST
♠A 8 5	1♣	1♡	♠J 3
♡J 4 3	1NT	2NT	♡Q 7 5 2
◇A K 6	3♣	No	◇Q 4
♣K Q 6 2			♣J 9 7 5 4

1NT might fail but 3♣ should be easy and you cannot be sure of defeating their 2◇ or 2♠.

Just because opener bids a suit, it does not mean that 3NT is safe in that area:

WEST	W	E	EAST
♠A K J	1♣	1◇	♠Q 9 7 3
♡K 9 4	1NT	2NT	♡Q J 7 2
◇K Q 7	3♣	3NT	◇A J 4 3
♣J 8 6 2	4♠	No	♣5

2NT-then-3NT = singleton or void in opener's suit.

(For a more dynamic approach to bidding after opener's 1NT rebid, see Appendix 2, page 140.)

EXERCISES ON BIDDING AFTER OPENER'S 1NT REBID

A. Playing 2♣ Checkback, what should responder rebid with these hands after 1♣ : 1♠, 1NT?

1. ♠ A J 9 7 2	2. ♠ A J 9 7	3. ♠ Q J 9 7 3	4. ♠ Q J 9 7 3	5. ♠ K 10 6 3 2
♡ Q J 5 3	♡ 3	♡ A K 9 8 2	♡ A K 9 8	♡ A J 5 4
♢ 7	♢ J 6 2	♢ 2	♢ 3 2	♢ K 9 3 2
♣ 8 7 4	♣ A Q 8 7 2	♣ Q 5	♣ A 4	♣ - - -

B. The bidding has started 1♢ : 1♡, 1NT : 2♣ (Checkback). What should opener do next?

1. ♠ A K J	2. ♠ J 3 2	3. ♠ 8 7 2	4. ♠ K Q 7	5. ♠ 9 8 2
♡ K J	♡ Q 7 4	♡ Q 7 4	♡ A J 2	♡ Q J 9
♢ A J 7 5 2	♢ A K 5 3	♢ A K 5 3	♢ A K 9 5 2	♢ A Q J 3
♣ 7 4 2	♣ A J 2	♣ A K 2	♣ 3 2	♣ A K J

C. The bidding has started 1♢ : 1♠, 1NT : 2NT (puppet, requiring opener to bid 3♣). What should responder do next with these hands after opener dutifully bids 3♣?

1. ♠ A J 8 7 3	2. ♠ A J 8 7 3	3. ♠ K Q J 5	4. ♠ K 8 7 5 2	5. ♠ Q 9 7 6
♡ 6 4 2	♡ A Q 7 5	♡ 5	♡ K 9 4 2	♡ K 3
♢ K Q 9	♢ 9 4 2	♢ K J 8 7 2	♢ - - -	♢ 7
♣ J 2	♣ 3	♣ J 6 4	♣ K J 10 4	♣ J 8 6 5 3 2

PARTNERSHIP BIDDING PRACTICE

How should the following hands be bid, using 2♣ Checkback? West is the dealer each time.

SET 3 — WEST	SET 3 — EAST	SET 4 — WEST	SET 4 — EAST
1. ♠ 9 7 4	1. ♠ 10 6 5 3 2	1. ♠ A 10 3	1. ♠ K Q 4 2
♡ K 8 6 3	♡ A 7 5 2	♡ A Q 10	♡ K J 7 4 2
♢ A Q	♢ K 8	♢ A Q 4	♢ 2
♣ A Q 6 2	♣ J 3	♣ 9 7 5 3	♣ J 6 2
2. ♠ K Q 10 8	2. ♠ A 5 2	2. ♠ A K Q	2. ♠ J 7
♡ 9 6 3	♡ A Q 8	♡ 6	♡ K 9 7 5 3 2
♢ 9 8 3	♢ K Q 6 4	♢ J 8 6 3	♢ K 9
♣ Q J 5	♣ K 6 3	♣ A Q 10 6 4	♣ K 7 2
3. ♠ 8 6	3. ♠ K J 2	3. ♠ 8 5 3	3. ♠ K Q J 7 4
♡ A Q 6 3	♡ K 8	♡ A Q 7 2	♡ K 6 3
♢ 8	♢ A K 7 4 3	♢ Q 8 5	♢ 9 4
♣ 8 7 5 4 3 2	♣ K 9 6	♣ A K Q	♣ J 6 4
4. ♠ J 9 8	4. ♠ K Q 7 5 2	4. ♠ 8 6 2	4. ♠ K Q 10 7 4
♡ A J 4 3	♡ K 7 5 2	♡ A Q 4	♡ K J 3
♢ K Q 8 2	♢ J 5	♢ J 7	♢ 9 4
♣ A K	♣ 8 4	♣ A K Q 3 2	♣ J 6 4
5. ♠ Q 5 2	5. ♠ J 7 3	5. ♠ A 7 3 2	5. ♠ J 10 4
♡ K 7 5 2	♡ A 9	♡ K 6 4 2	♡ A Q
♢ K 5 3 2	♢ A Q J 7 4	♢ K 10 9 3	♢ Q 7 5
♣ J 6	♣ K 9 2	♣ 3	♣ A K J 6 4
6. ♠ J 5	6. ♠ K 8 6 3 2	6. ♠ A 7 3 2	6. ♠ K Q 4
♡ Q 8 5	♡ J 7 6 4 2	♡ K 6 4 2	♡ Q J 3
♢ K Q J 5	♢ A 2	♢ K 10 9 3	♢ A Q J
♣ A K 7 2	♣ 4	♣ 3	♣ J 6 4 2

PLAY HANDS ON BIDDING AFTER OPENER'S 1NT REBID

(These hands can be made up by using pages 176-183)

Hand 5: Discarding losers — Card combination technique

Dealer North : N-S vulnerable

NORTH
- ♠ A K 3
- ♡ 10 3
- ◇ A Q 8 6 2
- ♣ A 5 4

WEST
- ♠ Q 7
- ♡ K 8 7 5
- ◇ J 9 4 3
- ♣ Q J 8

EAST
- ♠ J 10 6 5 2
- ♡ Q
- ◇ 10 7 5
- ♣ K 10 6 3

SOUTH
- ♠ 9 8 4
- ♡ A J 9 6 4 2
- ◇ K
- ♣ 9 7 2

WEST	NORTH	EAST	SOUTH
	1◇	No	1♡
No	1NT	No	2♣ (1)
No	3◇ (2)	No	4♡
No	No	No	

(1) 2♣ checkback (2) 17-18 points and five diamonds

Bidding: South is not quite strong enough to insist on game. Opposite a minimum 1NT rebid, a part-score will be enough. In reply to 2♣, opener's rebids at the 3-level show maximum values. South can be sure that North has two or three hearts. Else North's pattern would be 4-1-5-3 and so would have rebid 1♠ or 3-1-5-4 and would rebid 3♣ in reply to 2♣.

Lead: Queen of clubs. The other choices are far more dangerous.

Recommended play: South takes dummy's ♣A, plays a diamond to the king and crosses to dummy with a spade. Two clubs are discarded on the ◇A and ◇Q. Now it is time to tackle trumps. The ♡3 is led from dummy and South captures East's queen. A low heart is played from hand towards dummy's ten. If West wins this and leads a spade, take the ace, ruff a club and draw trumps.

If West ducks the second heart, ruff a club and lead the jack of hearts. Later ruff a club to hand and draw the last trump with your ♡9. You make 11 tricks, losing one trump and one spade.

Notes: (1) It is an error to lead the ♡10 on the first round of trumps and on this layout would create an extra trump loser. (Do not feel bad if you did this. A world-famous international made this very mistake in a world championship and thus lost a makeable slam.)
(2) If East were to follow low on the first heart, finesse the 9. If this loses, later cross to dummy with a spade and lead the ♡10 for a second trump finesse.

Hand 6: Reply to 2♣ checkback with a maximum — Catering for the normal break

Dealer East : E-W vulnerable

NORTH
- ♠ J 10 8 4
- ♡ A 10 5 4
- ◇ 9 8
- ♣ J 9 2

WEST
- ♠ A K Q 6 2
- ♡ 7 2
- ◇ 10 7 4 2
- ♣ 6 5

EAST
- ♠ 7 5
- ♡ Q J 8
- ◇ A J 6 3
- ♣ A K Q 4

SOUTH
- ♠ 9 3
- ♡ K 9 6 3
- ◇ K Q 5
- ♣ 10 8 7 3

WEST	NORTH	EAST	SOUTH
		1♣	No
1♠	No	1NT	No
2♣	No	3NT	All pass

Bidding: West's 2♣ checkback invites game and East's 3NT shows 17-18 points without 4 hearts and without 3 spades.

Lead: 3 of hearts. It is true that the heart lead does not work out well for the defence as it sets up a heart trick for declarer. Nevertheless it is normal to lead an unbid suit and it is usually preferable to lead an unbid major than an unbid minor. The diamond lead would turn out even worse.

Recommended play: North takes the ♡A and returns the ♡4. South wins and plays a third heart. It should be clear from the cards played by South and North that the hearts are breaking 4-4. To guard against a 4-2 break in spades, duck a spade at trick 4. North wins and a heart is cashed but declarer has nine tricks.

Notes: East must decide whether to cash the spades from the top and hope that they are 3-3 or duck a spade to ensure the contract if the spades are 4-2. Playing for spades 3-3 (36%) makes ten tricks and a top about 1/3 of the time, and fails, for a bottom, about 2/3 of the time. Ducking a spade works better when spades are 4-2, about 50% of the time. In a normal contract if the chance for an overtrick is below 50%, take the line which offers the best chance to make your contract.

Hand 7: Discarding losers — Playing for overtricks

Dealer South : Both vulnerable

NORTH
♠ A K J 9 6
♡ 8 6 2
♢ 5
♣ Q J 3 2

WEST
♠ 7 2
♡ 10 5 4
♢ K Q 10 6
♣ 10 8 7 5

EAST
♠ Q 8 5
♡ K Q J 7
♢ J 9 3
♣ 9 6 4

SOUTH
♠ 10 4 3
♡ A 9 3
♢ A 8 7 4 2
♣ A K

WEST	NORTH	EAST	SOUTH
			1♢
No	1♠	No	1NT
No	3♣ (1)	No	3♠
No	4♠	All pass	

(1) Game-force, spades and clubs

Bidding : North has a strong hand and must insist on game over 1NT. The 3♣ rebid shows at least 5-4 or 4-5 in the black suits and is forcing to game. South shows 3-card spade support with 3♠ and North has no further problem.

Lead: King of hearts. Wouldn't it be nice if all our opening leads were as easy as this?

Recommended play: Win with the ♡A, cash ♣A and ♣K, followed by ♢A and a diamond ruff. The ♣Q is cashed and a heart discarded from dummy. Next comes the ♣J. If East ruffs with the ♠Q or does not ruff at all, discard the last heart from dummy. You can ruff a diamond to hand, ruff a heart, play a spade to hand and ruff your last heart. This line brings in twelve tricks.

Notes: (1) At rubber bridge or at teams, where your primary concern is to make your contract and overtricks play a minor role, you would win ♡A and tackle trumps at once. Playing on clubs could cost the contract if a defender ruffs the first or second round of clubs.
(2) If trumps are played early and East comes in with the ♠Q, two hearts are cashed and declarer makes just ten tricks, almost certainly a bottom score. If overtricks are readily available, you must take them.
(3) If East dares to ruff the fourth club with the ♠5, declarer may make just eleven tricks. If declarer overruffs with the ten and concedes a heart, East wins and plays a third diamond. North ruffs a heart in dummy and may misguess spades for a second loser. Declarer also loses two tricks if declarer discards dummy's last heart instead of overruffing East. The diamond return is ruffed, a heart is ruffed, a spade to hand is followed by another heart ruff, but the fourth diamond from dummy promotes East's ♠Q.

Hand 8: Game try with a flat 8 count — Card combination — Timing

Dealer West : Nil vulnerable

NORTH
♠ K 7
♡ 9 7 5 3
♢ K 8 3
♣ 8 7 4 3

WEST
♠ 8 4 3
♡ Q 8 6 4
♢ A J
♣ A K Q J

EAST
♠ J 9 6 2
♡ A K 10
♢ 7 6 2
♣ 9 6 2

SOUTH
♠ A Q 10 5
♡ J 2
♢ Q 10 9 5 4
♣ 10 5

WEST	NORTH	EAST	SOUTH
1♣	No	1♠	No
1NT	No	2♣	No
3♡	No	3NT	All pass

Bidding: East's flat 8 is just enough to try for 3NT. You must be prepared to take a shot at game. You will not always be successful but with 25 HCP together, 3NT is about a 50% chance and that makes it acceptable. Using 2♣ checkback, East plans to rebid 2NT opposite any two-level rebid. West's 3♡ reply shows a maximum, 17-18 points, with four hearts. It does not deny three spades. With five spades, East would now bid 3♠.

Lead: 3 of diamonds. Not a particularly palatable choice but diamonds is the only unbid suit.

Recommended play: South plays the ♢Q. West should win and cash ♡A and ♡K. When the ♡J drops, cash the ♡10, come to hand with a club and cash the ♡Q, followed by the clubs.

Notes: (1) There is no benefit in ducking the first diamond and it could prove fatal. If South switched to the ♠5, the defence could collect four spade tricks. One down.
(2) It would be an error to cash the clubs before testing the hearts. After four rounds of clubs, there is no way to unravel the hearts to make four tricks when the jack falls singleton or doubleton.
(3) If the ♡J did not fall on the first two rounds of hearts, declarer can then run the clubs and hope the hearts are 3-3 or that an opponent discards a heart on the clubs.

CHAPTER 3

TRANSFERS AFTER 1NT — WEAK HANDS

The 4-Suit Transfer Structure

1NT : 2♣ remains Stayman. The transfer structure does not tamper with 2♣ Stayman.

1NT : 2◇ = 5 or more hearts
1NT : 2♡ = 5 or more spades
1NT : 2♠ = 5 or more clubs. If responder has a weak hand intending to sign off in 3♣, responder should hold six clubs or more.
1NT : 2NT = 5 or more diamonds. If responder has a weak hand intending to sign off in 3◇, responder should hold six diamonds or more.

While there are other systems of transfers at the two-level, the above 4-suit structure is preferred by most experts. The only loss with this scheme of transfers is the inability to sign off in 2◇. Just as Stayman prevents a signoff in 2♣, so the 2◇ transfer to hearts prevents a signoff in 2◇. Just as losing 2♣ is a small price to pay for the use of Stayman to explore major suit contracts, so losing a natural 2◇ is a small price to pay for all the benefits that flow from using transfers. It does mean that responder has to reach the 3-level if wanting to sign off in a minor. Responder may prefer to pass 1NT.

(For a new and superior structure for 1NT : 2♣ and transfers after opening 1NT, which enables you to sign off in 2◇ as one of many benefits, see Appendix 3.)

Advantages of Transfers

1. They enable the 1NT opener to be declarer more often, particularly useful when responder is very weak.

2. They enable responder to describe hand types which are difficult or impossible to show when using standard methods. These include :

Hands worth a raise to 2NT plus a 5-card major.

Game invitational hands with a 6-card major.

In addition, all two-suiters with game or slam potential can be shown below 3NT.

This expansion in bidding vocabulary greatly increases the efficiency of your bidding system. It does so without losing the ability to describe the hands traditionally shown in standard methods:

Weak hands with a 5-card major or 6-card minor.

Game-force hands with a 5-card or longer suit.

3. Opener is able to express degrees of support for responder's suit and also degrees of preference when responder reveals a two-suiter.

Allowing the NT opener to be declarer allows the opening lead to come up to the stronger hand. It also keeps the stronger hand concealed from the defenders' prying eyes. Although these are undoubted advantages, the major benefits flow from the vastly expanded flexibility for responder in being able to describe so many hands more accurately.

Transfers to a major when responder is weakish

1. Responder is very weak, not enough to invite game, and has a 5-card or longer major

Transfer to your major and pass when opener bids the major.

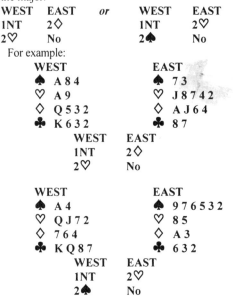

WEST	EAST	*or*	WEST	EAST
1NT	2◇		1NT	2♡
2♡	No		2♠	No

For example:

WEST	EAST
♠ A 8 4	♠ 7 3
♡ A 9	♡ J 8 7 4 2
◇ Q 5 3 2	◇ A J 6 4
♣ K 6 3 2	♣ 8 7

WEST	EAST
1NT	2◇
2♡	No

WEST	EAST
♠ A 4	♠ 9 7 6 5 3 2
♡ Q J 7 2	♡ 8 5
◇ 7 6 4	◇ A 3
♣ K Q 8 7	♣ 6 3 2

WEST	EAST
1NT	2♡
2♠	No

There is no suit quality requirement. You may transfer to any 5-card major. The theory is that the weak hand should produce more tricks with the major suit as trumps than in no-trumps. Opposite a worthless hand, a 1NT opener can usually make 3-4 tricks. A 5-card trump suit will generally produce two extra tricks so that you will be better off even if you do not make the contract.

Note that opener is bound to bid responder's suit, even if opener has only doubleton support. Opener has no option to reject the transfer.

2. Responder has enough to invite game and has precisely a 5-card major

Transfer to your major and rebid 2NT when opener bids the major.

WEST	EAST	*or*	WEST	EAST
1NT	2◇		1NT	2♡
2♡	2NT...		2♠	2NT...

For example:

WEST	W	E	EAST
♠ A J 5	1NT	2◇	♠ Q 7 3
♡ A 9	2♡	2NT...	♡ Q J 7 4 2
◇ Q J 7 6			◇ K 8
♣ 8 6 3 2			♣ K 7 4

With a minimum and no fit for responders major, opener will pass 2NT.

Responder will usually have a balanced hand to use the transfer plus 2NT rebid but this need not be so.

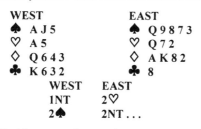

WEST	EAST
♠ A J 5	♠ Q 9 8 7 3
♡ A 5	♡ Q 7 2
◇ Q 6 4 3	◇ A K 8 2
♣ K 6 3 2	♣ 8

WEST	EAST
1NT	2♡
2♠	2NT . . .

While this may not be a perfect way to describe the East hand, it is the best available. It shows the 5-card major and the strength. If opener has 3-card or better support for spades, opener will revert to spades. If opener has a doubleton spade, opener will have length and hopefully strength in the suit in which responder is short. It is not open to East to transfer to spades and rebid 3◇ with the above hand. The transfer-then-new-suit sequence is forcing to game (see Chapter 4).

Opener's options after the 2NT rebid :

Minimum and doubleton in responder's suit : Pass

Maximum and doubleton in responder's suit : 3NT

Minimum and 3-4 cards in responder's suit :
Sign off in 3-of-responder's major.

Maximum and 3-4 cards in responder's major :
Sign off in 4-of-responder's major.

With 3-4 cards in responder's major, remember to add a point for an outside doubleton. Tend to be optimistic if you have 4-card support.

Examples:

WEST	W	E	EAST
♠ K J 10	1NT	2◇	♠ A Q 7
♡ 8 6	2♡	2NT	♡ Q J 7 4 2
◇ A J 6 3	No		◇ K 8 4
♣ Q J 3 2			♣ 8 7

WEST	W	E	EAST
♠ K J 3	1NT	2◇	♠ A Q 7
♡ K 6	2♡	2NT	♡ Q J 7 4 2
◇ A 7 6 3	3NT	No	◇ K 8 4
♣ Q J 3 2			♣ 8 7

WEST	W	E	EAST
♠ K J	1NT	2◇	♠ A Q 7
♡ A 6 3	2♡	2NT	♡ Q J 7 4 2
◇ A 7 6 3	3♡	No	◇ K 8 4
♣ 10 9 3 2			♣ 8 7

WEST	W	E	EAST
♠ K J	1NT	2◇	♠ A Q 7
♡ A 6 3	2♡	2NT	♡ Q J 7 4 2
◇ A Q 7 3	4♡	No	◇ K 8 4
♣ 10 9 3 2			♣ 8 7

3. Responder has enough to invite game and has a 6-card or longer major

Transfer to your major and raise your suit to the three-level when opener bids the major.

WEST	EAST	*or*	WEST	EAST
1NT	2◇		1NT	2♡
2♡	3♡ . . .		2♠	3♠ . . .

With a 6-card suit, responder should have 9-10 HCP. With 11-12 HCP and a 6-card major, be prepared to go to game. With a 7-card suit, drop the above HCP requirements by a couple of points.

Opener should pass with a minimum and bid the major suit game with a maximum. Even with a minimum, opener should raise to 4-major with three trumps and an outside doubleton.

Examples:

WEST	W	E	EAST
♠ A 8 5	1NT	2◇	♠ Q 7 3
♡ A 9	2♡	3♡	♡ Q J 8 7 4 2
◇ A J 5 4	No		◇ K 8
♣ 8 7 5 2			♣ Q 4

WEST	W	E	EAST
♠ A 8	1NT	2♡	♠ K 9 6 4 3 2
♡ A K 9 2	2♠	3♠	♡ Q J 8
◇ 9 8 5 4	4♠	No	◇ A
♣ Q J 2			♣ 9 6 4

WEST	W	E	EAST
♠ Q 8 5	1NT	2♡	♠ K 9 6 4 3 2
♡ A Q 9 2	2♠	3♠	♡ K J 8
◇ A 10 9 4	4♠	No	◇ 8
♣ 9 5			♣ K 6 4

Despite the minimum points, West should raise to game because of the 3-card support and the doubleton outside, giving West potential for an extra trick via a club ruff.

Opener's options after a transfer to a major

Opener has no option to refuse the transfer. Almost all the time opener simply bids responder's major. This is known as a 'simple accept'. With exceptionally good values, opener may 'super-accept'.

1NT : 2◇	1NT : 2◇
2♡ . . .	3♡ . . .
Simple accept	Super-accept

There are three key features for opener to consider :
1. 3- or 4-card support for responder's major.
2. A doubleton elsewhere to provide ruffing potential.
3. A maximum 1NT opening.
To super-accept, opener needs all three key features.

After the super-accept, responder may pass with a hand with no hope for game or raise to game with about 10 HCP or better (a shapely 9 count will do). Treat opener's super-accept as showing about 15 points or so in total value. With slam prospects, you may change suit as a cue-bid or use Blackwood. These areas are covered in Chapters 12-15.

Transfers to a minor when responder is weakish

1. Responder has a very weak hand: Transfer to your minor and pass when opener bids the minor.

WEST	EAST	*or*	WEST	EAST
1NT	2♠		1NT	2NT
3♣	No		3♢	No

Use these sequences only with a 6-card or longer minor and less than 11 HCP. You may sign off via a transfer to a major with a 5-card suit but you need at least a 6-card suit to sign off in 3-minor via a transfer. You are committing your side to two extra tricks (from 1NT to 3-minor). With only a 5-card minor you may as well play for 7 tricks in 1NT.

2. Responder has enough values to invite game and has a 5-card or longer minor: Do NOT transfer.

With 1NT : 2NT used as a transfer, the standard invitational 2NT response is lost. To cater for this hand type, start with 2♣ and follow up with 2NT.

Transfers to a minor are used only when you want to play in the 3-minor part-score or when you have enough for game. There is no transfer sequence available for invitational values and a long minor. *(See Appendix 3 where this feature is provided.)*

If the 2♣ response does not guarantee a major, the opponents should be alerted. If responder rebids 3NT after Stayman, responder will have a major (otherwise just bid 1NT : 3NT), but responder's 2NT rebid after Stayman carries no promise of a major.

3. Responder has enough values to invite game with a 4-card major and a longer minor: Do NOT transfer. Use 2♣ Stayman for this hand type.

A transfer followed by a new suit rebid by responder is a game-force (see Chapter 4). You cannot afford such a sequence with only invitational values. Use 2♣ Stayman. If opener bids your major, raise it. If not, rebid 2NT over opener's 2♢ or 2♠, but with four spades, bid 2♠ over 2♡.

Opener's options after a transfer to a minor

Opener may make only two bids: the simple accept (bid the minor suit shown) or super-accept the minor (bid the step in-between the transfer and the minor suit shown). No other rebid is permitted.

1NT : 2♠	1NT : 2♠
3♣ ...	2NT ...
Simple accept	Super-accept

1NT : 2NT	1NT : 2NT
3♢	3♣
Simple accept	Super-accept

To super-accept opener needs a maximum 1NT opening plus support for the minor, including a top honour (queen or better). The aim of the super-accept is to reach a sound 3NT where responder's minor will supply the bulk of the tricks. By showing a top honour in the minor, opener enables responder to gauge whether a suit like A-Q-x-x-x-x or K-Q-x-x-x-x is running. If so, prospects for 3NT may be rosy.

After the super-accept of a minor suit transfer

With a weakish hand, responder may :
1. Bid 3-minor anyway with a very weak hand and no prospects for game.
2. Rebid 3NT with game-invitational values or with a hand that has improved sufficiently from the fact that opener has a top honour in the long minor.

Responder's options with a strong hand are covered in Chapter 4.

Interference before responder has transferred

After 1NT : (Double) : ?

All suit bids are genuine in standard methods: 2♣ shows clubs and is not Stayman, while 2♢ / 2♡ / 2♠ show the actual suit bid and are not transfers. Given that their double is for penalties, it becomes important to be able to sign off in a minor at the two-level rather than at the three-level.

After 1NT : (Suit Bid) : ?

If they bid a suit over partner's 1NT, transfers no longer apply. A suit bid at the cheapest level is natural and not forcing. For other methods over interference, see Chapter 21 (and Appendix 4).

Expert methods after transfers

After responder's 2NT rebid (e.g., 1NT : 2♢, 2♡ : 2NT), opener may bid a new suit as a long suit trial bid, showing support for responder's major and looking for help in the trial suit. For example:

WEST	W	E	EAST
♠ K Q 6 2	1NT	2♢	♠ A 4
♡ K J 6	2♡	2NT	♡ Q 7 4 3 2
♢ A 7	3♣	3♡	♢ K Q 6
♣ 9 6 4 3	No		♣ 8 7 5

West's 3♣ expresses interest in 4♡ and asks for help in clubs. With no useful clubs, East signs off. Swap East's minor suits and East would bid 4♡.

Other ways to super-accept a major suit

1NT : 2♢	1NT : 2♢	1NT : 2♢
2NT ...	3♣ ...	3♡ ...
Super-accept	Super-accept	Super-accept

The 2NT rebid super-accept shows 4-card support for responder, a maximum 1NT with a 4-3-3-3 pattern with instant winners in the other suits (such as A-x-x or A-K-x). With such holdings you often make just as many tricks in no-trumps as in the major.

WEST	W	E	EAST
♠ A 9 6	1NT	2♢	♠ K 4
♡ K 6 3 2	2NT	3NT	♡ A Q 10 7 4
♢ A K 3	No		♢ 9 6 2
♣ 9 6 4			♣ 8 7 5

3NT has excellent chances. Had the bidding started 1NT : 2♢, 2♡, East would pass and if West had used 3♣ as the super-accept, East might bid the terrible 4♡.

Over 2NT, responder may sign off in the major or try 3NT. Responder may still wish to transfer and to do so, responder can use a rebid of 3♦ over 2NT to ask opener to bid the major suit anyway.

WEST	W	E	EAST
♠ A 8 6	1NT	2♦	♠ Q J
♥ K 9 6	2NT	3♦	♥ Q 10 7 5 4 2
♦ A K 3	3♥	No	♦ Q 2
♣ 10 4 3 2			♣ 8 7 5

Less than delighted by opener's super-accept, East wants to sign off in 3♥ but would still prefer opener to play it. 3♦ = 'Please bid my major anyway.' If East wanted to play in 4♥, East could bid 3♦ to effect the transfer and then raise to 4♥.

A minor suit bid by opener in reply to the transfer is also a super-accept (opener has no option to reject the transfer) and can be played in various ways. One of the best is as a long suit trial, a suit with 3+ cards including two or three losers (such as J-x-x-x, A-x-x, x-x-x or similar). If weak, responder can sign off in 3-major. With good help in the trial suit, bid game.

WEST	W	E	EAST
♠ J 10 6 2	1NT	2♥	♠ A Q 9 8 5 3
♥ A K 6	3♣	4♠	♥ Q 9 7
♦ K Q	No		♦ 8 7 2
♣ J 6 4 3			♣ 8

3♣ = super-accept for spades but needs help to reduce losers in clubs.

4♠ = good help in clubs despite the weak hand. If responder treats the super-accept as equal to a total value of 15-16 points, the decision to bid game becomes much easier.

WEST	W	E	EAST
♠ J 10 6 2	1NT	2♥	♠ A Q 9 8 5 3
♥ A K 6	3♣	3♠	♥ Q 9 7
♦ K Q	No		♦ 8
♣ J 6 4 3			♣ 8 7 2

With the worst holding in the trial suit East signs off at the three-level. Even that may prove too high.

After a minor suit trial bid as the super-accept, responder may still wish to transfer to make opener the declarer. For the transfer into game, responder can bid 4♦. In the above sequence, for example, East can bid 4♦ over 3♣ to have West the declarer in 4♠. To sign off at the three-level, responder can bid 3♦ over a 3♣ trial bid. If opener's trial bid is 3♦, the situation is trickier.

WEST	EAST	
1NT	2♦	If East wants to sign off in 3♥, there is no option other than bidding 3♥.
3♦	?	

WEST	EAST	
1NT	2♥	If East wants to sign off in 3♠, East should simply bid 3♠. It is better to use 3♥ as a natural and forcing bid or as a cue-bid than as a second transfer.
3♦	?	

How should the bidding go on these hands?

WEST	EAST
♠ A K 6 3	♠ Q J 10 4 2
♥ K 9 6 4	♥ A Q J 2
♦ A 8 3	♦ J 7 2
♣ 9 2	♣ 8

It would be easy enough to hit the second best spot on a sequence like this :

WEST	EAST
1NT	2♥
3♠	4♠
No	

4♠ is fine at rubber bridge or teams but at pairs you want to be in 4♥. When the hearts are 3-2, you score one trick more in 4♥ than in 4♠ because of the discard available when the side suit is spades.

It is not satisfactory for East to bid 4♥ over 3♠. Most would play this not as a choice of contract but rather as a cue-bid seeking a slam in spades.

It is possible to solve this dilemma by responder using 2♣ Stayman and that works well enough on the hand above. If opener bids 2♥ raise to 4♥. If opener bids 2♠, raise to 4♠. If opener bids 2♦, jump to 3♠ to show five spades and force to game.

One can also bid the hands via a transfer auction with a slight adjustment by opener. *When making a super-accept with 4-4 in the majors, opener bids the other major.* So:

WEST	W	E	EAST
♠ A K 6 3	1NT	2♥	♠ Q J 10 4 2
♥ K 9 6 4	3♥	4♥	♥ A Q J 2
♦ A 8 3	No		♦ J 7 2
♣ 9 2			♣ 8

If responder wants to sign off in 3♠, responder just has to bid that over 3♥. If responder wants to play in 4♠, responder can bid 4♠ or re-transfer to 4♠ via a rebid of 4♦. This allows the opener to be declarer whenever the final contract is spades.

The position is similar when responder has four spades and five hearts.

WEST	EAST	
1NT	2♦	West's 2♠ = a super-accept for hearts plus four spades. With four spades as well, East can bid 4♠.
2♠	?	

With no interest in spades, East can sign off by bidding 3♥ or 4♥. If East wants to transfer opener into a heart contract, East bids 3♦ as a re-transfer to 3♥ and then pass or raise to 4♥.

WEST	EAST	
1NT	2♦	It follows that if opener makes a direct super-accept, opener will not have four cards in the other major.
3♥ . . .		

It also follows that opener will not have a holding suitable for a trial bid or a maximum 4-3-3-3 pattern with A-x-x and A-K-x holdings.

EXERCISES USING TRANSFERS

A. Partner has opened 1NT. What is your response with each of these hands?

1.	♠ A 9	2.	♠ J 10 9 5 4	3.	♠ 2	4.	♠ 7 4	5.	♠ A 4
	♥ 8 7 5 3 2		♥ K 9 5		♥ 9 8		♥ 10 3 2		♥ K J 7 2
	◇ 7 2		◇ 7 5		◇ Q 6 3 2		◇ A K 8 7 4 3		◇ 4 3
	♣ K 6 4 3		♣ 9 7 2		♣ K 9 8 7 5 2		♣ K 4		♣ Q J 9 6 4

B. The bidding has started 1NT : 2◇ (transfer to hearts). What is opener's rebid with these hands?

1.	♠ 9 6 3	2.	♠ A K 9	3.	♠ 10 8 7	4.	♠ A J 7	5.	♠ A Q 6 4
	♥ K J 5 3		♥ 8 7		♥ A Q 6		♥ K Q 8 2		♥ A J 3
	◇ A 5		◇ K Q 5 2		◇ K Q 6 2		◇ A 10		◇ 7 4
	♣ K J 9 8		♣ Q 10 8 7		♣ K 9 5		♣ 9 8 6 3		♣ K 10 9 5

C. The bidding has started 1NT : 2◇, 2♥ : 2NT. What should opener do next?

1.	♠ 9 8 7 3	2.	♠ A 9 2	3.	♠ 9 8 2	4.	♠ 10 9 5 2	5.	♠ A 3
	♥ A 3		♥ K Q J 7		♥ Q 6 3		♥ K Q		♥ J 10 5 4
	◇ A J 10 2		◇ Q 8 4		◇ A K J 2		◇ A 8 7 2		◇ A 8 2
	♣ K Q 9		♣ J 6 3		♣ A 9 6		♣ Q J 6		♣ A 7 6 3

PARTNERSHIP BIDDING : How should the following hands be bid? West is the dealer each time.

SET 5 — WEST	**SET 5 — EAST**	**SET 6 — WEST**	**SET 6 — EAST**
1. ♠ J 10 9 3	1. ♠ 8 6	1. ♠ J 9 3	1. ♠ 8 6
♥ K 7 5	♥ Q 8 6 4 3 2	♥ A J 5	♥ K 4
◇ A 8 4	◇ K 5 2	◇ K Q J 4	◇ 8 5 2
♣ A J 3	♣ 7 2	♣ Q 6 3	♣ K J 10 8 7 2
2. ♠ A 7 4	2. ♠ 10 9 6 5 2	2. ♠ 8 5	2. ♠ A J 10 3
♥ A 3 2	♥ K 8 4	♥ 6 3	♥ A 4 2
◇ 9 7 5	◇ Q J 2	◇ Q 8 7 5 4 3 2	◇ J 6
♣ K J 6 5	♣ A Q	♣ 7 4	♣ A 9 6 2
3. ♠ Q J 9	3. ♠ A 8 7	3. ♠ A 7 4	3. ♠ 9 5
♥ A K J 8 3	♥ 10 7 2	♥ A K 6	♥ 9 5 3
◇ 5 4	◇ A 7 2	◇ Q 9 3	◇ A K 10 8 7 5
♣ 8 7 3	♣ K Q J 4	♣ 9 8 5 3	♣ J 2
4. ♠ 9 8 6 4 3 2	4. ♠ A K J 5	4. ♠ Q 10 7 2	4. ♠ A J 9
♥ 7 2	♥ 8 6 4	♥ K Q 8	♥ A J 5
◇ 4	◇ K Q J 5	◇ K 10 2	◇ 8 6
♣ A 7 5 3	♣ 9 2	♣ Q 9 2	♣ J 10 8 7 4
5. ♠ J 8 6 2	5. ♠ K Q 9 7 4	5. ♠ 9 4	5. ♠ A 7 6
♥ K Q 8	♥ 6 3	♥ A Q 9 8 3	♥ K 6 4 2
◇ K 4	◇ A 8 5 2	◇ 6 5 4	◇ A 8 2
♣ K Q 6 3	♣ 4 2	♣ A 6 2	♣ K 7 3
6. ♠ 8 7 3 2	6. ♠ A	6. ♠ Q 6	6. ♠ K J 9 7 5 3
♥ A J 2	♥ Q 10 5 4 3	♥ A 7 5 4	♥ 9 3
◇ 6 2	◇ K Q 4	◇ A Q 5	◇ K 6 4
♣ A K J 5	♣ 9 8 6 3	♣ Q 7 6 4	♣ K 2

PLAY HANDS ON TRANSFERS OVER 1NT
(These hands can be made up by using pages 176-183)

Hand 9: Transfer with a weak hand — Urgent discards — Opportunity to overruff

Dealer North : E-W vulnerable

NORTH
- ♠ Q 3
- ♡ J 9 6 4
- ◊ A K Q 8
- ♣ 9 7 6

WEST
- ♠ A 9
- ♡ Q 10 2
- ◊ J 7 6 4 3 2
- ♣ J 10

EAST
- ♠ J 10 8
- ♡ A K 5
- ◊ 10 9
- ♣ K Q 4 3 2

SOUTH
- ♠ K 7 6 5 4 2
- ♡ 8 7 3
- ◊ 5
- ♣ A 8 5

WEST	NORTH	EAST	SOUTH
	1NT	No	2♡
No	2♠	All pass	

Bidding: South's 2♡ is a transfer to 2♠ and North must accept the transfer. It would be dreadful for South to pass 1NT. The defence against 1NT is routine for two down.

South's pass of 2♠ indicates a weak hand. It often pays to compete in the pass-out seat in such auctions but the weak suit and the vulnerability should convince West to keep quiet.

Lead: Ace of hearts. The ♣K lead is also attractive but leading from an A-K suit has the advantage of retaining the lead, seeing dummy and partner's signal and then deciding whether to continue the suit led or to switch. West encourages and three hearts are cashed. West then switches to the jack of clubs.

Recommended play: North wins with dummy's ♣A and should immediately play the diamond winners to discard dummy's losing clubs. On normal breaks, all of dummy's clubs could be discarded without problem. Then a club could be ruffed in dummy in order to lead a trump towards the queen-doubleton in hand.

Here the diamonds break badly and East ruffs the third round. Should declarer overruff or discard dummy's third club? In such cases it is almost always right to discard the loser and not overruff. After winning with the 8 of spades, East leads a club, ruffed in dummy. Declarer now leads a low trump and whether West plays low or rises with the ace, declarer makes eight tricks.

Notes: (1) Had declarer overruffed with the ♠K and then led a trump, the contract can be defeated. West rises with the ace of spades and plays the ten of clubs. East lets West win that trick and then a diamond from West promotes the jack of spades for East and the sixth trick for the defence.

(2) The same could happen if declarer leads the king of spades from dummy. West wins and another diamond from West gives East an extra trump trick.

Hand 10: Super-accept — Choice of plays

Dealer East : Both vulnerable

NORTH
- ♠ A 8 4
- ♡ A K 10 9 7
- ◊ 10 9 3 2
- ♣ 5

WEST
- ♠ K Q 10
- ♡ 8 4
- ◊ Q 7 6 4
- ♣ K 9 8 4

EAST
- ♠ J 7 6
- ♡ 6 3 2
- ◊ K J 5
- ♣ 10 7 3 2

SOUTH
- ♠ 9 5 3 2
- ♡ Q J 5
- ◊ A 8
- ♣ A Q J 6

WEST	NORTH	EAST	SOUTH
		No	1NT
No	2◊	No	3♡
No	4♡	All pass	

Bidding: North has enough to justify a transfer followed by a rebid of 2NT (despite the singleton).

South is worth the super-accept even though holding only three trumps. The hand is maximum, there is an outside doubleton and the trump support is good. Even if South bids only 2♡, South will jump to 4♡ over North's 2NT rebid.

Lead: King of spades. Second choice: trump lead. It is more attractive to lead an unbid suit which has two or more touching honours than to lead an unbid suit which contains only one honour.

Recommended play: South wins with dummy's ace of spades and has two reasonable lines. Ten tricks are virtually assured by playing ace and another diamond. Declarer plans to ruff two diamond losers in hand with high trumps, returning to dummy once with a trump and once with a club ruff.

The other line is to play the ace of clubs and lead the queen of clubs, discarding a spade from dummy if West plays low. If this were to lose to East, declarer still has ten tricks by ruffing one diamond and discarding one on the jack of clubs. When West has the king of clubs, this line brings in an overtrick most of the time. Say West covers with the ♣K. This is ruffed in dummy, followed by a diamond to the ace and the jack of clubs on which a spade loser is discarded. Next a diamond is conceded and declarer later ruffs two diamonds in hand.

With a choice of plays, choose the line that may yield an extra trick even if that line is slightly riskier.

Hand 11: Minor suit transfer — Ruffing finesse — Compulsory duck — Defensive counter

Dealer South : Nil vulnerable

NORTH
♠ J 10 9
♡ 10 8 7 4
◇ K 9 8
♣ A Q 5

WEST
♠ 7 6 4
♡ - - -
◇ Q 7 5 4
♣ K J 8 4 3 2

EAST
♠ A 5 3 2
♡ K Q J 6
◇ A 2
♣ 10 7 6

SOUTH
♠ K Q 8
♡ A 9 5 3 2
◇ J 10 6 3
♣ 9

WEST	NORTH	EAST	SOUTH
			No
No	No	1NT	No
2♠	No	3♣	All pass

Bidding: North should not open 3rd-in-hand. To open light in third seat, you should have a strong suit. West's 2♠ is a transfer to clubs. East has a maximum 1NT but the club support is not good enough to give a super-accept. East therefore bids 3♣ and West has no further ambitions.

Lead: King of spades. A suit with two touching honours is preferable to a suit with only one honour. A singleton trump is usually a very poor choice.

Recommended play: East wins the ♠A and leads the king of hearts. If South plays low, a spade loser is discarded. When South plays the ace, dummy ruffs. A diamond to the ace enables East to discard two spades on the hearts. Next comes the ◇2 since declarer hopes to ruff at least one diamond in hand. If South plays low, declarer deduces North has the ◇K and so ducks the diamond. North wins and plays a spade, ruffed in dummy. A low diamond is ruffed in hand and when the ◇K falls, West's ◇Q is high. West loses two trumps and a diamond for +130.

Notes : (1) If East tackles trumps before going for the diamond ruff, North can draw declarer's trumps. East is now held to nine tricks and will fail if three diamonds are lost.

(2) South should insert the ◇10 when East leads a diamond at trick 6. If this is ducked, North allows South to hold the trick and a trump switch eliminates declarer's trumps. East should cover South's ◇10 with the queen. North wins but cannot afford to attack trumps. Declarer can ruff two diamonds in hand and still score ten tricks.

Hand 12: Minor suit transfer — Super-accept — Catering for a bad break

Dealer West : N-S vulnerable

NORTH
♠ K 10 8 3
♡ Q 10 3
◇ J 10 8 7
♣ Q J

WEST
♠ A Q 7
♡ A 9 5 4
◇ A 6 4
♣ 8 5 3

EAST
♠ 9 5 4
♡ 7
◇ K Q 9 5 3 2
♣ A 7 2

SOUTH
♠ J 6 2
♡ K J 8 6 2
◇ - - -
♣ K 10 9 6 4

WEST	NORTH	EAST	SOUTH
1NT	No	2NT	No
3♣	No	3NT	All pass

Bidding: It would not be far-fetched for East to bid 2♣, planning to rebid 2NT to invite opener to bid game if maximum. The 2NT diamond transfer is preferable since East would rather play in 3◇ than 2NT if West does not have a super-accept. West's 3♣ shows a maximum with a top honour in diamonds. East has no sensible way to check on the heart position (as 3 no-hearts is still not a legal bid) and should brazen it out with 3NT.
  When in doubt, choose 3NT and not a 5-minor contract.

Lead: 3 of spades. The long suit is the normal choice. You need a strong reason to avoid the lead likely to be the field's choice.

Recommended play: South plays the jack and West wins with the queen. North notes at once that the spade was a lucky lead. A heart or a club would have been less favourable.

West tackles the diamonds, starting with the ace. When South shows out, declarer is able to cope with the bad break. If North ducks the second diamond, finesse the 9. If North inserts the ◇10, capture it and return to hand with a spade to lead a third diamond, finessing dummy's 9 when North plays low. This produces ten tricks for +430.

Notes: (1) If West starts with a low diamond to dummy's king or queen, North will score a trick. To capture J-10-x-x, you must retain two higher honours in one hand to capture the two honours missing.

(2) If North did lead a heart, declarer should win and continue with the ◇A and a second diamond: 10, Q. Return to hand with a spade to the ace to lead the next diamond. Do not take the spade finesse. If the spade finesse loses, you might go down in 3NT. Here the safety of the contract is paramount since many pairs may miss game completely. When you have reached an excellent game on few points, make sure of the contract.

CHAPTER 4

TRANSFERS AFTER 1NT — STRONG HANDS

Transfers to a major when responder is strong

1. Responder has game values with a 5-card major and no second suit

Transfer to your major and rebid 3NT.

WEST	EAST	*or*	WEST	EAST
1NT	2♢		1NT	2♡
2♡	3NT...		2♠	3NT...

Opener should pass with a doubleton and almost always revert to the major with 3-4 card support. With 3-card support and a 4-3-3-3 hand, opener may pass 3NT if every outside suit is doubly stopped.

2. Responder has game values with a 6+ major and no interest in any other suit

Transfer to your major and then jump to game.

WEST	EAST	*or*	WEST	EAST
1NT	2♢		1NT	2♡
2♡	4♡		2♠	4♠
No			No	

There is another way to transfer to your major suit game if you are using South African Transfers.

1NT : 4♣ = 'Please bid 4♡.'

1NT : 4♢ = 'Please bid 4♠.'

South African Transfers are definitely preferable to reserving 1NT : 4♣ for Gerber, asking for aces. There are other (and better) ways to check on aces. South African Transfers may prevent a cheap lead-directing entry to the auction :

WEST	NORTH	EAST	SOUTH
1NT	No	2♢	2♠
No	No	3NT	No
4♡	No	No	No

This auction has allowed South to indicate a lead to North. This might be vital to the defence.

WEST	NORTH	EAST	SOUTH
1NT	No	4♣	?

While South may venture a two-level overcall, it is far less likely that South will come in over 4♣. Now when West bids 4♡, North has no clues suggesting a spade lead might be useful.

When you transfer, next player may double your artificial bid to indicate a lead to partner. That may influence your choice of which transfer route to take. If you want to reach 4♠, but a possible lead-directing double of 4♢ would be unwelcome, you may choose the 1NT : 2♡, 2♠ : 4♠ path instead.

It is not compulsory for responder to transfer. If it appears that the lead coming to responder's hand is preferable, responder may bid game at once: 1NT : 4♡ or 1NT : 4♠. Responder would have a 6+ major and holdings such as K-x, K-J-x, A-Q and A-J-x in the outside suits.

3. Responder has game values with both majors and at least a 5-4 pattern

Transfer to the longer major and then bid the other major. Only the first two-level response is a transfer. The next suit bid is genuine.

WEST	EAST	*or*	WEST	EAST
1NT	2♢		1NT	2♡
2♡	2♠...		2♠	3♡...

Opener has at least 5 hearts and 4 spades

Opener has at least 5 spades and 4 hearts

Change of suit after a transfer is forcing to game.

Showing a 5-5 pattern

WEST	EAST	*or*	WEST	EAST
1NT	2♡		1NT	2♡
2♠	4♡...		2♠	3♡
			3NT	4♡...

In both auctions, East is showing at least 5-5 in the majors. What is the difference? The principle known as 'Fast Arrival' says that the immediate jump to game is the weaker action. Thus, the jump to 4♡ over 2♠ shows game interest only. West should pass or give preference to spades. Where East bid 3♡ and then 4♡, this is 'Slow Arrival'. East has some ambitions for slam, particularly if West has useful help in the majors and instant winners in the minors.

4. Responder has a 5+ major and a 4-card minor

Unless you have ambitions for slam, it is better not to show the minor suit. Basic pairs strategy is not to play in a 5-minor contract unless there is no other possibility. Therefore, if you have game values only, do not show the minor. Opener's raise of the minor suit would be unwelcome.

WEST	W	E	EAST
♠ A 10 8 4	1NT	2♢	♠ 7 2
♡ J 6	2♡	3NT	♡ A Q 10 4 2
♢ A 6 3 2	No		♢ K Q J 4
♣ K Q 3			♣ 8 7

With no ambitions for slam, East should not introduce the diamonds. 5♢ may make but 3NT has reasonable chances for 10 tricks, thus outscoring 5♢ even if that makes an overtrick. 4♡ is a good spot but always tough to reach on a 5-2 fit.

With a 5-4 pattern, responder needs about 18 HCP before introducing a minor. With less than that, slam prospects are not great for the minor suit. With a 5-5 pattern, 15-16 HCP would be enough to show the minor if the two 5-card suits are strong.

♠ K Q   ♡ A J 10 7 4   ♢ K Q 10 5 3   ♣ 7

This is certainly enough for a 3♢ rebid after a transfer to 2♡.

Transfers to a minor when responder is strong

1. Responder is worth 3NT and has both minors or is one-suited with a long minor

Do NOT transfer. Just raise to 3NT.

WEST	East has opened 1NT and
♠ 5	South has passed.
♡ J 5 4	What action should West
◊ K 8 6	take?
♣ A K Q 6 3 2	

It is tempting to transfer to clubs and then rebid 3NT but that does not really solve your problem. What you need to know is whether partner is strong enough in spades. Showing the clubs does nothing to indicate your area of concern. You cannot solve this problem in standard methods. Take the percentage action: bid 3NT and avoid minor suit games.

(Appendix 3 includes a method which allows you to show a short suit to check if the suit is stopped.)

2. Responder has values for game but not for slam and has a 4-card major with a longer minor

Do NOT transfer. Use 2♣ to try to find the major suit fit. If that is not forthcoming, rebid 3NT and take your chances.

WEST	East has opened 1NT and
♠ 5	South has passed.
♡ A J 5 4	What action should West
◊ K 8 6	take?
♣ K Q 6 3 2	

West has enough for game but not nearly enough for a slam. West should bid 2♣. If East shows hearts, the partnership will reach 4♡. If East does not show hearts, West should rebid 3NT. If you fail, you fail . . . so what else is new? *(See Appendix 3.)*

3. Responder has enough for game and some prospects for slam, plus a two-suiter, at least 5-4, with the minor suit as the longer suit

Transfer to the long minor and then bid the second suit. We have seen that responder shows slam ambitions by a transfer to a major followed by a minor suit rebid. The same applies if responder transfers to a minor and then shows a 4-card major. Without slam ambitions, responder would have travelled via 2♣.

WEST	EAST
1NT	2♠
3♣	3♡ . . .

East is showing 5+ clubs and 4 hearts and some hopes for slam if a trump fit exists.

WEST	EAST
1NT	2NT
3♣	3♡ . . .

East is showing 5+ diamonds and 4 hearts and some hopes for slam if a trump fit exists. Even though West's 3♣ was a super-accept for diamonds, East's 3♡ bid is still natural. There could be a heart fit as well as a diamond fit.

Opener's options after responder has shown a two-suiter

Opener has five basic paths :

- Bid 3NT to deny support for either suit.
- Show weak support for responder's first suit.
- Show strong support for responder's first suit.
- Show weak support for responder's second suit.
- Show strong support for responder's second suit.

Where responder has shown a 5-card major, opener should support with 3+ trumps.

- Weak support for opener's first suit is shown by supporting that suit at *game level*.

WEST	EAST	West's 4♠, bidding the first
1NT	2♡	suit at game level, shows
2♠	3♡	weak support ('fast arrival').
4♠ . . .		

- Strong support for opener's first suit is shown by supporting that suit *below game level*.

WEST	EAST	West's 3♠, bidding the first
1NT	2♡	suit below game level, shows
2♠	3♡	strong support.
3♠ . . .		

What is weak support? What is strong support?

In Chapter 3 it was noted that there are three key features for opener to consider when responder transfers :

1. 3- or 4-card support for responder's suit.
2. A doubleton elsewhere to provide ruffing potential.
3. A maximum 1NT opening.

When responder has transferred to a major and opener has accepted the transfer, opener will not have all three of these features. With that, opener would already have given a super-accept. Therefore when responder shows a second suit and opener supports the original major:

Strong support = 2 of the 3 key features

Weak support = 0 or 1 of the 3 key features

- Weak support for opener's *second* suit is shown by raising that suit to game-level if it is a major.

WEST	EAST	West's 4♡, raising the
1NT	2♡	second suit to the four-level,
2♠	3♡	shows weak support for the
4♡ . . .		second suit.

- Strong support for opener's *second* suit is shown by a cue-bid, bidding an ace in an unbid suit.

WEST	EAST	West's 4♣, a new suit, is a
1NT	2♡	cue-bid. This shows strong
2♠	3♡	support for hearts plus the ace
4♣ . . .		of clubs.

When showing support for the second suit, 2 or 3 key features = strong support, 0 or 1 key feature = weak support. If you have strong support for the second suit but no ace available for a cue-bid, you will just have to raise the second suit.

When showing both majors, responder may have no slam ambitions. If so, even if opener shows strong support for either major, responder can simply sign off in game. Where responder has shown a minor suit, that in itself indicates slam interest.

WEST	EAST	
1NT	2♥	Opener's support of diamonds, while denying the ability to cue-bid 3♥ or 4♣, shows willingness to co-operate with East's slam ambitions in diamonds.
2♠	3♦	
4♦ . . .		

The next move is up to responder who may choose a cue-bid or use 4NT to ask for aces or key cards.

What if opener can support both suits?

If responder has shown both majors, support the major in which you have more cards. In particular, you should generally prefer a 4-4 fit to a 5-3 fit.

If responder has shown a major-minor two-suiter, prefer to show the support for the major. Opener's raise of the minor suit denies support for the major and denies the ability to cue-bid an outside ace.

Slam-going auctions
The 1NT : 3♣ / 3♦ / 3♥ / 3♠ sequences

A transfer sequence does not cope well with a one-suiter and slam prospects, especially for a major. This hand type is shown by a jump to the three-level. The suit bid is genuine, not a transfer. It promises a one-suiter and shows slam interest. With a two-suiter and slam interest, you would *definitely* adopt a transfer sequence, since opener can then show weak support or strong support for either suit. Without slam interest, there is always a convenient auction without needing the jump to the three-level.

After responder's jump to the three-level, opener rebids 3NT if holding only a doubleton in responder's suit (e.g., 1NT : 3♥, 3NT), raises the suit with weak support (0 or 1 key feature) or bids an outside ace with strong support (2 or 3 key features). For example, 1NT : 3♠, 4♦ shows good spade support, the ace of diamonds but no ace of clubs: with more than one ace, bid the cheaper. After receiving support, responder can make a cue-bid or use 4NT to ask for aces or key cards. (*For another approach here, see Chapter 13.*)

If opener bids 3NT, denying support, a new suit by responder is a cue-bid with the original suit set as trumps. Responder has a strong 6-card or longer suit. For example, 1NT : 3♠, 3NT : 4♦ . . . spades are set as trumps and responder is keen on slam. Responder has shown the ♦A and denied the ♣A.

What does this sequence mean:

1NT : 3♥, 3NT : 4NT ?

And what about :

1NT : 2♦, 2♥ : 4NT ?

It makes sense to play one of them as quantitative and the other as asking for aces. It does not matter much which way you play them provided you and partner have a clear understanding which is which.

After a transfer to a major

After opener has accepted the transfer, a jump in a new suit is not needed as a natural bid since a simple change of suit would be forcing. One method is to play this as a cue-bid with responder's major set as trumps. For example, 1NT : 2♥, 2♠ : 4♣ sets spades as trumps, indicates slam ambitions and shows the ♣A.

Why did responder not simply bid 1NT : 3♠? Because opener may then have bid 4♠ or cue-bid 4♥ or 4♦, cutting out the 4♣ bid. The transfer and then jump-as-a-cue-bid may save valuable bidding space.

The jump-shift cue does not apply to the sequence 1NT : 2♥, 2♠ : 4♥. Here responder has shown 5-5 in the majors and no slam interest (see page 27). The jump to 4♥ is not a cue-bid. The jump-shift cue does apply to 1NT : 2♦, 2♥ : 3♠ (♠A and 6+ hearts).

Another way to play the jump-shift after a transfer is as a splinter. Thus 1NT : 2♥, 2♠ : 4♣ would show a 6+ spade suit, a shortage in clubs and slam interest. It is in the nature of a short suit try for slam. If opener has no wasted values in responder's short suit opener should be keen to head for slam. Holdings with the king, queen or jack are usually wasted opposite responder's shortage.

After a transfer to a minor

Raising the minor suit to the four-level sets the minor suit as trumps and asks partner to start cue-bidding. For example, 1NT : 2♠, 3♣ : 4♣ . . .

The same applies if opener made a super-accept. For example, 1NT : 2♠, 2NT : 4♣ = clubs are trumps.

When responder rebids 3NT, the meaning will depend on whether opener gave a simple accept or a super-accept.

WEST	EAST	*or*	WEST	EAST
1NT	2♠		1NT	2NT
3♣	3NT		3♦	3NT

After a simple accept, responder's 3NT shows a hand close to slam values. If opener had given a super-accept, responder would have moved towards slam. Opener should push on with a maximum 1NT, particularly with Q-x or stronger in responder's suit.

WEST	EAST	*or*	WEST	EAST
1NT	2♠		1NT	2NT
2NT	3NT		3♣	3NT

After a super-accept, responder's 3NT shows a hand barely worth game. It is only because the hand has improved with the super-accept that responder is taking a shot at 3NT. Had opener given a simple accept, responder would have passed.

WEST	EAST	
1NT	2♠	Where responder has shown two suits and opener rebids 3NT, responder's rebid of the minor at the 4-level sets the minor suit as trumps and asks for cue-bidding.
3♣	3♥	
3NT	4♣ . . .	

This applies whether opener gave a simple accept or a super-accept.

Expert methods
Bidding after a super-accept of a major

After a super-accept of a major, a new suit would be a cue-bid.

WEST	EAST	
1NT	2♡	Responder's 4♢ shows interest
3♠	4♢	in slam plus the ace of diamonds

Responder's 4♢ shows interest in slam plus the ace of diamonds and denies the ace of clubs.

It also makes sense to treat 3NT as Blackwood after a super-accept of a major. Having received super support for the major, responder would have no reason to suggest 3NT as an alternative contract.

WEST	EAST	
1NT	2♡	Responder's 3NT offers opener
2♠	3NT	a choice of contracts. Opener has

Responder's 3NT offers opener a choice of contracts. Opener has not shown spade support.

WEST	EAST	
1NT	2♡	Responder's 3NT can be used as
3♠	3NT	an ace ask as opener has shown

Responder's 3NT can be used as an ace ask as opener has shown excellent support for responder.

Where opener has used a different form of super-accept such as a new suit (see page 22):

1NT : 2♡   If 3♣ is used as a long suit trial
3♣ . . .   for game responder's options are :
Bid the major at the three-level: Sign-off.
Bid the major at game level: Sign-off.
New suit = cue-bid with the major suit trumps.
3NT = Asking for aces as above.

WEST	EAST	*or*	WEST	EAST
1NT	2♡		1NT	2♢
2NT			2NT	

Here opener is showing a maximum 4-3-3-3 pattern with two aces and two kings. Responder's 3NT now would not be asking for aces but rather acceding to opener's suggestion to play in no-trumps despite the major suit fit. If that does not appeal, responder may sign off in 3-Major or 4-Major. It makes sense to use a change of suit here (other than the repeat transfer — see page 23) as a cue-bid. It is thus possible to play both cue-bids and splinters after the 2NT super-accept: a change of suit is a cue-bid and a jump-shift is a splinter.

Bidding after a super-accept of a minor

After a super-accept of a minor, a new suit is played as natural and not as a cue-bid.

WEST	EAST	
1NT	2♠	Even though opener has shown
2NT	3♡	excellent support for clubs and a

Even though opener has shown excellent support for clubs and a maximum 1NT responder's 3♡ still shows a 4-card heart suit. There may be a fit in hearts as well as in clubs. If East wants to start cue-bidding East can bid 4♣ over 2NT.

3NT over the super-accept of a minor is to play so that if responder simply wants to ask for aces after the super-accept, bid 4NT to ask or raise the minor to start cue-bidding and continue with 4NT to ask for aces. As opener has already shown a maximum 1NT it would not make sense here to use 4NT as a quantitative try for 6NT.

What does it mean if responder transfers to a minor and then jumps to game in a major?

WEST	EAST	*or*	WEST	EAST
1NT	2♠		1NT	2♠
2NT	4♡ / 4♠		3♣	4♡ / 4♠

Are these natural bids or are they cue-bids or perhaps splinters? Because there are always memory risks when a jump to game (which sounds natural) is used in a conventional sense it is recommended that these jumps are used as natural bids whether opener gave a simple accept or a super-accept. The hand type for responder would be a weakish 6-5 with no slam interest (7+ HCP would be enough for such a freak hand).

With a strong 6-5 and hopes for slam responder should transfer and then bid the major at the three-level. After a super-accept responder knows that slam is likely in the minor anyway. After a simple accept responder can suggest a slam or start cue-bidding by setting the minor suit:

WEST	EAST	
1NT	2♠	If responder bids 4♡ over 3NT
3♣	3♡	responder is showing a 6-5 and
3NT	?	suggesting slam. Opener may pass

4♡ or convert to 5♣, particularly with poor holdings (such as K-Q-x or K-Q-J opposite responder's short suits). Aces in the short suits would make a move towards slam attractive.

If responder bids 4♣ over 3NT this sets clubs as trumps and asks opener to start cue-bidding.

Interference after the transfer

If they bid a suit over the transfer:

Opener passes unless worth a super-accept. After opener's pass, further action is up to responder. If responder bids the suit shown originally, this is not forcing. A *new* suit by responder is still a game-force.

If they double the transfer bid:

The double of a transfer bid usually shows a strong holding in the suit doubled. One of the problems for the opening side is whether they should compete to the three-level if fourth player bids the suit shown by the doubler. This will often depend on the number of trumps opener holds.

Bid the major shown = doubleton only and no desire to compete to the three-level.

Pass = 3+ support and prepared to compete to three. If this comes back to responder, redouble asks opener to accept the transfer anyway.

Redouble = 4-card support and maximum values. Definitely wants to compete and invites game. This would show a maximum 1NT with two key features.

Super-accept = usual values (all 3 key features).

If they bid responder's major:

Pass = weak support and no desire to compete at the three-level. Double = 3+ support and desire to bid further. Super-accept = usual values.

EXERCISES USING TRANSFERS

A. Partner has opened 1NT. What is your response with each of these hands?

1. ♠ A K	2. ♠ A 9	3. ♠ 2	4. ♠ 7 4	5. ♠ K J 2
♡ K J 5 3	♡ K J 5 3	♡ K 8 6	♡ A K Q 8 2	♡ J 8 7 5 4 3 2
◇ 7 2	◇ 7 2	◇ A K 3 2	◇ A K 8	◇ A Q
♣ A Q J 4 3	♣ A J 6 4 3	♣ K J 8 7 5	♣ K 6 4	♣ 4

B. The bidding has started 1NT : 2♡, 2♠ : 3♡. What is opener's rebid with these hands?

1. ♠ K 6 3	2. ♠ 10 3	3. ♠ J 8 7	4. ♠ J 3	5. ♠ A Q 6 4
♡ K J 5 3	♡ A K 9 2	♡ A Q 6	♡ K 8 2	♡ A 4
◇ A 5	◇ A K 3	◇ K Q 6 2	◇ A 10 9 2	◇ 9 4 3
♣ J 10 8 6	♣ 8 7 6 3	♣ J 9 4	♣ A J 9 6	♣ Q 10 9 8

C. The bidding has started 1NT : 2♠, 3♣ : 3♡. What should opener do next?

1. ♠ 9 7 3	2. ♠ A K 2	3. ♠ A Q 9 2	4. ♠ A 9 5 2	5. ♠ K Q 10
♡ A J	♡ K 7 5 2	♡ 8 6 3	♡ K Q 7 5	♡ 5 4 2
◇ K J 9 6	◇ K 8 4	◇ A Q J 2	◇ 9 8 4	◇ A K J
♣ K 9 7 2	♣ 8 6 3	♣ 9 5	♣ A 6	♣ J 9 3 2

PARTNERSHIP BIDDING : How should the following hands be bid? West is the dealer each time.

SET 7 — WEST	SET 7 — EAST	SET 8 — WEST	SET 8 — EAST
1. ♠ K 7 2	1. ♠ A Q 9 6 5	1. ♠ A 10 3 2	1. ♠ K Q 6 4
♡ A 7	♡ K 3	♡ K 10 6 2	♡ A 9 7 5 3
◇ Q 10 5 3	◇ J 8 4 2	◇ A 7 4	◇ 8 6
♣ K 9 6 4	♣ A 7	♣ J 3	♣ A 4
2. ♠ K Q 5 2	2. ♠ 6	2. ♠ K 5 3 2	2. ♠ A 7 4
♡ A 5 2	♡ K J 10 7 4 3	♡ A Q J 6	♡ 8
◇ 6 4 2	◇ A K 3	◇ 6 5	◇ A K Q 9 8 7
♣ A 10 5	♣ Q 3 2	♣ K 8 3	♣ J 5 2
3. ♠ 9 6 3	3. ♠ A K J 4	3. ♠ K 7 4 2	3. ♠ A Q 8 5 3
♡ K Q 10	♡ 5	♡ Q 8 6	♡ A
◇ K 5	◇ A Q 10 9 7 2	◇ K 9	◇ A Q 8 7 5
♣ A J 8 4 3	♣ 7 6	♣ A 6 5 3	♣ 7 2
4. ♠ A K 7 2	4. ♠ 8 5	4. ♠ 10 7 6 3	4. ♠ A J
♡ K Q 5 4	♡ 9 2	♡ A 2	♡ K Q 8 4 3
◇ 9 6 5	◇ A K 4 3	◇ A 7 3	◇ 9
♣ J 2	♣ A K 9 5 3	♣ K Q 9 3	♣ A J 10 7 4
5. ♠ A K 4	5. ♠ 8 2	5. ♠ 8 7 4 3	5. ♠ K Q 10 5 2
♡ Q 3	♡ A J 10 5 4	♡ K 8 2	♡ A
◇ A 9 8 3	◇ K Q 7	◇ A K 4	◇ 8 2
♣ 10 7 3 2	♣ K 9 8	♣ Q 8 4	♣ A J 10 6 3
6. ♠ Q 7 3	6. ♠ A K 5 4 2	6. ♠ K 3	6. ♠ A Q J 6 4
♡ A 4 2	♡ K Q 9 8	♡ 8 4 2	♡ A K 5
◇ A Q 9	◇ J 3 2	◇ A J 9 7	◇ 5
♣ J 6 4 3	♣ 5	♣ A J 6 4	♣ K Q 3 2

PLAY HANDS ON STRONG TRANSFERS OVER 1NT
(These hands can be made up by using pages 176-183)

Hand 13: Transfer, then new suit — Choosing the 'better' trump fit at pairs

Dealer North : Both vulnerable

```
              NORTH
              ♠ A K 7 6
              ♡ K 8 6 2
              ◇ Q 7 2
              ♣ 9 6
WEST                        EAST
♠ 9 8                       ♠ 10 3
♡ 10 5 4                    ♡ 9 7
◇ K 9 5                     ◇ A J 10 6 3
♣ K Q 10 8 5                ♣ J 4 3 2
              SOUTH
              ♠ Q J 5 4 2
              ♡ A Q J 3
              ◇ 8 4
              ♣ A 7
```

WEST	NORTH	EAST	SOUTH
	1NT	No	2♡
No	2♠	No	3♡
No	4♡	All pass	

Bidding: South's sequence (transfer to spades and then 3♡) is a game-force with at least 5 spades and 4 hearts. At rubber bridge or teams North might choose the 5-4 fit which is often safer than the 4-4 fit. At pairs North should choose the 4-4 fit even though the spade support is stronger and the partnership may hold more spades than hearts. The 4-4 fit may not be safer (a terrible trump split is more likely when five trumps are missing) but it will often produce an extra trick, perhaps the overtrick which gives you a great score rather than just an average.

Lead: King of clubs. The strong unbid suit is normal.

Recommended play: South wins with the ♣A (it would be a serious error to duck since ten tricks would then be the limit) and should draw trumps. Next the spades are cashed starting with the ace and king and on the fifth spade declarer discards dummy's club loser. Ruff a club and concede two diamonds for 11 tricks. +650.

Notes: (1) If spades are trumps, the heart suit produces only four tricks. With hearts as trumps declarer can use the spades to obtain a vital discard and the club ruff means the heart suit has produced five tricks.
(2) If hearts were 4-1 (28% of the time) only ten tricks would be made, the same as having spades as trumps. 4♡ is slightly riskier than 4♠ since a 5-0 break would defeat 4♡ while a 4-0 break would not beat 4♠.

Hand 14: When to transfer when to avoid it — Catering for a bad break

Dealer East : Nil vulnerable

```
              NORTH
              ♠ A 9 2
              ♡ K 9 4
              ◇ J 10 9 6
              ♣ J 6 5
WEST                        EAST
♠ J 3                       ♠ Q 8 7 4
♡ A 8                       ♡ Q 6 5
◇ A K Q 5 3                 ◇ 7 4 2
♣ 9 8 4 2                   ♣ A K Q
              SOUTH
              ♠ K 10 6 5
              ♡ J 10 7 3 2
              ◇ 8
              ♣ 10 7 3
```

WEST	NORTH	EAST	SOUTH
		1NT	No
3NT	No	No	No

Bidding: Despite the two doubletons West bids 3NT. At pairs do not play in 5♣ or 5◇ if 3NT is feasible. 'Might 3NT make?' is the test. If the answer is 'Yes, it might' take your chances in 3NT. It would be wrong to transfer to diamonds and rebid 3NT. Firstly this does not highlight the problem suit(s) and it also suggests slam values. The West hand has no reasonable prospects for slam. If 3NT happens to go sour, what you desperately need is a partner who will not only be philosophical about the loss but will also console you and agree with your action. What a partner!

Lead: 3 of hearts. After 1NT : 3NT a major suit is usually best and the longer suit is the normal choice.

Recommended play: East ducks in dummy and North's king wins. North should return a heart (the 9, top from a remaining doubleton) and dummy wins. Declarer should cash the ◇A and return to hand with a club to lead a second diamond. When South shows out, the diamond is ducked to North. East wins the expected heart return, cashes the clubs and crosses to dummy in diamonds. With clubs 3-3 declarer scores an overtrick.

Notes: (1) At rubber or teams declarer would win the second heart and duck a diamond at trick 2. This secures the contract even if diamonds are 4-1. At pairs you play for the normal 3-2 break (68% chance) since this gives you an overtrick. However East should not simply start cashing diamonds. The 4-1 break would mean that there are only three diamond tricks and if the clubs were not 3-3 declarer would fail. The recommended play loses nothing if diamonds are 3-2 and caters for a 4-1 break with South having the singleton.
(2) After East returns to hand with a club and leads a diamond, if South were to follow declarer would win with a top diamond in dummy. If diamonds were 3-2, declarer would then cash the top clubs (in case they were 3-3) and the ♡Q followed by the diamond winners. If it turns out that South began with four diamonds declarer would then have to switch to clubs and hope they were 3-3.
(3) South should signal for a spade shift on the second round of diamonds, which is ducked to North. If the defenders cash their two spade tricks, declarer is held to nine tricks.

Hand 15: Choice of transfers — Discarding losers

Dealer South : N-S vulnerable

NORTH
♠ K 7 6 4
♡ 10 9 5
◇ A 7 2
♣ 10 7 4

WEST
♠ 8 3 2
♡ A Q 4 3
◇ K 8 5
♣ A J 6

EAST
♠ A Q J 10 9 5
♡ K
◇ 9 6 4
♣ K Q 5

SOUTH
♠ - - -
♡ J 8 7 6 2
◇ Q J 10 3
♣ 9 8 3 2

WEST	NORTH	EAST	SOUTH
			No
1NT	No	2♡	No
2♠	No	4♠	All pass

Bidding: East has the choice of jumping to 4♠ or transferring to 4♠. There is no clearcut benefit having the East hand as declarer and so East should transfer. East could choose 1NT : 4◇ (South African Transfer) but this might be doubled and a diamond lead could be unwelcome from East's point of view. A double of the 2♡ transfer is much less likely to be damaging.

Lead: 10 of hearts. North has no attractive lead. As the hearts contain a short sequence the heart lead is preferable to the club lead. It is normal to choose the stronger holding.

Recommended play: The ♡K wins trick 1. Declarer comes to hand with a club to the jack and cashes the heart winners to discard two diamond losers from dummy. Next comes the spade finesse, declarer running the ♠8. That works but North turns up with all the spades. After a second spade finesse, come to hand via the ♣A and repeat the spade finesse. The ace of spades drops North's king and declarer has 12 tricks +480.

Notes: (1) Not every transfer yields a tangible benefit. On this hand however, the transfer is worth two extra tricks. If East were declarer South would lead the queen of diamonds and the defenders would take the first three tricks. Declarer would now score only +420.
(2) 12 tricks are still there if North happened to lead a club. Win with the ♣K, cash the ♡K, return to hand with a club to the jack and pitch two diamonds on the hearts. Run the ♠8 and continue with a second spade finesse. Return to hand with a club to the ace and repeat the spade finesse.
(3) If the ♠K were with South then 4♠ by East would fail but 4♠ by West would make 11 tricks.
(4) Do not take the spade finesse before discarding dummy's diamonds. If it failed, you might go one down.

Hand 16: Transfer with two suits and a shortage — Urgent discards

Dealer West : E-W vulnerable

NORTH
♠ 10 9 2
♡ A K Q 3
◇ 9 5 3
♣ A 9 3

WEST
♠ A 6 5
♡ J 8 6 2
◇ 7 6 4
♣ K 8 4

EAST
♠ 8 7
♡ 10 9 5 4
◇ A 8 2
♣ Q J 10 2

SOUTH
♠ K Q J 4 3
♡ 7
◇ K Q J 10
♣ 7 6 5

WEST	NORTH	EAST	SOUTH
No	1NT	No	2♡
No	2♠	No	3NT
No	4♠	All pass	

Bidding: South has enough for game and should travel via a transfer to spades. After North bids 2♠ South should not show the diamonds. South is not interested in playing in 5◇ at pairs and to introduce the diamonds would indicate some interest in slam. South has only just enough for game.

South's 3NT offers North the choice of playing in 4♠ or in 3NT. With the 3-card support North should choose 4♠ even with the flat shape. For all North knows, South might have a singleton in diamonds or clubs and 3NT could be very risky.

Lead: Queen of clubs. Top-of-sequence is almost always best.

Recommended play: North should take the ace of clubs and shift to hearts, cashing the ace, king and queen to discard dummy's club losers. Next comes the ten of spades. Upon regaining the lead North draws trumps and then forces out the ace of diamonds. This makes 11 tricks for +450.

Notes: (1) 3NT could be defeated on a club lead. Even if you were to escape the club lead, a club switch after the defenders take their first ace would leave North-South with a terrible score.
(2) There is no reason to duck the opening lead. That would hold declarer to ten tricks (as two aces have to be lost) and +420 would be an awful score, probably a bottom.
(3) It would be a dreadful error to tackle trumps before playing out the heart winners. After winning the ♠A the defenders could cash two clubs and the ace of diamonds for one down.
(4) After discarding dummy's clubs, start on trumps and do not ruff a club or a heart in dummy. This could be fatal if trumps happened to be 4-1. Avoid shortening the long trump hand without a specific reason.

CHAPTER 5

BIDDING AFTER A 2NT OPENING

Standard Acol 2NT: 20-22 points

Problem: Responder with 4 points will usually pass and game could be missed.

WEST	W	E	EAST
♠ A Q 4	2NT	No	♠ J 7 2
♡ A 6 5			♡ 8 4 3 2
◇ K Q J 10			◇ 7 5 3
♣ A Q 7			♣ K 6 3

East passes and a good 3NT is missed. Do not blame East. Remove West's ♠Q or ♣Q and 3NT is silly.

A 3-point range for 2NT is awkward as there is no invitational bid. A 2-point range means that responder always knows the combined total within one point.

Recommended 2NT: 21-22 points.

With 20 points, open 1-suit and rebid with a jump in no-trumps. With more than 22, open 2♣ or 2◇ (your game-force opening) and rebid in no-trumps.

2NT : 3♣

There are two basic conventions that are popular:

Stayman 3♣, asking for opener's major suits. With no major, opener bids 3◇.

Baron 3♣, asking opener to bid 4-card suits up-the-line. If opener's only suit is clubs, opener rebids 3NT.

At pairs it is definitely superior to use Stayman. Playing Baron often means that the weaker hand becomes declarer in 4♡ or 4♠. With the great disparity in strength, it is a significant loss to have the weaker hand declarer frequently.

WEST	Stayman		EAST
♠ A K 8 4	W	E	♠ Q 9 7 2
♡ K 6 5	2NT	3♣	♡ 9 8 2
◇ A Q 3 2	3♠	4♠	◇ K J 6
♣ A Q	No		♣ 8 7 3

Here West is declarer and 4♠ is a good chance. Playing Baron the bidding would go:

	W	E
	2NT	3♣
	3◇	3♠
	4♠	No

With East declarer a heart or a club lead could produce a much worse result.

WEST	Stayman		EAST
♠ A Q 8 4	W	E	♠ K 9 7 2
♡ A J 6 5	2NT	3♣	♡ K 2
◇ K Q 7	3♡	3NT	◇ J 10 5 4
♣ A Q	4♠	No	♣ 8 7 3

Playing Baron the bidding would go:

	W	E
	2NT	3♣
	3♡	3♠
	4♠	No

With West declarer, a heart or a club lead is a benefit. With East declarer, a heart or a club lead may result in an extra trick lost.

The advantage of Baron is that it is easier to find minor suit slams on a 4-4 fit. This tiny plus is greatly outweighed by the weaker hand becoming declarer in the far more common major suit games.

Note how responder when playing Stayman rebids 3NT over 3♡ when holding four spades. The 3♣ response promises a major and so when opener bids 3♡, responder's 3NT says, 'That was not the major I wanted.' If opener has four spades opener can now bid 4♠ and become declarer.

After the 3♡ response, 3♠ by responder does show four spades but indicates slam interest. With slam potential and four spades, responder cannot afford to bid 3NT in case opener passes. As transfers to the minors are not generally used over 2NT, the 3♠ bid may be the beginning of a sequence where responder intends to show a minor suit next if opener does not have spade support.

WEST	W	E	EAST
♠ A J 8 4	2NT	3♣	♠ K 10 7 2
♡ A K 5 3	3♡	3♠	♡ 2
◇ A Q 2	4♣	4NT	◇ K J 6
♣ A 10	5♣	6♠	♣ K J 9 8 3

4♣ = cue-bid with spade support. 5♣ = 0 or 4 aces.

If West did not have spade support and rebid 3NT over 3♠, East would have continued with 4♣.

After 2NT : 3♣, 3◇ . . .

A major suit now by responder shows a 5-card major. Since 3◇ denied a major there would be no point in responder now showing a 4-card major. Responder's choice of 3♣ rather than a transfer suggests responder is at least 5-4 in the majors.

WEST	Stayman		EAST
♠ A K 8	W	E	♠ Q 9 7 5 2
♡ Q 10 5	2NT	3♣	♡ K 9 8 2
◇ K Q 2	3◇	3♠	◇ 6 4
♣ A K 4 3	4♠	No	♣ 8 7

If stronger, West would cue-bid with spade support.

Playing Baron you need a 2NT : 3♠ response to show the East hand. You cannot afford to use Baron 3♣ when 5-4 in the majors.

After any reply to Stayman, a bid of 4♣ or 4◇ by responder is natural and shows a 5-card suit. Opener can support via a raise or a cue-bid, and deny support with 4NT.

(A popular, modern method over 2NT is 3♣ 'Puppet Stayman', details of which can be found opposite.)

Bidding structure after 2NT

2NT : 3♣ = Stayman
2NT : 3♦ = Transfer to hearts
2NT : 3♥ = Transfer to spades
2NT : 3♠ = Optional. See later.
2NT : 3NT = To play
2NT : 4♣ / 4♦ = 6+ suit, slam values
2NT : 4♥ / 4♠ = To play
2NT : 4NT = Invitation to 6NT

After 2NT : 3♦ . . . *or* 2NT : 3♥ . . .

Opener will usually bid the major shown but may super-accept by jumping to game in the major. With 4-4 in the majors, opener should bid the other major to preserve the chance of the 4-4 fit.

WEST	W	E	EAST
♠ A Q 7 2	2NT	3♦	♠ K 9 6 3
♥ K Q 8 5	3♠	4♠	♥ A 6 4 3 2
♦ A J	No		♦ 6 4
♣ A J 4			♣ 8 7

4♠ will often produce 12 tricks, 4♥ will rarely bring in more than 11 tricks. If East had no interest in spades, East could sign off in 4♥ or, preferably, repeat the transfer to hearts via 4♦.

After 2NT : 3♦, 3♥ . . . *or* 2NT : 3♥, 3♠ . . .

Responder may pass, bid 3NT to offer a choice of contracts, raise to game in the major with a 6+ suit or bid a new suit below game as forcing.

WEST	W	E	EAST
♠ A Q 7 2	2NT	3♦	♠ 6 3
♥ A 5	3♥	Pass	♥ J 8 6 4 3 2
♦ A K J			♦ 6 4 3
♣ A 9 6 4			♣ 8 7

Transfers allow responder to bail out in a part-score, something not possible in standard methods. West would be very lucky to come to seven tricks in 2NT. In 3♥ there are reasonable chances for nine tricks.

2NT : 3♠ . . .

With 4 spades - 5 hearts, there is no problem in using transfers. Both suits can be shown below 3NT. When responder has 5 spades - 4 hearts, it is not appropriate to use a transfer sequence. After the transfer to spades you cannot afford to bid 4♥ with a 4-card suit. Opener may not have support for either suit. The sequence 2NT : 3♥, 3♠ : 4♥ shows responder has at least a 5-5 pattern in the majors.

The 5 spades - 4 hearts hand can be solved by using Stayman or by an immediate response of 3♠. Many partnerships use 2NT : 3♠ in this way. It is forcing to game and does not deny slam interest.

Another possible use for 2NT : 3♠ is to show a hand with both minors and slam interest. Opener can rebid 3NT to deny decent support for either minor (over 3NT, responder can still bid 4♣ or 4♦ to show a 5+ minor) or bid 4♣ or 4♦ to show support for the minor. Responder can continue via a cue-bid or 4NT to check on controls.

After 2NT : 4♣ or 4♦

These responses are natural and show a 6-card or longer suit with slam interest. Opener should cue-bid the cheapest ace. Responder will continue with a cue-bid or 4NT asking.

Expert methods

Many top pairs will open 2NT with a 5-card major if their methods do not provide some other way of showing the balanced 21-22 with a 5-major. If so, 2NT : 3♣ should be used to ask for a 5-card major.

Opener's replies are:

3♦ = No 5-card major, but one or two 4-card majors
3♥ or 3♠ = 5-card major
3NT = no 5-card major, no 4-card major

Over 3♦, responder can hunt for a 4-4 major fit:

2NT : 3♣, 3♦ : 3♥ = 4 hearts and forcing to game.
2NT : 3♣, 3♦ : 3♠ = 4 spades and forcing to game.

After 2NT : 3♣, 3♦ : 3♥ opener would bid 3♠ if holding four spades. The drawback to this approach is that responder is often declarer in 4♥ and 4♠.

Puppet Stayman over 2NT

This structure locates all the 5-3 and 4-4 fits and ensures opener becomes declarer as often as possible. Opener's rebids after 2NT : 3♣ are the same as above for 5-card major Stayman. Over opener's 3♦, if responder wishes to explore a 4-4 fit, responder bids the major in which there is no interest :

2NT : 3♣, 3♦ : 3♥ = 4 spades
2NT : 3♣, 3♦ : 3♠ = 4 hearts
2NT : 3♣, 3♦ : 4♦ = 4-4 in the majors

Over any rebid, opener can easily select the contract. With extras, responder can push on to slam.

Responder should choose the 3♣ response when holding a 4-card major or 3-card support for either major (unless wishing to stay in no-trumps with some 4-3-3-3). With a 5-card major, including 5-3 in the majors, responder should use a transfer.

2NT : 3♦ = transfer to hearts, showing 5+ hearts (and could have four spades also). Opener will usually bid 3♥ and bidding proceeds normally as after a transfer. Opener will refuse the transfer and bid 3♠ with 5 spades and 2 hearts. Responder may raise to 4♠, rebid 3NT or transfer to 4♥ via 4♦.

2NT : 3♥ = transfer to spades with 5+ spades but denying four hearts. Opener will almost always bid 3♠ and the bidding proceeds normally as after a transfer. Opener may reject the transfer and bid 3NT when holding five hearts and two spades. Responder may pass 3NT, bid 4♥ or transfer to spades via 4♦. (In this method 4♦ is always a transfer to responder's major.)

2NT : 3♠ = responder has 5 spades and 4 hearts, forcing. Opener chooses the contract. Responder may push on for slam after opener's rebid.

The only loss in the above structure is the rare occasion when opener is 5-2 in the majors and the partnership cannot stop in a 3-major sign off.

EXERCISES FOR BIDDING AFTER A 2NT OPENING

A. Partner has opened 2NT. What is your response with each of these hands?

1. ♠ J 9	2. ♠ J 9	3. ♠ J 9 8 4	4. ♠ J 9 8 4 3	5. ♠ 9 8 7 5 3 2
♡ K J 5 3	♡ K J 5 3 2	♡ K 9 8 6 2	♡ K 9 8 2	♡ 2
◇ 7 6 2	◇ 7 6 2	◇ 3 2	◇ 3 2	◇ 6 3 2
♣ 8 7 4 2	♣ 8 7 4	♣ 7 5	♣ 6 4	♣ 8 7 4

B. The bidding has started 2NT : 3♣, 3♡. What should responder do next?

1. ♠ K 6 3	2. ♠ K 8 7 4	3. ♠ K 8 7 4	4. ♠ K 8 7 4	5. ♠ K 4
♡ K 8 5 3	♡ K 9 6 2	♡ Q 6	♡ A 2	♡ K Q 9 4
◇ 7 5	◇ 6 3	◇ 9 6 2	◇ A 10 5 2	◇ A 4
♣ 9 8 4 2	♣ 7 6 3	♣ 8 7 5 3	♣ 10 9 6	♣ Q 10 9 8 2

C. The bidding has started 2NT : 3◇, 3♡ : 3♠. What is opener's rebid with these hands?

1. ♠ K 7 3	2. ♠ A K 2	3. ♠ A J 5 2	4. ♠ A K 5 2	5. ♠ A K 9 2
♡ A J	♡ K Q J 7	♡ K Q 7 5	♡ Q 9	♡ A J 3
◇ A K J 2	◇ Q J 4	◇ A 8	◇ A K 4	◇ A K 4 2
♣ K Q 7 2	♣ K Q 3	♣ A K 4	♣ K Q 10 4	♣ K 5

PARTNERSHIP BIDDING : How should the following hands be bid? West is the dealer each time.

SET 9 — WEST	SET 9 — EAST	SET 10 — WEST	SET 10 — EAST
1. ♠ Q J 9 6 5 3	1. ♠ A K	1. ♠ K 10 3 2	1. ♠ Q 7 6 4
♡ 9 3	♡ K Q J	♡ A J 10	♡ K 7 4
◇ 8 4	◇ A 9 6 5	◇ A K Q 4	◇ J 8 6
♣ 7 6 2	♣ K Q 4 3	♣ A 3	♣ 5 4 2
2. ♠ K Q 8	2. ♠ 5 2	2. ♠ A K 5 2	2. ♠ 8 7 4 3
♡ A 6 3	♡ J 8 7 5 4 2	♡ A Q 9 6	♡ 8 4
◇ A K Q 2	◇ 7 4	◇ A J	◇ Q 9 8 7
♣ Q J 5	♣ 8 6 2	♣ A 8 3	♣ Q J 2
3. ♠ K Q 8	3. ♠ 5 2	3. ♠ Q 8 5 3	3. ♠ K 7 4
♡ A K 6 3	♡ J 8 7 5 4 2	♡ 9 7 5 3 2	♡ A 8
◇ A K 8 2	◇ 7 4	◇ A 5	◇ K Q 2
♣ K 5	♣ 8 6 2	♣ 7 6	♣ A K Q 3 2
4. ♠ J 9 8 7 4 3 2	4. ♠ A 5	4. ♠ K J 9 2	4. ♠ A Q 4
♡ 9 2	♡ A Q 5	♡ K Q 8 4 3	♡ A J 5 2
◇ - - -	◇ A 9 6 5 3	◇ 9	◇ K J 7
♣ 9 6 3 2	♣ A K 4	♣ 10 8 4	♣ K Q J
5. ♠ K 4	5. ♠ Q J 2	5. ♠ A 8	5. ♠ K 10 6 5 2
♡ Q 8 7 3 2	♡ A 4	♡ K J 8 2	♡ Q 7 6 3
◇ 9 8 3	◇ K Q J 7 2	◇ A K Q 3	◇ 2
♣ 8 7 2	♣ A K J	♣ K Q 4	♣ 10 6 3
6. ♠ K 8 2	6. ♠ Q 9 7 5 3	6. ♠ J 8 6 3 2	6. ♠ K Q 4
♡ A K J 4	♡ Q 6 2	♡ Q 10 6 4 2	♡ A 8 5
◇ K Q J	◇ 9 7 4 2	◇ 9 7	◇ A Q 3 2
♣ A 4 2	♣ 3	♣ 4	♣ A Q 6

PLAY HANDS ON TRANSFERS OVER 2NT
(These hands can be made up by using pages 176-183)

Hand 17: Bailing out of 2NT — When to discard first, when to tackle trumps first

Dealer North : Nil vulnerable

	NORTH		
	♠ A 2		
	♡ A 7 5 4		
	◇ A 8 4 3		
	♣ A K Q		

WEST		EAST
♠ K 10 7		♠ Q 9
♡ J 10		♡ K Q 9 8
◇ K J		◇ Q 9 6 5 2
♣ 10 8 7 6 3 2		♣ J 5

	SOUTH
	♠ J 8 6 5 4 3
	♡ 6 3 2
	◇ 10 7
	♣ 9 4

WEST	NORTH	EAST	SOUTH
	2NT	No	3♡
No	3♠	All pass	

Bidding: South has an almost useless hand. Without transfers, South would pass since a bid of 3♠ would be forcing. Playing transfers, South is able to bid 3♡ showing 5+ spades and pass when North accepts the transfer with 3♠.

The transfer-then-pass sequence is best reserved for a 6-card major. With a 7-card suit, even with no points, it is worth taking a shot at game. With a 5-card suit it is usually best to pass 2NT.

Lead: King of hearts. Against no-trumps East would choose a diamond but against a suit contract it is more attractive to lead from a K-Q combination than from a suit with only one honour. To lead from ♣J-x holds no appeal.

Recommended play: North wins with the ♡A. It would not cost to duck but there is no benefit either. North should continue with ace and another spade. East wins with the queen and can continue with the hearts but the defence can take only two hearts and two spades. When North regains the lead, North can cash the clubs and discard a diamond loser from dummy.

Notes: (1) It would be an error for North to start on clubs at trick 2. There is no urgency for a discard since North still has the ◇A and can discard a diamond loser from dummy later. If North were to play the clubs at once East will ruff the third round. If dummy overruffs, declarer should lose two spades, two hearts and a diamond, while if dummy discards, declarer should lose two tricks in the red suits, the club ruff and two spades.
(2) Note that nine tricks are available in spades while in no-trumps North has only six tricks available.

Hand 18: Treatment of a two-suiter — Judging which honour to play with K-J opposite junk

Dealer East : N-S vulnerable

	NORTH	
	♠ 9 6 4	
	♡ 10 5	
	◇ Q J 10 8 7	
	♣ Q 5 4	

WEST		EAST
♠ A Q 5 2		♠ K J 8 3
♡ A Q J 9		♡ K 7 6 4 2
◇ A 4		◇ 3 2
♣ K J 6		♣ 8 3

	SOUTH
	♠ 10 7
	♡ 8 3
	◇ K 9 6 5
	♣ A 10 9 7 2

WEST	NORTH	EAST	SOUTH
		No	No
2NT	No	3◇	No
3♡	No	3♠	No
4♠	No	No	No

Bidding: East has shown 5 hearts and 4 spades. West should choose spades as trumps even though this means the weaker hand will be declarer. *Being in the best contract is 90% of your task. Having it played from the right side is 10%. Do not sacrifice the contract for the sake of having the stronger hand as declarer. If you can be in the best contract and have it played from the right side, that is a bonus. If not, still choose the best spot.*

Lead: 5 of diamonds. It is usually better to lead from an unbid suit headed by the king than one headed by the ace.

Recommended play: East wins the diamond lead with dummy's ace and draws trumps. Next come the hearts. East overtakes the fourth round and cashes the fifth heart on which dummy's diamond loser is discarded. East continues with a club. If South rises with the ace, East has 12 tricks. South should play low and East has to guess whether to finesse the jack or the king. If East calls for dummy's jack, East makes 11 tricks while if dummy's king is played, East scores 12 tricks.

Notes: (1) On the first diamond North should play the ◇Q. If North can later signal South the count in diamonds, South will know East began with two diamonds only and so it is safe to duck the club lead.
(2) A tiny clue might guide East into picking the clubs correctly. South led a diamond rather than a club. With ♣A South would be reluctant to lead a club. Without the ♣A South might have chosen a club lead rather than the diamond. As South chose a diamond, perhaps holding the ♣A was the reason.
(3) In hearts, East-West can make only 11 tricks even if the clubs are picked correctly. In spades East-West can make 12 tricks. Note that if East uses Stayman West bids 3♡. It would be very tough then to reach 4♠.

Hand 19: Choice of transfers — Discarding losers

Dealer South : E-W vulnerable

NORTH
♠ K 10 9 6 3
♡ Q 8 7 2
♢ 9 5
♣ 7 4

WEST
♠ Q 4 2
♡ 5
♢ A 10 8 7 6
♣ Q 8 6 3

EAST
♠ J 8 5
♡ J 10 9 6 4
♢ K 2
♣ 10 9 5

SOUTH
♠ A 7
♡ A K 3
♢ Q J 4 3
♣ A K J 2

WEST	NORTH	EAST	SOUTH
			2NT
No	3♠	No	3NT
No	No	No	

Bidding: 3♠ shows 5 spades and 4 hearts. With no fit for either major, South chooses 3NT.

North might bid this hand type via Stayman as follows :

WEST	NORTH	EAST	SOUTH
			2NT
No	3♣	No	3♢
No	3♠	No	3NT
No	No	No	

3♢ = no major and then 3♠ = five spades.

Lead: 7 of diamonds. The long suit is the normal choice.

Recommended play: East wins with the ♢K at trick 1 and returns the ♢2. South plays an honour, captured by West who plays a third diamond. South wins in hand and discards a heart from dummy (a tough decision). With eight tricks on top, there is no rush to try the club finesse for the ninth trick. Best is to play the ace of spades and duck the next spade into the East hand (safe as East is known to be out of diamonds). Win the return from East, cash one top club in case the queen drops and then play off the hearts, ending in dummy. Test the spades by cashing the ♠K. When spades turn out to be 3-3, you have ten tricks without needing the club finesse.

Notes: (1) Knowing from the bidding that South figures to have only two spades, a thoughtful West might play the ♠Q on the second round of spades. If that persuades South that West has Q-J-x in spades, South might switch to the club finesse and so fail.
(2) If declarer discards a club from dummy on the third diamond, East should play a club when in with the ♠J. Now South has to guess whether the club finesse is necessary before finding out how the majors break. If you decide to discard from a major, keep the length in spades where if things go well you score more tricks.

Hand 20: Transfer with a weak hand — Coping with a bad break

Dealer West : Both vulnerable

NORTH
♠ J 10 8 4 3
♡ - - -
♢ 10 7 6 4
♣ Q 7 5 2

WEST
♠ K Q
♡ A K 6 2
♢ A K Q J
♣ 9 8 3

EAST
♠ 9 7 6
♡ J 10 9 5 4 3
♢ 8 2
♣ 10 6

SOUTH
♠ A 5 2
♡ Q 8 7
♢ 9 5 3
♣ A K J 4

WEST	NORTH	EAST	SOUTH
2NT	No	3♢	No
4♡	No	No	No

Bidding: West should open 2NT despite the weakness in clubs. There is no other opening bid to describe the shape and the strength as accurately as 2NT. Take your chances!

East transfers to hearts with the intention of passing 3♡. East should not pass 2NT. On a spade lead and return West has no more than seven tricks against competent defence.

After the 3♢ transfer, West should super-accept with 4♡. West has a maximum 2NT, 4-card heart support and a doubleton outside as ruffing potential.

Lead: Jack of spades. Prefer the top of a near sequence to leading from a suit headed by one or two honours.

Recommended play: East might well wish West loads of luck as dummy is revealed. South wins the ace of spades and should cash the top clubs. If South plays a third club, this is ruffed in dummy. A heart to the ace reveals the bad news. Needing to return to dummy to take the heart finesse, declarer plays ♢A, ♢K and ruffs the third diamond. The jack of hearts is led and if South plays low, so does declarer.

Notes: (1) At trick 1 it is clear West began with ♠K-Q. Even if West did not drop an honour, South should shift to clubs. If South fails to cash the clubs early, West can discard club losers on the diamond winners.
(2) Normally 4♡ would be child's play. If trumps are 2-1 (about 78% of the time), declarer can just draw trumps and claim. If South cashed two clubs and then led a diamond or a spade, West would reach dummy by ruffing a club. If South had five diamonds and two clubs, making declarer ruff the club in dummy would almost certainly defeat the contract.

CHAPTER 6
SPLINTERS

What do you understand by 1♡ : 4◇? Or 1♣ : 3♠? In standard methods these are played as pre-empts but such a treatment is not very profitable. Firstly, the occurrence is rare and to pre-empt after partner has opened is seldom useful and rarely necessary. To pre-empt beyond 3NT can be downright foolish.

For these reasons many tournament players have assigned a different meaning to the double jump in a new suit after partner has opened the bidding. Known as 'splinters' because they indicate the tiniest part of the hand, these jumps show good trump support (normally at least four trumps), sufficient high card values for game and a singleton or a void in the suit bid. The strength will vary according to what has been shown so far.

Responder's immediate splinter to a major
1♡ : 3♠ / 4♣ / 4◇ and 1♠ : 4♣ / 4◇ / 4♡

Expectancy is 4+ trumps, 11+ HCP and a void or a singleton in the suit bid. Opener should consider the splinter as a short-suit try for a slam. Opposite a singleton, the ace is a good card but the other honours are wasted ('duplication'). For the following layouts, imagine that a major suit is trumps.

Situation (1)		Situation (2)	
◇ J x x	◇ K Q x	◇ J x x	◇ A x x
♣ x	♣ A x x	♣ x	♣ K Q x

In (1) the singleton is opposite the ace and no other high cards. The partnership should lose only one trick in the minors. In (2), with the singleton opposite K-Q-x the partnership could easily have three minor losers if the defenders start on the diamonds early.

Opposite a void, even the ace is often wasted.

Situation (3)		Situation (4)	
◇ K Q J x	◇ A x x	◇ K Q J x	◇ x x x
♣ - - -	♣ x x x	♣ - - -	♣ A x x

In (3) with nothing wasted opposite the void, there are no minor suit losers. In (4) you have to lose a diamond. The ♣A contributes almost nothing.

The best holding facing the short suit is three or four low cards. That allows you to ruff two or three times to eliminate two or three losers. A doubleton facing the singleton is not so great since you can ruff only once and a singleton facing a singleton is no asset at all. Again, this is known as 'duplication'. A 5-card holding facing the singleton can also have problems. There may not be enough trumps in dummy to ruff all the losers in a long suit, particularly if the opponents start leading trumps. Opposite a singleton A-x-x, A-x-x-x, x-x-x and x-x-x-x are excellent holdings and opposite a void, x-x-x or x-x-x-x are best.

After responder's immediate splinter, opener should sign off in game with a minimum opening hand unless you have one of the excellent holdings opposite responder's short suit. Opener should look for slam with a minimum opening if opener has an excellent holding facing the shortage, or with sufficient extra values to compensate for the duplication opposite the shortage.

WEST	W	E	EAST
♠ A Q 8 6 3	1♠	4◇	♠ K 9 7 5 2
♡ A 6	?		♡ K 5 3
◇ K 7 6			◇ 5
♣ 6 3 2			♣ A Q 8 4

West should sign off in 4♠. West has a minimum opening and the ◇K is now wasted. If the club finesse fails, there are three losers.

WEST	W	E	EAST
♠ A Q 8 6 3	1♠	4◇	♠ K 9 7 5 2
♡ A 6	?		♡ K 5 3
◇ 6 3 2			◇ 5
♣ K 7 6			♣ A Q 8 4

West should move towards 6♠, which is an excellent slam. Although holding only a minimum opening, West has an ideal holding opposite the diamond shortage. When bidding for slam, you may ask with 4NT or cue-bid (see Chapters 12-15).

WEST	W	E	EAST
♠ A Q 8 6 3	1♠	4◇	♠ K 9 7 5 2
♡ A 6	?		♡ K 5 3
◇ K Q 2			◇ 5
♣ K 6 3			♣ A Q 8 7

West should move on to 6♠. Although there is severe duplication in diamonds, West has much more than a minimum opening. In such cases, ask yourself 'If I remove the wasted high cards opposite the shortage, would I be looking for a slam?' If after removing the duplication you still have a decent opening hand, the answer should be yes. Here if West considers the ◇K-Q-x as ◇x-x-x, West still has a sound opening and with an ideal diamond holding, would certainly be looking for slam.

WEST	W	E	EAST
♠ A Q 8 6 3	1♠	4◇	♠ K 9 7 5 2
♡ A 6	4♠ . . .		♡ K J 3
◇ K 7 6			◇ 5
♣ 9 3 2			♣ A K Q 8

Even if opener signs off, responder may push on with sufficient extra values. The minimum would be 16 HCP or a 5-loser hand. If worse than that, responder should respect opener's sign off. Here with great support, 16 HCP and 5 losers, East should continue with 4NT and finish in 6♠.

Responder's immediate splinter to a minor

1♣ : 3◇ / 3♡ / 3♠   and   1◇ : 3♡ / 3♠ / 4♣

Expectancy is 4+ trumps, no 4-card major, at least 13 HCP and a singleton or void in the suit bid.

With strong support for a major, you want to play in the major suit game. With strong support for a minor, there remains the question of whether you would be better off in 3NT. Except for the rarely used 1◇ : 4♣ sequence, the splinter responses to a minor do not commit the partnership to a minor suit contract. If opener is very strong in responder's short suit (at least a double stopper), opener should choose 3NT.

WEST	W	E	EAST
♠ J 9 3 2	1♣	3♡	♠ A 7 5
♡ K Q J 2	?		♡ 8
◇ K			◇ A Q 5 4
♣ A 7 5 4			♣ K 8 6 3 2

With such strong hearts facing the shortage, West should choose 3NT which is not only more likely to succeed than 5♣ but often leads to a better score.

If opener does not fancy 3NT, treat the splinter as a short suit try for slam. Again with an ideal holding opposite the shortage, slam is a good bet.

WEST	W	E	EAST
♠ K Q	1♣	3♡	♠ A 7 5
♡ 9 7 3 2	?		♡ 8
◇ J 2			◇ A Q 5 4
♣ A Q J 5 4			♣ K 8 6 3 2

With the ideal holding in hearts, West bids 4♣ indicating no desire for no-trumps and slam interest in clubs. It is best to treat the splinter as game-forcing and not treat 4♣ here as a sign-off. With good controls, East here should bid 4NT and finish in 6♣.

It is even possible to suggest a contract in some other suit :

WEST	W	E	EAST
♠ K Q J 3	1♣	3♡	♠ A 7 5
♡ K 5 2	?		♡ 8
◇ K 3			◇ A Q 5 4
♣ Q J 5 4			♣ K 8 6 3 2

Sometimes one stopper opposite the singleton will do for 3NT but most of the time it is too risky. Here West can bid 3♠ to suggest 4♠ on a 4-3 fit and East should raise to 4♠. The 4-3 fit is reasonable if the short hand is doing the ruffing. Here 5♣ is safe enough but 4♠ will succeed most of the time for a better score.

Opener's splinter rebid after a major response

When opener has enough to raise responder's major to game, opener can also use the splinter structure. For example:

WEST EAST	
1♣ 1♠	West has enough for 1♣ : 1♠, 4♠ and has a singleton or void in diamonds.
4◇ . . .	

The same applies to sequences like 1♣ : 1♡, 3♠ or 1◇ : 1♠, 4♡, and so on. Responder can sign off in game or head for a slam.

With a balanced hand of 19-20 points with support for responder's major, opener should travel via the 2NT rebid. For example:

WEST	W	E	EAST
♠ A 4 3	1♣	1♡	♠ K 9
♡ K Q 9 8	2NT	3NT	♡ A 5 4 3
◇ A 2	4♡	No	◇ J 5 3
♣ A Q 9 4			♣ 8 7 5 2

Opener's 2NT shows 19-20 points and is forcing to game. Removing 3NT to 4♡ shows the 4-card support. Naturally if East had rebid other than 3NT opener would also show the heart support then.

It thus follows that sequences like 1♣ : 1♡, 4♡ or 1◇ : 1♠, 4♠ will be neither balanced nor have a singleton or a void. The pattern must be 5-4-2-2.

WEST	W	E	EAST
♠ A 4	1♣	1♡	♠ K 9 7
♡ K Q 9 8	4♡	No	♡ A 5 4 3
◇ 10 2			◇ J 5 3
♣ A K J 9 4			♣ 8 7 2

After an auction starts 1♠ : 2♡, a rebid of 3♣ or 3◇ by opener is forcing and so it is sensible to use a jump to 4♣ or 4◇ as a splinter raise of hearts. The same would apply after responder's jump-shift. Opener's jump in a new suit would be a splinter.

Opener can also splinter with the second rebid.

WEST	W	E	EAST
♠ K Q 6 3	1♡	2♣	♠ A 7 5 4
♡ A K 9 8 3 2	2♡	2♠	♡ 6
◇ 2	4◇ . . .		◇ J 8 7
♣ J 8			♣ A K Q 3 2

Too weak to reverse, West rebids 2♡ but over 2♠, West shows the good support and diamond shortage with the jump to 4◇. East-West should now reach 6♠.

Opener's splinter rebid after a minor response

After 1♣ : 1◇, opener's jump-rebid to 3♡ or 3♠ has little value as a natural bid and can be harnessed as a splinter with 4-card diamond support.

After a two-level response in a minor, you need to weigh up the value of a jump-shift as a natural rebid or as a splinter. For example:

WEST	EAST	
1♠	2♣	Change of suit is forcing after a two-level response, so is the jump to 3♡ needed as natural?
3♡ . . .		

After 1♠ : 2♣ a rebid of 2♡ is therefore forcing and a natural jump to 3♡ is used to show a good hand with 5-5 in the majors. The splinter jump to 3♡ would show at least 4-card support for the minor, 16+ HCP and a singleton or void in hearts. You cannot have both and have to choose which method to play. The 3-level splinter avoids the jump to 4-minor on hands too good for 3-minor and still leaves open the option for 3NT.

Responder's splinter rebid

Where opener has rebid with a change of suit, the only suit left will be the fourth suit. A simple bid of the fourth suit is played as conventional and forcing. A jump in the fourth suit is played as natural and game-forcing.

WEST	EAST	
1♦	1♠	East's 3♥ shows game values
2♣	3♥ . . .	and 5-5 in the majors. With no natural 2♥ bid available, the jump

here is natural and not a splinter.

Where opener's rebid is in the suit opened, change of suit is natural and forcing and so a jump in a new suit can sensibly be played as a splinter. If opener's suit is a major, the splinter will show just 3-card support. With better support responder could have splintered on the first round.

WEST	W	E	EAST
♠ A 6 3	1♥	2♣	♠ J
♥ K Q 6 5 4 2	2♥	?	♥ A 7 3
♦ K 6 3			♦ A Q 8 4
♣ 2			♣ A K 10 8 5

How should East continue? The splinter jump to 3♠ expresses East's values well: 3-card support for hearts, short in spades and too strong for a mere jump to 4♥. After the 3♠ splinter East-West have a firm basis to reach 7♥.

If opener's suit is a minor, responder may have genuine support for the minor:

WEST	W	E	EAST
♠ 3	1♣	1♠	♠ K Q 7 5 2
♥ K 5 2	2♣	3♦	♥ Q 8 4
♦ A K 3	3NT	No	♦ 2
♣ Q J 5 4 3 2			♣ A K 8 6

East's 3♦ shows club support, short diamonds and game values. With strong diamonds, West chooses 3NT. Although 5♣ should make easily, 3NT has no problems and will often score an overtrick.

Expert methods

Splinters after overcalls

Just as you can splinter after an opening, so you splinter after an overcall to show good high card strength as well as the support and shortage requirements. Although a slam is unlikely after the opponents have opened, it is not impossible if there is no duplication facing the shortage.

WEST			EAST
♠ K Q J 6 3			♠ A 7 5 4
♥ K 5 2			♥ Q J 8
♦ 3			♦ A K 5 4 2
♣ A 8 5 4			♣ 2

SOUTH	WEST	NORTH	EAST
1♣	1♠	No	4♣
Dble	4NT	No	5♥
No	6♠	All pass	

With a strong overcall and an ideal holding in East's known short suit, West heads for slam.

Splinters after powerful two openings

This is a very fruitful area for splinters. After a negative response to an artificial strong opening of 2♣ or 2♦, responder can show useful values in support of opener's suit plus the shortage. This will often be enough to encourage opener to head for slam.

WEST	W	E	EAST
♠ A K Q 6 3 2	2♣	2♦	♠ 8 7 5 4
♥ - - -	2♠	4♣	♥ 8 6 4 3 2
♦ K Q J 3	4♥	5♦	♦ A 7 4
♣ A Q 4	7♠	No	♣ 2

After West rebids 2♠, East has a great hand with the 4-card support, the singleton and the ace as well. The jump to 4♣ shows the shortage and now West can see there are no club losers. West cue-bids 4♥ to show first-round control in hearts and East's 5♦ shows first-round control there (see Chapters 14-15 for cue-bidding). That is enough for West to bid 7♠.

WEST	EAST	
2♣	2♦	It follows that if a weak responder
2♠	3♠ . . .	simply raises opener's suit, then either responder has no short suit

(the likely explanation) or has only three trumps.

Splinters after a 1NT opening

1NT : 3♣ / 3♦ / 3♥ / 3♠*

These sequences are commonly used to show one-suiters with slam interest (see Chapter 2). Some partnerships prefer to use the jumps to the three-level as splinters, indicating concern about 3NT as the best spot. The splinter jump here shows enough for game with a singleton or void in the suit bid. The splinter after 1NT would deny a 5-card major and the 1NT : 3♠ splinter ought to deny four hearts.

With the short suit well-stopped, opener can bid 3NT without any interest in a suit contract.

With the danger suit stopped and major suit interest, opener can bid the major first. Without support, responder makes a natural bid. Having already shown the shortage, responder can bid 3NT without support for opener's major.

WEST	W	E	EAST
♠ A K 7 2	1NT	3♥	♠ Q 5
♥ J 8 7	3♠	3NT	♥ 4
♦ A Q 3	4♥	5♦	♦ K J 8 7 6 2
♣ 9 5 2	No		♣ A K 10 6

3♥ = 0 or 1 heart, 3♠ suggests spades, 3NT = no support for spades, 4♥ = not sure where to go, and asking East to choose the contract. East must have a 5+ minor and here East has an easy 5♦ bid.

Playing splinters, the strong single-suiters can be shown via a transfer and raise to the four-level (for the minors) or a 4NT rebid (for the majors). The sequence transfer-to-a-major followed by a jump to 4♣ or 4♦ can be used either as a splinter or for the single-suiter with slam interest.

---

*Splinters after 1NT: *See also Appendix 3.*

EXERCISES ON SPLINTERS

A. West has opened 1♡. North passes. What should East bid with each of these hands?

1.	♠ A J 10 7	2.	♠ J 9 7 2	3.	♠ 2	4.	♠ 8	5.	♠ A K Q
	♡ Q J 5 3 2		♡ A Q 5 3		♡ A K 9 8 4		♡ K 9 8		♡ A J 7 5 4
	◇ 7		◇ A K 4 3		◇ A 3 2		◇ K 8 4 3		◇ - - -
	♣ 8 7 4		♣ 7		♣ 9 8 7 5		♣ A K 7 6 3		♣ 10 9 4 3 2

B. The bidding has started 1♠ : 4♣ (splinter). What should opener do next?

1.	♠ A Q J 6 2	2.	♠ A Q J 6 2	3.	♠ A Q J 6 2	4.	♠ K J 8 7 4	5.	♠ A J 9 8 2
	♡ 8 5 3		♡ A 2		♡ 6 2		♡ A 2		♡ K J 9
	◇ K 5		◇ K Q 3		◇ A K		◇ 9 7 3 2		◇ A J 3 2
	♣ Q 9 8		♣ Q J 2		♣ 9 8 6 2		♣ K Q		♣ 2

C. The bidding has started 1♡ : 2◇, 2♡. What should responder do next with these hands?

1.	♠ 7	2.	♠ A 7 2	3.	♠ 4	4.	♠ 5	5.	♠ 6
	♡ 6 5		♡ Q 7 5		♡ K Q 7		♡ K 9 2		♡ K 8 3
	◇ K Q J 9 3		◇ A Q 9 7 6 2		◇ K Q 7 6 2		◇ A K Q J 4		◇ Q J 7 4 2
	♣ A K J 7 2		♣ 5		♣ A 7 6 2		♣ K 10 9 4		♣ A J 6 5

PARTNERSHIP BIDDING : How should the following hands be bid? West is the dealer each time.

	SET 11 — WEST		SET 11 — EAST		SET 12 — WEST		SET 12 — EAST
1.	♠ A J 7 4 2	1.	♠ 10 8 6 5 3	1.	♠ A J 5 2	1.	♠ 4
	♡ K 8 6 3		♡ A Q 2		♡ K Q 7 5 4		♡ J 9 8 3 2
	◇ 3		◇ A K 4 2		◇ A K		◇ Q 8
	♣ A 7 6		♣ 5		♣ 8 2		♣ K 9 7 4 3
2.	♠ A J 7 4 2	2.	♠ 10 8 6 5 3	2.	♠ 6	2.	♠ A K 9 7 5
	♡ K 8 6 3		♡ A Q 2		♡ 8 5 3		♡ Q
	◇ 3		◇ A K 4 2		◇ A K 5		◇ Q 7
	♣ K Q 6		♣ 5		♣ A J 10 6 4 2		♣ K 8 7 5 3
3.	♠ K 6	3.	♠ A 9 5 2	3.	♠ 5 3	3.	♠ A K J 7 4
	♡ A Q 6 3		♡ K 8 5 4 2		♡ A J 7 2		♡ K Q 8 6 3
	◇ A K 5 4 3 2		◇ 8		◇ 5		◇ 9 4
	♣ 3		♣ 7 4 2		♣ A K 10 9 7 4		♣ 2
4.	♠ K 6	4.	♠ A 9 5 2	4.	♠ A K Q 6 2	4.	♠ 7 3
	♡ A Q 6 3		♡ J 7 5 2		♡ K Q 6 4 3		♡ A J 9 7 2
	◇ A K 5 4 3 2		◇ 8		◇ Q 9 2		◇ A 8 4
	♣ 3		♣ K 9 8 4		♣ - - -		♣ J 7 4
5.	♠ K J 8 6	5.	♠ A Q 7 4	5.	♠ A K Q 6 2	5.	♠ 7 3
	♡ K J		♡ Q 6 2		♡ K Q 6 4 3		♡ A J 9 7 2
	◇ A 9 4		◇ 8 7 2		◇ Q 9 2		◇ J 8 4
	♣ A Q J 7		♣ K 4 3		♣ - - -		♣ A 7 4
6.	♠ K J 8 6	6.	♠ A Q 7 4 3	6.	♠ A K Q 8 6 3	6.	♠ 9 7 5 2
	♡ K 9		♡ Q 6 2		♡ A K Q J		♡ 5 3 2
	◇ A 9		◇ J 8 2		◇ - - -		◇ K 9 8 3 2
	♣ A Q J 7 2		♣ K 4		♣ A 5 3		♣ 2

PLAY HANDS ON SPLINTERS

(These hands can be made up by using pages 176-183)

Hand 21: Judging game or slam potential — Setting up a winner for a discard

Dealer North : N-S vulnerable

NORTH
♠ 9 7 6 4
♡ - - -
♢ A 9 8 7 3
♣ A 10 9 5

WEST
♠ A 8 3
♡ K 9 8 5 2
♢ 6
♣ K J 7 2

EAST
♠ K 5 2
♡ A J 7 6 4
♢ Q J 4 2
♣ Q

SOUTH
♠ Q J 10
♡ Q 10 3
♢ K 10 5
♣ 8 6 4 3

WEST	NORTH	EAST	SOUTH
	No	1♡	No
4♢	No	4♡	All pass

Bidding: West's 4♢ splinter shows a strong hand (normally 11 HCP or more) with 4+ support for opener and a singleton or void in diamonds. The splinter is best considered as a short suit try for slam. East has a poor holding in the splinter suit with the Q-J of diamonds wasted opposite the singleton. The ace is the only good card opposite a singleton. The diamond duplication effectively reduces East's opening bid from 13 HCP to 10 HCP including a singleton queen and so East signs off in 4♡. With a very powerful hand, West could still bid on.

Lead: Queen of spades. Top of sequence is always attractive. A trump lead also appeals on splinter auctions but not from Q-10-x.

Recommended play: Win with the ♠K in hand and lead a low heart to the king. The bad break reveals a loser in trumps. A low club is led from dummy. If North rises with the ♣A and returns a spade, win with dummy's ace and discard a spade loser on the king of clubs. Cash the ♡A and concede just three tricks, a heart, a diamond and a club.

Notes: (1) If North ducks the club from dummy (and it could be right to do so . . . suppose East were void in clubs), East wins with the queen. Now declarer can score an overtrick. Play a diamond to make dummy void. Win the spade return with the ace and lead the king of clubs. When North plays the ace, you ruff, cash the ace of hearts and ruff a diamond in dummy. Discard your spade loser on the jack of clubs and cross-ruff from there. The defence comes to just one heart and one diamond.

(2) If North does duck the first club, it is important that declarer does not cash the ace of hearts before giving up a diamond. Otherwise, South could cash the ♡Q and draw a third round of trumps. This would prevent declarer scoring three ruffs in dummy and three in hand and restrict declarer to ten tricks.

Hand 22: Card valuation opposite a shortage — Ruffing in dummy vs. establishing a long suit

Dealer East : E-W vulnerable

NORTH
♠ K Q 7 3
♡ K 7 3
♢ A 8 6 4 2
♣ 3

WEST
♠ 9 6
♡ Q 10 5 2
♢ Q 9 7 5
♣ Q 9 6

EAST
♠ 5 2
♡ J 9 8 4
♢ J 10
♣ A K 10 5 4

SOUTH
♠ A J 10 8 4
♡ A 6
♢ K 3
♣ J 8 7 2

WEST	NORTH	EAST	SOUTH
		No	1♠
No	4♣	No	4NT
No	5♢	No	6♠
No	No	No	

Bidding: After North's splinter, South should be very enthusiastic about slam prospects. South has only a minimum opening but the club holding is ideal. Three or four useless cards opposite the shortage means that no significant high cards are wasted. South checks on aces and bids the slam when just one ace is missing. Using 4NT Roman Key Card Blackwood, North's reply would be 5♠ (two key cards plus the trump queen — see Chapter 12.) South would then be more confident about bidding the slam.

Lead: 6 of spades. After a splinter auction, a trump lead is fine.

Recommended play: South wins the trump lead in hand and leads a club. If the defenders do not lead a second trump, declarer can ruff the three club losers in dummy. The defenders should play a second trump and now declarer can score only two ruffs in dummy. Declarer should tackle the diamonds next: king of diamonds, diamond to the ace and ruff a diamond, heart to the king and ruff another diamond. This establishes dummy's fifth diamond as a winner and declarer can now ruff two clubs in dummy and discard the other club loser on dummy's diamond winner.

Notes: (1) When leading a trump, it is standard to lead lowest, even from a doubleton.

(2) If the opening lead is not a trump (a heart, the suit with two honours, would be next choice), declarer wins and concedes a club. Now the defence cannot stop declarer ruffing three club losers in dummy.

Hand 23: Second round splinter — Cue-bid to suggest a slam

Dealer South : Both vulnerable

NORTH
- ♠ A 10 9 6
- ♡ - - -
- ◇ 10 7 6 4 3
- ♣ J 7 5 4

WEST
- ♠ J 3 2
- ♡ A K 10 9 6 5
- ◇ A 8
- ♣ 8 6

EAST
- ♠ 5
- ♡ Q 8 3
- ◇ K Q 5 2
- ♣ A K 9 3 2

SOUTH
- ♠ K Q 8 7 4
- ♡ J 7 4 2
- ◇ J 9
- ♣ Q 10

WEST	NORTH	EAST	SOUTH
			No
1♡	No	2♣	No
2♡	No	3♠	No
4◇	No	4NT	No
5♡	No	6♡	All pass

Bidding: With only three trumps, East must not splinter at once. East changes suit and when West rebids 2♡, East can now splinter with 3♠ to show a singleton or void in spades, 3 hearts and the values for at least game. West has an ideal spade holding opposite the singleton and so suggests slam possibilities with the cue-bid of 4◇. East checks on aces and bids the slam. (With 4NT RKCB, West would bid 5♣ to show 0 or 3 key cards — see Chapter 12.)

Lead: 4 of diamonds. Spades or clubs are less appealing.

Recommended play: Win with the king of diamonds and concede a spade. If a diamond is returned, win with the ace and ruff a spade. Next comes the queen of hearts and when North shows out, finesse the 10 of hearts and draw trumps. The other spade loser is discarded on the queen of diamonds.

Notes: (1) Note how easy it can be to make a slam with just 26 HCP and a decent trump fit when there are no wasted high cards opposite a short suit.
(2) If North had J-x-x-x in trumps, the defence would prevail by starting with two rounds of spades.
(3) If North-South were sure 6♡ would make, the sacrifice in 6♠ would be worth taking but how to find it?
(4) West could try for an overtrick by hoping clubs are 3-3, but this risks failing in the slam when North has fewer than three clubs and can over-ruff West on the third round. As the 3-3 club break is only 36%, the risk is not worth taking. The slam is an excellent contract, which many may miss, and so the overtrick is not as important as giving yourself the best chance of making the slam.

Hand 24: Splinter by a very weak hand — Cue-bidding to slam

Dealer West : Nil vulnerable

NORTH
- ♠ A K Q J 8 2
- ♡ K Q 3
- ◇ - - -
- ♣ A Q 7 2

WEST
- ♠ - - -
- ♡ J 10 9 8 6 5
- ◇ A K 6
- ♣ 9 8 6 3

EAST
- ♠ 9 7 6
- ♡ - - -
- ◇ Q J 10 7 4 2
- ♣ K J 10 5

SOUTH
- ♠ 10 5 4 3
- ♡ A 7 4 2
- ◇ 9 8 5 3
- ♣ 4

WEST	NORTH	EAST	SOUTH
No	2♣	No	2◇
No	2♠	No	4♣
No	4◇	No	4♡
No	7♠	All pass	

Bidding: South's 4♣ splinter shows spade support and a singleton or void in clubs. The 4◇ cue-bid shows the ace of diamonds or a diamond void and 4♡ shows first-round control of hearts (certainly the ace, given the splinter in clubs). That is enough for North to bid the grand slam.

If playing Benjamin Twos, North would open 2◇, South would give a 2♡ negative and the rest of the auction would be the same.

Lead: 7 of spades or queen of diamonds. Against a grand slam a trump lead is often the safest.

Recommended play: On a trump lead, win in hand, cash ♣A and ruff a club, ruff a diamond, ruff a club, ruff a diamond and ruff your last club. Return to hand with a diamond ruff and draw trumps.

Notes: (1) If declarer tries to come to hand with a heart, East ruffs and the grand slam is defeated. That is very unlucky for North but even such a tiny risk is unnecessary. It is quite safe to come to hand each time via a diamond ruff.
(2) If a diamond is led, ruff, cash ♣A, ruff a club, ruff a diamond, ruff a club, ruff a diamond, ruff the last club and then lead a trump to draw trumps.
(3) If East intervenes with 2◇, South passes and West might raise to 3◇. North would bid 3♠ and if East passes, South can then splinter with 5♣. North would cue-bid 5◇, South 5♡ and North again jumps to 7♠. If the East-West interference is more violent, North-South may be unable to find the grand slam.

CHAPTER 7
OPENER'S STRATEGY

The Suit Quality Test

    Number of Cards in Suit
  + Number of Honours in Suit
  = Suit Quality (SQ)

For example:

    K Q 8 7 4 3 = Suit Quality of 8
              (6 cards + 2 honours)

When assessing suit quality, the jack and ten are counted only if the suit also contains a higher honour (ace, king or queen). Thus :

    J 8 6 4 3 = SQ 5

5 cards but do not count the jack since the suit does not contain a higher honour.

    K J 8 6 3 = SQ 7 (5 cards + 2 honours)

The Suit Quality Test is useful when the quality of a suit is relevant to your bidding decision. For example, for a pre-empt you should have a decent suit. How decent? The SQ should equal the number of tricks for which you are bidding. Thus a weak two opening should have a suit quality of 8 (6-card suit and at least two honours), a 3-level pre-empt should have a suit quality of 9, and so on.

Suit quality is not relevant for opening bids of one-in-a-suit, but can be useful when rebidding. With a suit quality of ten, you can insist on your suit as trumps. SQ 10 = 6-card suit with four honours or a 7-card suit with three honours. For example:

WEST	EAST	
1♠	2♦	After East has responded 2♦ to the 1♠ opening, what should West rebid with these hands?
?		

(1)	(2)	(3)
♠ K Q 8 4 3 2	♠ K Q 8 4 3 2	♠ K Q J 10 3 2
♡ A J 8	♡ A J 8	♡ A 8 2
◇ 5 3	◇ 5 3	◇ 5 3
♣ K 3	♣ A K	♣ A K

(1) This is only a minimum opening. Bid 2♠.
(2) 17 HCP = a strong opening. Bid 3♠.
(3) This has the same strength as (2) but your suit has a Suit Quality of 10. You can show this with a rebid of 4♠. Thus the jump to game shows the same strength as a jump rebid but promises a better suit. SQ of 10 means the suit is playable opposite a singleton, and even opposite a void the suit may have only one loser.

K-Q-x-x-x-x opposite a singleton will have three losers most of the time. K-Q-J-10-x-x opposite a singleton will usually play for just one loser. One advantage of being able to show such suit quality is that responder is able to head for a slam, even with the barest support because of the knowledge that the trump suit should be all right.

The 5-3-3-2 hand with five hearts

With 15 HCP or more, open 1♡. There should be no significant rebid problem. With 12-14 points, the bidding becomes awkward if partner replies 1♠ and your hearts are too flimsy to rebid 2♡.

(1)	(2)	(3)
♠ K 4 3	♠ Q 2	♠ 8 2
♡ A J 8 7 2	♡ A Q 9 7 3	♡ 10 8 6 4 2
◇ 5 3	◇ 5 3 2	◇ A Q 3
♣ K J 3	♣ A J 7	♣ A K 5

With (1), open 1♡. Over 2♣ or 2◇, rebid 2♡. Over 1♠, raise to 2♠. The 3-card raise is not ideal but is acceptable with Q-x-x or better.

With (2), open 1♡ and rebid 2♡ over 1♠, 2♣ or 2◇. A suit quality of seven will do for this rebid.

With (3), you might open 1NT and hide the weak five-card suit. The alternative is to open 1♡ and rebid 2♣ or 2◇ in a strong 3-card minor. This shows the five hearts (higher suit followed by lower suit = 5-4 pattern at least) and is only a 'minor' distortion.

Opening in third seat

It is permissible to open light in third seat and it is not unusual to open with 10-11 HCP in third seat. However, the light opening bid should be used only when the suit you are opening is strong. Do not open on a weak hand just for the sake of opening. Open despite your weak points if you are indicating a good lead for your partner. Once partner has passed and you have 12 HCP or less, chances for game for your side are remote. Unless you can make a pre-emptive bid, opening the bidding on light values will often help your opponents. If they win the contract, declarer may be able to place the missing cards because of your opening bid. Better to pass in third seat unless your bid has some constructive purpose.

Tricks and therefore matchpoints are often thrown away with the opening lead. If you can stop partner from the usual rotten opening lead, you will see a significant improvement in your duplicate scores. A good test for opening light in third seat is this: Would you be happy to overcall in the suit you are opening? If yes, you are worth an opening bid in third seat. If not, do not open light.

Another good test is this: Does the suit you are opening third-in-hand have a Suit Quality of seven? If so, it is worth opening light. If not, prefer to pass.

Third-seat 1NT openings should be sound. With a balanced 12 HCP, prefer to open in third seat on a strong 4-card suit with a SQ of 7. For example:

♠ A K Q 8 After two passes, unless you are
♡ J 3   going to open 1♠ with this hand,
◇ 6 3 2   don't bother. Rather pass than
♣ J 8 5 4 open 1NT or 1♣.

1♠ shows partner what to lead and forces the opponents to start bidding their suits at the two-level. 1NT is much riskier. 1♣ has no lead-directing value and no hindrance value either.

Having opened light in third seat, you are expected not to bid again. On the above hand, you would pass any response from partner. If you open in third seat and do bid again, you are showing full opening values, normally 13 HCP or more.

If you have a good 5-card major (SQ of 8 or better), be prepared to open with a weak two, even though you are normally expected to have a 6-card suit.

♠ 8   After two passes, open 2♡,
♡ K Q J 7 3 weak, or do not open at all. If you
◇ 9 7 4   open 1♡, you have no good
♣ Q J 4 2 action if partner responds 1♠.

Another advantage is partner will usually pass 2♡.

The Drury 2♣ Convention

Because it is common to open light in third seat, it is easy for responder to bid too high. The Drury Convention is designed to check whether opener's third seat opening is genuine.

After a major suit opening, the 2♣ response by a passed hand is 'Drury' and asks : 'Is your third seat opening full value?'

In reply:

2◇ = 'No, I have opened light.'

All others = Natural and genuine opening bid. Any rebid other than 2◇ usually leads to game at least.

After 2◇, responder can sign off in opener's major at the two-level or make some other natural bid. This may avoid reaching the three-level with two 10-11 point hands.

If 2♣ is doubled, redouble indicates very strong clubs (and requests responder to pass if possible), pass suggests good clubs and other actions have the normal meaning. If the opponents bid over 2♣, pass by opener shows the weak opening and other bids show a full value opening bid.

Psyching

A psyche (derived from 'psychic bid') is simply a bluff bid. It is a bid that does not come close to the requirements for the bid chosen (for example, an opening bid of 1♡ with only 4 points). Psyches are perfectly legal provided that partner is not aware that you are psyching. Partner must be just as fooled as the opponents.

Psyching is of course highly dangerous. Partner often bids too high or, believing you have strength when you have none, doubles the opponents for penalties and they make their contract easily. As a result, psyching undermines partnership confidence and can do considerable damage to a partnership.

Nevertheless, psyching does have a place in the armoury of every strong pair. Practised judiciously and rarely (say once every three sessions or so), you can score some good results. Even better, your victims will in future often think you are psyching when you are not.

Conditions are favourable for psyching when:

● They are vulnerable and you are not
● Partner is a passed hand
● The opponents are stronger than you and partner

There is less value in psyching against weaker opposition. If they are weaker you will beat them by your superior skill. If the opponents are stronger, some additional strategy such as psyching may help.

● The player on your right has doubled

WEST	NORTH	EAST	SOUTH
No	1♡	Dble	?

SOUTH   Many players with these cards
♠ 8 3   would choose to psyche 1♠ and
♡ K J 7 3 2 so hope to steal the enemy's suit.
◇ 9 7   If doubled, they can sooner or
♣ 9 7 3 2 later return to hearts.

This particular psyche is known as a 'baby psyche' because it is so common that these days only a baby would be fooled by it. The best defence against a suspected psyche over a partner's takeout double is to double for penalties. With strong spades, West should double 1♠ by South.

The victims of a successful psyche are often very upset and may call the Director. Frequent psychers have the Director at their table regularly. Frequent psyching may also lead to a presumption that a pair has an undisclosed understanding.

You may find that Drury 2♣ is barred except for competition at the highest level. This is a pity since Drury is so useful but administrators feel Drury can be used to guard against a third-hand psyche.

Opening in fourth seat

There is less pressure to open in fourth seat since you can simply pass out the bidding. In fourth seat, by all means open all 13-point or stronger hands but be conservative below 13 points. This is a good approach for 10-12 point hands in fourth seat:

Add your HCP to the number of spades you hold. If the total is 15 or more, be prepared to open.

When each side has about 20 points, each side can usually make eight tricks in its trump fit. Owning the spade suit is therefore very important. It means you can bid up to 2♠ and the opponents will have to bid to the three-level to prevent your making 2♠. Therefore be reluctant to open with 10-12 points if short in spades but by all means open with length and strength in spades.

In fourth seat, weak twos are played as 8-12 points (since you would not open with less than 8 HCP in fourth seat). A good 5-card suit (SQ of 8) is enough.

EXERCISES

A. West : Pass, North : Pass. What should East do with each of these hands?

1. ♠ A J 9 7	2. ♠ A 2	3. ♠ A K J 6 2	4. ♠ J 6 3 2	5. ♠ A K J 9
♡ Q J 5 3	♡ K Q J 3	♡ 7 4	♡ 9 8 4 3	♡ Q 7 5
◊ 7	◊ 7 5 3 2	◊ 8 4 2	◊ A K Q	◊ J 3 2
♣ Q 8 7 4	♣ 8 4 3	♣ 7 6 2	♣ 8 4	♣ Q 6 4

B. There have been three passes to South. What should South do with each of these hands?

1. ♠ A Q J 3	2. ♠ 4	3. ♠ K 8 7	4. ♠ 7	5. ♠ A K Q 9 8 2
♡ 8 5	♡ A 6 2	♡ A Q J 9 8 2	♡ 9 2	♡ - - -
◊ K 5	◊ K Q J 3	◊ J 8 4	◊ Q J 7 5	◊ 8 3
♣ Q 9 8 4 2	♣ Q 7 5 4 2	♣ 3	♣ A K J 9 8 4	♣ Q J 7 4 2

C. What is your opening bid as dealer and rebid plan with these hands?

1. ♠ K J 7	2. ♠ K 7	3. ♠ K 6 3 2	4. ♠ K 3 2	5. ♠ K 3 2
♡ A J 6 4 2	♡ 8 6 4 3 2	♡ A J 6 2	♡ A K J 6 2	♡ A K J 6
◊ J 3	◊ A K 2	◊ A 3	◊ J 3	◊ J 3 2
♣ K 8 2	♣ K 8 4	♣ A Q J	♣ A Q J	♣ A Q J

PARTNERSHIP BIDDING: How should the following hands be bid? West is the dealer each time.

SET 13 — WEST	SET 13 — EAST	SET 14 — WEST	SET 14 — EAST
1. ♠ 9 7 4	1. ♠ 10 6 5	1. ♠ J 10 3 2	1. ♠ 8 7 5
♡ K 8 6 3	♡ A Q J 5 2	♡ 7 6 2	♡ 9 8 4
◊ K 6	◊ A 2	◊ J 6 3 2	◊ A K Q
♣ A 7 6 2	♣ 8 5 3	♣ J 5	♣ 8 6 4 2
2. ♠ K 9 8 4	2. ♠ A Q J 7	2. ♠ 5 3	2. ♠ Q J 8 7 6 2
♡ 9 6 3	♡ Q 2	♡ J 9 8 7 5 2	♡ 6 4 3
◊ A 9 8	◊ K 6 4 3	◊ J 8	◊ 9 6 2
♣ Q J 5	♣ 10 6 2	♣ J 7 6	♣ 3
3. ♠ 8 6	3. ♠ J 7 5 2	3. ♠ A J 5 3	3. ♠ K Q 10 7 4
♡ J 8 7 6 3 2	♡ A K Q 4	♡ A Q 7 2	♡ K J 6 3
◊ 8	◊ 7 5 4 3	◊ 8 5	◊ A J
♣ A K 4 2	♣ 6	◊ 7 6 4	♣ 9 3
4. ♠ A 8 7 4	4. ♠ K 6 5 2	4. ♠ J 2	4. ♠ A K 10 9
♡ A 9 7 2	♡ 3	♡ A Q J 7 3	♡ 8 6 5
◊ A K J	◊ Q 5 2	◊ Q 10 6 2	◊ K 7 5
♣ K 2	♣ A J 10 9 4	♣ 7 4	♣ 9 6 5
5. ♠ A 5 2	5. ♠ K Q 7 4	5. ♠ K	5. ♠ A 3 2
♡ J 7 5 3 2	♡ A 9	♡ K Q J 10 7 6 2	♡ 4
◊ Q 5	◊ 8 6 3 2	◊ Q J 7	◊ A K 9 2
♣ A Q 4	♣ 7 6 2	♣ A 4	♣ K Q 6 5 2
6. ♠ A J 2	6. ♠ K 5	6. ♠ K Q J 6 2	6. ♠ 4 3
♡ K Q 7 5 4	♡ J 9 3	♡ A J	♡ Q 8 4
◊ K 5	◊ A 7 2	◊ Q J 7	◊ A K 9 2
♣ A Q 4	♣ K 8 6 3 2	♣ A J 4	♣ K Q 5 2

PLAY HANDS ON OPENER'S STRATEGY
(These hands can be made up by using pages 176-183)

Hand 25: Opening in third seat — Drury Convention — Card reading

Dealer North : E-W vulnerable

NORTH
♠ K 7 6 4
♡ A Q
♢ 10 7 5
♣ Q 10 8 3

WEST
♠ Q 9 2
♡ 9 5 3 2
♢ A J 8 6 3
♣ 5

EAST
♠ 8
♡ 10 8 6 4
♢ Q 9 2
♣ A K J 9 4

SOUTH
♠ A J 10 5 3
♡ K J 7
♢ K 4
♣ 7 6 2

WEST	NORTH	EAST	SOUTH
	No	No	1♠
No	2♣	Dble	2♢
No	2♠	All pass	

Bidding: North's 2♣, Drury, asks about South's opening and 2♢ indicates a light opening. North therefore signs off in 2♠. Without Drury, North might well jump to 3♠ over 1♠, which is hopeless as the cards lie and might go two down. East's double of 2♣, an artificial bid, asks partner to lead a club.

If not vulnerable, East might chance a takeout double of 2♠ and East-West would then land in 3♢ or 3♡. At adverse vulnerability, the risk is not worthwhile.

Lead: 5 of clubs. Without East's double, West might well have led a heart and that may have turned out better for the defence.

Recommended play: East takes the first three club tricks and West signals for a diamond switch. East shifts to the 2 of diamonds (showing an honour). South plays low and West wins with the jack followed by the ace of diamonds. If West continues with a third diamond, South ruffs, cashes the ace of spades and leads the jack of spades, letting it run if West plays low. South thus scores eight tricks.

Notes: (1) After East has turned up with A-K-J in clubs, South knows West has the ace of diamonds, as East would have opened with 12 HCP. If East also turns up with the ♢Q, that marks West with the ♠Q.
(2) If East continues with a club at trick 4, South should discard a diamond, as West will have the ♢A. West ruffs and now declarer has no problem with the trump suit. If South ruffs the fourth club, West makes a trump trick and declarer will fail after losing two diamond tricks later.
(3) If West takes the ♢A, cashes ♢J and switches to a heart, declarer can play dummy's third diamond to locate the ♢Q (although that is risky if West discarded diamonds on the clubs). Even without that, declarer should figure East has the ♢Q and play West for the ♠Q. With ♢A-Q-J-x-x, West would almost certainly have doubled South's artificial 2♢.

Hand 26: Opening in third seat — Competitive bidding

Dealer East : Both vulnerable

NORTH
♠ A J 10 7 5
♡ A 10 2
♢ 10 8 3
♣ A J

WEST
♠ 9 3
♡ Q 9 7 3
♢ A K Q
♣ 7 6 4 3

EAST
♠ 6 2
♡ K J 8 5 4
♢ J 7 6 2
♣ 9 2

SOUTH
♠ K Q 8 4
♡ 6
♢ 9 5 4
♣ K Q 10 8 5

WEST	NORTH	EAST	SOUTH
		No	No
1♢	1♠	Dble	3♠
No	4♠	All pass	

Bidding: West should not open 1♣ or 1♡. If not prepared to open 1♢, do not open at all. With 5-3 in the majors, North should overcall 1♠ rather than double. Prefer the double if you are 4-3, 4-4 or 5-4 in the majors. East's double shows 4+ hearts and 6+ points. If playing the jump to 3♠ as pre-emptive, South could bid 2♢ to show the strong passed hand or jump to 3♣ to show a maximum pass with spade support. If South did bid 2♢, West should double to insist on a diamond lead.

Lead: 2 of diamonds. Definitely after a third-in-hand opening.

Recommended play: West wins and cashes two more diamonds. West would then switch to a heart. North wins and draws trumps. The heart losers can be ruffed in dummy or discarded on the clubs. 10 tricks.

Notes: (1) If West opened 1♣, East would lead a club. If West passes originally, East might well lead a club, a trump or even a heart. On anything but a diamond lead, North can make thirteen tricks: draw trumps, discard the diamond losers on the clubs and ruff two hearts in dummy. Once you see how rotten partner's usual leads are, you will be eager to indicate a good lead with your third seat opening.
(2) Even though the diamond lead does not defeat 4♠, East-West will score very well by holding the contract to ten tricks. At many tables, North will be allowed to make thirteen tricks.

Hand 27: Opening in third seat — Competitive bidding

Dealer South : Nil vulnerable

NORTH
- ♠ A K J 9
- ♡ 6 5
- ◇ 8 7 3
- ♣ Q 8 4 3

WEST
- ♠ 8 7 2
- ♡ Q J 2
- ◇ K 10 6 5
- ♣ A 10 5

EAST
- ♠ 6 5 4
- ♡ A K 10 9 7
- ◇ A 9 2
- ♣ K 9

SOUTH
- ♠ Q 10 3
- ♡ 8 4 3
- ◇ Q J 4
- ♣ J 7 6 2

WEST	NORTH	EAST	SOUTH
			No
No	1♠	2♡	2♠
4♡	No	No	No

Bidding: If North is not prepared to open 1♠, North should pass. It would not be worth opening 1♣. West has a tough decision whether to bid 3♡ or 4♡. On the actual layout, 4♡ is not much of a contract but West would expect East to be shortish in spades (at most a doubleton) on the North-South bidding. If West did bid 3♡, East should pass, even though East might think West is short in spades.

Lead: 3 of spades. One usually leads partner's suit. When partner has opened in third seat and the opponents win the contract, it is even more important to lead partner's suit.

Recommended play: North wins the lead with the king of spades and cashes the ace. North continues with a third spade, won by South. When South exits safely with a trump, declarer has no way to avoid losing a diamond trick. This defence holds the contract to nine tricks. Even if East-West stopped in 3♡, this figures to give North-South a respectable score.

Notes: (1) Had North passed, South would have a tough lead, with a trump or the ◇Q as the recommended choices. A trump lead gives declarer nothing but on the ◇Q lead, declarer can make eleven tricks (win ◇A, draw trumps ending in hand, finesse ◇10 and discard a spade on the thirteenth diamond).
(2) On a trump lead, if declarer wins and plays a diamond to the 9, South would have to find the spade switch to hold declarer to nine tricks.
(3) A club lead, unattractive from J-x-x-x, would also give declarer eleven tricks. Declarer captures North's queen, plays a heart to the queen and a heart back to the ace, finesses the 10 of clubs, discards a diamond on the ♣A, plays ◇A, ◇K and ruffs a diamond, plays a trump to dummy to draw the last trump and cashes the thirteenth diamond for a spade discard.

Hand 28: Opening in fourth seat — Competitive bidding

Dealer West : Both vulnerable

NORTH
- ♠ K J 4 2
- ♡ 9 5 3
- ◇ A 9 6
- ♣ J 8 6

WEST
- ♠ 9 3
- ♡ K J 10 7 2
- ◇ J 10 4
- ♣ K Q 5

EAST
- ♠ 10 8 7
- ♡ A Q 8
- ◇ 8 5 3
- ♣ A 9 7 2

SOUTH
- ♠ A Q 6 5
- ♡ 6 4
- ◇ K Q 7 2
- ♣ 10 4 3

WEST	NORTH	EAST	SOUTH
No	No	No	1◇
1♡	Dble	2♡	2♠
3♡	No	No	No

Bidding: East has no suit strong enough to justify a light third-seat opening. In fourth seat, with a borderline opening, add the number of spades to your HCP. If the total comes to 15 or more, it is worth opening. Here South has 15 on the fourth-seat count and should open 1◇, not 1NT. West has a routine overcall and North's negative double shows four spades (if not using the negative double in that way, North would bid 1♠). East raises to 2♡ and South is worth 2♠. It is important not to sell out at the two-level in such auctions and so West competes to 3♡.

Lead: 2 of spades. No reason to select a different suit.

Recommended play: South should win with the ace of spades and switch to the king of diamonds. North encourages and a low diamond goes to North's ace. North cashes the king of spades and leads a third diamond to South's queen, defeating the contract by one trick.

Notes: (1) South can tell that there are no more than two spade tricks for the defence and so starts setting up extra tricks. South could continue with ♠Q at trick 2 to try to hold the lead and then switch to diamonds.
(2) If East-West had passed out 2♠, North-South would have no trouble making eight tricks.
(3) Note the importance of the spade suit. Swap the majors and South should pass the hand in (11 HCP and only two spades = 13). With the majors reversed, if South did open, East-West could make 2♠ and North-South would need to compete to 3♡, one down.

CHAPTER 8

RESPONDER'S STRATEGY & JACOBY 2NT

Suit Quality Test for Responder

Just as the Suit Quality Test is useful for overcalls, pre-empts and opener's rebid (see Chapter 7), so it can be used for responses and responder's rebids.

WEST	EAST	
1♣	4♡	Responder's immediate jump to game should be based on a hand with seven playing tricks, about 6-9 HCP and a 7+ suit which has a Suit Quality of 10+.
1♢	4♠	

Beware of the 1♠ : 4♡ sequence if you are using that as a splinter raise of spades.

With a single-suiter (6+ suit) and 10 HCP or more, prefer to start with a simple change-of-suit response.

WEST	EAST	
1♣	1♡	Jump-rebid your suit to the three-level with 10-12 points and a suit quality below 10.
1♠	3♡	

WEST	EAST	
1♣	1♡	Jump-rebid to game in your major with 10-12 points and a suit quality of 10+.
1♠	4♡	

W	E	EAST (1)	EAST (2)
1♢	1♠	♠ K Q 8 6 5 3	♠ K Q J 10 5 3
2♣	?	♡ A 6 2	♡ A 6 2
		♢ 8 2	♢ J 2
		♣ Q 7	♣ 6 3

With (1), rebid 3♠. The suit quality of the spades is only 8. With (2), you have a suit quality 10 and should therefore rebid with a jump to 4♠.

Once you hit 13 HCP or more with a strong single-suiter, your rebid will depend on whether opener made a narrow range rebid (e.g., rebid of suit opened) or with a wide-range rebid (change of suit). After opener has rebid the suit opened, it is sensible to play that a jump-rebid by responder is forcing. For example:

W	E	EAST (1)	EAST (2)
1♢	1♠	♠ K Q 8 6 5 3	♠ K Q J 10 5 3
2♢	?	♡ A 6 2	♡ A 6 2
		♢ A 2	♢ A 2
		♣ Q 7	♣ 6 3

With (1), it could be very silly to jump to 4♠ (which might fail if opener is void or singleton in spades, with 3NT laydown). With no fourth-suit forcing available, treat the jump to 3♠ as forcing after opener's rebid in the suit opened. (With 10-12 points, you may be too high, but that's life.) With (2) your spades are SQ 10 and you should rebid 4♠.

When opener's rebid is a change of suit, use fourth-suit forcing with strong hands. This frees the jump-rebid for 10-12 point hands. For example:

W	E	EAST (1)	EAST (2)
1♢	1♠	♠ A Q 8 6 5 3	♠ A Q J 10 5 3
2♣	?	♡ A 6 2	♡ A 6 2
		♢ A 2	♢ A 2
		♣ 7 2	♣ 7 2

Both of these are too strong for a rebid of 3♠ or 4♠. As opener may yet have a strong hand, you do not want to give up on slam chances. Use 2♡ fourth-suit forcing. Over opener's next bid of say, 2NT, 3♣ or 3♢, follow up with 3♠ on (1) and 4♠ on (2). The 3♠ rebid is now forcing: after fourth-suit, responder's next bid below game is forcing.

The same principle can apply after a jump-shift:

W	E	EAST (1)	EAST (2)
1♢	2♠	♠ A Q 8 6 5 3	♠ A Q J 10 5 3
3♣	?	♡ Q 6 3	♡ Q 6 3
		♢ A 5	♢ A J
		♣ A J	♣ K 2

With (1), bid 3♠ while with (2), you should rebid 4♠, showing the self-sufficient suit. That may enable opener to bid on to a slam. If not prepared to stop in game, rebid 3♠ even with a suit of SQ 10.

Fourth-Suit Forcing

WEST	EAST	
1♠	2♣	Where the fourth-suit bid comes at the three-level, it is sensible to play the sequence as forcing to game.
2♡	3♢	
?		

Where the fourth-suit bid occurs at the two-level, it is common to play that a minimum rebid by opener can be passed but thereafter any rebid by responder below game is forcing.

WEST	EAST	
1♢	1♠	At this point, 2♠, 2NT, 3♣ or 3♢ by opener is not forcing. Over any of these, responder's 3♠ or minor-suit support is forcing.
2♣	2♡	
?		

WEST	EAST	
1♢	1♠	Responder's jump-rebid in the fourth suit is played as natural, showing at least 5-5 in the suits bid and forcing to game.
2♣	3♡	
?		

There is only one sequence where the fourth suit rebid occurs at the one-level.

WEST	EAST	
1♣	1♢	It is best to play this sequence as natural and East's 1♠ is forcing, showing 4+ spades but only 6+ points (like 1♠ : 1♠ at once).
1♡	1♠	
?		

To create a fourth-suit auction, you need to make a jump-rebid to 2♠:

WEST	EAST	
1♣	1♢	The jump to 2♠ *denies* four spades, but shows 10+ points. Bidding continues as in a normal fourth-suit auction.
1♡	2♠	
?		

Raising opener's major

There are four basic hand types which responder wishes to convey:

(1) The weak raise, 6-9 points

Most show this range with a raise to the two-level.

(2) The pre-emptive raise, less than 10 HCP, 4+ trumps and an unbalanced hand

This is shown by a jump-raise to game.

(3) The invitational raise, 10-12 points

(4) The game-forcing raise, 13+ points

Playing limit raises

1♡ : 3♡ or 1♠ : 3♠ = 4+ support, 10-12 points

This invitational raise figures to be balanced. With 10-12 points, 4+ support and a singleton or a void you have enough for game. With an unbalanced hand with 4+ trumps and below 10 points, use:

1♡ : 4♡ or 1♠ : 4♠, the pre-emptive raise

That leaves the 13+ raise. In Acol, this is shown by a change of suit, followed by a jump to game when responder is in the 13-15 range (the 'delayed game raise') and by a jump shift followed by support when responder has 16+ points.

Growing in popularity is a response of 2NT to cover the 13+ raise. This is known as:

The Jacoby 2NT Response

This shows support for opener's major, 13 points or more and a balanced hand. (If unbalanced, use a splinter response.) You can afford to give up a natural 2NT response, since with a balanced 10-12, you can change suit and follow up with 2NT.

The Jacoby 2NT response leaves the three-level available for opener to describe the hand further. For example, after 1♠ : 2NT —

3♣ / 3♢ / 3♡ = singleton or void in the suit bid

3♠ = extra length, extra strength, no short suit

3NT = extra strength, no extra length, no shortage

4♣ / 4♢ / 4♡ = strong second suit (at least two of the top three honours in a 5-card or longer suit)

4♠ = minimum opening, 11-13 points

Other structures for opener's rebids are possible (see Appendix 4 for *The Jacoby 2NT Two-Step*).

After opener's rebid, responder can sign off with a minimum 2NT or if the hands do not fit well (wasted honours opposite opener's short suit). With excess values or if the hands do fit well, responder can push on to slam, either by asking for aces / key cards or via a cue-bidding sequence (see Chapters 12-15).

The Jacoby 2NT response is highly recommended. If you appreciate the benefit of splinters (see Chapter 6), then the value of Jacoby 2NT will be obvious. A splinter response allows the responder to show a shortage. Jacoby 2NT enables opener to show a short suit and again the partnership can benefit from knowing how well the hands fit.

WEST	W	E	EAST
♠ K J 6 3	1♡	2♢	♠ A 7
♡ A K 10 7 6 2	2♡	4♡	♡ Q 8 4 3
♢ 7 2	No		♢ A K 5 4
♣ 4			♣ 9 3 2

It would be easy enough to bid the hands as shown and miss the excellent slam. If the bidding began 1♡ : 2NT, 3♣ (singleton club), slam might be reached.

The Jacoby 2NT response promises 4+ support. With only 3-card support, choose a change of suit sequence and support later.

Expert Methods

W	E	EAST (1)	EAST (2)
1♠	?	♠ J 8 6 5 3	♠ K 10 5 3
		♡ 6 2	♡ 2
		♢ 9 7 2	♢ K 7 4 2
		♣ J 8 4	♣ 6 5 3 2

Hand (1) has no suitable action in standard methods. With no short suit, a jump to 4♠ is not recommended and the strength is not close to a normal single raise to 2♠. Few would want to pass, however, with such excellent support. Hand 2 is very strong for a single raise, given the 4-card support, the singleton and only eight losers.

Some partnerships have adopted two pre-emptive raises. This is one such structure for 5-card majors:

1♡ : 2♡ or 1♠ : 2♠ = 6-9 points, 3+ support

1♡ : 3♡ or 1♠ : 3♠ = pre-emptive raise, 0-5 points, 4+ support (less than two defensive tricks): Hand 1.

1♡ : 4♡ or 1♠ : 4♠ = standard pre-emptive raise

To cover the stronger hand types, some use:

Bergen Raises

1♡ / 1♠ : 3♣ = 6-9 points and 4+ support (Hand 2)

1♡ / 1♠ : 3♢ = 10-12 points and 4+ support

1♡ / 1♠ : 2NT = Jacoby 2NT raise

Some scope exists for trial bids over the 3♣ reply. The theory underlying the 3♣ response is that strong players are sure to compete over 1♡ : 2♡ or 1♠ : 2♠. When you have nine trumps or more between you, it is worthwhile for your side to compete to the three-level. Therefore, if you know that you have nine or more trumps, you may as well commit your side to the three-level at once. There is also some pre-emptive value in the 3♣ response.

After the 3♢ response, opener can sign off in the major at the 3-level or 4-level. With slam interest, opener can bid the other major (artificial slam try) or bid 4♣ or 4♢ as a splinter try for slam.

Another method which uses the above pre-emptive jump-raise to the three-level is —

Power Raises

To show the better hands, the Power System uses:

2NT = 6-9 points, 4+ support (Hand 2)

Power 2♣ (1♡ / 1♠ : 2♣) = artificial, 10-12 points

Power 2♢ (1♡ / 1♠ : 2♢) = artificial, 13+ points

These artificial responses can be grafted on to any standard system. The strength is shown at once and you show the support on the next round. One benefit of the Power structure is there is plenty of room for trial bids after 1♡ / 1♠ : 2NT, and with the stronger hands, you may be able to set the trump suit at the two-level (e.g., 1♠ : 2♢, 2♡ : 2♠). This allows your slam-bidding sequences to start at the lowest possible level.

Forcing Minor Suit Raises

A popular approach known as Inverted Minor Raises works like this:

1♣ : 3♣ or 1◇ : 3◇ = weak raise, 6-9 points, the sort of hand that normally raises to the two-level.

1♣ : 2♣ or 1◇ : 2◇ = strong raise, 10+ points, forcing for one round. A rebid of 3♣ / 3◇ by either opener or responder (sooner or later) shows a minimum hand for the values promised and the bidding can end in 3-minor. If responder has enough for game, responder will naturally keep the bidding alive until at least game is reached.

This method has the great advantage of enabling responder to cope with very strong hands with minor suit support. Since there is no upper limit to responder's strength, the single raise may be the prelude to a slam auction.

In these days of highly competitive bidding, forcing minor suit raises can be taken one step further. No self-respecting duplicate opponents would ever allow the bidding to die out after . . .

WEST	NORTH	EAST	SOUTH
1♣	No	2♣	No
No	?		

Therefore it makes sense for East-West to bid more as the opponents will force you to reach the three-level anyway. Accordingly, this approach has much to recommend it:

1♣ : 3♣ or 1◇ : 3◇ = pre-emptive raise, 0-5 points normally, perhaps six points if there is no more than one king in the hand.

1♣ : 2♣ or 1◇ : 2◇ = 6+ points, unlimited and forcing for one round.

These retain their meaning over a simple overcall.

Subsequent bidding

After a pre-emptive raise, opening will usually pass unless wishing to pre-empt further. On the odd occasion, opener will have the right values to take a stab at 3NT (long, strong minor and outside aces).

WEST	W	E	EAST
♠ A 3	1♣	3♣	♠ 7 5
♡ J 7 2	3NT	No	♡ 8 4 3
◇ A K			◇ 8 5 4
♣ A K 7 5 4 2			♣ Q J 8 6 3

After the forcing raise to 2-minor

3-minor by opener = no game interest opposite the 6-9 range or opposite the usual limit raise of 10-12. Responder bids on only with game-forcing values. To sign off at once, opener will have a hand in the 11-13 point range.

2NT by opener = balanced 17-18. Responder can still sign off in 3-minor.

3NT by opener = balanced 19-20.

New suit by opener at the cheapest level = game interest, generally 14 points or more. The suit bid by opener need not be a genuine suit. It may be just a stopper-showing bid.

Jump-rebid in a new suit = splinter, game-forcing.

Jump-to-4-agreed-minor by either partner = forcing to game and starts a slam-going auction.

Opener will choose a new suit rebid with the balanced 15-16 type and also stronger balanced hands if concerned about an unguarded suit. The new suit bid may also be the start of describing non-balanced hand types (such as a 6-5 pattern).

After a new suit rebid by opener, responder will sign off in 3-minor with 6-8 points, but should choose some other action with a stronger hand. Responder's 2NT rebid is also non-forcing after a new suit rebid by opener. It shows 6-8 points and suggests 2NT as the contract if opener has the 15-16 balanced hand.

If either partner bids beyond 3-agreed-minor, this commits the partnership to game.

WEST	W	E	EAST
♠ A K J	1◇	2◇	♠ Q 5
♡ 7 2	2♠	2NT	♡ K 3
◇ A K 7 4 2	3NT	No	◇ Q 8 5 3
♣ A 5 3			♣ 8 7 6 4 2

West has enough to jump to 3NT over 2◇ but is naturally concerned about the heart position. 2♠ shows values in spades and, as 2♡ has been bypassed, denies a stopper in hearts. East's 2NT shows a minimum hand but promises a stopper in the danger suit, hearts. That is enough for West.

WEST	W	E	EAST
♠ A K J	1◇	2◇	♠ 10 4 2
♡ 3	3♡	3NT	♡ A K
◇ A Q J 10 4	No		◇ K 8 5 3
♣ A 7 5 3			♣ J 6 4 2

3♡ is a splinter, showing a singleton or void in hearts and enough values for game. Even though East has a strong hand in this context, the wasted strength in hearts suggests 3NT is a more likely prospect than 6◇.

WEST	W	E	EAST
♠ J 7	1◇	2◇	♠ 9 5 4
♡ J 5 2	3♣	3◇	♡ Q 6
◇ A K 7 4 2	No		◇ Q 9 8 6
♣ A Q J			♣ K 8 7 2

Opener's 3♣ shows extra values and is a try for game. East's 3◇ rejects the invitation.

WEST	W	E	EAST
♠ J 7	1◇	2◇	♠ 9 5
♡ 7 2	3♣	3♡	♡ A Q
◇ A K 7 4 2	4◇	4♡	◇ Q 9 8 6 5 3
♣ A Q J 3	5♣	5◇	♣ K 8 7
	No		

West shows extra values with 3♣ and East makes one final effort to reach 3NT by showing the heart stopper. West bids 4◇ in case East is much stronger and is interested in slam. 4♡ and 5♣ are both cue-bids (see Chapters 14 and 15). With no control in spades, East signs off in 5◇ and as West has no spade control either, West goes no further.

EXERCISES ON RESPONDER'S STRATEGY

A. Partner 1♢ : You : 1♡ : Partner 2♣. What is your rebid with each of these hands?

1.	♠ A 9	2.	♠ K 5 4	3.	♠ A J 7 2	4.	♠ A 7 2	5.	♠ A 7 2
	♡ K J 9 8 7 3		♡ K Q J 10 8 2		♡ A Q 8 4		♡ A Q 8 4 2		♡ A Q 8 4 3 2
	♢ Q 2		♢ Q 5		♢ Q 2		♢ Q 2		♢ Q 2
	♣ 6 4 2		♣ J 4		♣ 7 5 4		♣ J 5 4		♣ J 5

B. Partner has opened 1♡, pass on your right. What would you respond with these hands?

1.	♠ K 6 3	2.	♠ K 6 3	3.	♠ 7	4.	♠ 8 7 2	5.	♠ J
	♡ K J 5 3		♡ K J 5 3 2		♡ Q 6 5 3 2		♡ Q 6 5 3 2		♡ K Q 8 2
	♢ A 5		♢ 9 5 2		♢ 6 2		♢ 6 2		♢ A K 4
	♣ 9 8 6 2		♣ A K		♣ K 10 8 7 3		♣ 8 7 3		♣ 9 8 6 3 2

C. You opened 1♠ and partner replied 2NT (Jacoby raise). What is your rebid?

1.	♠ Q J 7 3 2	2.	♠ A J 7 3 2	3.	♠ A 9 7 4 2	4.	♠ A 10 7 5 2	5.	♠ A J 7 4
	♡ A Q 4 3		♡ A Q 4 3		♡ 3		♡ K Q		♡ Q J 4
	♢ 2		♢ 2		♢ A K J 4 2		♢ Q 7 2		♢ K Q 2
	♣ K 9 2		♣ A K 2		♣ Q 5		♣ J 10 6		♣ A Q 9

PARTNERSHIP BIDDING: How should the following hands be bid? West is the dealer each time.

	SET 15 — WEST		SET 15 — EAST		SET 16 — WEST		SET 16 — EAST
1.	♠ 3	1.	♠ A 8 6	1.	♠ A J 7 4 2	1.	♠ K Q 8 6
	♡ K 7 5		♡ Q 8 6 4 3		♡ K Q 3		♡ A J
	♢ A J 4 3 2		♢ K 9		♢ K 8 4 3		♢ A 5 2
	♣ A Q 3 2		♣ K 7 5		♣ 5		♣ 8 7 4 2
2.	♠ Q 7	2.	♠ A K J 6 5 2	2.	♠ A J 7 4 2	2.	♠ K Q 8 6
	♡ A 9 7 3 2		♡ 8		♡ K Q 3		♡ 8 7 4 2
	♢ A 7		♢ K Q 3		♢ K 8 4 3		♢ A 5 2
	♣ K 6 5 3		♣ Q J 2		♣ 5		♣ A J
3.	♠ 9 4 3 2	3.	♠ A 8 7 5	3.	♠ A K 7 4 3 2	3.	♠ Q 9 8 6
	♡ A K J 8		♡ 7 2		♡ 9 6		♡ A K 3
	♢ 4		♢ K J 7 5 2		♢ K 8 3		♢ A 7 5
	♣ K J 6 2		♣ 8 4		♣ A K		♣ 7 5 2
4.	♠ A J 9	4.	♠ 7 5 2	4.	♠ J	4.	♠ A 7 6 2
	♡ K J 6 2		♡ Q 5		♡ Q 8 4 3 2		♡ A K 9 6 5
	♢ 4		♢ A K 9 6 5		♢ Q 7		♢ A 6
	♣ A 8 5 3 2		♣ K J 4		♣ A K J 7 4		♣ Q 9
5.	♠ 8	5.	♠ 7 5 2	5.	♠ 4	5.	♠ A 7 6
	♡ A K 8 2		♡ Q 5		♡ Q 8 4 3 2		♡ A K 9 6 5
	♢ J 7 3		♢ A K 9 6 5		♢ K 7		♢ A 3
	♣ A 8 6 3 2		♣ K J 4		♣ A K 8 7 4		♣ Q J 3
6.	♠ 7 3	6.	♠ K Q 10 4 2	6.	♠ K Q 8 4 2	6.	♠ A J 9 7
	♡ A 9 5 3		♡ Q J 7 2		♡ Q J 7		♡ A 3
	♢ Q J 6 2		♢ K 4		♢ K 4		♢ A Q J 3
	♣ A 6 3		♣ 7 5		♣ Q 7 5		♣ 8 3 2

PLAY HANDS ON RESPONDER'S STRATEGY
(These hands can be made up by using pages 176-183)

Hand 29: Jacoby 2NT — Locating a missing queen

Dealer North : Both vulnerable

WEST	NORTH	EAST	SOUTH
	1♡	1♠	2NT
No	4♡	All pass	

NORTH
♠ 10 8
♡ Q J 8 5 4
♢ A 10 6
♣ A J 10

WEST
♠ Q 7 6
♡ 7
♢ Q 7 5 2
♣ 8 7 4 3 2

EAST
♠ A K J 5 2
♡ 10 6 2
♢ 8 4
♣ Q 9 6

SOUTH
♠ 9 4 3
♡ A K 9 3
♢ K J 9 3
♣ K 5

Bidding: When playing Jacoby, the 2NT heart raise still applies after a 1♠ overcall. After a two-level overcall, however, 2NT would be natural and you bid the enemy suit with the game force raise. North has a minimum opening with no short suit and no strong second suit and shows that with the game rebid.

  If not playing Jacoby, South would respond 2♢ and raise 2♡ to 4♡, the delayed game raise.

Lead: Ace of spades. Obvious choice.

Recommended play: West signals encouragement and East continues with the ♠K and a third spade ruffed by North. Trumps are drawn in three rounds, followed by the ♣K, ♣A and the ♣J ruffed in dummy. Declarer plays West for the queen of diamonds: cash the ♢K followed by the ♢J, letting the jack run if West plays low. When the diamond finesse works, declarer scores an overtrick.

Notes: (1) North's 4♡ is absolutely safe but the overtrick is essential to secure a good score.
(2) There is no benefit in taking a club finesse either way. Even if this succeeds there is no useful discard.
(3) It may seem attractive to play East, the bidder, for the ♢Q. North can place East with five spades for the overcall, three hearts (discovered when drawing trumps) and ♣Q-x-x (discovered on the play of the clubs). East therefore cannot hold more than two diamonds and so West began with 4+ diamonds. East could have ♢Q-x but you need a powerful reason to counter the 2-1 odds in favour of West's holding the queen.
(4) On the hearts, West should discard two clubs. One diamond discard is safe but looks suspicious.

Hand 30: Jacoby 2NT — Setting up an endplay — Passive defence

Dealer East : Nil vulnerable

WEST	NORTH	EAST	SOUTH
		1♠	No
2NT	No	3♠	No
4♠	No	No	No

NORTH
♠ A 6
♡ 6 5 3 2
♢ A 9 7 5 3
♣ Q 2

WEST
♠ J 8 5 3 2
♡ K 8
♢ K J 2
♣ K J 10

EAST
♠ K Q 10 9 7
♡ A Q
♢ 6 4
♣ A 7 5 4

SOUTH
♠ 4
♡ J 10 9 7 4
♢ Q 10 8
♣ 9 8 6 3

Bidding: Although Jacoby 2NT shows 13+ points, West should choose 2NT, given the excellent trump support. It would be far too timid to treat West as a limit raise. 3♠ by East shows an extra spade (if playing 4-card suits) and extra strength, but no short suit. (If playing 5-card majors, East would rebid 3NT: extra strength, but no extra length and no short suit.) West is keen to sign off at the first opportunity and East has nothing to spare. (Some pairs use 3NT by opener as Blackwood after Jacoby 2NT. If so, opener repeats the major with 14+ HCP and no shortage.)

Lead: Jack of hearts. The other suits are much riskier.

Recommended play: Win ♡A and play a heart to the king. Then lead the ♠J from dummy. If North plays low, continue with a second spade. North has to give declarer a ruff and discard or solve the diamond or club position.

Notes: (1) The hearts are cashed at once in order to endplay North if North began with singleton ♠A.
(2) If ♠J is led from dummy, it is hard for North to rise with the ♠A (South might have ♠Q or ♠K bare). If North takes the first spade (e.g., the spade is led from the East hand), North should exit with a spade. Declarer should then tackle clubs. The normal play with this club combination is a first round finesse but even if South has the ♣Q, there is no useful discard on the fourth club. Here East should cash ♣A and then finesse ♣J. The second round finesse gives you a better chance to endplay North. In with the ♣Q, North has to give East a ruff and discard via a third heart or eliminate East's guess in diamonds. If East takes a first round club finesse, North should exit with the second club and let East guess the diamonds.

Hand 31: Jacoby 2NT — Slam technique

Dealer South : N-S vulnerable

NORTH
- ♠ A 2
- ♡ A Q 7 4
- ◇ K 7 2
- ♣ 9 7 6 2

WEST
- ♠ J 10 9 7
- ♡ 2
- ◇ J 10 8 6
- ♣ A Q 10 5

EAST
- ♠ 8 6 5 4
- ♡ 8 6 5
- ◇ Q 9
- ♣ K J 8 3

SOUTH
- ♠ K Q 3
- ♡ K J 10 9 3
- ◇ A 5 4 3
- ♣ 4

WEST	NORTH	EAST	SOUTH
			1♡
No	2NT	No	3♣
No	4NT	No	5◇
No	6♡	All pass	

Bidding: If you appreciate the value of splinters, you will adore using the Jacoby 2NT, which allows opener to show a short suit. If the bidding had started 1♡ : 2♣, 2◇ : 4♡ (the delayed game raise), it would be nigh impossible to reach 6♡.

3♣ showed a singleton or void in clubs and with only one club loser and 4 outside losers, North could see the slam potential. Playing Roman Key Card Blackwood (Chapter 12) South would answer 4NT with 5♡ (two key cards but no trump queen).

Lead: Jack of spades. Prefer the stronger sequence.

Recommended play: South should win with the king of spades and lead the singleton club at once. Win any return, say a spade taken by the ace. Draw two rounds of trumps with ♡K and ♡J, cash ♠Q and discard a diamond from dummy, followed by ◇K, ◇A and a diamond ruffed with a top trump in dummy. Ruff a club to hand and ruff the last diamond in dummy. South has only trumps left.

Notes: (1) The slam is excellent with just 26 HCP and many pairs will stop in game. It is important to play the hand as safely as possible. You could ruff three clubs in hand but this line has no superiority unless the opponents start with two rounds of clubs, thus helping your entry position.
(2) You could win ♠A, cash ♠K and ♠Q discarding a diamond, and follow with ◇K, ◇A, third diamond ruffed high in dummy. If you ruff low, you will be overruffed. However, it is slightly safer to draw two rounds of trumps before playing to ruff the diamonds as long as you keep two top trumps in dummy.
(3) You must not start with three spades, ♡K,♡J, ◇K, ◇A, diamond ruff because then you have no easy way back to hand. East can win the club exit and lead a third trump. Playing the club first solves this.

Hand 32: Rebid with a weak hand after Jacoby 2NT — Playing it safe

Dealer West : E-W vulnerable

NORTH
- ♠ 10 9 7 2
- ♡ 8 4
- ◇ 9 8 4
- ♣ K J 9 5

WEST
- ♠ Q J 6
- ♡ K Q 9 6 5
- ◇ Q J
- ♣ Q 10 2

EAST
- ♠ A 4
- ♡ A J 7 2
- ◇ A K 10 7
- ♣ 8 7 4

SOUTH
- ♠ K 8 5 3
- ♡ 10 3
- ◇ 6 5 3 2
- ♣ A 6 3

WEST	NORTH	EAST	SOUTH
1♡	No	2NT	No
4♡	No	No	No

Bidding: West may have to check twice to ensure that this is worth an opening bid. It certainly looks like 13 low card points. Over 2NT, West is anxious to bid 4♡. If ever there was a minimum opening, this is it. Although East has a strong hand, East has too many losers to push on over 4♡ which will usually be an 11-13 point 5-3-3-2 hand.

If the bidding began 1♡ : 2◇, 2♡ East has a tougher time as the West hand might be a bit better or could be distributional.

Lead: 10 of spades. A near-sequence is usually better than leading from a suit with broken honours or from a rag suit.

Recommended play: West rises with dummy's ♠A, draws trumps and then runs the diamonds, discarding two club losers. A spade is played and declarer makes eleven tricks, losing one spade and one club.

Notes: (1) A club lead would give the defence three tricks but North has no way of telling.
(2) North's lead might be from K-10-9-x but it would be foolish for declarer to take the first round spade finesse. Firstly, it is not likely that North has led from the ♠K. Secondly, declarer has eleven safe tricks by rising with the ♠A. It is silly to jeopardise a normal contract when an overtrick is perfectly safe. Thirdly, other tables might receive a club lead and be held to ten tricks. Therefore, make sure of eleven.
(3) If declarer received a trump lead or a diamond lead, declarer would draw trumps, cash the diamonds and discard two clubs. Later declarer could safely try the spade finesse for an extra trick.

CHAPTER 9

WEAK TWOS

In standard Acol, game force hands are opened with 2♣ and the 2♦ / 2♡ / 2♠ openings show a powerful 5-card or longer suit and usually 8-9½ playing tricks. One of the drawbacks of this approach is the rarity of such powerful hands.

Modern methods are concerned with frequency of occurrence. You need to be able to deal with the hands that come up again and again, not with those that occur relatively rarely. Consequently, most duplicate partnerships have adopted weak twos which allow you to enter the bidding more often. The more action you generate, the better. Used in a disciplined fashion, weak twos enable partner to judge further action accurately and still make life tough for the opponents who usually have to start their auction at the three-level.

There are two basic approaches when using weak two openings. In standard American style:

2♦ / 2♡ / 2♠ = weak twos, showing the suit bid
2♣ = artificial, 23+ points, game-forcing

Benjamin Twos Style

2♡ / 2♠ = weak twos, showing the major bid
2♦ = artificial, 23+ points, game-forcing
2♣ = artificial, 8½-9½ playing tricks, i.e., about one trick short of game, long suit not yet disclosed

Most pairs use weak twos in the majors. Very few use a weak 2♦ opening which has little pre-emptive or constructive value. It is better to adopt the Benjamin Twos structure which deals more effectively with the strong hands. Another choice gaining in popularity is to use the Multi-2♦ opening (see Chapter 23).

WEAK TWOS IN THE MAJORS

To open with a weak two, you should have:

1. A 6-card suit, headed by the queen or better and containing at least two honours. It can be fun to open a weak two on J-8-6-4-3-2, but it can do untold harm. If partner is on lead and starts with A-x or K-x, this will do more damage than good.

When vulnerable, you may open a weak two with a 7-card suit if the hand is not worth a 3-opening.
2. 6-10 HCP. With 11 HCP and a good 6-card suit, choose a 1-opening.
3. 7-8 losers. A minimum weak two has 8 losers and a maximum has 7.
4. No 4-card major. Do not to open a weak two with a 4-card holding in the other major. You may miss your best spot.
5. No freak shape. 6-3-2-2 and 6-3-3-1 patterns are normal. 6-4-2-1 is acceptable if the 4-card suit is a minor. 6-4-2-1s may be 6-loser hands.

One singleton is permitted for a weak two but not two singletons and not a void. Hands with such extreme shape have too much playing strength and partner will often be unable to appreciate the value of the combined hands. With these freak shapes, if you are unable to start with a 1-opening or a 3-opening, prefer to pass than open a weak two.

Weak Twos in third or fourth seat

Once partner has passed and you have no more than 10 points, prospects for game are poor. The above requirements therefore become more flexible. In third seat, the range expands to 6-12 HCP and it is not taboo to have a 7-card or 5-card suit rather than the normal 6-card holding. If it is a 5-card suit, it should contain three honours (e.g., A-K-J-x-x). In fourth seat, the range is played as 8-12 HCP, partly because it is so unlikely that there would be no opening bid ahead of a 7-point or weaker hand in fourth seat and partly because with 7 HCP or less, you are probably far better off to pass the hand in. A weak two in third or fourth seat may contain a void.

Some players open a weak two in first or second seat on a strong 5-card suit. Although it increases the frequency of opening, this practice cannot be recommended. In order to compete effectively at the three-level and to find decent sacrifices, partner needs to know the combined trump length. Opening weak twos on 5-card *and* 6-card suits makes it nigh impossible for partner to gauge the combined trump length correctly.

Examples

♠ A Q 8 7 6 3	♠ A Q 8 7 6 3	♠ K J 10 5 4 2
♡ 9 6	♡ 9 6	♡ 3
♦ 7 3 2	♦ 7 3 2	♦ A J 8
♣ 6 3	♣ K 6	♣ 7 4 2
Open 2♠	Open 2♠	Open 2♠
Minimum	Maximum	Maximum

Even though the third hand has 8 losers, it is treated as a maximum because of the 9 HCP and strong spade suit. A minimum weak two usually has two high card winners and a maximum will usually have three.

♠ 6 3	♠ 6 3	♠ 5
♡ Q J 9 8 6 2	♡ A K Q 9 6 2	♡ A K 8 6 3 2
♦ K 3 2	♦ 7 3	♦ 10 8 5 3
♣ 6 3	♣ 9 6 5	♣ Q 2
Open 2♡	Open 2♡	Open 2♡
Minimum	Maximum	Maximum

♠ 6 3	♠ - - -	♠ A 9 8
♡ J 8 7 6 4 2	♡ K J 10 8 6 2	♡ A Q J 9 3 2
◇ K 3 2	◇ 8 7 6 3	◇ 5 3
♣ A 3	♣ A 4 2	♣ 7 2
Pass.	Pass in 1st or	Open 1♡.
Suit quality	2nd seat. Open	Hand too
too poor for 2♡.	2♡ in third seat.	strong for 2♡.

♠ K Q J 9 8 3	♠ K J 8 7 6 4 3	♠ K Q J 10 5
♡ 6	♡ 6	♡ 3
◇ Q J 9 8 4	◇ 9 3 2	◇ J 8 5 3
♣ 2	♣ Q 4	♣ 7 4 2
Open 4♠.	Open 2♠ if vul,	Open 2♠ in
Too freakish	3♠ if not vul.	3rd seat. Pass
for 2♠.		1st or 2nd seat.

When are you maximum, when minimum?

6-7 HCP is normally a minimum, 9-10 = maximum.
8 losers = minimum, 7 losers = maximum.
6-4-2-1: 7 losers = minimum, 6 losers = maximum.
Three cover cards = maximum.
Two cover cards = minimum.
'Cover card' = ace, guarded king or guarded queen (Q-x-x or better).

Bidding structure after a weak two

1. Raises of opener's suit are pre-emptive, not invitational. Opener is not to bid again.

2. Change of suit is forcing. A new suit is a good 5-card or longer suit and a very strong hand. Opener should raise with 3 trumps or with Q-x or better support. The change of suit normally indicates a singleton or void in opener's suit.

3. The OGUST 2NT Response

2NT asks opener to describe the strength of the hand and the strength of the 6-card major. Opener bids 3♣ / 3◇ with a minimum and 3♡ / 3♠ / 3NT if maximum. **Minors minimum, majors maximum.**

Opener's reply also indicates whether opener holds one, two or three of the top honours (A, K or Q) in the major. The cheapest reply in each case shows just one top honour.

After 2♡ : 2NT or 2♠ : 2NT —

3♣ = Minimum, 1 top honour	*Memory guide*	
3◇ = Minimum, 2 top honours	*for honours:*	
3♡ = Maximum, 1 top honour	**1-2, 1-2-3**	
3♠ = Maximum, 2 top honours		
3NT = 3 top honours (A-K-Q-x-x-x in the major)		

After the reply to 2NT, 3-of opener's-major is to play and any game bid is a sign off, too. 4NT is Blackwood and a new suit is played as a cue-bid with opener's major agreed as the trump suit.

If they double the weak two for takeout: Redouble is strong, looking for penalties. 2NT is still Ogust while a new suit is genuine but is a rescue-bid which opener should pass.

If they overcall with 2NT or a suit: If they bid 2♠ over 2♡, 2NT is still Ogust. In other cases, 3-of-opener's-major becomes an invitation to game. A new suit is forcing and double is for penalties.

If they overcall after responder has bid 2NT Ogust:

Make your normal reply if still available. If your normal reply is not available, double if their bid is your answer and pass if your reply is lower-ranking.

Responder's strategy after a weak two

Singleton or void in opener's suit

Below 16 HCP: Pass. Your side does not have the values for game. With no fit with opener's suit, you are high enough already.

16 HCP or more: Bid a new suit (forcing) with a strong 5-card or longer suit or use the Ogust Convention (2NT — see later). With 16-18 HCP and no long, strong suit, bid 2NT and if opener shows a maximum, try 3NT, but opposite a minimum, sign off in 3-of-opener's major.

With 19 HCP or more, you should be in at least game, even opposite a minimum weak two. Bid a new suit or bid 3NT. If the quality of opener's suit is relevant, you can use the Ogust 2NT response.

If responder bids 3NT, that is to play and opener should normally pass. However, with a major which has a suit quality of 10 (6-card suit with 4 honours), it is better to remove 3NT to 4-Major. Such a suit plays well enough opposite a singleton or a void.

With 2+ cards in opener's suit

A maximum weak two can have six playing tricks. With tolerance (doubleton) or support (3+ trumps) for opener's major, responder should therefore try for game with four winners. Even a bit more than three sure tricks will justify a move towards game.

Counting your tricks in support of opener:

A, K or Q of trumps = 1 trick

Outside suits: Count only your quick tricks, the winners in the first two rounds of a suit:

A-K = 2, A-Q = 1½, A = 1, K-Q = 1 and K-x = ½

With support for opener, you can count one trick for an outside singleton and two tricks for a void.

With 3 trumps and less than 2½ tricks: Raise to the three-level as a pre-empt.

With 4+ trumps and up to 3 tricks: Raise to game pre-emptively.

With 3½-4 tricks: Use the Ogust 2NT Convention. Bid game opposite a maximum, but sign off at the three-level in opener's major opposite a minimum.

With 4½-5½ tricks: Bid game, expecting to make. Whether opener has 5 or 6 tricks, game should be a reasonable bet.

With 6 or more tricks: Use the Ogust 2NT response and explore slam possibilities.

EXERCISES USING WEAK TWOS IN THE MAJORS

A. You are the dealer, neither side vulnerable. What do you do with each of these hands?

1. ♠ 9 7 3	2. ♠ A K 9 7 6 2	3. ♠ A K	4. ♠ K 9 5 2	5. ♠ A Q J 9 8 7
♡ A J 9 8 5 4	♡ K J 7	♡ J 9 8 6 3 2	♡ A J 7 5 4 3	♡ 2
◇ K J 2	◇ 8 4	◇ J 10 7	◇ 8 7	◇ J 2
♣ 7	♣ 5 2	♣ 9 5	♣ 6	♣ J 9 3 2

B. Partner has opened 2♡. What is your response with each of these hands?

1. ♠ A 9 2	2. ♠ A 9 7 4	3. ♠ K Q 9 8	4. ♠ 7 4 3 2	5. ♠ K J 10 2
♡ K J 5 3	♡ K 3	♡ 6	♡ A 9 2	♡ 2
◇ 7	◇ Q J 7 2	◇ A Q 9 6 2	◇ A K 8 6	◇ A K 9 3
♣ Q J 7 4 3	♣ 8 6 4	♣ J 8 7	♣ K 4	♣ K Q J 4

C. The bidding has started 2♠ : 2NT. What is opener's rebid with these hands?

1. ♠ K Q 9 6 3 2	2. ♠ A K Q 6 4 2	3. ♠ A J 8 7 4 2	4. ♠ Q J 7 6 4 2	5. ♠ A Q 9 6 4 3
♡ 5 3	♡ 2	♡ 6 4	♡ 8 2	♡ 4
◇ J 8 5	◇ 8 6 3	◇ K Q	◇ 10 6	◇ J 7 4
♣ 9 7	♣ 7 4 3	♣ 9 6 2	♣ A 5 4	♣ K 8 2

PARTNERSHIP BIDDING : How should the following hands be bid? West is the dealer each time.

SET 17 — WEST	SET 17 — EAST	SET 18 — WEST	SET 18 — EAST
1. ♠ K 3	1. ♠ 9 5 2	1. ♠ 7	1. ♠ A Q 9 4
♡ K Q 9 7 5 3	♡ A 6 2	♡ A Q J 6 4 3	♡ 7
◇ 8 6 4	◇ A K J 3	◇ 9 7 2	◇ K Q 6 4 3
♣ 7 2	♣ K Q 4	♣ J 10 3	♣ K 8 4
2. ♠ K Q 5 3	2. ♠ 6 4	2. ♠ Q 2	2. ♠ A K 4 3
♡ A 5	♡ K J 10 7 4 3	♡ K Q 8 6 5 3	♡ 2
◇ J 6	◇ K 3	◇ 6 5	◇ A K 9 8
♣ 9 8 5 4 2	♣ J 6 3	♣ 9 8 3	♣ K Q J 10
3. ♠ A K 8 6 3 2	3. ♠ Q 9 7 5	3. ♠ 5 2	3. ♠ A K 4 3
♡ 5 3 2	♡ 8	♡ K Q J 10 9 6	♡ 2
◇ 5	◇ A 9 7 2	◇ 6 5	◇ A K Q 9 8
♣ 6 4 3	♣ A J 5 2	♣ 9 8 3	♣ K Q J
4. ♠ A J 9 6 4 3	4. ♠ K 8 7 5 2	4. ♠ A Q 10 7 6 5	4. ♠ J 4 2
♡ 9 7 2	♡ 5 4	♡ 7 3	♡ A K 5 2
◇ 8 3	◇ 9	◇ 9 5 2	◇ A Q 4 3
♣ K 9	♣ Q 8 5 4 2	♣ K 8	♣ 9 5
5. ♠ A 9 7 4 2	5. ♠ K Q J 8 3	5. ♠ A K 8 7 4 3	5. ♠ Q 10 5 2
♡ Q 3	♡ 10 5 4	♡ 5 4 2	♡ A 9 3
◇ A 9 8 3	◇ 2	◇ 3 2	◇ A 8 5
♣ 7 2	♣ A 9 6 4	♣ 8 6	♣ A 10 4
6. ♠ 9 6 2	6. ♠ A K 5 4	6. ♠ A K Q 8 7 3	6. ♠ 9 6 4 2
♡ A J 7 6 4 2	♡ 8 5	♡ 7 2	♡ A 8 5
◇ 7	◇ A J 3 2	◇ 9 7	◇ K Q J
♣ Q 8 7	♣ K J 2	♣ 6 4 3	♣ A 7 2

PLAY HANDS ON WEAK TWO OPENINGS
(These hands can be made up by using pages 176-183)

Hand 33: 3NT vs. 4-Major — Establishing a long suit

Dealer North : Nil vulnerable

NORTH
- ♠ 6
- ♡ A K J 9 8 3
- ◇ J 10
- ♣ 7 4 3 2

WEST
- ♠ Q 10
- ♡ 6 4
- ◇ 7 6 5 4 3
- ♣ K Q 10 9

EAST
- ♠ K J 9 7
- ♡ 7 5 2
- ◇ K Q 9 2
- ♣ J 6

SOUTH
- ♠ A 8 5 4 3 2
- ♡ Q 10
- ◇ A 8
- ♣ A 8 5

WEST	NORTH	EAST	SOUTH
	2♡	No	4♡
No	No	No	

Bidding: South has four clear-cut winners (three aces and the queen of trumps plus good potential for an extra trick — a potential ruff in diamonds and a spade suit that might be established). That justifies bidding game rather than checking on opener's strength. If South did use 2NT (Ogust), North would bid 3♠ (maximum points and two top honours in hearts). South could see that 3NT would be available but should still choose 4♡ where there would be better chances for overtricks.

Lead: King of diamonds. J-x is usually a poor lead. Better to choose the suit where the honours are touching (diamonds) than the suit where the honours are split (spades).

Recommended play: North wins with the ◇A and should immediately set about establishing the spades. Ace of spades, ruff a spade, heart to the ten, ruff a spade, heart to the queen, ruff a spade. Two spade winners are now set up in dummy. Draw the last trump and then cross to the ♣A to cash the spades. 11 tricks.

Notes: (1) If trumps are drawn at once, declarer is relying on clubs 3-3, less than a 40% chance.
(2) A better plan is to ruff a club with one of dummy's top trumps: win ◇A and play ace and another club, but the opponents can thwart this plan by switching to trumps and eliminating dummy's ruffing power.
(3) When setting up a long suit, use the trump entries to dummy before using the outside entries.
(4) Note how much better you do in 4♡ (450) than in 3NT (400). The possibility of overtricks is a vital consideration at pairs.

Hand 34: Using Ogust 2NT — Establishing a long suit

Dealer East : N-S vulnerable

NORTH
- ♠ 5 3
- ♡ 6 5 4 2
- ◇ K Q 10
- ♣ J 9 6 5

WEST
- ♠ K 9 2
- ♡ J 10
- ◇ A J 2
- ♣ A Q 10 8 7

EAST
- ♠ A Q J 10 6 4
- ♡ Q 9
- ◇ 7 5 4
- ♣ 3 2

SOUTH
- ♠ 8 7
- ♡ A K 8 7 3
- ◇ 9 8 6 3
- ♣ K 4

WEST	NORTH	EAST	SOUTH
		2♠	No
2NT	No	3♠	No
4♠	No	No	No

Bidding: West can count 3½ tricks in support of spades. Add the heart shortage and the club length and there is enough potential to try for game. East has 9 HCP but eight losers. Because of the strong spades (Suit Quality 10), East should bid 3♠ to show maximum points and two top honours in spades. The jack and the ten do not count as top honours.

Lead: Ace (or king) of hearts. Most top players prefer to lead the ace from A-K-x or longer. After cashing two hearts, South should switch to a diamond. From the bidding and play so far, South can tell that North has diamond strength.

Recommended play: East should take the ace of diamonds at once, cross to hand with a trump to the ace and lead a club. When South plays low, finesse the queen. If that lost, declarer would be two down. When the ♣Q wins, cash the ♣A and ruff a third club high. Play a low spade to dummy's 9 and ruff a fourth club. Dummy's last club is now a winner. Cross to the king of spades, cash the club and discard a diamond loser.

Notes: (1) If two rounds of trumps are drawn before starting on the clubs, declarer is one entry short to set up the clubs if they divide 4-2.
(2) If East ruffs the third round of clubs low, South overruffs. Two down.
(3) With only two clubs in hand, finesse the queen of clubs, not the ten.
(4) Declarer succeeds even if the first round of diamonds is ducked. The advantage of taking the first diamond comes when clubs are 3-3 with the ♣K with South. After finessing ♣Q, cashing the ♣A and ruffing a club, there are two club winners established in dummy and both diamond losers can be discarded.

Hand 35: Action after a weak two — Card reading — Playing for the overtrick

Dealer South : E-W vulnerable

	WEST	NORTH	EAST	SOUTH
				No
	2♠	No	No	No

NORTH
- ♠ 7 4
- ♡ J 10 9 8
- ◇ K Q 9
- ♣ K J 6 5

WEST
- ♠ A K 10 6 5 3
- ♡ 7 4 2
- ◇ J 7 2
- ♣ 9

EAST
- ♠ 9 8 2
- ♡ Q 5 3
- ◇ A 6 4
- ♣ A Q 7 4

SOUTH
- ♠ Q J
- ♡ A K 6
- ◇ 10 8 5 3
- ♣ 10 8 3 2

Bidding: East has fewer than three quick tricks and so prospects for game are poor. If the opposition compete, East would be worth a push to 3♠ as East knows the partnership has 9 trumps.

Most club players would pass out 2♠ on the South cards but many top players would compete with a double. This is not so risky as South is a passed hand. North may well bid 3♡ which would not play well (2 spades, 2 clubs, 2 club ruffs and a diamond to be lost) but it may push East-West to 3♠.

Lead: Jack of hearts. Choose the sequence that is solid (hearts) rather than the suit where there are only two honours in sequence (diamonds) or the suit with no sequence (clubs).

Recommended play: Declarer plays low in dummy and so does South. After three rounds of hearts, South shifts to the 3 of diamonds. Declarer plays low and North's 9 forces the ace. Trumps are drawn in two rounds and the contract is now secure.

Should declarer take the club finesse to try for an overtrick? If the finesse works, declarer can discard a diamond loser and make nine tricks. If the finesse fails, the opponents can probably cash two diamonds and defeat the part-score.

Notes: (1) Deciding whether to jeopardise the contract for an overtrick is a common problem at pairs. If your contract is excellent and the finesse is 50%, it is not worth the risk. If your contract is poor, you should take any reasonable risk to try to improve your score. If your contract is normal as here, it usually does not pay to risk the contract if the chance for an overtrick is 50% or worse.

(2) Here the club finesse is almost a certainty. South passed as dealer but has turned up with A-K in hearts and Q-J in spades. That makes 10 points. If South had the king of clubs, that would make 13 HCP and South would almost certainly have opened despite the poor spade holding. Therefore take the club finesse.

Hand 36: Weak two in fourth seat — Card reading — Discovery play

Dealer West : Both vulnerable

WEST	NORTH	EAST	SOUTH
No	No	No	2♡
No	No	No	

NORTH
- ♠ J 10 8
- ♡ A 9 8
- ◇ A Q 10
- ♣ 10 7 5 4

WEST
- ♠ A K 7 2
- ♡ 7 5 4
- ◇ 9 6 2
- ♣ A 6 3

EAST
- ♠ Q 9 6 4
- ♡ K
- ◇ 8 7 5 4
- ♣ Q J 9 8

SOUTH
- ♠ 5 3
- ♡ Q J 10 6 3 2
- ◇ K J 3
- ♣ K 2

Bidding: In fourth seat, the weak two is usually played as 8-12 HCP. With less, pass the deal in. With 3 hearts, West's shape does not justify coming in over 2♡. With only 2½ tricks, North has no reason to push higher. With the shortage in hearts and four cards in each other suit, East has the right shape to compete. Again, most club players would pass while most experts would compete with a double. West would bid 2♠, which makes easily, and North would compete to 3♡. Do not sell out at the two-level when your side has a trump fit.

Lead: Ace of spades. East encourages and West continues with the king of spades and a third spade.

Recommended play: South ruffs the third spade and the natural inclination is to tackle trumps next. However, South should cross to dummy with a diamond and lead a club to the king. West wins and may return a club. South ruffs the third club and leads a heart to the ace. When the king drops singleton, South makes nine tricks and the vital overtrick.

Notes: (1) The standard play in hearts is to lead the queen and let it run if West plays low.
(2) Since the club finesse has to be taken some time, there is little risk in taking it early. If East has the ace of clubs, South can later play the hearts in the normal fashion.
(3) When West turns up with the ace of clubs as well as the A-K of spades, that makes 11 HCP. As West passed as dealer, West cannot hold the king of hearts as well. Since the finesse must lose, play the ace. Playing on clubs early is a 'discovery' play. Locating the ace of clubs helps you in the play of the hearts.

CHAPTER 10
THE BENJAMIN 2♣ OPENING

A sound approach for those who play weak twos is the use of 2♣ and 2◇ for strong hands. The Benjamin Twos structure uses 2◇ for game-going hands and 2♣ for hands about one trick short of game. The 2♣ opening caters for the 19-21 point hand with a 6+ suit, a hand that could not be shown in standard Acol. The typical problem looks like this:

♠	A K 2	Suppose you open 1◇ and
♡	A 6	partner responds 1♡?
◇	A K J 9 8 4	What now?
♣	6 2	

You are too strong for 3◇, which shows 16-18 points and is not forcing. 3NT is just a gamble with nothing in clubs and to bid 1♠ with a 3-card suit should leave you cold.

The Benjamin 2♣ opening solves the problem. You open 2♣ and rebid 3◇ showing the strength and the good suit.

♠	A Q	Similarly, suppose you open
♡	A K 4	1♣ on this hand. What is your
◇	6 2	rebid if partner bids 1♡? What
♣	A K 10 9 8 4	about after a 1♠ response?

You are strong enough for game but which game? Over 1♡, there is no satisfactory rebid. Over 1♠, many would choose a 2♡ reverse, but this does not come risk-free. Opening 2♣ Benjamin and rebidding 3♣ shows the strength and the nature of the hand.

As the popularity of the Benjamin 2♣ increased, problems began when players used it on unsuitable hands with any 19-21 points. 2♣ is fine for the 19-21 point hand with a 6-card or longer suit. It may be used for other powerful hands but it does not work well if you open 2♣ willy-nilly on any 19-21 point hand, particularly two-suiters or a 4-4-4-1 pattern.

The playing strength for the 2♣ opening should be about 8½-9½ tricks. You should open 2♣ when you are worried that partner may pass your 1-opening and you may thus miss a game. In general, an 8-trick hand (5 losers) is not strong enough. Opposite that, you need two tricks to make 4♡ or 4♠ a good bet. With two tricks or even 1½ tricks, partner will have enough to respond to a 1-opening. When just one ace or one useful king in partner's hand is all you need for game, it is sensible to start with 2♣. In other words, open 2♣ when you are about one trick short of game.

Open 2♣ with an unbalanced hand and 8½-9½ playing tricks. The HCP strength should be 16-22 if not balanced. Below 16 HCP, start with a 1-opening, or a pre-empt if below 10 HCP. The 2♣ opening may also be used for balanced hands of 23-24 points. If stronger, choose the 2◇ opening (see Chapter 11).

Open 2♣ with —
(a) 23-24 HCP and a balanced hand
(b) 21-22 HCP and an unbalanced hand
(c) 21-22 HCP and a 5-3-3-2 with a 5-card major
(d) 18-20 HCP and a 6+ suit. 18 HCP is borderline.
   With poor short suit holdings (J-x, Q-x), choose the jump-rebid sequence such as 1♡ : 1NT, 3♡ . . .
(e) 16-18 HCP and a 7+ suit. 16 HCP is borderline.

Avoid opening 2♣ with a two-suiter unless you have 21-22 HCP. Two-suiters in the 18-20 HCP range are usually shown via a 1-opening followed by a jump-shift, such as 1♡ : 1NT, 3♣.

Do not open 2♣ with a balanced 19-20 points. Opposite this strength and shape, you need partner to have 6 points or more to make game a good bet. With that, partner will respond to your 1-opening. If partner cannot respond to a 1-opening, you are better off being passed out at the 1-level than reaching 2NT with 19-20 HCP opposite nothing or just one or two points. With a balanced 21-22, open 2NT.

As a rough guide, then, open 2♣ with —

23-24 HCP and a balanced hand
21-22 HCP and a 5+ suit
19-20 HCP and a 6+ suit
17-18 HCP and a 7+ suit

RESPONDING TO 2♣

2◇ = Artificial negative response, 0-7 HCP and less than 1½ quick tricks.

All other responses = positive responses, 8+ HCP or 1½ quick tricks or better.

Quick tricks: A-K = 2, A-Q = 1½, A = 1, K-Q = 1 and K-x = ½.

CHOOSING YOUR POSITIVE RESPONSE

It is playable for a 2-Major response to be based on just a 4-card suit but it is recommended that any suit reply shows a 5-card or longer suit and that the 2NT response is a balanced hand of 8 HCP or more.

What should you do with a positive response and a 4-4-4-1 pattern? The good news is that this is a rare shape. You should bid your cheapest 4-card suit and hope for the best. Partner will expect a 5-card major but it is not worth changing your whole bidding structure to cater for one infrequent pattern.

Almost always a 2-Major response is a 5-card or longer suit and it pays to treat it as such.

With a two-suiter, bid your longer suit first and bid the higher suit first with a 5-5 or 6-6 pattern.

OPENER'S REBID

(a) After the 2♦ negative response

Any rebid by opener can be passed. Opener should choose from :

2♥ / 2♠ = 5+ suit, 8½ tricks or 21-22 HCP. If you have opened 2♣ with a 4-4-4-1 and 21-22 HCP, bid your cheaper 4-card major.

3♥ / 3♠ = 6+ suit and exactly 9 playing tricks

4♥ / 4♠ = 6+ suit and 9½ playing tricks

3♣ / 3♦ = 8½-9½ tricks, usually 6+ suit (it may be a 5-card suit occasionally)

4♣ / 4♦ = 9½-10 tricks, 6+ suit, unsuitable for a try at 3NT

5♣ / 5♦ = 10½ tricks, 7+ suit, unsuitable for 3NT

3NT = long, solid minor suit with at least two outside suits stopped and nine running tricks or thereabouts. A typical 3NT rebid might look like one of these:

♠	A 3	♠	8 2
♥	9 6 4	♥	A K
♦	A K Q J 8 7 2	♦	A 5 2
♣	A	♣	A K Q J 9 2

While 3NT may not be a certainty, you are more likely to take nine tricks in no-trumps than eleven tricks in your minor opposite a negative response where responder has less than 1½ quick tricks.

It is reasonable to take a chance on one unguarded suit with a 3NT rebid but it is sensible to have at least two cards in such a suit. With a void or a singleton, a rebid of 3NT is too risky. Prefer a rebid in your minor suit.

2NT = the balanced 23-24 point hand. This rebid is not forcing but responder would pass only with a very weak hand. With two points or stronger, it is worth trying for game. After the 2NT rebid, bidding proceeds as after a 2NT opening, with 3♣ Stayman, 3♦ and 3♥ transfers, and so on (see Chapter 5).

(b) After a positive response

Any positive response is forcing to game and so any bid below game is forcing. Opener's rebid is natural. Bid your longer suit first and the higher suit with a 5-5 or 6-6 pattern. With a 4-4-4-1 and a singleton in responder's suit, rebid in no-trumps.

Responder's suit may be supported with 3-card or better support but it will often work out better to show your own long suit first and support responder on the next round. This will help responder assess the fit for slam purposes. Particularly if you have only 3-card support, prefer to describe your hand first (e.g., with a 2NT rebid or a change of suit) and show the support later.

A jump-rebid after a positive response is best played as a splinter: 4+ support for responder and a singleton or void in the suit bid. For example,

♠	A K 6 3	Open 2♣. If partner bids 2♥,
♥	A Q 2	bid 3♣ and support the hearts
♦	2	later. If partner bids 2♠, jump to
♣	A K J 7 3	4♦ (splinter).

After a 2NT positive response, it is sensible to play 3♣ as Stayman.

RESPONDER'S REBID

(a) After the 2♦ negative response

You may pass any rebid by opener but you are not obliged to pass. You should certainly bid again with one sure winner in your hand or with 5-7 HCP. You may raise opener's suit with three trumps or better support. Where opener's rebid is in a major, you should be eager to raise the major. Where opener's rebid is 3♣ or 3♦ and you have enough to bid, angle towards 3NT if possible rather than raise the minor. A risky 3NT will usually result in a better score than a minor suit game.

A new suit by responder will be a 5+ suit while a no-trump rebid would show about 5-7 points and no 5+ suit of your own. A no-trump rebid is acceptable with a powerful 4-4-4-1.

A jump rebid by responder is a splinter (4+ support for opener and a singleton or void in the suit bid).

♠	9 8 7 3 2	In reply to 2♣, you bid 2♦
♥	2	negative. If opener rebids 2♥,
♦	A 8 3 2	bid 2♠, but if opener's rebid is
♣	9 6 4	2♠, you are worth 4♥ (splinter).

After the negative 2♦ response, it is more useful to treat responder's jump-rebid in a new suit, such as 4♥ here, as a splinter than as natural. With long hearts, bid 3♥ over 2♠ and rebid 4♥ if you wish.

If the bidding has started 2♣ : 2♦, 3♥ or 3♠, you may raise the major suit with doubleton support or better and the slightest chance for a trick. A king or better would be enough.

(b) After a positive response

The partnership is committed to game at least. As opener's hand is limited, even though very strong, it is usually up to responder to initiate slam auctions.

A rebid of 3NT by responder indicates a minimum positive response and insufficient for a slam. Other game rebids by responder including supporting opener's suit to game also suggest slam is unlikely.

Raising opener's suit below game shows slam prospects. As opener has a hand of around four losers or about nine winners, responder should envisage slam potential with three winners or more if a trump fit has come to light. With 12 HCP or more or four winners or better, slam figures to be a good bet anyway.

EXERCISES ON THE BENJAMIN 2♣ OPENING

A. You are the dealer, neither side vulnerable. What do you do with each of these hands?

	1.	2.	3.	4.	5.
♠	9 7 3	A K Q 9 7 6 2	A K Q	A Q J 7 2	A Q 8
♡	A K J 8 5 4	J 3	10 9 8 6 3	8	2
◇	A K J	8	A K Q 3	A Q J	A K 2
♣	7	K Q J	J	A K J 9	A K 9 8 4 2

B. Partner has opened 2♣. What is your response with each of these hands?

	1.	2.	3.	4.	5.
♠	K J 8 7 4	K J 8 7 4	K J 8 7	9 2	K J 10 2
♡	6 3	7	7 5	Q J 9 3	2
◇	7 2	A 7 6 4	J 7 4	A K 9 8 6 2	Q J 8 4
♣	Q 7 4 3	8 6 4	A J 8 7	4	K 8 4 2

C. The bidding has started 2♣ : 2◇. What is opener's rebid with these hands?

	1.	2.	3.	4.	5.
♠	A 4 3	A 4 3	A K	A K J 8	A Q 9 6 4
♡	A K Q 8 5 3	6 2	6	A K	K Q 7
◇	A K	A K	A Q 4 2	Q 8 2	A 6
♣	6 2	A K Q 8 5 3	A K 9 8 6 2	A Q J 4	A K 8

PARTNERSHIP BIDDING : How should the following hands be bid? West is the dealer each time.

	SET 19 — WEST		SET 19 — EAST		SET 20 — WEST		SET 20 — EAST
1.	♠ A K 3 ♡ A K Q 8 7 3 2 ◇ 9 2 ♣ 8	1.	♠ 8 6 5 2 ♡ 10 4 ◇ J 8 7 3 ♣ 10 7 4	1.	♠ J 3 ♡ 5 2 ◇ A K Q ♣ A K Q J 8 6	1.	♠ K Q 10 9 4 2 ♡ K 8 4 ◇ 7 5 2 ♣ 3
2.	♠ A K 3 ♡ A K Q 8 7 3 2 ◇ 9 2 ♣ 8	2.	♠ 8 ♡ 10 4 ◇ J 7 5 4 3 ♣ 9 7 5 4 2	2.	♠ 2 ♡ K Q 5 3 2 ◇ K 6 5 ♣ 9 7 4 2	2.	♠ A K J 8 3 ♡ 6 ◇ A Q J 2 ♣ K Q J
3.	♠ 6 3 ♡ 5 4 2 ◇ Q 7 4 3 ♣ 8 6 5 2	3.	♠ A K Q J 9 4 2 ♡ 8 3 ◇ A 2 ♣ K Q	3.	♠ A Q J 8 7 3 ♡ 6 3 ◇ K 9 ♣ A K Q	3.	♠ K 5 2 ♡ Q J 8 7 2 ◇ Q J 4 ♣ J 9
4.	♠ 7 6 ♡ A 7 4 2 ◇ 7 6 4 3 ♣ 6 5 2	4.	♠ A K Q J 9 4 2 ♡ 8 3 ◇ A 2 ♣ K Q	4.	♠ Q 9 6 4 2 ♡ A 3 ◇ 9 7 5 2 ♣ A 10	4.	♠ 3 ♡ K Q J ◇ A K Q J 4 3 ♣ K J 5
5.	♠ 7 6 3 2 ♡ J 8 7 2 ◇ 7 6 4 3 ♣ 6	5.	♠ A 8 ♡ 5 4 3 ◇ A ♣ A K Q J 9 8 2	5.	♠ K Q ♡ A 10 9 8 7 5 3 ◇ A K Q ♣ 5	5.	♠ 8 6 ♡ K Q 6 2 ◇ J 5 ♣ A K 8 7 3
6.	♠ K Q ♡ A K J 7 6 4 ◇ A K ♣ 8 7 4	6.	♠ A 5 4 3 ♡ 8 5 3 2 ◇ J 8 3 2 ♣ 2	6.	♠ Q 10 5 4 2 ♡ A 8 3 2 ◇ 9 5 ♣ 8 4	6.	♠ A K 8 7 ♡ 9 4 ◇ A K Q ♣ A K J 6

PLAY HANDS ON THE BENJAMIN 2♣ OPENING
(These hands can be made up by using pages 176-183)

Hand 37: Rebidding to show nine tricks — Competitive action

Dealer North : N-S vulnerable

	NORTH		
	♠ K Q 9 8		
	♡ 10		
	◇ Q 9 3 2		
	♣ K 7 6 4		
WEST		**EAST**	
♠ 7		♠ A 4 2	
♡ 6 4 2		♡ A K Q 9 8 7 3	
◇ 10 8 7 5		◇ A 4	
♣ J 9 8 3 2		♣ Q	
	SOUTH		
	♠ J 10 6 5 3		
	♡ J 5		
	◇ K J 6		
	♣ A 10 5		

WEST	NORTH	EAST	SOUTH
	No	2♣	No
2◇	No	3♡	No
4♡	No	No	No

Bidding: East has a strong hand but not enough to insist on game. After West's 2◇ negative, showing 0-7 points, East's jump to 3♡ shows a good 6-card or longer suit and exactly nine playing tricks. Had East's rebid been 2♠ or 3♠, West would have passed, but the heart support and the singleton spade are certainly enough to raise to 4♡. Note that if East would have opened 1♡, West should pass this and an excellent game might be missed.

Lead: 5 of spades. South has no attractive lead. The bidding suggests a trump lead, but J-x in trumps can be risky. A spade lead here is the least of evils.

Recommended play: The play is much the same regardless of the lead. On a spade lead, win the ace of spades, ruff a spade, play a heart to the ace, ruff a spade, play a diamond to the ace and draw trumps. Making 11 tricks. On a trump lead, win ace of hearts, cash ace of spades, ruff a spade, diamond to the ace and ruff the last spade, leading to the same result.

Notes: It is difficult for North-South to enter the auction but 4♠ is an excellent spot for North-South. After a heart lead won by East and say, the ♣Q switch, taken by the ace, declarer leads a spade to the king. If East wins and returns a spade, take this in dummy and lead a diamond to the king. Return to dummy with a trump to draw the last trump and lead a second low diamond. East's ◇A does not capture an honour and declarer can discard the club loser on the ◇Q later. This line is available no matter how the defenders wriggle.

At any other vulnerability, North might make a delayed takeout double of 4♡ (on the auction, it cannot sensibly be a penalty double by a passed hand) and South would bid 4♠. After West passes 4♠, East cannot see four tricks in defence and so should push on to 5♡ which makes. At adverse vulnerability, it is very, very tough for North to risk the double of 4♡.

Hand 38: Rebidding with a solid minor

Dealer East : E-W vulnerable

	NORTH		
	♠ 10 6 5 4		
	♡ 8 6 3		
	◇ 5 3		
	♣ J 8 6 4		
WEST		**EAST**	
♠ K Q 8 7 2		♠ A 9	
♡ K 4 2		♡ Q J 10 7 5	
◇ 9 8 4		◇ 10 6	
♣ 7 5		♣ Q 10 9 2	
	SOUTH		
	♠ J 3		
	♡ A 9		
	◇ A K Q J 7 2		
	♣ A K 3		

WEST	NORTH	EAST	SOUTH
		No	2♣
No	2◇	No	3NT
No	No	No	

Bidding: South has 22 HCP and four losers, not enough to choose a game-force opening. After the negative response, South's best shot is 3NT. Without a spade lead, nine tricks are almost certain and a spade lead will be fatal only if the opponents can take five or more tricks at once. Certainly 3NT is more likely to succeed than 5◇. With four losers, South can hardly expect partner to cover two of those losers after the 2◇ negative response. Note that North would pass a 3◇ rebid.

Lead: 7 of spades. There is no reason to choose other than the normal long suit lead.

Recommended play: East wins with the ace of spades and may well try a switch to the queen of hearts (hoping for K-x with South and A-x-x with West). South wins and has nine tricks on top.

Notes: (1) When South runs the diamonds East cannot afford to discard two clubs. Otherwise declarer makes four club tricks and eleven tricks in all.

(2) If East returns a spade, West can cash two more spades. A fourth spade (or a cunning 8 of spades at trick three) would give declarer ten tricks. East should signal with the queen of hearts on the third spade.

Hand 39: Rebids by opener and responder — Defensive technique

Dealer South : Both vulnerable

NORTH
- ♠ J 5 4
- ♡ K Q J 6 4 2
- ◇ Q 3
- ♣ J 2

WEST
- ♠ A Q 7 6 2
- ♡ 5 3
- ◇ 8 7 6 4
- ♣ 10 3

EAST
- ♠ K 10 9
- ♡ A 10 9
- ◇ J 10 9 5 2
- ♣ 6 5

SOUTH
- ♠ 8 3
- ♡ 8 7
- ◇ A K
- ♣ A K Q 9 8 7 4

WEST	NORTH	EAST	SOUTH
			2♣
No	2♡	No	3♣
No	3♡	No	4♡
No	Pass	No	

Bidding: Even with only 16 HCP, South has nine playing tricks and should open 2♣ rather than 1♣. Opening 1♣ and rebidding with a jump to 3♣ shows a 6+ suit, 16-18 points and 5-6 losers. A 4-loser hand is too strong for that sequence. North's 2♡ shows 8+ points and a 5-card or longer suit. Repeating the hearts then shows a 6+ suit, allowing South to raise with just a doubleton. Note that if 2♡ could be just a 4-card suit, the 3♡ rebid might be just five hearts, making life very tough for opener.

Lead: Jack of diamonds. Nothing else has greater appeal.

Recommended play: Declarer wins in dummy and should lead a spade, hoping to ruff a spade in dummy.

Notes: (1) If declarer leads a spade and the defence tries to counter the threat of the ruff by playing ace and another heart, declarer makes twelve tricks. The defence should switch to a trump but not play the ace. Then if declarer leads a second spade, the defence can win, cash the ace of hearts and a third spade.

(2) If declarer leads a spade and the defence does not switch to a trump, the contract cannot be beaten.

(3) If declarer leads a heart to the king at trick two and East wins with the ace, the contract cannot be defeated. If East fails to switch to a spade, declarer makes twelve tricks and if East does switch to a spade, the contract can be held to ten tricks.

(4) East can see that there are no tricks for the defence in the minors and the only hope to beat the contract is to take four tricks in the majors. If East lets the king of hearts hold, the defence can later win the ace of hearts to draw dummy's last trump and cash their spade tricks.

Hand 40: Slam bidding — Playing for an overtrick

Dealer West : Both vulnerable

NORTH
- ♠ 8 7 6 5
- ♡ K 3
- ◇ K Q 10 9
- ♣ 8 7 3

WEST
- ♠ A K 3
- ♡ A Q J 10 8 7
- ◇ A J 8
- ♣ 6

EAST
- ♠ J
- ♡ 9 5 4 2
- ◇ 7 6 3
- ♣ A K Q J 5

SOUTH
- ♠ Q 10 9 4 2
- ♡ 6
- ◇ 5 4 2
- ♣ 10 9 4 2

WEST	NORTH	EAST	SOUTH
2♣	No	3♣	No
3♡	No	4NT	No
5♠	No	5NT	No
6◇	No	6♡	All pass

Bidding: As West has shown 8+ tricks, East with 4+ winners should look for slam once the heart fit is located. East might splinter with 4♠ over 3♡ but given West's known strength, it is unlikely that the diamond suit is unguarded.

5NT, the king ask, is either a grand slam try or aimed at reaching 6NT. If using Roman Key Card Blackwood (see Chapter 13), West would reply 5♣ (showing 0 or 3 key cards) and East would bid 6♡ at once since one key card is known to be missing.

Lead: King of diamonds. No reason for any other lead.

Recommended play: Declarer wins with the ace of diamonds. Declarer should continue by playing three top clubs and discarding the diamond losers. Next comes the heart finesse, losing. West wins any return, draws the last trump and ruffs the spade loser in dummy. Making twelve tricks.

Notes: (1) At teams or rubber bridge where safety first is vital and overtricks are usually of little significance, the best play is to cash the ace of hearts at trick two and if the king of hearts has not dropped, tackle the clubs next. The standard play in hearts is to lead the nine and let it run if South plays low.

(2) At pairs duplicate, the overtrick may be vital since 6♡ figures to be found by most pairs. Taking the heart finesse is far more likely to avoid a heart loser than playing for the drop. There is a slight risk in playing the clubs first but the risk is worthwhile in giving you a better chance to avoid a loser in trumps. As it happens, both lines bring in twelve tricks.

CHAPTER 11

THE BENJAMIN 2♦ OPENING

Playing Benjamin Twos, the 2♣ opening caters for hands about one trick short of game, while the 2♦ opening covers the hands which are forcing to game.

Open 2♦ with —

(a) Any balanced hand of 25 HCP or more
(b) Any non-balanced hand of 23 HCP or more
(c) Any hand of 16-22 HCP with 10 playing tricks or better (3 losers or fewer) and a long major.
(d) Any hand of 16-22 HCP with 10½ playing tricks or better (2½ losers or fewer) with a long minor as the dominant suit.

Hands just short of a 2♦ opening should start with 2♣ (see Chapter 10), or 2NT if 21-22 balanced.

RESPONDING TO 2♦

2♡ = Artificial negative response, 0-7 HCP and less than 1½ quick tricks.
Quick tricks: A-K = 2, A-Q = 1½, A = 1, K-Q = 1 and K-x = ½.

Any hand of 0-5 HCP should give the negative response. Most hands of 6-7 HCP should also bid 2♡ negative but holdings such as A-K (2 tricks), an ace plus a king in another suit (1½ tricks) or an A-Q suit (1½ tricks) are worth a positive response.

All responses other than 2♡ = positive response, 8+ HCP or 1½ quick tricks or better.

Any positive response indicates slam is likely. Opener has 23+ points and responder has 8+, or opener has 10+ tricks and opener has 1½ or better. In each case, the slam potential is good.

The function of the negative response is to deny values suitable for a slam. If opener has three losers and responder has less than 1½ quick tricks, slam is not likely to be a good bet.

The sequence 2♦ : 2♦, 2NT can be used to show a balanced 25-27 HCP, forcing to game. Further bidding, if any, follows the same structure as after a 2NT opening (3♣ Stayman, transfers, etc.). For details, see Chapter 5. Use 2♦ : 2♡, 3NT for 28-30 HCP. Responder can raise no-trumps to invite slam.

CHOOSING YOUR POSITIVE RESPONSE

With positive values, it is best to play that any suit reply shows a 5-card or longer suit. The 2NT response is a balanced hand of 8 HCP or more. If your suit is hearts, you will have to bid 3♡ over 2♦, as 2♡ is the negative reply. With a 4-4-4-1, bid your cheapest 4-card suit and hope for the best. With a two-suiter bid your longer suit first, and with a 5-5 or 6-6 pattern, start with the higher-ranking suit.

OPENER'S REBID

(a) After the 2♡ negative response
(i) Opener has a balanced hand

25-27 HCP: Rebid 2NT, forcing to game. Further bidding is the same as after a 2NT opening (see Chapter 4). For 23-24 points balanced, see Chapter 10.
28-30 points: Rebid 3NT. Then, 4♣ by responder is Stayman, 4♦ is natural and forcing. Any suit game is to play. Jumps to 5♡ or 5♠ invite slam. 4NT shows 3-4 points balanced and invites 6NT.
31-32 points: Rebid 4NT.
33 points: Rebid 5NT, allowing partner to bid a suit at the six-level rather than 6NT.
34 points: Rebid 6NT (you should be so lucky!).

(ii) Opener has an unbalanced hand

Rebid in a suit, *forcing to game.* Responder will treat the suit bid as a 5+ suit. With a huge 4-4-4-1, bid your cheapest 4-card suit and bid naturally later. With a two-suiter, bid your longer suit first. Start the higher-ranking suit with a 5-5 or 6-6 pattern. Opener's jump-rebid in a suit below game (e.g., 2♦ : 2♡, 3♠) shows a solid suit. This sets opener's suit as trumps and asks responder to bid any ace. With no ace, responder bids opener's suit.

(b) After a positive response

After a 2NT response, 3♣ is Stayman and any other suit promises a 5+ suit (there are no transfers by the strong opener). 3NT over 2NT = the 25-27 point balanced opening.

After a suit response, opener may raise responder's suit with 3+ trumps. Raising responder below game (e.g. 2♦ : 2♠, 3♠) sets responder's suit as trumps and asks responder to bid the cheapest ace (see Chapter 14 on Cue-bidding). If opener changes suit, the first suit bid will be a 5+ suit and responder should support if possible. Opener's second bid suit may be only a 4-card suit. Opener's 3NT rebid shows 25-27 balanced and leaves slam bidding to responder.

RESPONDER'S REBID

After a negative response, unless opener rebid 2NT, the bidding must continue until game is reached, no matter how weak responder's hand. Support opener if possible. If not, bid your own long suit (5+ cards) or bid no-trumps with no long suit.

After a positive response, bidding is natural and most auctions should lead to a slam. Try to agree on a trump suit before asking for aces and try to allow opener, the stronger hand, to do the asking. You should play that a positive response followed by a suit raise is forcing.

EXERCISES ON THE BENJAMIN 2◇ OPENING

A. Partner has opened 2◇. What is your response with each of these hands?

	1.	2.	3.	4.	5.
♠	9 7 3	K 7 6 2	3	Q J 7 2	8
♡	8 2	6 3 2	6 3	K 8 5 2	A 9 8 2
◇	9 7 5 3 2	8 4	A Q 9 4 3	Q J 4	Q 8 5 2
♣	7 6 3	K 8 4 2	K J 7 4 2	9 2	K 9 8 4

B. The bidding has started 2◇ : 2♡. What should opener rebid with each of these hands?

	1.	2.	3.	4.	5.
♠	A Q 8 7 4	7 4	A K Q J 8 7 2	A K 6 2	K Q J
♡	6	A K J 10 7 2	K Q J	K Q	A K 9 4
◇	A K Q	A K	---	A K 10 8	A K J
♣	A K Q 3	A K Q	K Q 7	A K 7	A K J

C. The bidding has started 2◇: 2♡, 2♠. What is responder's rebid with these hands?

	1.	2.	3.	4.	5.
♠	4 3	K 7 6 2	8 7 4 2	Q 8 7 2	3
♡	K Q 7 6 3	6 3 2	J 6 4	6 4	Q 7 4 3
◇	8 6 4 2	8 4	8	9 7 4 2	8 6 5 3
♣	6 2	K 8 4 2	A 9 7 3 2	7 4 2	7 4 3 2

PARTNERSHIP BIDDING : How should the following hands be bid? West is the dealer each time.

	SET 21 — WEST		SET 21 — EAST		SET 22 — WEST		SET 22 — EAST
1.	♠ A K 6 3	1.	♠ J 8 5 2	1.	♠ J 8 3	1.	♠ A K Q
	♡ A J		♡ 9 5		♡ K 5 2		♡ A 6
	◇ A Q J 10		◇ K 6 3		◇ K J 10		◇ A Q 5 2
	♣ K Q J		♣ 8 5 4 3		♣ 8 7 6 3		♣ A K 4 2
2.	♠ 7 3	2.	♠ A K J 6 2	2.	♠ K Q J 8	2.	♠ A 3
	♡ 8 7 5 3		♡ A K 6 2		♡ K Q J 6 2		♡ A 9 3
	◇ 9 6 4		◇ A K Q		◇ A K		◇ 7 2
	♣ 8 5 3 2		♣ 7		♣ A 3		♣ K 9 7 6 5 2
3.	♠ A K Q J 9 4	3.	♠ 8 7 3	3.	♠ A Q J 8	3.	♠ K 5 2
	♡ 8 3		♡ K Q 6		♡ K Q		♡ A 8 7 2
	◇ A J		◇ 9 8 6 4 2		◇ A 9 5		◇ K J 4
	♣ A K Q		♣ 7 2		♣ A K Q 2		♣ J 9 5
4.	♠ A 6 3 2	4.	♠ K Q J 8 5 4	4.	♠ 4 2	4.	♠ A K Q 6 3
	♡ 8 7 3 2		♡ A K Q		♡ A 8 4 3		♡ K Q J 9 2
	◇ 9 8 7 2		◇ A		◇ 9 8 5 2		◇ A K
	♣ 8		♣ A Q 4		♣ 1 0 6 3		♣ A
5.	♠ 1 0 9 6 5 2	5.	♠ A Q	5.	♠ K Q 7 2	5.	♠ J 9 6
	♡ 8 7 5 2		♡ A K 6 3		♡ A J		♡ K Q 6
	◇ Q J 2		◇ A K 5 3		◇ A K Q		◇ 7 5 4
	♣ 6		♣ K Q 5		♣ A K Q J		♣ 8 6 3 2
6.	♠ A K Q 7 3 2	6.	♠ ---	6.	♠ 5 2	6.	♠ A K J 7 4
	♡ A 9 6		♡ 8 7 5 4 3 2		♡ K 9 6 3 2		♡ A 1 0
	◇ A K		◇ J 7 5 2		◇ A 7 3		◇ K Q J
	♣ A J		♣ 8 4 3		♣ Q 4 2		♣ A K 6

PLAY HANDS ON THE BENJAMIN 2◇ OPENING
(These hands can be made up by using pages 176-183)

Hand 41: No-trumps versus minor suit games — Entries

Dealer North : E-W vulnerable

NORTH
- ♠ 2
- ♡ K Q
- ◇ A Q J 9 8 6
- ♣ A K Q J

WEST	NORTH	EAST	SOUTH
	2◇	No	2♡
No	3◇	No	3♠
No	4♣	No	5◇
No	No	No	

WEST
- ♠ A 10 8 7
- ♡ A 6
- ◇ K 5 2
- ♣ 10 9 5 3

EAST
- ♠ K Q 9
- ♡ J 10 9 8 3
- ◇ 7
- ♣ 8 7 4 2

SOUTH
- ♠ J 6 5 4 3
- ♡ 7 5 4 2
- ◇ 10 4 3
- ♣ 6

Bidding: North is borderline between a 2♣ and a 2◇ opening. If the decision is close, prefer to insist on game. North's 3◇ over 2♡ commits the partnership to game. South's 3♠ shows a 5+ suit but does not promise any values. North might consider 3NT but with only one stopper in the suit likely to be led and diamonds not solid, it is preferable to aim for a suit contract. If North's diamonds were A-K-Q-x-x-x, 3NT would be the choice. South supports diamonds over 4♣ and 5◇ is less encouraging than 4◇.

Lead: Jack of hearts. Obvious choice.

Recommended play: West wins with the ace of hearts and might as well return a heart. There is no rush to switch to a spade (which could help declarer with K-x in spades). North wins and should tackle the trumps. It is normal to finesse for the king but to do this declarer needs to reach dummy. Therefore North continues with the ace of clubs and a second club, ruffed in dummy, followed by the 10 of diamonds. If West plays low, the ◇10 is run. When it wins, declarer leads dummy's remaining diamond, again finessing, and then draws trumps. Making 11 tricks.

Notes: (1) Note the likely outcome in 3NT. East leads the jack of hearts and a heart is returned. With no entry to dummy, declarer can do no better than make six tricks.
(2) In 5◇, if North leads the low diamond from dummy and finesses the jack, the finesse wins but, unable to take a second finesse, North will lose a trump trick to West.

Hand 42: Positive response — Choosing the right slam

Dealer East : Both vulnerable

NORTH
- ♠ Q 10 7 5
- ♡ 10 9
- ◇ 10 9 8 6 5 3
- ♣ 5

WEST	NORTH	EAST	SOUTH
		2◇	No
3♣	No	3♡	No
3♠	No	4NT	No
5◇	No	6♣	All pass

WEST
- ♠ A K J 2
- ♡ 3
- ◇ 4 2
- ♣ 10 9 8 7 6 3

EAST
- ♠ 8
- ♡ A K Q J 2
- ◇ A Q J
- ♣ K Q J 2

SOUTH
- ♠ 9 6 4 3
- ♡ 8 7 6 5 4
- ◇ K 7
- ♣ A 4

Bidding: West chooses 3♣, long suit first, when giving a positive. Although East has club support, East should try to find a fit in hearts before agreeing on the minor. West's 3♠ shows four spades, five clubs and denies three hearts. Playing simple Blackwood, East asks for aces and settles for 6♣ when one ace is missing. If playing Roman Key Card Blackwood, 4NT would set spades as trumps, so that East should bid 4♣ over 3♠ to set the trump suit. West can then cue-bid 4♠ and East can then use 4NT to check on the key cards. With one ace missing, East again settles for 6♣.

Lead: 10 of diamonds. Normal unbid suit and top of sequence.

Recommended play: Win ◇A, cash two top hearts and discard the diamond loser, then lead trumps.

Notes: (1) If you take the diamond finesse at trick 1, you fail quickly.
(2) If you win ◇A and lead trumps at once, you fail almost as quickly.
(3) The best spot on these cards is 6NT played by East. Over 3♠, East could bid 4NT and follow up with 5NT asking for kings. After finding one ace and one king, East could take a chance and bid 6NT. The risk is that West has the ace of clubs and the king of diamonds and a spade lead might defeat 6NT. However, unless the player on lead holds A-K of spades, a spade lead would be unlikely. Using 4NT RKCB over 3♠ locates two key cards and again it is reasonable, although no certainty, to play in 6NT rather than 6♣.

Hand 43: Locating the trump fit — Card reading in defence

Dealer South : Nil vulnerable

NORTH
♠ Q 10 5 3
♡ J 9 8 6 4
◇ 6 2
♣ 10 8

WEST
♠ 9 8 2
♡ K Q 7 5 2
◇ 10 9 8 7 4
♣ - - -

EAST
♠ 7 4
♡ 10 3
◇ A K J
♣ 9 7 6 5 4 2

SOUTH
♠ A K J 6
♡ A
◇ Q 5 3
♣ A K Q J 3

WEST	NORTH	EAST	SOUTH
			2◇
No	2♡	No	3♣
No	3♡	No	3♠
No	4♠	All pass	

Bidding: With 24 HCP, South should start with the 2◇ game force opening. After the 2♡ negative, South bids longer suit first and 3♣ commits the partnership to game. North bids 3♡, showing 5+ hearts but not promising any significant values. South now shows the second suit with 3♠ and North raises. As the cards lie, 3NT would make but more often, 3NT would fail while 4♠ would make eleven tricks.

Lead: 10 of diamonds. Top of sequence. You need a strong reason to choose other than the unbid suit.

Recommended play: The contract should be defeated. East wins with the king of diamonds and returns the 2 of clubs for West to ruff. West plays another diamond to East's ace and the next club ruff beats 4♠.

Notes: (1) On the bidding East knows South started with five clubs and with two clubs in dummy and six in hand, East can tell that West is void in clubs.
(2) If West leads anything but a diamond, declarer has a comfortable eleven tricks by drawing trumps.
(3) If East wins the lead and cashes the other diamond, the contract can no longer be defeated. If East then fails to find the club ruff, declarer comes to eleven tricks.
(4) On the North-South cards, even without a diamond lead, there are only ten tricks in no-trumps. Playing in 4♠ will almost always produce eleven tricks (even if trumps were 4-1). It is only the vile club break that takes 4♠ down.

Hand 44: Slam bidding — Finding the right fit

Dealer West : N-S vulnerable

NORTH
♠ J 9 5 4 3
♡ - - -
◇ 10 9 8 5 4
♣ K J 9

WEST
♠ A K Q 8 7 6
♡ A K Q 9 3
◇ 2
♣ A

EAST
♠ 2
♡ J 7 6 5 4
◇ A 7 3
♣ 8 7 6 2

SOUTH
♠ 10
♡ 10 8 2
◇ K Q J 6
♣ Q 10 5 4 3

WEST	NORTH	EAST	SOUTH
2◇	No	2♡	No
2♠	No	3♡	No
4NT	No	5◇	No
7♡	No	No	No

Bidding: West has only one loser and thus twelve playing tricks. After the 2♡ negative, West rebids in the longer suit first. East's 3♡ rebid shows 5+ hearts but does not promise any points. West should insist on hearts as trumps and now has enough to bid 6♡. It costs nothing to check whether East has the missing ace and when East does show up with the ace of diamonds, West can confidently bid the grand slam in hearts. As East is declarer and bound to be somewhat anxious, West should reveal the good trumps first.

Lead: King of diamonds. The obvious choice.

Recommended play: The play is routine. Win the lead, draw trumps and then start on the spades. East needs to ruff spades twice to establish the sixth spade as a winner.

Notes: (1) West should not consider 7NT, which would require a 3-3 break in spades. If West's spades were as good as A-K-Q-J-x-x, it would be reasonable to expect the suit to run at no-trumps, even opposite a void but the same cannot be said for A-K-Q-x-x-x.
(2) Although it does not affect the outcome, North should not discard a spade as trumps are drawn. 'Keep length with dummy' is a sound principle when deciding what to keep and what to discard.
(3) After drawing trumps, East should not play for ruffs in dummy. When the choice is to set up a long suit or to take ruffs, play first to set up the long suit.
(4) It would be a sharp lesson if East elected to play two top spades before drawing trumps.
(5) A minor flaw in using the Benjamin 2◇ is that a negative response of 2♡ leads to the weak hand being declarer in heart contracts. That does not matter on this deal. It is a loss one is prepared to accept in exchange for the many benefits that flow from using the strong 2♣ and 2◇ openings.

CHAPTER 12

ROMAN KEY CARD BLACKWOOD (1)

In the constant quest for greater accuracy, one of the great products of the 1980s was Roman Key Card Blackwood (RKCB), popularised by Eddie Kantar. There are many who are happy to stick with the same bridge they have been playing for years, but for those who are ambitious, slam bidding without RKCB is like bidding your hand with your eyes shut. Once you are used to RKCB, you will not want to return to the good ol' Black. Obviously both partners will need to know RKCB.

In reply to 4NT *simple* Blackwood, the answers are 5♣ = 0 or 4 aces, 5♦ = 1 ace, 5♥ = 2 aces and 5♠ = 3 aces. After the reply, 5NT asks for kings and the replies are in similar vein: 6♣ = 0, 6♦ = 1, 6♥ = 2, 6♠ = 3 and 6NT = all four.

Simple Blackwood may still be relevant if no trump suit has been agreed. After a trump suit has been set, 4NT = RKCB.

Roman Key Card Blackwood

4NT asks for five cards: the four aces *and* the king of trumps. These five cards are called the key cards. Not every king is a key card, only the king of trumps. The standard replies to 4NT RKCB are:

5♣ = 0 or 3 Key Cards
5♦ = 1 or 4 Key Cards
5♥ = 2 Key Cards, but no queen of trumps
5♠ = 2 Key Cards plus the queen of trumps

Eddie Kantar has now recommended that the 5♣ and 5♦ replies be transposed. Wise though this may be, the above replies are firmly ingrained into bridge thinking. If you wish to amend the above with your partner, by all means do so.

There are five key cards and in theory, one player could hold all five. It would be even rarer, though possible, for the other player to have a hand which would justify asking for key cards. The replies to show all the key cards are:

5NT = 5 Key Cards, but no queen of trumps
6♣ = 5 Key Cards plus the queen of trumps

If partner is asking and hears 5NT or 6♣, that should be enough to jolt the memory. There can hardly be any more that partner needs to know, but a six-level asking bid is still possible (see Chapter 13).

Note:
(1) The answers of 5♥ and higher include the location of the queen of trumps.
(2) The answers of 5♣ and 5♦ give no information about the location of the queen of trumps. An extra asking bid is necessary if you need to find out whether partner holds the trump queen.

WHICH SUIT IS TRUMPS?

1. If a suit is bid and supported, that suit is trumps :

WEST	EAST	WEST	EAST	WEST	EAST
1♠	2♦	1♠	2♥	1♠	2♦
2♥	4♠	4♥	4NT	2♥	3♣
4NT				3♦	4NT

♠s are trumps   ♥s are trumps   ♦s are trumps

2. If no suit has been supported, the RKCB ask refers to the last bid suit as trumps.

WEST	EAST	WEST	EAST	WEST	EAST
1♠	2♦	1♠	2♥	1♥	1♠
4NT		3♣	4NT	3NT	4NT

♦s are trumps   ♣s are trumps   ♠s are trumps

3. If no genuine suit has been bid, 4NT is played as simple Blackwood.

WEST	EAST	
1NT	2♣	The 2♦ reply to Stayman said
2♦	4NT	merely 'No major suit.' As no
?		genuine suit has been shown, 4NT
		is just simple Blackwood.

The importance of the king of trumps

WEST	W	E	EAST
♠ J 7 6	1♥	3♠	♠ 2
♥ A Q 8 6 3	4NT	5♦	♥ 9 7 5 2
♦ A K 10 6	5♥	No	♦ Q J 9 3
♣ 6			♣ A K Q 4

East's 3♠ is a splinter raise, short in spades. With little wasted in spades, West sees slam prospects. East's 5♦ reply shows 1 or 4 key cards, obviously only one as West has two. West knows that either two aces are missing or one ace and the trump king. 6♥ figures to be a poor bet in either case. On the actual cards, 6♥ needs South to have the doubleton king in hearts, about a 21% chance.

WEST	W	E	EAST
♠ J 7 6	1♥	3♠	♠ 2
♥ A Q 8 6 3	4NT	5♥	♥ K 7 5 2
♦ A K 10 6	6♥	No	♦ Q J 9 3
♣ 6			♣ A Q 4 3

This time East bids 5♥ showing two key cards but no trump queen. With just one key card missing and a singleton spade opposite, West can bid the small slam with fair confidence. 6♥ is a 90% chance.

Note that East has the same pattern, same HCP, the same losers on each hand. Using simple Blackwood East shows one ace each time. If West now pushes on, the poor slam is reached on the first hand. If West signs off in 5♥ over 5♦, an excellent slam is missed on the second hand. Simple Blackwood does not solve this sort of problem. RKCB does.

WEST	W	E	EAST
♠ A Q 8 6 3	1♠	4♦	♠ 9 7 5 2
♡ K Q 6	4NT	5♡	♡ A J 5
♦ A K 7 6	6♠	No	♦ 5
♣ 6			♣ A K 8 4 2

East's 4♦ is a splinter raise, short in diamonds. 5♡ showed two key cards without the queen of trumps. West has two key cards and knows that one key card is missing, either an ace or the king of trumps. Either way, 7♠ will not be a good contract.

As it is, 7♠ needs South to have the doubleton king of spades, about a 21% chance. Poor odds.

WEST	W	E	EAST
♠ A Q 8 6 3	1♠	4♦	♠ K 7 5 2
♡ K Q 6	4NT	5♣	♡ A J 5
♦ A K 7 6	7♠	No	♦ 5
♣ 6			♣ A 8 5 4 2

East's 5♣ shows 0 or 3 key cards. From East's 4♦ bid and the West cards, West can tell that it must be three. East could not have enough for the 4♦ splinter with no key cards. Knowing East has at least K-x-x-x in trumps, ♡A, ♣A and a singleton diamond, West is able to bid the grand slam.

East again has the same pattern, the same HCP, the same losers on each of the above hands. Using simple Blackwood East shows two aces each time and one king in reply to 5NT. But which king?

Not knowing which king East holds, West cannot judge whether the grand slam is a sensible risk or a foolish one. This kind of guesswork can be eliminated by using RKCB.

The importance of the queen of trumps

Where the reply to 4NT RKCB is 5♡ or 5♠, the asker knows whether the trump queen is held or not.

WEST	W	E	EAST
♠ A J 6 4 3	1♠	4♦	♠ K 7 5 2
♡ A K Q 6	4NT	5♡	♡ J 10 3
♦ A 7 6	6♠	No	♦ 5
♣ 6			♣ A K 8 4 2

5♡ shows two key cards but no queen of trumps. West knows that East holds the ♠K and the ♣A but no ♠Q. The grand slam will therefore be a poor bet and West settles for 6♠. With nine trumps missing the queen and jack, the chance for no loser (the 2-2 split) is 42%. Even with the jack of trumps, the chance for no trump loser is only a bit over 50%.

WEST	W	E	EAST
♠ A J 6 4 3	1♠	4♦	♠ K Q 5 2
♡ A K Q 6	4NT	5♠	♡ J 10 3
♦ A 7 6	7♠	No	♦ 5
♣ 6			♣ A J 8 4 2

5♠ shows two key cards plus the queen of trumps. With those cards and a singleton diamond opposite, West can see that all losers are covered. Although not a certainty, the grand slam should be a good chance. Simple Blackwood has no provision for finding the trump queen or finding the trump king.

Locating the trump queen after a 5♣ or 5♦ reply

Over 5♣ or 5♦, if you need to know whether partner holds the queen of trumps, bid the cheapest suit outside trumps. This asks: 'Do you have the queen of trumps?' If no, partner makes the cheapest bid possible ('Step 1'). If yes, partner bids one more than the cheapest bid ('Step 2').

If clubs are trumps

Over the 5♣ reply, 5♦ asks for the ♣Q.
Answers: 5♡ = No, 5♠ = Yes.
Over the 5♦ reply, 5♡ asks for the ♣Q.
Answers: 5♠ = No, 5NT = Yes.

If diamonds are trumps

Over the 5♣ reply, 5♦, the agreed trump suit, would be a sign-off. Therefore, over 5♣ or 5♦, 5♡ asks for the ♦Q.
Answers: 5♠ = No, 5NT = Yes.

If hearts are trumps

Over the 5♣ reply, 5♦ asks for the ♡Q.
Answers: 5♡ = No, 5♠ = Yes.
Over the 5♦ reply, 5♠ asks for the ♡Q since 5♡, the agreed suit, would be a sign-off.
Answers: 5NT = No, 6♣ = Yes.

If spades are trumps

Over the 5♣ reply, 5♦ asks for the ♠Q.
Answers: 5♡ = No, 5♠ = Yes.
Over the 5♦ reply, 5♡ asks for the ♠Q.
Answers: 5♠ = No, 5NT = Yes.

Strategy for small slams

Assuming that the values for a small slam exist:
1. If two key cards are missing, stay out of slam.
2. If one key card is missing but the trump queen is held, bid the small slam.
3. If one key card *and* the trump queen are missing, bid six with ten or more trumps, and also with nine trumps if you hold the trump jack. The slam will be better than 50%. With fewer than nine trumps or with nine trumps but not holding the trump jack, stay out of the slam. Slam figures to be below 50%.

Strategy for grand slams

Assuming the losing trick count or other assessment method indicates the potential for thirteen tricks :
1. If you hold ten trumps or more, the partnership should have all five key cards but need not have the trump queen.
2. With nine trumps or fewer, you need all five key cards plus the queen of trumps to make seven a good bet. If you can count thirteen tricks, bid seven. With thirteen winners in top cards, bid 7NT. With a strong trump fit and no losers in the first three rounds of any suit, seven should be a good contract.
3. If you need to know about partner's holding in a suit outside trumps, you can ask for kings (if 5NT is available) and you can also make a Control Asking Bid. These are both covered in Chapter 13.

EXERCISES ON ROMAN KEY CARD BLACKWOOD

A. Hearts have been set as trumps and partner bids 4NT RKCB. What is your reply with these hands?

1. ♠ K Q 7 3	2. ♠ K 8 7 3	3. ♠ Q 8 7 3	4. ♠ 7 4 3	5. ♠ A 8
♡ A 8 6 2	♡ A Q 6 2	♡ A K 6 2	♡ A K Q 2	♡ A K Q 2
◇ J 3 2	◇ J 3 2	◇ J 3 2	◇ K J 2	◇ A 8 5 2
♣ A K	♣ A K	♣ A K	♣ A 6 4	♣ A J 4

B. Diamonds are trumps and in reply to 4NT partner has shown one key card. What should you do next?

1. ♠ K Q 2	2. ♠ A K Q	3. ♠ K Q J	4. ♠ A K	5. ♠ A
♡ 6	♡ 6	♡ 7	♡ A	♡ A
◇ A K 7 6 4	◇ A Q 7 6 4	◇ A K Q 7 4 2	◇ A K 1 0 8 4	◇ A Q J 9 6 2
♣ K Q 8 3	♣ K Q J 5	♣ A K J	♣ K Q J 4 2	♣ A K Q J 10

PARTNERSHIP BIDDING : How should the following hands be bid? West is the dealer each time.

SET 23 — WEST	SET 23 — EAST	SET 24 — WEST	SET 24 — EAST
1. ♠ A Q J 7 2 ♡ A K Q J ◇ A K Q ♣ 7	1. ♠ 8 6 5 4 ♡ 9 8 ◇ J 5 3 ♣ K 8 6 3	1. ♠ A Q ♡ A 8 7 3 ◇ 7 2 ♣ Q 9 8 4 2	1. ♠ 4 ♡ K J 10 6 2 ◇ A K Q 5 4 ♣ A K
2. ♠ A Q J 7 2 ♡ A K Q J ◇ A K Q ♣ 7	2. ♠ K 6 5 4 ♡ 9 8 ◇ J 5 3 ♣ 8 6 3 2	2. ♠ A 7 ♡ A Q 7 3 ◇ 7 2 ♣ Q 9 8 4 2	2. ♠ 4 ♡ K J 10 6 2 ◇ A K Q 5 4 ♣ A K
3. ♠ 8 6 5 4 ♡ 9 8 ◇ J 5 ♣ A K 8 6 3	3. ♠ A Q J 7 2 ♡ A K Q J ◇ A K Q ♣ 7	3. ♠ A K J 8 2 ♡ A K Q 6 ◇ 9 5 4 ♣ Q	3. ♠ 9 5 4 ♡ J 7 ◇ A K J 3 2 ♣ K J 9
4. ♠ K 6 5 4 ♡ 9 8 ◇ J 5 ♣ A 8 6 3 2	4. ♠ A Q J 7 2 ♡ A K Q J ◇ A K Q ♣ 7	4. ♠ A K J 8 2 ♡ A K Q 6 ◇ 9 5 4 ♣ Q	4. ♠ Q 5 4 ♡ 7 2 ◇ A K J 3 2 ♣ K 7 3
5. ♠ K Q J ♡ Q 9 8 7 5 ◇ A K Q 3 ♣ 3	5. ♠ A 6 ♡ A 6 3 2 ◇ 8 7 2 ♣ K Q 6 4	5. ♠ K 8 7 3 ♡ A K ◇ A J 8 6 2 ♣ 4 3	5. ♠ A J 10 6 4 ♡ 6 ◇ K 5 ♣ A K Q 5 2
6. ♠ K Q J ♡ Q 9 8 7 5 ◇ A K Q 3 ♣ 3	6. ♠ A 6 ♡ A K 3 2 ◇ 8 7 2 ♣ Q 8 6 4	6. ♠ K Q 7 3 ♡ A J ◇ A J 8 6 2 ♣ 4 3	6. ♠ A J 10 6 4 ♡ 6 ◇ K 5 ♣ A K Q 5 2
7. ♠ A 9 6 5 ♡ A K ◇ 8 3 ♣ A 8 7 4 2	7. ♠ Q 8 7 4 3 2 ♡ 8 ◇ A K Q 7 ♣ K 6	7. ♠ A ♡ A K 8 7 5 2 ◇ K Q J 2 ♣ A K	7. ♠ 10 9 6 ♡ 9 6 3 ◇ A 5 4 ♣ Q 9 7 6
8. ♠ A K 6 5 ♡ A 9 ◇ 8 3 ♣ A 8 7 4 2	8. ♠ Q 8 7 4 3 2 ♡ 8 ◇ A K Q 7 ♣ K 6	8. ♠ A ♡ A K 8 7 5 2 ◇ K Q J 2 ♣ A K	8. ♠ 10 9 6 ♡ Q 6 3 ◇ A 5 4 ♣ 9 7 6 2

PLAY HANDS ON ROMAN KEY CARD BLACKWOOD
(These hands can be made up by using pages 176-183)

Hand 45: Precaution play — Catering for a bad break

Dealer North : Both vulnerable

NORTH
♠ K Q 10 6 3
♡ A J 8 7
♦ K 6 4
♣ 8

WEST
♠ - - -
♡ K Q 10 5
♦ 9 8 5 3 2
♣ 10 7 4 2

EAST
♠ J 8 7 5
♡ 9 4 3 2
♦ Q J 10
♣ J 3

SOUTH
♠ A 9 4 2
♡ 6
♦ A 7
♣ A K Q 9 6 5

WEST	NORTH	EAST	SOUTH
	1♠	No	4NT
No	5♠	No	7♠
No	No	No	

Bidding: With a solid suit, excellent support and control in hearts and diamonds, South has the values for slam and should take control of the bidding by asking for key cards at once. If the bidding started 1♠ : 3♣, 3♡ : 3♠, North should cue-bid 4♡ to show slam interest and then South would bid 4NT. 5♠ shows two key cards plus the queen of spades. South need not be concerned about a parking spot for the diamond loser. Even if North had no kings outside trumps, the club suit should provide North with all the discards needed for any red suit losers.

Lead: Queen of diamonds. Routine.

Recommended play: North should win the lead in hand and tackle the trumps. Missing J-x-x-x, it is correct to leave one top trump in each hand. Start with the king of spades. When the bad break appears, lead a low spade towards dummy and insert the 9 when East plays low. Cash the ace and king of spades to draw East's trumps and then start on the clubs. You need to ruff the fourth round of clubs to set up the suit. Cash your red suit winners ending with the ace of diamonds in dummy, and dummy is high.

Notes: (1) If North starts trumps by leading a spade to the ace, there is a trump loser. One down.
(2) If the first diamond is won in dummy, the timing is a little different. At trick 2, a trump to the king reveals the bad break. Continue with a club to the ace, ruff a club, cash the queen of spades, finesse the nine of spades and draw East's last trump with the ♠A. Dummy needs an entry after the clubs are set up.

Hand 46: Catering for a bad break — Handling a tenace combination

Dealer East : Nil vulnerable

NORTH
♠ J 8 7 5
♡ - - -
♦ K Q 5 3
♣ J 7 6 4 2

WEST
♠ 3
♡ K J 7 6 2
♦ 10 7 2
♣ A Q 9 3

EAST
♠ A K Q 6 4 2
♡ A 9 5 4 3
♦ A
♣ 8

SOUTH
♠ 10 9
♡ Q 10 8
♦ J 9 8 6 4
♣ K 10 5

WEST	NORTH	EAST	SOUTH
		1♠	No
2♡	No	4NT	No
5♡	No	7♡	All pass

Bidding: Do not open 2♣ or 2♦ with a huge two-suiter unless you have loads of HCP. If the opponents intervene, it can become awkward to show both suits economically. Here East opens 1♠, planning to jump shift in hearts next. After 2♡, East knows that there is a huge fit in hearts. With only one loser outside, East asks at once with 4NT. 5♡ showed two key cards but no ♡Q. Even though the ♡Q is missing, East knows that there are at least 10 trumps between the two hands and the odds are almost 80% that the missing trumps will split 2-1.

Lead: King of diamonds. The other choices are much worse.

Recommended play: Win the ace of diamonds and start on trumps at once. Even though the normal break is 2-1, you should still guard against a 3-0 break whenever possible. Your K-J in hearts is a tenace and allows a finesse later if necessary. When holding a tenace in one hand, best technique is to cash the winner(s) opposite the tenace first. Here, this means that you should start with the ace of hearts. When North shows out you can finesse the jack of hearts on the next round. Draw the last trump and set up the spades next by ruffing the fourth round.

Notes: (1) It would be an error to play the king of hearts first. Here this costs you the grand slam. If North has the Q-10-8, you can do nothing to capture the queen. Since you can deal only with Q-10-8 with South, you cater for that possibility by playing the ace of hearts first.
(2) After drawing trumps you should not start ruffing losers in dummy. When you have a choice of setting up winners or ruffing losers, setting up winners comes first. Here that means that after trumps have been drawn you should set up the spades.

Hand 47: Setting up the right secondary suit — Minimising the risks

Dealer South : N-S vulnerable

NORTH
♠ 10 8 5 2
♡ 10 9 7 2
♢ Q 10 3
♣ J 8

WEST
♠ K Q 7 3
♡ A J
♢ A J 8 6 2
♣ 4 3

EAST
♠ A J 9 6 4
♡ 4
♢ K 5
♣ A K Q 5 2

SOUTH
♠ - - -
♡ K Q 8 6 5 3
♢ 9 7 4
♣ 10 9 7 6

WEST	NORTH	EAST	SOUTH
			No
1♢	No	1♠	No
3♠	No	4NT	No
5♣	No	5♢	No
5♠	No	7♠	All pass

Bidding: With a void, South should not open 2♡. In reply to 4NT, 5♣ = 0 or 3 key cards. Checking the unseen HCP, East can tell it must be three. West could not have the values to jump rebid 3♠ with no key cards. Having found the ♠K, ♡A and ♢A, East next asks for the trump queen via 5♢ and 5♠ says 'I have the ♠Q'. That covers all of East's losers in the first three rounds of every suit and so East bids the grand slam.

Lead: King of hearts. The obvious choice.

Recommended play: Declarer wins and starts on the trumps with the ♠K. When the 4-0 break appears, East must not draw all North's trumps. Best is to continue with ♣A, ♣K and ruff a low club with the ♠Q. Next lead a spade and finesse the 9, followed by the ace and jack of spades to draw North's trumps.

Notes: (1) When trumps are played, South should discard low hearts and keep the clubs and diamonds.
(2) Drawing four rounds of trumps relies on clubs 3-3, or diamonds 3-3 with the ♢Q onside. If South does not discard a club, declarer should fail if declarer starts by drawing all of North's trumps.
(3) After ♠K reveals the bad break, it would work, as the cards lie, to play ♢K, ♢A and ruff a diamond. However, this line requires diamonds 3-3. Playing on clubs works if clubs are 3-3 or 4-2.
(4) If declarer ruffs the third club low in dummy, North overruffs. Declarer can afford to ruff high.

Hand 48: Handling a tenace combination — Making the maximum number of tricks

Dealer West : E-W vulnerable

NORTH
♠ A K Q 9 5 4
♡ A J 9 5
♢ A 4
♣ 2

WEST
♠ 8 6
♡ Q 10 8 7
♢ K J 3
♣ J 10 8 4

EAST
♠ J 10 7 3
♡ - - -
♢ 9 8 6 5 2
♣ Q 7 6 5

SOUTH
♠ 2
♡ K 6 4 3 2
♢ Q 10 7
♣ A K 9 3

WEST	NORTH	EAST	SOUTH
No	1♠	No	2♡
No	4NT	No	5♡
No	6♡	All pass	

Bidding: Although North has excellent spades, North should make hearts the trump suit. The spades will provide South with discards for any minor suit losers. North has four losers, South's 2♡ should have eight losers or fewer, so North can recognise slam potential. In addition, a strong trump fit plus a running suit is a sign that slam is likely. With control in each suit, North is well placed to ask with 4NT. South's 5♡ = two key cards but no queen of trumps. As the trump queen is missing, North should give up on any ambitions for a grand slam.

Lead: Jack of clubs. Almost a sequence.

Recommended play: Win with the ace of clubs and start on trumps. As dummy's A-J is a tenace, you should *cash the winner opposite the tenace first*. Start with the king of hearts. When East shows out, lead a low trump and cover West's card. If West plays the 7 or 8, play the 9. Cash the ace of spades and ruff a spade to return to your own hand. Cash the other top club while you are in hand to discard the diamond loser. Then repeat the trump finesse. Draw West's last trump and dummy is high. Although the grand slam is not a good bet, the recommended line brings in thirteen tricks thanks to the heart position.

Notes: (1) With four trumps missing including the queen, the chance for no loser is only a touch above 50%. You need better odds to justify a grand slam. With ten trumps, missing three including the queen, the chance for no loser is much better, almost 80% and that would make a grand slam worthwhile if there is no other problem on the deal.
(2) If declarer starts by leading a low heart to the jack, there will be a trump loser. You can still make the slam, but you will not score well as thirteen tricks are available.
(3) If you fail to cash the ♣K after ruffing a spade, there is no later entry to reach the ♣K and you will again hold yourself to twelve tricks. You must make the most tricks possible to score well at pairs.

CHAPTER 13

ROMAN KEY CARD BLACKWOOD (2)

10 trumps = the trump queen

When the partnership holds ten trumps including the ace and king but no queen and no jack, the chance for no loser (the 2-1 break) is 78%, almost 4 out of 5. When ten trumps are held missing the queen, but including the ace and king plus the jack in the same hand as a higher honour, such as:

K-J-x-x-x opposite A-x-x-x-x, or

A-K-J-x-x-x opposite x-x-x-x

or equivalent holdings, the chance for no loser is 89%, about nine times out of ten (either a 2-1 break or the queen onside if trumps are 3-0). As the chance of a loser is so low in these cases, it pays you to *show the trump queen if you know that the partnership holds at least ten trumps.*

WEST	W	E	EAST
♠ A 8 7 6 3	1♠	2♡	♠ 2
♡ A J 8 6 3	4♣	4NT	♡ K 9 7 5 2
◇ A 8	5♣	5◇	◇ K J
♣ 6	5♠	7♡	♣ A K J 7 2

4♣ = splinter, strong raise of hearts, short in clubs
5♣ = 0 or 3 key cards, clearly three on the bidding
5◇ asks for the trump queen
5♠ says 'I have the queen of hearts'. As West knows the partnership holds ten trumps at least, West 'shows' the trump queen. East can then bid the grand slam with reasonable confidence.

5NT asking for kings

After the answer to 4NT, a rebid of 5NT asks for kings outside the trump suit. Since the trump king was already included as a key card in reply to 4NT, it is not shown again in reply to 5NT.

Replies to the 5NT king ask :
6♣ = No king
6◇ = 1 king
6♡ = 2 kings
6♠ = 3 kings

These king answers are the same as the answers to 5NT simple Blackwood.

The 5NT king ask also applies if it is available after the reply to the trump queen ask.

Suppose hearts are trumps:

WEST	EAST		
...	...	4NT = RKCB	
		5♣ = 0 or 3 key cards	
4NT	5♣	5◇ = Ask for the trump queen	
5◇	5♠	5♠ = I have the trump queen	
5NT ...		5NT = Asking for kings	

The king ask may be necessary if looking for a grand slam or for playing in 6NT rather than in a suit small slam (or 7NT rather than a suit grand slam).

Other Asking Bids

While the 5NT ask for kings can be useful, it may be necessary to find a king or queen in a specific suit. The king in one suit may be useless, in another suit (opposite A-Q-J-x, for example), it may be gold. Once you are familiar with RKCB, you may wish to add extra asking bids. The principles are:

After the reply to 4NT:
Cheapest suit (excluding trumps) = Trump queen ask
Any other suit bid (excluding trumps) = Control Ask
5NT = Asking for kings (excluding the trump king)
After the reply to the trump queen ask:
Any suit except trumps = Control Ask
5NT if available = Asking for kings outside trumps
Replies to the Control Ask

The ace is known from the reply to the RKCB ask.

Step 1 = No king, no queen in the asked suit
Step 2 = Queen in asked suit but no king
Step 3 = King in asked suit but no queen
Step 4 = King and queen in the asked suit
Step 5 = King + queen + jack in the asked suit

WEST	W	E	EAST
♠ A K J 7 2	2◇	2♡	♠ Q 6 5 4
♡ A K Q	2♠	3♣	♡ 9 8 2
◇ A Q J 9 3	4NT	5♣	◇ K 5
♣ ---	5◇	5♠	♣ 9 8 6 4
	6◇	6NT	
	7♠	No	

2◇ = artificial game-force, 2♡ = artificial negative, 5♣ = 0 or 3 key cards, clearly none, 5◇ = ask for trump queen, 5♠ says 'I have the trump queen', 6◇ = 'What is your diamond holding?' and 6NT = 'I have the king of diamonds but not the queen.' West has found the cards necessary to bid the superb 7♠. Had East bid 6♡ (no diamond honour), West would have settled for 6♠. Note that 5NT asking for kings would not have helped West. If East had shown one king, West would be unable to tell whether it is the king of diamonds (gold) or the king of clubs (dross).

WEST	W	E	EAST
♠ K Q 8	1♡	2NT	♠ A 7 2
♡ A Q J 6 3	3◇	4♡	♡ K 9 7 5
◇ 6	4NT	5♣	◇ A 9 7
♣ A K J 8	6♣	6♡	♣ Q 6 2
	7NT	No	

Even though West's singleton (3◇) is useful, East is so minimum that the sign off in 4♡ is best. West has more than enough to push on. 5♣ showed 0 or 3 key cards (West can tell it must be three). 6♣ asked for East's holding in clubs and 6♡ showed the queen of clubs but no king. West now knows enough to bid the grand slam in no-trumps.

Ambiguity with the 5♣ and 5♢ replies

When you hear a 5♣ reply to 4NT you can usually tell whether it is no key cards or whether it is three. If you hold 3+ key cards yourself, obviously partner has none. Even when you hold two key cards or fewer, you can usually tell. You will know partner's minimum HCP from the bidding and by looking at your own high cards, you work out what partner could hold with no key cards at all. For example:

♠	K Q	Partner opens 1♣, you bid 1♡
♡	A Q J 6 3 2	and partner raises to 2♡. When
♢	A K 4	you later bid 4NT, partner bids
♣	J 2	5♣, 0 or 3 key cards. Which is it?

For partner to have zero key cards, partner's high cards at best would be ♠J, ♢Q-J and ♣K-Q. That is 9 HCP, inconsistent with the opening bid and so partner must have the three missing key cards.

The same applies when the answer is 5♢, one or four key cards. For example:

♠	A Q J 7 3	You open 1♠, partner bids
♡	K Q J 6 3	2NT, Jacoby (13+ points). Later
♢	K Q	you bid 4NT and partner bids 5♢.
♣	J	Is it one key card or four?

Suppose partner holds just one key card. The most partner could have would be one ace, K-Q in clubs and the ♢J. That is only 10 HCP, too weak for a Jacoby 2NT reply. Except for chronic overbidders, partner must have four key cards and you are worth a shot at 7NT.

There are still occasions when you will not be certain whether partner has the lower number of key cards or the higher. In that case, assume the worst and sign off in the trump suit. *If partner has the higher number of key cards, partner must bid on.* The asker should not need more than three cards (or four) for the slam to be reasonable. So, pass the sign-off with the lower number, bid on with the higher number.

WEST	WEST	EAST
♠ K 9 6 4 3 2		1♢
♡ 2	1♠	3♠
♢ A 9 5 3	4NT	5♣
♣ K 2	?	

Has East three key cards or none? East might have either of these hands:

EAST 1	EAST 2
♠ Q J 8 5	♠ A J 8 5
♡ K Q J	♡ A 8
♢ K Q J 6 2	♢ Q 7 6 4 2
♣ 8	♣ A 8

With East 1, slam is ridiculous, but with East 2, 6♠ is a good bet, although not a certainty.

West should sign off in 5♠. East 1 will pass, but East 2 will bid again.

When bidding on with the higher number of key cards, treat the sign off bid as the ask for the queen of trumps. So, Step 1 = No queen, Step 2 = Queen. East 2 above bids 5NT : 3 key cards but no ♠Q.

Using RKCB below 4NT

If you and partner use 4♣ Gerber for aces, you can adapt RKCB and play Roman Key Card Gerber. The basic replies to the 4♣ ask would be:

4♢ = 0 or 3 key cards
4♡ = 1 or 4 key cards
4♠ = 2 key cards, no queen of trumps
4NT = 2 key cards plus the queen of trumps

The Gerber 4♣ Convention is not recommended, particularly because it conflicts with splinters and is not compatible with cue-bidding (see Chapters 14-15) and most experts strongly prefer splinters and cue-bidding to Gerber.

For those who like Gerber, there is good news. You can play RKCB at a level even lower than 4♣.

If a major suit is bid and supported to the three-level, 3NT should be used as RKCB rather than as a natural attempt to play in 3NT.

Where a primary major suit fit has been found, the likelihood that 3NT is superior *and* that you can tell that 3NT *is* superior is remote. It is therefore sensible to treat 3NT in auctions such as these as RKCB:

WEST	EAST	WEST	EAST	WEST	EAST
1♢	1♠	1♠	2♡	2♢	2♡
3♠	3NT	3♡	3NT	2♠	3♠
				3NT	

3NT RKCB should be used only after major suit agreement and then only after a direct raise. 3NT in these auctions is not RKCB:

WEST	EAST	WEST	EAST	WEST	EAST
1♠	2♣	1♣	1♠	1♠	2♢
3♠	3NT	3♢	3NT	2♡	2NT
No major suit		No major suit		3♣	3♠
agreement		agreement		3NT	

In the final auction, East's 3♠ is belated support and West's 3NT should be suggestion of contract.

Naturally, you and partner need to agree on using 3NT as RKCB. It would certainly help opposite East 1 in the previous column:

WEST	W	E	EAST
♠ K 9 6 4 3 2		1♢	♠ Q J 8 5
♡ 2	1♠	3♠	♡ K Q J
♢ A 9 5 3	3NT	4♣	♢ K Q J 6 2
♣ K 2	4♠	Pass	♣ 8

No-one wants to reach 5♠ off three aces. A similar benefit applies to this example:

WEST	W	E	EAST
♠ A Q 8 7 2	2♢	2♡	♠ 10 6 5 4
♡ A K Q J	2♠	3♠	♡ 8 7 3
♢ A K Q	3NT	4♣	♢ 6 4 2
♣ 6	4♠	Pass	♣ K Q 4

Better to stop in 4♠ than to reach 5♠ and complain about your wretched luck when North has ♠K-J-x.

Using 3NT RKCB follows the same structure as for 4NT RKCB but all bids are one level lower. 3NT RKCB can also be used after 1NT where opener gives a super-accept of a transfer and after the Jacoby 2NT reply to a major suit opening.

RKCB after minor suit agreement

After minor suit agreement at the two-level or three-level, 3NT is to play. After minor suit agreement at the four-level, 4NT RKCB can push the partnership overboard when two key cards are missing, especially when the trump suit is clubs.

One way to overcome this problem is to treat a minor suit raise to the four-level as starting a key card auction. This structure allows you both to ask for key cards and to show key cards. For example:

WEST	EAST	
1♥	2♣	4♦ = RKCB Asking
4♣	?	4♥ = offer to play in 4♥
		4♠ / 4NT / 5♣ =RKCB replies
		(0 or 3 / 1 or 4 / 2 key cards)

The same would apply to auctions featuring a raise of diamonds to the four-level. For example:

WEST	EAST	
1♦	1♠	4♥ = RKCB
3♦	4♦	4♠ / 4NT / 5♣ / 5♦ = RKCB
?		replies (the usual four replies).
		Here 4♠ is not needed as natural.

Thus, after minor suit agreement at the four-level, Step 1 is the RKCB ask. The other bids up to 5-of-the-agreed-minor are normally the RKCB replies as though partner had asked. To sign off, bid Step 1 (RKCB ask) and sign off after the reply.

This method is incompatible with cue-bidding after minor suit agreement (see Chapters 14-15), but the RKCB asking approach has much merit.

Expert Methods

Showing kings simultaneously with your answer to the trump queen ask

WEST	EAST	
...	...	4NT = RKCB
4NT	5♦	5♦ = 1 or 4 key cards
5♥	?	5♥ = Ask for the trump queen
		East : 5♠ = No, 5NT = Yes

Without the trump queen, you must bid Step 1, but when you have the trump queen you can give partner extra information. In the above sequence, what would 6♣ mean over 5♥? Or 6♦? Some play these bids to show the trump queen plus a very good suit. The occasions for this use would be rare. A better idea is to use these bids to show kings. Thus, 6♣ shows the trump queen plus the king of clubs, 6♦ would show the trump queen plus the king of diamonds and no king of clubs.

This approach does lose the chance to make a control ask for the queen in a particular suit. If you wish to overcome this, you use the extra steps only when you lack the queens in the suit bypassed. Thus, 6♣ would show the queen of trumps, the king of clubs but no queen of clubs. Likewise, 6♦ = trump queen plus the king of diamonds but denies the king of clubs, queen of clubs and queen of diamonds. Naturally, you do not bypass your agreed trump suit at the six-level.

WEST	W	E	EAST
♠ Q 8 2	1♣	2♠	♠ A K J 6 5 3
♥ A J 3	3♠	3NT	♥ 5
♦ K Q 2	4♦	4♥	♦ A J 6 3
♣ K 5 4 2	5♣	5♦	♣ A 3
	6♣	7NT	

3NT = RKCB
4♦ = 1 or 4 key cards (East knows it is one)
4♥ = Asking for the queen of trumps
5♣ = I have the trump queen plus the king of clubs but no queen of clubs.
5♦ = Control Ask in diamonds
6♣ = Step 4, showing the king + queen of diamonds, but no jack of diamonds (see page 75).

East knows virtually all of West's hand and can count thirteen tricks. Note how economical the bidding is after starting with 3NT RKCB and how helpful it was for West to show the ♣K with 5♣.

RKCB after a pre-empt by partner

After partner's pre-empt, there is little merit in changing suit to a minor. It is useful to play:
3♦ / 3♥ / 3♠ : 4♣ = RKCB
3♣ : 4♦ = RKCB. 3♣ : 3♦ may be seeking 3NT.

Weak Key Card Responses

When partner has a very limited hand (such as a negative reply to a 2♣ or 2♦ opening), partner cannot have very many key cards. It can be useful to use a different set of replies for a poor hand:
Step 1 = No key card, no queen of trumps
Step 2 = Queen of trumps but no key card
Step 3 = One key card, no queen of trumps
Step 4 = One key card + the queen of trumps
Step 5 = Two key cards, no queen of trumps (if this is possible for the weak hand)

Showing key cards in other auctions
After 1NT : 3♣ / 3♦ / 3♥ / 3♠ (see page 29)

Where these response show a 5+ suit, opener bids 3NT without support, but with support, opener can show key cards at once. For example, after 1NT : 3♠ —
3NT = Doubleton spade only
4♣ = spade support, 0 or 3 key cards
4♦ = spade support, 1 or 4 key cards
4♥ = spade support, 2 key cards, no trump queen
4♠ = spade support, 2 key cards + trump queen

After a demand opening

If opener supports responder after a game-force opening, treat the raise as RKCB. Responder shows key cards by steps at once. It is better for opener to receive the key card information, as the stronger hand has fewer losers to cover. For example, after 2♦ : 3♣, 4♣ : ?, responder would continue:
4♦ = 0 or 3 key cards, clubs set as trumps
4♥ = 1 or 4 key cards
4♠ = 2 key cards, no trump queen
4NT = 2 key cards + trump queen

EXERCISES ON ROMAN KEY CARD BLACKWOOD (2)

A. Spades are trumps. West bids 4NT, East 5♦, West rebids 6♣. What is East's next bid on these hands?

1. ♠ A K 4 2	2. ♠ K 8 7 3	3. ♠ 9 8 7 3	4. ♠ 7 4 3	5. ♠ A 8 7 2
♥ Q 9 8 2	♥ K Q 6 2	♥ A K 6 2	♥ K 8 2	♥ Q 2
♦ A 3	♦ J 3	♦ K Q	♦ K J 5 2	♦ K 8 5 2
♣ A 6 3	♣ K 6 5	♣ J 7 4	♣ A Q 9	♣ K Q 8

B. Hearts are trumps. In reply to 4NT, you bid 5♣. What next if partner bids (a) 5♥ *or* (b) 5NT?

1. ♠ A 8 7 3	2. ♠ K Q 5	3. ♠ A J 4	4. ♠ 5	5. ♠ 5
♥ K Q 6 2	♥ J 6 4 3	♥ A 8 7 3 2	♥ A K 3 2	♥ A K Q 6 2
♦ J 3	♦ K Q J 6 4	♦ A 7	♦ A 1 0 8 4	♦ A 6 2
♣ A 6 5	♣ 3	♣ 9 6 4	♣ K J 4 2	♣ K 8 7 5

PARTNERSHIP BIDDING: How should the following hands be bid? West is the dealer each time.

SET 25— WEST	SET 25 — EAST	SET 26 — WEST	SET 26 — EAST
1. ♠ K J 7 3	1. ♠ A Q 4	1. ♠ K Q 6	1. ♠ A J 8 7 3 2
♥ A 8 7 6	♥ K 9 5 3 2	♥ Q 8 4	♥ A K J 2
♦ A 6 2	♦ 4	♦ Q 7 2	♦ A
♣ K 9	♣ Q J 10 5	♣ J 9 4 2	♣ A K
2. ♠ K J 7 3	2. ♠ A Q 4	2. ♠ Q 10 9 7 2	2. ♠ A K 6 4 3
♥ A 8 7 6	♥ K 9 5 4 3 2	♥ A	♥ K Q J 10 2
♦ A 6 2	♦ 4	♦ A K 3	♦ 7
♣ K 9	♣ Q J 10	♣ 9 7 4 2	♣ A 6
3. ♠ 3	3. ♠ A 9 7	3. ♠ 8 6 4 3	3. ♠ K Q J 7 5 2
♥ A J 7 6 4	♥ K 8 3 2	♥ 6 2	♥ A K Q
♦ K Q J	♦ A 8 4 3 2	♦ K 5 4	♦ A Q J
♣ A J 6 2	♣ 7	♣ K 8 7 2	♣ A
4. ♠ 3	4. ♠ A 9 7	4. ♠ A K J 8 2	4. ♠ Q 5 4 3
♥ A J 7 6 4	♥ K 9 8 5 3 2	♥ K 8 6 3	♥ A Q 7
♦ K Q J	♦ A 8 4	♦ A 4 3	♦ K Q 5
♣ A J 6 2	♣ 7	♣ 2	♣ A 7 3
5. ♠ K Q J	5. ♠ 3	5. ♠ A K Q 8 2	5. ♠ J 5 4 3
♥ Q J 8 7	♥ A 10 9 5 2	♥ K 8 6 3	♥ A Q 7
♦ A	♦ K Q J 5 3	♦ A 4 3	♦ K Q 5
♣ Q 10 8 7 3	♣ K J	♣ 2	♣ A 7 3
6. ♠ A 6 2	6. ♠ 3	6. ♠ K Q 7 3	6. ♠ A J 10 6 4
♥ K 8 7 3	♥ A 10 9 5 2	♥ A K	♥ 6
♦ A	♦ K Q J 5 3	♦ J 8 6 4 2	♦ A 5
♣ A 6 5 4 2	♣ K J	♣ Q 3	♣ A K J 10 2
7. ♠ A 6	7. ♠ 3	7. ♠ 5	7. ♠ A 9 6
♥ 9 6 2	♥ A K Q	♥ K Q 7 5	♥ A 9 6 4 3 2
♦ A 4	♦ K Q 8 5 3	♦ A K 8 6 3 2	♦ Q
♣ A Q J 5 4 2	♣ K 9 6 3	♣ K 9	♣ A 5 4
8. ♠ Q J 6 4 2	8. ♠ K	8. ♠ A J	8. ♠ 10 9 5
♥ K	♥ 5 2	♥ A Q J	♥ K 3 2
♦ A K	♦ Q 8 5 2	♦ K Q J 6	♦ A 5
♣ K J 5 4 2	♣ A Q 8 7 6 3	♣ A K 6 4	♣ Q J 9 7 2

PLAY HANDS ON ROMAN KEY CARD BLACKWOOD (2)

(These hands can be made up by using pages 176-183)

Hand 49: Asking bids — Endplay

Dealer North : Nil vulnerable

NORTH
- ♠ K 7 5 4 2
- ♡ A K 5 2
- ◊ A K Q
- ♣ A

WEST
- ♠ Q 10 9
- ♡ J 10
- ◊ 8 7 4
- ♣ J 9 6 4 2

EAST
- ♠ 6
- ♡ Q 9 8 6
- ◊ J 10 9 2
- ♣ Q 10 5 3

SOUTH
- ♠ A J 8 3
- ♡ 7 4 3
- ◊ 6 5 3
- ♣ K 8 7

WEST	NORTH	EAST	SOUTH
	2◊	No	2NT
No	3♠	No	4♠
No	4NT	No	5◊
No	5♡	No	5♠
No	5NT	No	6◊
No	6♡	No	6♠
No	No	No	

Bidding: 5◊ = one key card. Over 5♠ (no queen of trumps), North was worth 6♠ but tried to find whether 6NT was playable. 6◊ showed one king, 6♡ asked in hearts and 6♠ = no king, no queen in hearts. If South had ♠A, ♣K and ♡Q, North should be prepared to play in 6NT.

Lead: Jack of diamonds. Prefer the solid sequence.

Recommended play: Win with the ace of diamonds and cash the king of spades. Unblock the ace of clubs and then lead a low spade. When East shows out, win with dummy's ace, cash the ♣K and ruff a club. Play off your diamond winners, followed by the ace and king of hearts. Then throw West in with the third spade. With no hearts left, West has to give you a ruff-and-discard.

Notes: (1) If North fails to play off the ace of clubs before the second round of trumps, North will have no way to complete the elimination of the minor suits.

(2) When East shows out on the second spade, it seems that a trump loser and a heart loser are inevitable. The only hope is for the hand with the spade winner to be short in hearts.

(3) 6NT would make if there were no spade loser, about a 50% chance. From North's point of view, when the bidding shows that there are not twelve tricks on top, 6♠ looks safer, especially as South need not have the jack of spades and might have a doubleton heart.

Hand 50: Asking bids — Dummy reversal

Dealer East : N-S vulnerable

NORTH
- ♠ 8 7 2
- ♡ 10 9 8 7
- ◊ K J 9 6
- ♣ 10 2

WEST
- ♠ K Q 5
- ♡ J 5 4 3
- ◊ A 8 5
- ♣ A K 7

EAST
- ♠ A 4 3
- ♡ A K Q 6 2
- ◊ 2
- ♣ Q 8 6 3

SOUTH
- ♠ J 10 9 6
- ♡ - - -
- ◊ Q 10 7 4 3
- ♣ J 9 5 4

WEST	NORTH	EAST	SOUTH
		1♡	No
2NT	No	3◊	No
3NT	No	4♣	No
4◊	No	4♠	No
5♣	No	5♡	No
7♡	No	No	No

Bidding: 2NT = Jacoby (game-force raise). 3◊ = shortage in diamonds. 3NT = RKCB. 4♣ = 0 or 3 key cards (West can tell it must be three). 4◊ = ask for the trump queen. 4♠ = 'Yes, I have it.' 5♣ = Control Ask. 5♡ = ♣Q, no ♣K. West can now see the first three rounds of every suit covered and so has enough to bid the grand slam. West can count only 12 tricks in no-trumps.

Lead: Jack of spades. Choose the solid sequence.

Recommended play: Win the lead and play the ace of hearts. If everybody had followed, the rest would be child's play after drawing trumps. With trumps 4-0, you can hope for clubs 3-3 or that North has four or more clubs so that you can ruff the fourth round in dummy. Neither of those lines has a high chance of success. Far better is to switch to a diamond to the ace and ruff a diamond, club to the ace and ruff a diamond. Then cash the king and queen of hearts, cross to dummy. With only six spades and seven clubs, it is slightly safer to cross to dummy with the second round of spades. Draw North's last trump with the ♡J, discarding your club loser. This play, ruffing in the long trump hand, is known as a dummy reversal.

Notes: (1) It would be wrong for East to draw four rounds of trumps at the start. If East does this, South should discard diamonds since East showed a singleton diamond in the bidding.

(2) If East plays clubs before drawing trumps, North ruffs the third round.

Hand 51: Opening lead — Playing for the overtrick

Dealer South : E-W vulnerable

NORTH
- ♠ A 7 6 4
- ♡ 4
- ♢ K Q 8
- ♣ A 8 6 3 2

WEST
- ♠ Q J 10
- ♡ J 9 3
- ♢ A J 7 6 2
- ♣ Q 4

EAST
- ♠ 3
- ♡ 10 8 7 5
- ♢ 10 9 5 4
- ♣ J 10 7 5

SOUTH
- ♠ K 9 8 5 2
- ♡ A K Q 6 2
- ♢ 3
- ♣ K 9

WEST	NORTH	EAST	SOUTH
			1♠
No	4♡	No	4NT
No	5♡	No	5♠
No	No	No	

Bidding: 4♡ = splinter, strong raise in spades and short in hearts. With only four losers, South must try for a slam. As North has a singleton heart and at least four trumps, South sees that the heart losers can be ruffed in dummy and can envisage a grand slam opposite three aces and the queen of spades. North's 5♡ reply shows that one ace is missing as well as the ♠Q and so South signs off.

Lead: Queen of spades. A solid trump sequence will not give away a trick but as will be seen later, West has a better lead.

Recommended play: Declarer wins and cashes a second round of spades. There is no problem making 5♠, but South should try for an overtrick. Continue with the top hearts, discarding two diamonds from dummy. Then lead your fourth heart. If West ruffs, the other diamond loser is discarded. West will probably discard and the heart is ruffed in dummy. A club to the king is followed by the fifth heart, now a winner. Whether West ruffs or not, dummy's last diamond is discarded and South's diamond loser is ruffed in dummy. 12 tricks.

Notes: (1) South could also try for an overtrick, hoping that clubs are 3-3 and so South's diamond could be discarded on an established club winner. Given that West has three spades and East one, the club play is not as good as playing hearts. The hearts figure to be 4-3 most of the time and clubs figure not to be 3-3.
(2) Against 6♠, West would lead the ace of diamonds but there is a strong case for leading the ♢A even against 5♠. At pairs, it is vital to hold declarer to the minimum number of tricks. As North has shown a strong hand and South has tried for slam, West with 11 HCP should realise that East will have almost nothing. Therefore West should try for a diamond trick at once by leading the ace.

Hand 52 : Handling a tenace combination — Making the maximum number of tricks

Dealer West : Both vulnerable

NORTH
- ♠ Q 9 5 4 3
- ♡ 9 8 5 3 2
- ♢ K Q 8
- ♣ - - -

WEST
- ♠ - - -
- ♡ A K Q 6 4
- ♢ 10 9 7 4 2
- ♣ A 7 6

EAST
- ♠ A J 7
- ♡ J 10
- ♢ A J
- ♣ K Q 10 9 5 2

SOUTH
- ♠ K 10 8 6 2
- ♡ 7
- ♢ 6 5 3
- ♣ J 8 4 3

WEST	NORTH	EAST	SOUTH
1♡	No	2♣	No
2♢	No	2♠	No
3♣	No	4♣	No
4NT	No	5♡	No
6♢	No	7NT	All pass

Bidding: 2♠ = fourth suit. 3♣ = a 1-5-4-3 or 0-5-5-3 pattern. 4♣ sets clubs as trumps and 4NT = two key cards for clubs. (Over 4♣, 4♢ = RKCB — 'I want to ask', 4♡ = 0 or 3, 4♠ = 1 or 4, 4NT = 2 key cards, no ♣Q, 5♣ = 2 key cards + the ♣Q.) Over 4NT, 5♣ = sign off and 5♢ = ask in diamonds. 5♡ is a Control Ask in hearts and 6♢ shows the K + Q but no J. East can count to 13 tricks with six clubs, five hearts and two aces.

Lead: King of diamonds. Clear-cut against 7NT.

Recommended play: Win ♢A and cash ♣K. If everyone followed to this, the rest would be easy: cash jack and ten of hearts, cross to ♣A, cash the hearts to discard the ♢J and the spade losers, and claim. When the clubs are 4-0, the situation is awkward. You run the 10 of clubs but you cannot afford to cash ♡J-10 as there is no entry back to dummy's clubs. So, run ♣10, then cash ♣A, cross to ♡10 and run the clubs and cash the ♠A. In the ending, declarer has ♡A K Q 6 and East has ♠J-7, ♡J and ♢J. North is squeezed and with four cards left cannot hold on to four hearts and the ♢Q. If the ♢Q is thrown, dummy's ♢J is high and if North throws a heart, play the ♡J and overtake it. West's ♡6 will be a winner.

Notes: (1) If North had started with J-x-x-x in clubs, the play would be much easier.
(2) If East-West reached 7♣, the play should follow the recommended line. After a heart lead against 7♣, East should return to hand via the ♢A and not a heart after ♣K, ♣10 and club to the ace.

CHAPTER 14
CUE-BIDDING (1)

Cue-bidding is a method of exploring slams by showing precisely which aces and which kings are held. It is also able to locate singleton and void holdings. It is thus superior to simple Blackwood or the Gerber Convention. It works well when used in conjunction with Roman Key Card Blackwood.

What is a cue-bid?

A cue-bid is a change of suit after suit agreement in a game-forcing auction. East's last bid in each of these auctions would be taken as a cue-bid:

WEST	EAST	WEST	EAST	WEST	EAST
1♣	2♠	1♦	1♡	1♠	2♡
3♠	4♦	3♡	3♠	3♡	4♣

Where the suit agreed is a minor suit and the raise is to the three-level, new suit bids at the three-level are stopper bids, angling for 3NT.

WEST	EAST	3♦ is a stopper bid, not a cue-
1♠	2♣	bid. The partnership needs to
3♣	3♦ . . .	agree whether 3♦ *shows* a

stopper or *asks* for a stopper.

Most play that 3♦ shows a stopper and the focus is on whether a heart stopper is held. Some play that 3♦ asks partner to bid 3NT if a stopper in diamonds is held. Partnership agreement is needed here. If you have no preference, stopper *asks* are recommended.

After minor-suit agreement at the four-level, change of suit is played as a cue-bid in standard methods. In the previous chapter, it was suggested that using RKCB rebids at that point are valuable. You and partner will need to settle this.

After cue-bidding has begun, there are no cue-bids in the trump suit itself. A bid in the agreed trump suit is a sign-off, saying: 'I have no further cue-bid to make. I am unable or unwilling to go higher.'

When should you choose to cue-bid?

A cue-bid is appropriate when the bidding reveals slam potential and a key-card ask is unsuitable. The most common situations for cue-bidding are:
1. You hold a void, *OR*
2. You lack control in a suit (you do not have the ace, king or a singleton in that suit).

What does a cue-bid show?

Cue-bids aim to reveal control of suits outside trumps. To say that you have 'control' of a suit generally refers to first- and second-round control and means that the opponents are unable to cash the first two tricks in that suit (rather important for a slam, isn't it?). To have control, you need to hold the ace or king or void or singleton in that suit.
First-round control = ace or void
Second-round control = king or singleton

When does cue-bidding start?

The first cue-bid usually occurs at the four-level. If hearts are trumps (e.g., 1♣ : 1♡, 3♡ . . .) 3♠ will be the first cue-bid. Where a minor suit has been raised to the four-level, it will be assumed for Chapters 14 and 15 that cue-bidding is used.

PRIMARY CUE-BIDS

A primary cue-bid shows first-round control of the suit bid. The first cue-bid made is a primary cue. A new suit cue-bid will also be a primary cue unless the ace or void in that suit has already been shown or denied.

Rule 1: Do not differentiate between an ace or a void when making a primary cue.

Rule 2: With more than one primary cue available, bid the cheapest possible. If you bypass a suit other than trumps, you deny first round control in that suit.

WEST	EAST	3♠ is a primary cue. It promises
1♦	1♡	the ace of spades or a void in
3♡	3♠ . . .	spades.

WEST	EAST	4♣ is a primary cue, showing ace
1♦	1♡	or void in clubs *and denying* ace
3♡	4♣ . . .	or void in spades.

WEST	EAST	4♦, a primary cue, shows ace or
1♦	1♡	void in diamonds *and denies* ♠A
3♡	4♦ . . .	or void *and denies* ♣A or void.

WEST	W	E	EAST
♠ A K Q J 8 7	2♦	2♡	♠ 9 5 4 3
♡ - - -	2♠	3♠	♡ 9 7 4 2
♦ K Q J 3	4♣	4♦	♦ A 5
♣ A K Q	7♠	No	♣ 7 4 2

4♣ and 4♦ are primary cues. Note that asking for key cards would not solve West's problem (does East have an ace and if so, which one?).

WEST	W	E	EAST
♠ A K Q J 8 7	2♦	2♡	♠ 9 5 4 3
♡ - - -	2♠	3♠	♡ A 7 4 2
♦ K Q J 3	4♣	4♡	♦ 6 5
♣ A K Q	6♠	No	♣ 7 4 2

4♡ denied the ♦A and so West knows to reject the grand slam.

WEST	W	E	EAST
♠ A K Q J 8 7	2♦	2♡	♠ 9 5 4 3
♡ K Q J 5	2♠	3♠	♡ A 7 4 2
♦ A K Q	4♣	4♡	♦ 6 5
♣ - - -	7♠	No	♣ 7 4 2

4♣ and 4♡ are primary cues. Note the void in clubs, the cheaper bid, is shown ahead of the ♦A.

WEST	W	E	EAST
♠ A K Q J 8 7	2◊	2♥	♠ 9 5 4 3
♥ - - -	2♠	3♣	♥ K J 4 2
◊ K Q J 3	4♣	4♠	◊ 6 5
♣ A K Q	6♠	No	♣ 7 4 2

4♠, the return to the trump suit, denied the ♥A and the ◊A and therefore West knows there is no grand slam.

SECONDARY CUE-BIDS

A secondary cue-bid shows second-round control of the suit bid. It promises either the king or a singleton in that suit.

A secondary cue-bid means that you can win the second round of the suit bid, either with the king or by ruffing when you have the singleton. If you are known to have a balanced hand, then the secondary cue-bid must be based on the king.

A cue-bid is a secondary cue if —

(a) It is a bid in a suit in which a primary cue has already been made, *OR*

(b) It is a bid in a suit which the bidder previously bypassed and thus denied first-round control there.

Rule 3: Do not make a secondary cue if you can still make a primary cue. A secondary cue normally denies first-round control in any unbid suit outside the trump suit. Show your primary controls first. Only when your primary controls are exhausted, start on your secondary controls.

Rule 4: Do not differentiate between a king and a singleton when making a secondary cue-bid.

Rule 5: With two or more secondary cue-bids available, bid the cheapest possible. Bypassing a suit to make a secondary cue denies second-round control in each suit bypassed other than trumps.

WEST	EAST	
1◊	1♥	3♠ and 4♣ are primary cues. 4♠ is a secondary cue, showing ♠K or a singleton spade. 4♠ denies first-round control of diamonds as 4◊ was bypassed. (Rule 3)
3♥	3♠	
4♣	4♠ ...	

WEST	EAST	
1◊	1♥	3♠ and 4♣ are primary cues. 5♣ is secondary (the ♣K or club singleton), *and denies* first round diamond control (Rule 3) and second round spade control (as 4♠ was bypassed — Rule 5).
3♥	3♠	
4♣	5♣ ...	

WEST	EAST	
1◊	1♥	4♣ and 4◊ are primary cues. 4♠, a secondary cue, shows ♠K or singleton. 4♠ is secondary as 4♠, bypassing 3♠, denied first round spade control.
3♥	4♣	
4◊	4♠ ...	

WEST	EAST	
1◊	1♥	4♣ and 4◊ are primary cues. 5◊ is a secondary cue, (◊K or a singleton diamond) and, bypassing 4♠ and 5♣, denies second round in spades and clubs
3♥	4♣	
4◊	5◊ ...	

WEST	W	E	EAST
♠ A K Q 8 6 5	2◊	3♥	♠ 9 4 3
♥ - - -	3♠	4♣	♥ Q 10 9 8 2
◊ K Q 8 3	5♣	5◊	◊ A 4
♣ A Q 3	5♥	6♣	♣ K 8 4
	7♠	No	

East raises to 4♠ in order to allow the stronger hand to take control of slam bidding. The strong hand has fewer losers and can usually judge the final contract better than the weaker hand. After a game force opening and a positive reply, supporting partner's suit should be played as forcing.

5♣, 5◊ and 5♥ are primary cues. As 5♣ was a primary cue, 6♣ is a secondary cue.

WEST	W	E	EAST
♠ A K Q 8 6 5	2◊	3♥	♠ J 4 3
♥ - - -	3♠	4♣	♥ Q J 10 8 6
◊ K Q 8 3	5♣	5◊	◊ A 4
♣ A Q 3	5♥	5♠	♣ J 10 4
	6♠	No	

5♠, the return to the trump suit, denies the ability to make another cue. Therefore, East has no ♣K, no club singleton and so West rejects the grand slam which figures to be 50% at best.

With a major suit as trumps

Situation A: Suit agreement at the three-level, two or three primary cues followed by a sign-off in 4-major.

Message: Only mild slam interest. Slam not clear-cut.

WEST	EAST	
1♥	1♠	4♣ and 4◊ are primary cues. 4♠ is a sign-off indicating East has no more than a modest interest in slam.
3♠	4♣	
4◊	4♠ ...	

WEST	EAST	
1♠	2◊	4♣, 4◊ and 4♥ are primary cues. 4♠ is a sign-off by East, indicating that East has no significant extra values. West may still bid on, of course.
3♣	3♠	
4♣	4◊	
4♥	4♠ ...	

Situation B: Suit agreement at the four-level. Two primary cues followed by a sign-off in 5-major.

Message: Strong slam interest but no control in the unbid suit. Partner is asked to bid six with control in the missing suit, or pass with no control.

WEST	EAST	
1◊	2♥	4♠ and 5◊ are primary cues. The 5♥ sign-off = no club control and asks West to bid 6♥ with club control and to pass 5♥ without club control.
3♣	3♥	
4♥	4♠	
5◊	5♥ ...	

Situation C: Primary and secondary cues in two suits only, followed by sign-off in 5-major.

Message: Pass with no control in the unbid suit, bid on if you have control.

WEST	EAST	
1♠	2♥	4♣ / 4♠ are primary cues. 5♣ is a secondary cue. The 5♥ sign-off = 'I have no diamond control. Pass if you also cannot control diamonds, bid 6♥ if you can.'
3♥	4♣	
4♠	5♣	
5♥ ...		

EXERCISES ON CUE-BIDDING (1)

A. Suppose the bidding has started 1♢ : 1♡, 3♡. What should responder bid next with these hands?

1. ♠ A Q 4 2	2. ♠ J 7	3. ♠ 9	4. ♠ 7	5. ♠ Q 8 7 2
♡ Q J 9 8 2	♡ K Q 8 6 4 2	♡ A K J 6 4 2	♡ A Q 7 5 2	♡ A K Q 2
♢ A 3	♢ 3	♢ A 8 3	♢ K 8 2	♢ A 2
♣ 9 6	♣ A 6 5 2	♣ K Q 3	♣ K Q 9 3	♣ J 8 2

B. W: 1♡, (N: 3♠), E: 4♡, (S: No), W: 5♣. What should East bid now with these hands?

1. ♠ J 8	2. ♠ Q 8	3. ♠ A J 7	4. ♠ 8 5	5. ♠ 6
♡ K Q 6 2	♡ K 6 4 3 2	♡ A 9 6 3 2	♡ Q J 7 6 4	♡ A 10 7 5 2
♢ J 3 2	♢ A 6 4 3 2	♢ A 5	♢ A 8 4 2	♢ A 6 2
♣ K Q 6 5	♣ 3	♣ 9 7 4	♣ J 4	♣ K Q 5 4

PARTNERSHIP BIDDING: How should the following hands be bid? West is the dealer each time.

SET 27— WEST	SET 27 — EAST	SET 28 — WEST	SET 28 — EAST
1. ♠ A K Q J 3 2 ♡ - - - ♢ K Q J 2 ♣ A K Q	1. ♠ 9 7 5 4 ♡ 8 7 6 2 ♢ A 4 ♣ 5 4 2	1. ♠ J 6 2 ♡ K J 2 ♢ A K J 5 ♣ K 3 2	1. ♠ A K Q 7 5 ♡ A Q 7 6 3 ♢ 3 ♣ A 6
2. ♠ A K Q J 3 2 ♡ - - - ♢ K Q J 2 ♣ A K Q	2. ♠ 9 7 5 4 ♡ A 7 6 2 ♢ 6 4 ♣ 5 4 2	2. ♠ A J 8 7 2 ♡ A ♢ 9 6 3 2 ♣ K 7 4	2. ♠ K 6 4 3 ♡ K Q J ♢ 7 ♣ Q J 8 6 2
3. ♠ A K Q J 3 2 ♡ - - - ♢ K Q J 2 ♣ A K Q	3. ♠ 9 7 5 4 ♡ K Q J 2 ♢ 6 4 ♣ 5 4 2	3. ♠ K 9 7 4 3 2 ♡ 3 ♢ K Q 4 ♣ A 7 2	3. ♠ A Q J 8 ♡ K 9 6 5 ♢ A J 9 5 ♣ 9
4. ♠ 9 7 5 4 ♡ 8 7 6 2 ♢ A 5 3 2 ♣ 5	4. ♠ A K Q J 8 3 2 ♡ - - - ♢ K Q J ♣ A Q 2	4. ♠ A K J 8 6 2 ♡ - - - ♢ A K 7 4 ♣ 9 8 6	4. ♠ Q 7 5 4 3 ♡ A K 7 ♢ Q J 5 2 ♣ 2
5. ♠ 9 7 5 ♡ 8 7 6 3 2 ♢ A 5 ♣ 8 5 4	5. ♠ A K Q J 8 3 2 ♡ - - - ♢ K Q J ♣ A Q 2	5. ♠ A K J 8 6 2 ♡ - - - ♢ A K 7 4 ♣ 9 8 6	5. ♠ Q 7 5 4 3 ♡ K Q J 3 ♢ Q J 5 2 ♣ - - -
6. ♠ 9 7 5 ♡ Q J 10 7 3 ♢ A 7 ♣ K 7 3	6. ♠ A K Q J 8 3 2 ♡ - - - ♢ K Q J ♣ A Q 2	6. ♠ Q J 7 3 2 ♡ A 4 2 ♢ J 8 6 ♣ K Q	6. ♠ 6 4 ♡ K Q J 9 7 ♢ A K Q 7 5 ♣ J
7. ♠ J 5 3 ♡ Q J 4 ♢ A K Q 8 ♣ Q J 2	7. ♠ A K Q 6 2 ♡ 6 ♢ 6 4 2 ♣ A K 6 3	7. ♠ Q J 7 3 2 ♡ A 4 2 ♢ J 8 6 ♣ A Q	7. ♠ 6 4 ♡ K Q J 9 7 ♢ A K Q 7 5 ♣ J
8. ♠ Q 9 4 2 ♡ Q J 5 ♢ 7 ♣ A K Q 9 6	8. ♠ A K 10 6 3 ♡ 7 6 2 ♢ A K Q ♣ J 8	8. ♠ A J 7 3 2 ♡ A 4 2 ♢ J 8 6 ♣ A 4	8. ♠ 6 4 ♡ K Q J 9 7 ♢ A K Q 7 5 ♣ J

PLAY HANDS ON CUE-BIDDING (1)
(These hands can be made up by using pages 176-183)

Hand 53 : Suit without control — Squeeze play

Dealer North : N-S vulnerable

NORTH
♠ K 5 3
♡ K 8 4
◇ A K Q 8
♣ 5 4 3

WEST
♠ 7 4
♡ A Q 3
◇ J 10 7 3
♣ Q J 10 9

EAST
♠ 10 9 8
♡ 10 9 7 6 5 2
◇ 9 5
♣ 7 2

SOUTH
♠ A Q J 6 2
♡ J
◇ 6 4 2
♣ A K 8 6

WEST	NORTH	EAST	SOUTH
	1◇	No	1♠
No	1NT	No	3♣
No	4♠	No	5♣
No	5◇	No	6♠
No	No	No	

Bidding: 4♠ = weak preference (3♠ would have been stronger). North is minimum in high cards and has flat shape. Over 4♠, South should be concerned about control in diamonds. Therefore South cue-bids 5♣ and when North can bid 5◇, South takes a shot at 6♠, which figures to be a reasonable chance.

Lead: Queen of clubs. Even though South bid clubs, this is safe. The ♡A is not attractive. South must have heart control to jump to 6♠ over 5◇.

Recommended play: On the ♣Q lead, win with the ♣A and draw trumps, ending in hand. Lead the ♡J, taken by West who plays a second club. South wins, crosses to the ◇K, cashes the ♡K to discard a club and then ruffs a heart. West is down to ◇J-10-7-3 ♣10. South now leads the last trump and West is squeezed in diamonds and clubs.

Notes: (1) It would work if South wins the lead and plays the ♡J at once, but there is a slight risk of a club ruff and there is no advantage in delaying trumps.
(2) On the third spade, West can safely discard a club but should hang on to the diamonds ('keep length with dummy').
(3) If West switches to a diamond after winning ♡A, the play goes the same way. South needs to keep track of the club spots. If South's ♣8 is not high, then South has to hope that the diamonds will provide four tricks. Note South's play of the last trump before playing off the diamonds. If the diamonds are 3-3, that can wait. The last trump may squeeze somebody.

Hand 54: Lack of control in side suit — Play it as safe as you can

Dealer East : E-W vulnerable

NORTH
♠ A Q 10 6 3
♡ 7 6 2
◇ A K Q
♣ J 8

WEST
♠ - - -
♡ 10 9 4
◇ J 8 6 5
♣ 10 7 5 4 3 2

EAST
♠ J 8 7 5
♡ A K 8 3
◇ 10 9 4 3 2
♣ - - -

SOUTH
♠ K 9 4 2
♡ Q J 5
◇ 7
♣ A K Q 9 6

WEST	NORTH	EAST	SOUTH
		No	1♣
No	1♠	No	3♠
No	4◇	No	5♣
No	5◇	No	5♠
No	No	No	

Bidding: Opening hand opposite opener who can jump-rebid = slam potential if a trump fit exists. North should recognise slam prospects upon hearing 3♠. With two suits unguarded, North should choose a cue sequence. 4◇ and 5♣ = primary cues and 5◇ is a secondary cue. The focus is clearly on heart control. South's 5♣ bypassed 4♡ and so denied the ♡A and 5♠ denies second round control in hearts. Therefore North passes 5♠.

Lead: Ace of hearts. What could be easier?

Recommended play: East cashes two hearts and exits with a heart or a diamond. North should start at once on trumps by cashing the ace (or queen) first. When missing J-x-x-x, keep one top trump in each hand. When West shows out, play a spade to the 9, finessing against East's jack, and draw East's remaining trumps. After trumps are drawn, you have only winners left.

Notes: (1) Do not play diamonds or clubs before starting trumps. This may not cost but there is no benefit either. With nothing but winners outside trumps, draw trumps at once. Play a club early and East ruffs.
(2) Playing the king of spades on the first round of trumps is an error. As the cards lie, this gives East a trump trick and declarer will fail.

Hand 55: Splinter with a void — Catering for a bad break

Dealer South : Both vulnerable

NORTH
♠ 9 7 4
♡ - - -
♢ K 8 7 4
♣ K 7 5 4 3 2

WEST
♠ A K Q 8 5
♡ A Q 8 6 2
♢ - - -
♣ J 9 6

EAST
♠ J 10 6 3 2
♡ K 9 5 4
♢ A Q J 3
♣ - - -

SOUTH
♠ - - -
♡ J 10 7 3
♢ 10 9 6 5 2
♣ A Q 10 8

WEST	NORTH	EAST	SOUTH
			No
1♠	No	4♣	No
4♢	No	5♣	No
5♢	No	5♡	No
7♠	No	No	No

Bidding: 4♣ = splinter, showing good spade support and a shortage in clubs. 4♢ is a primary cue, showing ace or void in diamonds. The cheaper first-round control is shown first. 5♣ is a primary cue in the splinter suit and normally shows a void. Bypassing 4♡, it also denies the ♡A. 5♢ is a secondary cue, bid deliberately ahead of 5♡ to enable responder to show second-round heart control. 5♡ = secondary cue, the ♡K.

Lead: 4 of spades. Choose a safe lead against a grand slam.

Recommended play: Draw trumps and then tackle the hearts, starting with ♡K. When North shows out, lead a low heart. If South plays low, finesse the ♡8. If South plays ♡10 or ♡J, take the ♡A, ruff a club in dummy and lead a heart, finessing the ♡8. Ruff a club in dummy and discard your other club loser on the ♢A.

Notes: (1) If East bid 5♠ over 5♢ to deny heart control, West would settle for 6♠. If East jumped to 6♠ over 5♢, this would promise second round heart control and West would bid 7♠.
(2) When missing J-10-x-x in a key suit, you need to retain two honours in the one hand to capture the two honours missing if the 4-0 break occurs. Therefore start the hearts by playing off the king first.
(3) After drawing trumps, you must not ruff a club, cash ♢A, ruff a diamond, ruff a club and then start on the hearts. You are now an entry short to capture South's hearts. When faced with the choice of taking ruffs or establishing a long suit, set up the long suit first.

Hand 56 : Inferential cue — Jettison play— Ruffing finesse

Dealer West : N-S vulnerable

NORTH
♠ 10 9 2
♡ 8 7 6 5 4
♢ K J 10
♣ 5 2

WEST
♠ A 5 3
♡ A K
♢ Q 4 2
♣ Q J 10 9 8

EAST
♠ K Q J 7 6 4
♡ 3
♢ A 7 6 5 3
♣ A

SOUTH
♠ 8
♡ Q J 10 9 2
♢ 9 8
♣ K 7 6 4 3

WEST	NORTH	EAST	SOUTH
1♣	No	1♠	No
1NT	No	3♢	No
3♠	No	4♣	No
4♡	No	5♣	No
5♡	No	6♠	All pass

Bidding: East's 3♢ shows a game-forcing 5-5 and West's 3♠ = strong preference. 4♣ and 4♡ are primary cues (4♡ denying the ace of diamonds). 5♣ is a secondary cue designed to find whether West has the king of diamonds. West's 5♡ shows second-round heart control and denies the king of diamonds. East gives up on any grand slam hopes and relies on West's strong preference 3♠ in bidding 6♠.

Lead: Queen of hearts. Lead the solid sequence.

Recommended play: Win ♡A and cash ♡K, discarding the ace of clubs. Then lead the ♣Q and discard a diamond when North plays low (ruffing finesse). If South takes the ♣K, win the return, draw trumps, ending in dummy and discard your diamond losers on the remaining club winners.

Notes: (1) A diamond lead would defeat the slam.
(2) Declarer might win the heart lead and decide to draw trumps and play ace and another diamond. This is a bit better than 50% but fails on the actual layout. The recommended line is superior.
(3) Jettisoning the ♣A is necessary on the actual deal since the West hand has so few entries.
(4) If South ducks the ♣Q and then ducks the ♣J next, North can ruff the third club with say, the ♠2. East can still succeed: overruff with the ♠6 (not the 4), cash ♠K and play ♠7 to the ace, lead ♣9 and discard a diamond. South wins but declarer can cross with ♠4 to ♠5 in order to reach the last club winner.

CHAPTER 15
CUE-BIDDING (2)

THIRD-ROUND CUE-BIDS

A tertiary cue shows third-round control of the suit bid, either the queen or a doubleton. The rules and guidelines for tertiary cues are equivalent to the rules for secondary cues.

Hands which can locate third-round controls are rare as the bidding is usually too high. Systems which can create a game-force and agree a trump suit at a low level have greater possibilities for third-round cues. The main objective of cue-bidding is to find specific first-round and second-round controls.

Third-round control can also exist in short suit holdings such as voids or singletons:

Void = first, second and third round control
Singleton = second and third round control
Ace-singleton = first, second and third round control
Ace-doubleton = first and third round control
Ace-king-doubleton = first, second and third round control
A-K-x = first and second round control
A-Q-x = first and third round control
K-x = second and third round control
K-Q-x = second and third round control
x-x or Q-x-x = third round control

When a minor suit is trumps

In Chapter 13, it was suggested that key cards be shown after minor suit agreement at the four-level. If the partnership is not using that approach, then cue-bidding will apply.

Situation A: Minor suit agreement at the four-level and responder returns to 4-of-opener's-major. This is intended as a natural bid, not a cue-bid.

WEST	EAST	
1♠	2♣	4♠ is intended as a natural bid,
4♣	4♠...	not forcing, not a primary cue. East has a limit spade raise.

WEST	W	E	EAST
♠ A K 9 8 5	1♠	2♦	♠ J 6 2
♡ A J	4♦	4♠	♡ K Q 2
◇ K Q 10 6	No		◇ A J 5 2
♣ J 8			♣ 7 3 2

Situation B: Minor suit agreement at the four-level. Three primary cues followed by a sign-off in 5-minor.
Message: Only borderline slam interest. Bid on only if you have extra values.

WEST	EAST	
1♠	2♣	4◇ is a primary cue (3◇ would
3♣	4◇	be a stopper probe for 3NT). 4♡
4♡	4♠	and 4♠ are primary cues. The
5♣		5♣ sign-off = 'I have no extra values, just a minimum opening.'

WEST	W♡	E	EAST
♠ J 4	1♡	2♣	♠ A K 6 2
♡ A K 9 7 2	4♣	4♠	♡ 6
◇ 3	6♣	No	◇ Q 5 2
♣ A K 6 5 3			♣ Q J 9 7 2

4♠ is a primary cue, showing slam interest and first-round control in spades *and denying* first-round control in diamonds, as 4◇ was bypassed. West bids 6♣ since there is no chance for a grand slam with the ◇A missing but West has sufficient values to make 6♣ a worthwhile chance.

Situation C: Minor suit agreement at the four-level. Two primary cues followed by a sign-off in 5-minor.
Message: No control in the unbid suit. Pass if you also have no control, bid on if you have control.

WEST	EAST	
1♡	2♣	4◇ and 4♡ are primary cues.
4♣	4◇	The 5♣ sign-off says, 'I have no control in spades. Bid 6♣ if you
4♡	5♣...	have spade control, else pass.'

WEST	W	E	EAST
♠ A K J 6 5	1♠	2◇	♠ 9
♡ 2	4◇	4♡	♡ A K 7
◇ A K 9 4 3	4♠	5◇	◇ Q J 8 7 5 2
♣ 9 5	No		♣ Q 4 2

4♡ and 4♠ are primary cues. The 5◇ sign-off = no control in clubs. With no control in clubs either West passes.

This is the one drawback to cue-bidding. It is too precise. When a cue-bidding auction fails to reach slam it is often because the partnership lacks control in one suit. The cue-bidding sequence reveals that. Regrettably, it also reveals it to the opponents and they invariably lead the danger suit. Had the auction been less informative, you may have received a more favourable lead, which may have given you one or more overtricks.

When to end a cue-bidding sequence

Once cue-bidding has begun, it continues until one partner or the other has sufficient knowledge to place the contract or until the sequence is broken by 4NT RKCB or by the 5NT Trump Ask (see later). If you know that six is a good chance but seven is out of the question, bid six. Do not continue with a cue-bidding sequence which can help only the opponents.

If seven is still a chance, by all means keep on cue-bidding. Persist with cue-bidding if you need more information and cue-bidding is able to provide what you need. You will often recognise that the information you need for seven (such as a key queen) cannot be found. Stop the cues and bid six.

Raising a major suit to the 5-level

If the bidding has reached 4♡ / 4♠ (the agreed major), raising to 5♡ / 5♠ says: 'Bid six if you have strong trumps.' What counts as strong trumps depends on what has been shown so far. Usually two of the top three trumps or A-J-10 in the major is enough to bid six. Since 4NT RKCB can usually find the top trump honours, the raise to 5-Major often occurs when a void is held. In that case the answer to RKCB may be ambiguous.

Cue-bids at the 5-level and at the 6-level

A cue-bid at the six-level is looking for a grand slam (since you are already committed to the six-level) and promises that no first-round controls are missing. The same applies to a cue-bid at the five-level *above* the agreed trump suit. As this commits you to the six-level anyway, it must be looking for a grand slam and also promises that no first-round controls are missing. You may sometimes be able to show a number of controls economically with a cue beyond five of the agreed trump suit. For example:

WEST	W	E	EAST
♠ A Q J 5 2	1♠	2♢	♠ - - -
♡ 7	3♢	4♡	♡ A 6 3 2
♢ J 8 7 4	5♡	7♢	♢ A K Q 6 5 2
♣ A 6 5	No		♣ K Q 9

East chooses 2♢ rather than 3♢ as it is not economical to jump-shift with a two-suiter. After 3♢, 4♡ is a primary cue, showing slam interest. A bid of 3♡ would be a stopper probe for 3NT.

West's 5♡ is a secondary cue but because it is at the five-level *above* the agreed trump suit, it simultaneously promises first-round control in all unbid suits. Thus it shows not only the second-round heart control but also the ace of spades and the ace of clubs. That is enough to enable East to bid 7♢. Notice how much more efficient the 5♡ cue is than a primary cue of 4♠.

Blackwood or RKCB after cue-bidding has begun

It is possible to revert to 4NT asking (or even 3NT asking) after one or more cue-bids have been made. There are many possible reasons. Perhaps you need to check whether the key cards in trumps are held, perhaps you need to check whether a primary cue was a void or an ace, perhaps you had an unguarded suit and have now found partner has control in that suit. The answers to 4NT are the normal replies used by the partnership. If an ace has already been cue-bid, it is still shown in reply to the 4NT ask.

WEST	EAST	
1♢	1♠	4♣ and 4♢ are primary cues. 4NT
3♠	4♣	has its normal meaning, RKCB or
4♢	4NT	simple Blackwood, according to partnership agreement.

Cue-bidding by inference

A 1NT opener or a natural 2NT bidder can make a cue-bid without raising the trump suit.

WEST	EAST	
1NT	3♠	If East's 3♠ is natural, 3NT =
?		no support for spades. With
2NT	3♠	support for partner, raise to the four-level = weak support, new
?		suit = cue and a strong raise.

Assuming responder's bid is natural and RKCB support bids are not being used:

2NT : 3♡, 3♠ = heart support + the ace of spades
2NT : 3♡, 4♣ = heart support, ♣A but no ♠ A
1NT : 3♠, 4♢ = spade support, ♢ A but no ♣ A

Where a change of suit is forcing, a jump-shift is often played as a splinter, particularly when the jump is to the four-level.

WEST	EAST	
		3♣ by West would have been
1♠	2♡	forcing. 4♣ by West is generally
4♣ . . .		played by experts as a splinter.

However, if splinters are not being used, the jump to 4♣ can be played as an inferential cue-bid, showing good support for hearts, the values to raise to at least 4♡ plus the ace of clubs.

Cue-bid after a splinter

If a player has made a splinter and later cue-bids the splinter suit, that shows that the splinter was a void. It could logically be ace singleton, but many prefer not to splinter with ace singleton since partner's king or king-queen are less likely to be wasted values opposite the ace.

The 5NT Trump Ask

RKCB and splinters have taken away much of the need for cue-bidding. 4NT can locate the top trumps and splinters can locate shortages. Still, there are many situations where cue-bidding is valuable and may be the only way to solve the slam problems at hand. Once cue-bidding has started, you can use 4NT to check on the top trumps but what if the cue-bids have taken you beyond 4NT? In that case you need to use the 5NT Trump Ask to locate the top trump honours. A bid of 5NT without using 4NT first asks partner for the ace, king, queen of trumps (not the jack). The 5NT trump ask should be used only if there are no losers outside the trump suit and a grand slam is possible.

Replies to 5NT

6♣ = no top trump
6♢ = one top trump
6♡ = two top trumps
6♠ = three top trumps

Other schemes are possible, but 5NT comes up so rarely, it is better to have a simple set of replies which will not tax the memory and will be remembered easily when the situation arises. If you wish to play something more complex, see *Bridge Conventions, Defences and Countermeasures*.

EXERCISES ON CUE-BIDDING (2)

A. The bidding has started 1NT : 3♠ (one-suiter, slam try). What should opener rebid with these hands?

1. ♠ A 8 4 2	2. ♠ K 8 7	3. ♠ 9 8 6 2	4. ♠ A 4 3	5. ♠ K 8
♥ 8 2	♥ K 6 2	♥ A K 6	♥ K Q 6 2	♥ Q J 2
◇ K Q J 2	◇ A J 3	◇ 9 3	◇ K Q 5 2	◇ K 8 5 2
♣ A 6 3	♣ J 10 3 2	♣ A Q 7 3	♣ 8 4	♣ A 9 8 3

B. Hearts are trumps. What would your reply be to the 5NT Trump Ask?

1. ♠ A 8 7	2. ♠ K Q 5	3. ♠ A J 4	4. ♠ A 4	5. ♠ 9
♥ K 6 2	♥ J 6 4 3	♥ A K 7 6 3 2	♥ A Q 7 6 4	♥ A K Q 5
◇ J 9 7 3 2	◇ 4	◇ - - -	◇ 4	◇ A Q J 9
♣ A K	♣ A K J 7 3	♣ J 9 6 4	♣ K Q 8 7 2	♣ A 10 4 2

PARTNERSHIP BIDDING : How should the following hands be bid? West is the dealer each time.

SET 29— WEST	SET 29 — EAST	SET 30 — WEST	SET 30 — EAST
1. ♠ J 9 7	1. ♠ A K 8 6 5 4 2	1. ♠ K Q 6 3	1. ♠ A J 8 7 5
♥ 8 6 3 2	♥ A	♥ Q 8 4	♥ A K 2
◇ A K Q	◇ 6 4 3 2	◇ - - -	◇ J 8 7
♣ 10 5 2	♣ A	♣ A K Q 9 4 2	♣ 6 3
2. ♠ A Q 9 7 3	2. ♠ K 8 6 5 4	2. ♠ K Q 6 3	2. ♠ J 8 7 5 4
♥ 3 2	♥ A K 6	♥ Q 8 4	♥ A K 2
◇ A J	◇ K 8 4 3	◇ - - -	◇ A J 8
♣ A 8 4 2	♣ 7	♣ A K Q 9 4 2	♣ 6 3
3. ♠ 10 8 7 5 4 2	3. ♠ K Q J 3	3. ♠ A Q J 6	3. ♠ K 2
♥ 6	♥ A K Q 2	♥ K 9 4 2	♥ A Q 8 7 5
◇ A 8	◇ K Q J 4 2	◇ 7	◇ K 9 3
♣ A 6 3 2	♣ - - -	♣ A K 4 3	♣ Q J 5
4. ♠ A 9 7 4 2	4. ♠ K Q J 3	4. ♠ K 2	4. ♠ A Q J 6
♥ 8 4	♥ A K Q 2	♥ A Q 8 7 5	♥ K 9 4 3 2
◇ A 8 3	◇ K Q J 4 2	◇ A 5 2	◇ K 4 3
♣ 7 5 2	♣ - - -	♣ A 9 3	♣ 7
5. ♠ A Q 10 6 3	5. ♠ K 9 7 2	5. ♠ Q J 8 7 2	5. ♠ A K 5 4 3
♥ A J 8 7	♥ 6 3	♥ A J 3	♥ K Q 7
◇ A 7 4	◇ K 6	◇ 4 3	◇ K Q 5 2
♣ 2	♣ A K Q J 4	♣ A 8 2	♣ 3
6. ♠ A 10 8 7 2	6. ♠ K 9 6 3	6. ♠ A K Q 7 5 2	6. ♠ 9 8 4 3
♥ 5 4	♥ A K 7 2	♥ Q 5	♥ K 6 2
◇ A K	◇ Q 7 5 2	◇ A K Q J	◇ 8 5
♣ A K 6 2	♣ 8	♣ A	♣ 7 4 3 2
7. ♠ A 10 8 7 2	7. ♠ K Q 6 3	7. ♠ A 5 3	7. ♠ 7 2
♥ 5 4	♥ A K 7 2	♥ K Q J 7 5	♥ A 9 6 4 3
◇ A K	◇ Q 7 5 2	◇ A 8 2	◇ Q
♣ A K 6 2	♣ 8	♣ 7 2	♣ A K Q 8 5
8. ♠ A 10 8 7 2	8. ♠ K Q 6 3	8. ♠ A 7	8. ♠ 10 9 5
♥ 5 4	♥ K Q 7 2	♥ A Q J 4 3	♥ K
◇ A K	◇ Q 7 5 2	◇ K Q J 6 2	◇ A 9 8 5 4
♣ A K 6 2	♣ 8	♣ 4	♣ A J 7 2

PLAY HANDS ON CUE-BIDDING (2)
(These hands can be made up by using pages 176-183)

Hand 57: Splinter — Trump Ask — Catering for a bad break

Dealer North : E-W vulnerable

NORTH
- ♠ A 9 8 7
- ♡ A 8 2
- ◇ - - -
- ♣ K Q 10 7 6 2

WEST
- ♠ 10
- ♡ J 6 4 3
- ◇ K Q 10 4
- ♣ J 8 4 3

EAST
- ♠ 4 3 2
- ♡ K 10 7 5
- ◇ A 9 6 5 3
- ♣ 5

SOUTH
- ♠ K Q J 6 5
- ♡ Q 9
- ◇ J 8 7 2
- ♣ A 9

WEST	NORTH	EAST	SOUTH
	1♣	No	1♠
No	4◇	No	5♣
No	5NT	No	6♡
No	7♠	All pass	

Bidding: 4◇ = splinter, strong spade raise and short in diamonds. North has just enough because of the 5-loser hand. 5♣ = primary cue. On hearing that, North figures the clubs should provide whatever discards South needs and the only remaining problem is the trump position. 5NT asks for South's top trumps and 6♡ = two of the top three honours. That is enough for North to bid the grand slam.

Lead: King of diamonds. The normal choice.

Recommended play: Ruff in dummy, cash ♠A and play a spade to the king, ruff another diamond, cross to the ace of clubs and draw the last trump, discarding a heart from dummy. Continue with a club to the king, cash the ♣Q and ruff a club. Dummy's clubs are now high. Cross to ♡A and run the clubs, discarding your remaining red suit losers.

Notes: (1) North could cue-bid 5◇ over 5♣ but there is no need to do this. South would sign off in 5♠ (no heart control) and North could still continue with 5NT.
(2) Once South cue-bids 5♣ North should figure there are no losers outside trumps.
(3) It is easy to go wrong. If declarer ruffs the diamond lead and draws three rounds of trumps, declarer is one trick short when the clubs do not break (it would be fatuous to finesse the ♣10). South should foresee the possibility of a 4-1 club break and ruff a second diamond just in case.

Hand 58: Cue-bid in support of a minor — Vienna Coup

Dealer East : Both vulnerable

NORTH
- ♠ 9 8 7 2
- ♡ Q J 10 6 3 2
- ◇ 6
- ♣ 4 2

WEST
- ♠ Q 4
- ♡ 4
- ◇ A K Q 9 8 7 3
- ♣ A 8 6

EAST
- ♠ A 10 6
- ♡ K 8 7
- ◇ J 10 5
- ♣ K Q 7 3

SOUTH
- ♠ K J 5 3
- ♡ A 9 5
- ◇ 4 2
- ♣ J 10 9 5

WEST	NORTH	EAST	SOUTH
		1NT	No
3◇	No	3♠	No
6◇	No	No	No

Bidding: 3♠ is a cue-bid in support of diamonds. 1NT : 3◇ natural shows a strong single-suiter. Without support, opener would bid 3NT. With support, opener cue-bids the cheapest ace. This is one of the few areas where one can cue-bid at the three-level in support of a minor.

As 3♠ denied the ace of hearts, West knows there is no grand slam. 6◇ is reasonable since many pairs will miss this slam, but as it happens 6NT is on. West could have cue-bid 4♣ and rebid 6NT over East's 4♡ cue-bid showing the ♡K.

Lead: Queen of hearts. Choose the solid sequence.

Recommended play: Duck the first heart, ruff the ♡J continuation and draw trumps. It appears that a 3-3 break in clubs is necessary, but it does not cost to run all your trumps first. Errors in discarding are common. First, cash the ace of spades to isolate your ♠Q as a 'menace' against the player with the ♠K. This play of cashing an ace opposite a potential threat card is known as the Vienna Coup.

Then run all your trumps, keeping dummy's clubs intact. Be on the lookout for the ♠K. South is squeezed at trick 9. If the ♠K has not appeared, just play off your clubs. Dummy's fourth club will be a winner.

Notes: (1) West could also transfer to diamonds and follow up with 4◇ to start a cue-bidding sequence.
(2) A spade lead does not defeat 6◇: win ♠A and play off seven rounds of diamonds, keeping ♡K and four clubs in dummy. At trick 8, South has to discard from ♠K ♡A ♣ J-10-9-5. This is a triple squeeze.
(3) The same triple squeeze would operate in 6NT on, say, a diamond (or ♣J) lead. Win the lead, cash ♠A and rattle off all the diamonds. South cannot hang on to ♠K, ♡A and all the clubs.

Hand 59: Inferential cue-bid — Trump endplay

Dealer South : Nil vulnerable

NORTH
- ♠ A K Q 10 5
- ♡ 9 8 2
- ◇ 10 2
- ♣ A K Q

WEST
- ♠ ---
- ♡ 7 6 5 4
- ◇ Q J 8 6 3
- ♣ 10 7 6 5

EAST
- ♠ J 8 7 3
- ♡ Q J 10
- ◇ 9 7 5
- ♣ J 9 4

SOUTH
- ♠ 9 6 4 2
- ♡ A K 3
- ◇ A K 4
- ♣ 8 3 2

WEST	NORTH	EAST	SOUTH
			1NT
No	3♠	No	4◇
No	5♣	No	5♡
No	6♠	All pass	

Bidding: It is awkward to show the powerful one-suiter with a transfer. The sequence 1NT : 3-Major is used to cover this hand type. 4◇ is an inferential primary cue, showing spade support and a maximum 1NT. (Without spade support, South would rebid 3NT and with a weaker hand, South would raise to 4♠.) North cue-bids 5♣ because of the worry of the unguarded hearts. When South cue-bids 5♡, North bids the small slam. With 12-14 HCP opposite, North does not have enough to look for 7♠.

Lead: Queen of hearts. Simple when you have a sequence.

Recommended play: The bad break with J-x-x-x offside makes it appear that you have an inevitable spade loser as well as the certain heart loser. Do not panic. If the other suits break normally you may yet survive. The key to such hands is to reduce your trump length to the same length as the opponent with the trumps. If you can force that opponent to lead trumps when all the other suits have been eliminated, you can succeed.

So, win the heart, play a spade to the ace, play off the diamonds and ruff a diamond (trump reduction). Next cash your club winners (stripping the clubs from the East hand) and your other heart winner. Finally, exit with your last heart. If West wins the third heart, you fail but if East wins it, East will have only spades left and will have to lead into your K-Q-10 tenace. The seemingly certain trump loser has vanished.

Notes: (1) 6NT is the best contract and makes 12 tricks almost all the time. On this layout, 6NT would fail.
(2) If East's hearts were say, Q-J-4, it would be vital for East to unblock the heart suit and keep only the 4, so that declarer cannot force East on lead. East would have to hope that the ♡10 was with West.

Hand 60: Primary and secondary cue-bids — Double squeeze

Dealer West : Nil vulnerable

NORTH
- ♠ 8 4
- ♡ Q 10 5
- ◇ 10 6 2
- ♣ 10 9 8 5 4

WEST
- ♠ A J 2
- ♡ K 3 2
- ◇ A J 8 5
- ♣ K J 2

EAST
- ♠ K Q 9 7 5
- ♡ A 6
- ◇ 3
- ♣ A Q 7 6 3

SOUTH
- ♠ 10 6 3
- ♡ J 9 8 7 4
- ◇ K Q 9 7 4
- ♣ ---

WEST	NORTH	EAST	SOUTH
1◇	No	1♠	No
1NT	No	3♣	No
3♠	No	4♣	No
4◇	No	4♡	No
5♣	No	5◇	No
5♡	No	5NT	No
6◇	No	7♠	All pass

Bidding: 3♣ = at least 5-4 in spades-clubs. 3♠ = strong preference, particularly because of the excellent values in both black suits. 4♣ / 4◇ / 4♡ = primary cues. 5♣ / 5◇ / 5♡ are secondary cues. 5NT asks for the A / K / Q of trumps and 6◇ shows one top trump. That enables East to bid the grand slam..

Lead: King of diamonds. Second choice, a trump.

Recommended play: The slam looks simple: five spades, five clubs and three red suit winners. Win ◇A, draw trumps (North discards a diamond on the third spade) and lead a club. When South shows out, do not give up. Win the club, ruff a diamond, cross to dummy with a club and ruff a third diamond. On this third diamond, North has to let a heart go (if a club is discarded, your fifth club is good). Next, cash ♣A and ♣Q, leaving yourself with ♣7 and ♡A-6. South has to discard from ◇Q and ♡J-9-8. If ◇Q is thrown, dummy's ◇J is good and you discard a heart from dummy. If South keeps ◇Q and throws a heart, you throw ◇J from dummy. Now ♡A and a heart to the king sees you make trick 13 with the ♡3! You have executed a double squeeze. Well done!

Notes: (1) Were it not for West's 1◇ opening, South would be keen to show the red two-suiter.
(2) East might well choose to bid 7NT and the play would be similar. Instead of ruffing diamonds, declarer would cash five spades and discard the low diamonds on the fourth and fifth spade. The rest is the same.
(3) South has to keep the diamond guard (dummy's ◇J is the 'menace' against South) and North has to keep all the clubs (East's fifth club is the 'menace' against North). If each keeps a minor suit guarded, neither can keep a guard in the hearts.

CHAPTER 16
TACTICS AT IMPS

Playing pairs, the challenge is to do better than all the other pairs on each board. At teams, your team of four players plays a match against one other team-of-four and your aim is to defeat just that team. A teams match may be short (perhaps just two boards) or long (20-board matches are common in the qualifying rounds of major tournaments). Most international tournaments are teams events.

Suppose Team A is playing Team B. At one table, one A pair sits North-South and one B pair sits East-West. Each board played at that table is moved to another table where the other A pair sits East-West and the other B pair sits North-South. The board is replayed and when scoring up, the difference in scores achieved at each table on each board is calculated. As only the scores involved in those two tables are taken into account, teams bridge is the fairest of all tournament bridge. The luck factor is virtually eliminated as your team has the same chance to do well on exactly the same boards as your opposing team.

Teams bridge is scored using IMPs (International Match Points) according to the following table :

Difference in scores	IMPs	Difference in scores	IMPs
0-10	0	750-890	13
20-40	1	900-1090	14
50-80	2	1100-1290	15
90-120	3	1300-1490	16
130-160	4	1500-1740	17
170-210	5	1750-1990	18
220-260	6	2000-2240	19
270-310	7	2250-2490	20
320-360	8	2500-2990	21
370-420	9	3000-3490	22
430-490	10	3500-3990	23
500-590	11	4000-up	24
600-740	12		

Suppose you score +400 in 3NT and on the same board, your teammates score +50. You add the two results together and so your team has scored +450. This equals +10 IMPs for your team, −10 for them.

Suppose you are −110 at your table and your teammates' score on the same board is +50. Add the scores together and you are −60. This equates to −2 IMPs for your side and +2 IMPs for them.

The effect of the IMP-scale is to reduce the impact of large gains and losses. If your team loses 500 points on a board, that is −11 IMPs. Lose 1000 and the score is −14 IMPs. The second 500 points is only 3 additional IMPs.

For each match, you tally up the IMPs won by your side (+) and deduct the IMPs scored by the opponents (−). The difference is the margin of your win or loss. This difference is often converted into Victory Points. This is a simple VP scale :

IMP Difference	VPs
0-1	5-5
2-4	6-4
5-8	7-3
9-13	8-2
14-19	9-1
20+	10-0

On this scale, each match is out of 10 Victory Points, the winner scoring the VPs on the left of the VP column and the loser scoring the VPs on the right. Victory Point scales also reduce the impact of large results. A win by 50 IMPs is the same as a win by 20 IMPs on the above scale. VP scales also eliminate minus-IMP scores from results sheets.

Scoring simply in + and - IMPs is fairer than using a conversion to Victory Points, but VP scales are widely used and many other Victory Point scales exist. The World Bridge Federation has produced a more complicated series of VP scales (varying according to the number of boards in the match) where a drawn match is 15-15, but the winners can score no more than 25 VPs while the losers can at worst be minus 5 VPs. The maximum result on the WBF scale is 25 to minus-5.

IMP Strategy

Just as pairs strategy is based on the method of scoring, so IMPs strategy relates to the scoring approach. One of the most striking differences is in regard to overtricks. At pairs, because you are striving to beat so many pairs, you want to achieve the highest score reasonably possible. +400 in 3NT will score 0 matchpoints at pairs if all the others score +430. At teams the difference between +400 and +430 is only 1 IMP, while the difference between making 3NT for +400 and failing for −50 is 10 IMPs. The upshot is you do not jeopardise your contract at teams for the sake of a possible overtrick. Making your contract is the primary aim.

At pairs, safety plays which sacrifice a possible overtrick in order to ensure your contract by guarding against a bad break are shunned most of the time. At teams such safety plays are a vital ingredient of your declarer technique. Your aim as declarer is far clearer at teams: make your contract.

Defending at teams is also simpler: defeat their contract is your objective, not to restrict declarer to the minimum number of overtricks. If you can see the setting trick, grab it. Do not wait around hoping for more than one down unless you can see that it is perfectly safe to do so.

Strategy for part-scores

At pairs, although it is sensible to strive for a safe part-score, it is quite common with 23-24 points to choose 1NT rather than a minor suit fit. At teams, you should always choose the safest contract. An 8-card or better trump fit will almost always be safer than 1NT or 2NT. Naturally you still strive for games but with only part-score values there is nothing wrong with a minor suit.

It is still vital to compete for part-scores and the strategies covered in Chapters 17-18 are just as important for teams as for pairs. There is one slight difference: playing teams there is less emphasis on competing above them at the three-level. If they are in 3 ◇ and you might bid 3 ♠, at pairs you are quick to bid 3 ♠ if your side is known to have nine trumps. At teams, this approach is still relevant but you should have some prospects of making your contract (e.g., via an assessment by the losing trick count).

Very often, both sides will fail at the three-level. If they were making 3 ◇, −110, and you would be going down for −100 in 3 ♠, the difference is 0 at teams but could be vital at pairs. If you were going to make +140 and you collect +100 by defending against 3 ◇, your loss is only 1 IMP. However, if both sides would fail, it is foolish to be −100 when you could be +100. That is a difference of 5 IMPs and enough of those could cost you the match.

The non-vulnerable game

In deciding whether to try for a game when not vulnerable, you should be just a touch more optimistic than at pairs. At pairs, games are worth bidding if they are 50-50. At teams, if you bid say 4 ♠ and they stop in 3 ♠, then if ten tricks are made, you score +420 not vulnerable and they score +170. The difference is +6 IMPs. If only nine tricks are made, you are −50 while they are +140, a loss of 5 IMPs. Thus, bidding the game gains you little more than stopping in the part-score. If you are two down for −100, then the loss is 6 IMPs, the same as the gain for success. In general, if you have a borderline decision, prefer to bid the game when you are not vulnerable unless you can detect some risk of being doubled for penalties.

The vulnerable game

Here there is a significant difference in approach. At pairs, 50% is still the guideline but at teams, vulnerable games are worth bidding if the chance for success is around the 40% mark. Again, suppose you bid 4 ♠ and they stop in 3 ♠. If ten tricks are made, you score +620 vulnerable and they score +170. The difference of +450 translates into +10 IMPs. If only nine tricks are there, you are −100, they are +140, a loss of 6 IMPs for the 240 difference. Thus you gain 10 IMPs when you are right and lose only 6 IMPs when you are wrong.

Even if you are two down in 4 ♠, the loss is 340, 8 IMPs, still 2 IMPs less than the gain for bidding the game. If you are doubled and go two down, you lose 12 IMPs, just 2 IMPs more than your gain when your decision is right.

Recommended approach: Do stretch to bid your vulnerable games. Be bold but not reckless.

The practical advice is that you retain all your basic bidding structure but you should invite game with one point less than normal. While game on 25 points is usually about a 50% chance, you should be prepared to be in game with just 24 points when vulnerable. Bid game if you can count 24 points or more, invite game if there might be 24 points between you. When replying to an invitation, make your normal decision. Partner has already fudged the extra point when inviting.

Minor suit games

At pairs, you avoid 5 ♣ and 5 ◇ like the plague. If you can make eleven tricks in a trump contract, you can make ten tricks in no-trumps most of the time. At pairs, the difference between 430/630 and 400/600 is likely to be critical. At teams it is of little consequence. In other words, at teams there is no reason to avoid game in a minor if you judge that this is likely to be safer than 3NT.

Small slams

To be worth bidding, a small slam should have a 50% or better chance for success. 33 points or more gives you the required edge. The losing trick count will help you gauge whether slam is likely to succeed with fewer than 33 points.

If your side has below 30 points, assume the other side will not bid the slam. With an ace and a king missing, be prepared to stay out of the slam. If you have plenty of points together, the other side is likely to be in the slam and so should you unless you can tell the slam is worse than 50%.

Grand slams

Bid these only if you can tell that they are virtually laydown. A grand slam that needs a 3-2 trump break is all right but only just. A grand slam that needs a finesse is poor odds. Be satisfied to have reached a good small slam. Often the opponents will have stopped in game.

Sacrifices

At pairs, if they bid 4 ♡ and can make it for 620, sacrificing in 4 ♠ doubled for only −500 is a triumph. At teams, you gain only 3 IMPs while if you are wrong and they were failing in 4 ♡, you are −500 when you could have +100, a gain of 12 IMPs. In other words, if you are right 4 times out of 5, you still only break even. Do not sacrifice at teams unless they are likely to make their contract and your sacrifice might succeed or go only one off. Two down is acceptable at favourable vulnerability.

EXERCISES ON TACTICS AT IMPS

A. Both sides are vulnerable. The bidding has started 1NT from partner, Pass on your right. What action would you take with these hands : (a) at pairs?   (b) at teams?

1. ♠ K 10 7 4 2	2. ♠ K 8 7	3. ♠ 10 9 6	4. ♠ J 4 3	5. ♠ 8
♡ 9 8 2	♡ K 8 2	♡ 9 7 6	♡ K Q 6 2	♡ Q J 2
◊ K Q J	◊ Q 7 3	◊ K 3	◊ K 9 5 2	◊ A J 5 2
♣ 6 3	♣ K J 9 5	♣ A Q J 10 3	♣ Q 6	♣ A K 9 8 3

B. In each of the following situations, you are South with the hand given. What is your next action at teams? State whether vulnerability is relevant and whether your answer would be different at pairs.

1.

WEST	NORTH	EAST	SOUTH
			1◊
No	1NT	No	?

♠ K 3
♡ A J
◊ K J 10 9 7
♣ Q J 5 2

2.

WEST	NORTH	EAST	SOUTH
			1NT
No	2♡	No	2♠
No	3♡	No	?

2♡ = transfer to spades;   3♡ = natural

♠ K 8 6 3
♡ A 8 5 4
◊ Q 8
♣ A 9 2

3.

WEST	NORTH	EAST	SOUTH
1◊	No	1♠	No
2♠	No	No	?

♠ K 7
♡ Q J 8 6 4
◊ 9 7
♣ A 10 5 2

4.

WEST	NORTH	EAST	SOUTH
	1◊	No	1♠
No	1NT	No	?

♠ K 9 6 3
♡ 7 3
◊ K 10 4 2
♣ 9 7 2

5.

WEST	NORTH	EAST	SOUTH
			1◊
No	1NT	No	?

♠ 8 3
♡ A J
◊ K Q 7 6 3
♣ A K 5 2

6.

WEST	NORTH	EAST	SOUTH
No	No	1♠	?

♠ K 3 2
♡ 8 4
◊ K Q 8 7 3
♣ A 5 2

7.

WEST	NORTH	EAST	SOUTH
		1♡	?

♠ 8
♡ 8 5
◊ K Q 7 4 3
♣ A 9 8 5 2

8.

WEST	NORTH	EAST	SOUTH
	1♠	No	2♡
No	4♡	No	4NT
No	5♣	No	5◊
No	5♠	No	5NT
No	6◊	No	?

5♣ = 0 or 3 key cards; 5♠ = ♡Q; 6◊ = one king

♠ K Q 2
♡ A J 8 6 4 3
◊ A 7
♣ 5 2

9.

WEST	NORTH	EAST	SOUTH
	1♠	No	2NT
No	4♣	No	4NT
No	5♠	No	?

♠ K J 6 3
♡ A 7 6 2
◊ A K 3
♣ Q J

10.

WEST	NORTH	EAST	SOUTH
	1♠	No	1NT
No	2NT	No	?

♠ 8 3
♡ A J 2
◊ Q 7 6 3
♣ 10 6 5 2

PLAY HANDS ON IMP TACTICS
(These hands can be made up by using pages 176-183)

Hand 61: 3NT vs 5♣ — Safety play at IMPs

Dealer North : Both vulnerable

NORTH
♠ A 8 6
♡ A K J
♢ J 10 9 5 4
♣ 8 3

WEST
♠ J 10 9 4
♡ Q 9 5
♢ Q 6
♣ J 10 6 5

EAST
♠ K 7 3 2
♡ 10 8 7 4 3
♢ A K 8
♣ 9

SOUTH
♠ Q 5
♡ 6 2
♢ 7 3 2
♣ A K Q 7 4 2

WEST	NORTH	EAST	SOUTH
	1NT	No	3NT
No	No	No	

Bidding: At pairs, South's 3NT reply is routine but even at teams you should be reluctant to try for 5-minor after partner has opened 1NT if you have only marginal game values and no singleton or void. It is true that North may have a weak holding in diamonds or one of the majors but this is not very likely as North has at most one point in clubs. In addition how would you find out where partner's weakness lies? Take a shot at 3NT on hands like this and take your medicine when it goes wrong.

Lead: 4 of hearts. Your aim is to defeat 3NT and the best chance is via your long suit as you have outside entries.

Recommended play: North captures West's queen and immediately ducks a club. If West returns a heart, North wins and cashes the rest of the clubs followed by the ♠A and top heart. Nine tricks.

Notes: (1) 5♣ is a terrible contract even if clubs were 3-2.
(2) If West shifts to the jack of spades after taking the club, North should rise with the ♠A. To play low would risk failing if East won and the defence took three diamonds.
(3) At pairs, North would not duck a club. The normal 3-2 club split (about 2/3 of the time) would bring in an overtrick most of the time. At pairs you should play for the most tricks on the most common breaks. At teams five club tricks are enough to make your game. Simply duck the club and you make nine tricks without any heartaches.

Hand 62: Choosing the right slam — Safety play

Dealer East : Nil vulnerable

NORTH
♠ 8 6 4 3
♡ 4
♢ 10 9 8 7 3
♣ 8 3 2

WEST
♠ A J
♡ A 9 6 5
♢ A Q 6
♣ A K 7 6

EAST
♠ Q 10 9 2
♡ K J 7 3
♢ K 4 2
♣ Q 5

SOUTH
♠ K 7 5
♡ Q 10 8 2
♢ J 5
♣ J 10 9 4

WEST	NORTH	EAST	SOUTH
		No	No
2NT	No	3♣	No
3♡	No	4NT	No
5♢	No	6♡	All pass

Bidding: At pairs, with most pairs bidding slam, East might take a shot at 6NT which fails on the actual layout. At teams, it is usually safer to play in the suit slam if the high card values are borderline for slam. 5♢ showed 1 or 4 key cards for hearts and East can tell it must be four. East can tell that West cannot have enough to make 7♡ a good bet and so settles for 6♡.

Lead: 10 of diamonds. Safest from an uninspiring collection.

Recommended play: Win with the ♢K and take the spade finesse at once. Continue with the ♡K and lead a low heart towards your A-9-6. If South plays low, insert the 9. When this holds, cash the ♡A, ♣Q, ♣K and ruff a club. Then take your diamond winners and black aces. You lose just one trump trick.

Notes: (1) If South inserts the ♡10 on the second round of hearts, take with ♡A. When North shows out, continue with ♣Q, ♣K, ruff your low club with ♡J and lead a heart towards ♡9-6.
(2) In 6NT you need four heart tricks. In 6♡, you can afford to lose a heart if the ♠ K is onside.
(3) You have to take the spade finesse some time. By taking it early, you can gauge how best to play the hearts. If the spade finesse lost, you take the best line for four heart tricks: ♡A and then finesse ♡J. The safety play to make sure you do not lose two tricks in hearts is to cash the king and lead low towards A-9-6. If South follows, you should be safe. If South shows out, rise with ♡A, cash ♠A, cross to ♣Q and lead ♠Q. You may still need a little extra luck but that is your best line.

Hand 63: Choosing the right slam — Strip and throw-in

Dealer South : N-S vulnerable

```
              NORTH
              ♠ 9 4 3
              ♡ Q 8 5 2
              ◇ A 7 6
              ♣ A K 8
WEST                          EAST
♠ K J 6                       ♠ 8 7 5 2
♡ 9 4                         ♡ 10 3
◇ J 8 4 2                     ◇ Q 10 5 3
♣ J 10 9 6                    ♣ 7 5 2
              SOUTH
              ♠ A Q 10
              ♡ A K J 7 6
              ◇ K 9
              ♣ Q 4 3
```

WEST	NORTH	EAST	SOUTH
			1♡
No	2NT	No	3NT
No	4♡	No	4♠
No	5♣	No	6♡
No	No	No	

Bidding: After the Jacoby 2NT raise, South's 3NT = 16+ HCP and no singleton or void. With an absolute minimum, North signs off but there is no stopping South. 4♠ is a cue-bid, aimed at locating club control, and when North cue-bids 5♣, South knows enough to bid 6♡. For 7♡, South needs North to hold ♠K, ♡Q, ◇A and ♣A-K. With so much, North would not have signed off over 3NT.

Lead: Jack of clubs. No contest.

Recommended play: South wins, draws trumps, cashes ◇K, ◇A, ruffs a diamond and plays off the clubs ending in dummy. Having stripped the minor suits, a spade is led from dummy and South inserts the ten when East plays low. West wins with the jack but has to return a spade into South's A-Q or give declarer a ruff-and-discard.

Notes: (1) At pairs, it would be sensible to play in 6NT where declarer would take two finesses in spades. To reach 6NT, South would bid 4NT over 4♡ and bid 6NT after finding North with two key cards, the ♡Q and one king. 6NT would make 75% of the time but on this layout, 6NT would fail. In 6NT you do not have the strip-and-throw-in play available. If the opening lead is not ruffed, 6♡ is foolproof unless hearts are 4-0. At teams you play in the safer slam.
(2) In 6♡ it would be silly to take two spade finesses. Why settle for 75% when 100% is available?
(3) South should insert the ♠10 just in case East has K-J-x in spades. You may as well make all the tricks if both spade honours are onside.
(4) It makes no difference here but West should play back a spade when in with the ♠J. The ruff-and-discard is sure to cost. The spade return may work.

Hand 64: Choosing the right slam at IMPs — Setting up dummy's suit

Dealer West : E-W vulnerable

```
              NORTH
              ♠ J 10 8 5
              ♡ 9
              ◇ 9 8 2
              ♣ 10 9 5 4 3
WEST                          EAST
♠ A 9 6 4 3                   ♠ K Q 2
♡ K Q 2                       ♡ A J 8 6 4 3
◇ K 6 4                       ◇ A 7
♣ A 8                         ♣ J 2
              SOUTH
              ♠ 7
              ♡ 10 7 5
              ◇ Q J 10 5 3
              ♣ K Q 7 6
```

WEST	NORTH	EAST	SOUTH
1♠	No	2♡	No
4♡	No	4NT	No
5♣	No	5◇	No
5♠	No	5NT	No
6◇	No	7♡	All pass

Bidding: The jump to 4♡ shows 15+ HCP and 3+ hearts. A 5◇ cue-bid would be too awkward and so East chooses 4NT. The 5♣ reply shows 0 or 3 key cards, clearly three as West has shown a strong hand. 5◇ asked for the queen of trumps and 5♠ said, 'I have it'. East's 5NT asks for kings outside trumps and 6◇ shows one. East can count twelve tricks in top cards and hopes to set up an extra trick via dummy's spades.

Lead: King of clubs. Easy against a grand slam.

Recommended play: Win ♣A, draw trumps and continue with ♠K, ♠Q, ♠A and ruff a spade. Dummy's fifth spade is now a winner on which your club loser is discarded.

Notes: (1) At pairs, it would be reasonable to take a shot at 7NT. This would make if spades were 3-2 or if North started with singleton 10 or J. 7♡ makes despite a 4-1 break in spades and therefore 7♡ is the contract you should be in at teams.
(2) Playing in 7NT, East has 12 tricks. Win ♣A, and cash ♠K, ♠Q, ♠A. When spades do not break, declarer should play off all the hearts. North can afford to discard all the clubs after South's ♣K lead but if North lets go a seemingly innocuous diamond, South will be squeezed when the last heart is played.

CHAPTER 17
PART-SCORE COMPETITIVE BIDDING (1)

Your side has not entered the bidding early

When the opposition bidding dies out at a low level, should you pass it out and defend or should you back into the auction? In the following auctions, should South sell out or come into the bidding?

(1) WEST	NORTH	EAST	SOUTH
1♢	No	1♠	No
2♢	No	No	?

(2) WEST	NORTH	EAST	SOUTH
1♢	No	1♠	No
2♠	No	No	?

There is a significant difference between the two auctions. In (1), there is no evidence of a trump fit for East-West. Indeed, East could be singleton or even void in diamonds. Where the bidding has not revealed a good trump fit, there is no urgency to compete. You should re-open only if you have something worthwhile to bid. That would be unusual given your silence on the previous round. A poor 6-card suit, too weak to overcall initially, would be justification or a shortage in declarer's suit. In (1), South might back in with 2♡ with something like:

♠ 7 3   ♡ 10 8 6 4 3 2   ♢ 4   ♣ A K 9 7

If their last bid was 1NT, you should bid only if you have a reasonably clear-cut action. Otherwise you are risking a substantial penalty.

In (2), it is highly likely that East-West have at least eight spades together. If they have a definite trump fit, you should be eager to compete and should almost never sell out at the two-level.

The 3-over-2 rule

If the opponents bid and raise a suit and stop at the two-level, be quick to bid in the pass-out seat.

When they have a trump fit and about half the HCP between them, they can usually score eight tricks. If they have about half the HCP, then so does your side. If they have a trump fit, your side does too (almost always). Your job is to dislodge them from the safety of the two-level and push them to the jeopardy of the three-level.

You must be prepared to go the three-level yourself and possibly fail at the three-level. Even if you do not make your contract at the three-level, the cost will usually be less than what they would have scored if you had left them to play in two. Your bonus comes when they push on to the three-level. You have pushed them one higher than they wished to be and perhaps you can now defeat them. Having pushed them to the three-level, pass and defend. Do not push once more.

This advice about being prepared to compete applies only if there have been two passes to you. If you also pass, the bidding is over. The advice does not apply in the direct seat, when the last bid was on your right. In auction (2), North is in the direct seat over 1♢ and over 2♠. To bid in the direct seat, you need full values for your action. To bid in the pass-out seat needs courage more than points. Suppose North did double 2♠. What would you expect North to hold?

As the action is in the direct seat, North should have about opening points or better with hearts and clubs, the unbid suits. North's failure to double 1♢ is sure to be due to inadequate support for spades.

Suppose in auction (2) South doubles 2♠. What can you expect from South?

South should hold at least four hearts and four clubs, but the point count is almost irrelevant. If they have 18-19-20-21-22 HCP their way, then your side will have the balance of 22-21-20-19-18 HCP. So, suppose in auction 2, North-South have 20 HCP. Then if South has 12, partner will have 8, while if South has 7, partner will have 13. What South has does not matter, since the combined partnership total will be close to the 20-point mark.

Suppose you have decided to take action in the pass-out seat. What actions are available?

The Delayed Overcall

(3) WEST	NORTH	EAST	SOUTH
1♡	No	2♡	No
No	?		

One option for North is to bid 2♠, 3♣ or 3♢, a delayed overcall. If the suit you bid could have been overcalled at the one-level, poor suit quality explains the failure to bid earlier. Expectancy for a delayed overcall is a 5-card suit but the suit does not require any suit quality. A 2♠ delayed overcall might be:

♠ J 8 7 4 2   ♡ A 2   ♢ K Q   ♣ 7 5 3 2

An important consequence is that partner need not be anxious later in the defence to lead your suit. The failure to overcall at once marks you with a poor suit. In (3) above, North might bid 3♣ with:

♠ A 5   ♡ K 2   ♢ K 9 3   ♣ J 8 6 5 3 2
(bad suit in a good hand), or with:

♠ 9 2   ♡ 8 7 4   ♢ 5 2   ♣ A K 8 6 3 2
(good suit in a poor hand)

After a delayed overcall by partner, never raise partner's suit if the opponents do not bid and almost never bid on if they have been pushed to the three-level. Do not be impressed if you hold 13-14 points. Partner has already taken your values into account when making the delayed overcall.

The delayed double

The delayed double is generally used when you are short in their suit and hold 3-4 cards in the unbid suits. If they have bid and raised a major, then the delayed double should include four cards in the other major and tolerance for the minors. If they have bid and raised a minor, the delayed double should be at least 4-3 in the majors.

(4)	WEST	NORTH	EAST	SOUTH
	1♠	No	2♠	No
	No	?		

To double, North should have at least 4 hearts and at least 4-3 in the minors. A shortage in clubs is permitted as long as North is prepared to remove a 3♣ reply to 3♦ (6 diamonds or a reasonable 5).

The reason for not doubling earlier is lack of strength. To double 1♠ North should have about the same strength as an opening hand. For a delayed double, the shape is important but the high card strength is largely irrelevant.

In reply to a delayed double, partner should choose the best suit at the cheapest level. Do not make a jump reply to a delayed double! Do not become excited because you seem to hold a good hand. The fact that the opponents have stopped at the two-level has marked you with some strength. Partner will have deducted the points in hand from 20 to make an estimate of your likely strength. If you feel you have a really good hand, you can be reasonably confident that the doubler will have a bad hand to compensate.

The aim is to push them to the three-level. Once that has been achieved, neither the doubler nor partner should push again. Push them once, not twice. 'Do not go to the well too often.' Bid again and a penalty double is imminent.

After you have pushed them to the three-level it is rarely right to make a penalty double after a delayed overcall or a delayed double. They have robbed you of nothing so that a penalty double is not needed. Defeating their contract will already gain a decent score for you. A penalty double at the three-level is warranted if the hand belongs to your side, if you have say 23 HCP or more and they have 17 or less. If that were the case, your side would have been in the bidding earlier.

The delayed 2NT overcall

(5)	WEST	NORTH	EAST	SOUTH
	1♠	No	2♠	No
	No	?		

What action should North take with :

♠ 9 5 3 2   ♡ 4   ♦ K Q 5 2   ♣ K J 3 2

Since they have bid and raised a suit and stopped at the two-level, it is right to take action, but North cannot afford to double. What if partner bids 3♡? You are then beyond anything that resembles sanity. An overcall or 3♣ or 3♦ lacks suit length and how can you tell which minor to bid?

The solution is to use a delayed 2NT overcall as a request to partner to bid but to choose only a minor suit. A delayed double says, 'Pick any suit' while a delayed 2NT says 'Pick one of the minors'.

The delayed 2NT cannot sensibly be a genuine no-trump hand. With a powerful balanced hand, you would have taken action on the previous round (1NT overcall or double). This use of 2NT follows the concept of the unusual 2NT overcall where an immediate overcall of 2NT shows at least 5-5 in the minors, about 6-11 HCP and a willingness to sacrifice should the opponents bid a major suit game. The delayed 2NT is usually 4-4 or 5-4 in the minors (with 5-5 you might have bid 2NT on the previous round). It might be 5-5 in the minors if the suit quality of the minors is poor.

The North hand after auction (5) above is ideal for the delayed 2NT. The 4-card holding in spades means that partner should be singleton or void in spades and therefore partner is very likely to have length in one of the minors.

Possible outcomes of the 3-over-2 rule

(a) You let them play at the two-level	−110
(b) You bid at the three-level and make	+110
(c) You bid at the three-level and fail	−50 / −100
(d) They bid to the three-level and fail	+50 / +100
(e) They bid three and make it	−140
(f) They double you at the three-level	−500

If you leave them unchallenged in a major suit at the two-level, you will be scoring −110 most of the time. If you take one of the foregoing delayed actions and commit yourself to the three-level, you will do better in three situations (b, c and d). If they push on to the three-level and make it, you are no worse off. Making three in 2♠ or making three in 3♠ is the same result.

Occasionally you will have a horror result, doubled and down some large number. If all of the above results were equally likely, the recommended strategy is still sensible. You come out in front 60% of the time (b, c and d), break even 20% of the time (e) and suffer 20% of the time (f). In fact, (f) is the least likely result. Most of the time you can make eight tricks in your trump fit and most of the time you will not be doubled. They have only about half the HCP and as they have a trump fit, a penalty double is not appealing. Experience indicates (b, c and d) occur about 70% of the time, (e) about 20% and (f) about 10% of the time. The important thing is not to focus on the bad times. When a calamity does occur, reflect on all the great results you have had.

Suppose the bidding has started:

(6)	WEST	NORTH	EAST	SOUTH
	1♡	No	2♡	No
	No	Dble	No	?

What action should South take with:

♠ 7 4   ♡ 8 6 3   ♦ Q J 5 2   ♣ A 9 6 4

It is not clear which minor to choose. Partner could be 4-3 in the minors, perhaps even 5-3. Why risk picking the wrong minor? Why not use the 2NT reply to a *delayed* double to ask partner to choose the minor? It would be rare to want to play in 2NT opposite a delayed double. The partnership can hardly have the strength to make 2NT viable. In reply to an immediate takeout double, 2NT is a natural, strong balanced hand (commonly 10-12 points). In reply to a delayed double, use 2NT for the minors.

When is it unwise to follow the 3-over-2 rule?

(a) Do not compete if a trump fit may not exist.

If the bidding does not reveal a good trump fit their way, usually after responder has given merely a preference, you need not compete as vigorously.

(7) WEST	NORTH	EAST	SOUTH
1♥	No	1NT	No
2♦	No	2♥	No
No	?		

They have stopped at the two-level but they have not bid and raised a suit. South's 2♥ preference need not be more than a doubleton and perhaps they are playing in a 7-card trump fit. Be wary of bidding here if you hold three cards in opener's suit as East is quite likely to score a defensive ruff in hearts if you buy the contract.

(b) Do not compete if they are playing in their third suit as trumps. For example:

(8) WEST	NORTH	EAST	SOUTH
1♦	No	1♥	No
1♠	No	2♠	No
No	?		

The only place left for you is clubs and they know so much about their hand patterns that a defensive cross-ruff is quite likely. When they finish in their third suit as trumps, declarer is quite likely to play the hand as a crossruff. Your best defence is to lead trumps at each opportunity.

(c) Do not compete against notorious underbidders.

You may know the regular underbidders in your club. If not, keep track of those pairs who are often scoring +170 when the field is in game. Once you have established who these chronic underbidders are, do not bother to compete against them in the part-score zone without full values. It is quite likely that they have missed a game and if you give them a second chance, they may bid on to game. Let sleeping dogs lie. The stronger your opponents, the safer it is to compete when they have stopped at the two-level. Strong players rarely miss game.

(d) If an opponent takes a long time before passing partner's two-level raise, do not back in.

The person who trances (thinks for a long time) and then passes is considering a game-invitation. If you come in, they will frequently push on to game and make it. *Do not protect against a trancer.*

The 3-over-3 rule

When the opponents have competed to the three-level over your two-level bid, should you pass and defend or should you bid three over their three? Most of the time you will better off defending. Often neither side can make nine tricks, so why should you fail when they are about to fail? Do not assume that because they have bid to the three-level, they are bound to make nine tricks. The opponents are quite fallible.

One of the best guidelines in this area uses the number of trumps held by your side as the basis for your decision:

At the three-level:

With eight trumps for your side: Pass and defend.
With nine trumps for your side: Bid 3-over-3.

Note that this guideline applies only when the bidding is already at the three-level. At the two-level, follow the 3-over-2 rule.

If both sides have a trump fit and one side has nine trumps, one side figures to make nine tricks (not necessarily the side that has the nine trumps, though). If this is so, then if your side is the one making the nine tricks, it obviously makes sense to bid 3-over-3. If their side is going to make nine tricks, you should still bid 3-over-3, choosing to go one down (you figure to make eight tricks) rather than let them make their three-level part-score.

The partnership should be able to tell whether eight or nine trumps are held. If your side has bid and raised a suit, you should have eight trumps together. If either partner has an extra trump, then the partnership should hold nine trumps. If neither partner has an extra trump, then you have only eight trumps together. Playing 5-card majors, a raise of opener's major shows 3+ support. If responder actually has four trumps, responder knows the partnership has nine trumps and so responder is the one to take the push to 3-over-3.

This is a trouble area for those pairs who may raise partner's 4-card major with only 3-card support. It is much harder for such pairs to gauge whether the partnership has seven or eight or nine trumps.

If you are going to take the push to 3-over-3, it often pays to take the push at once. For example:

(9) WEST	NORTH	EAST	SOUTH
1♠	No	2♠	No
No	2NT	?	

If East intends to bid 3♠ later, East may as well bid 3♠ now. This shows no extra strength, just an extra trump. The advantage comes when South is unable to indicate the preferred minor and so North may have a tougher choice of lead.

The 4-over-3 rule

Do not bid a part-score hand to the four-level. If they outbid you at the three-level, pass and defend rather than push on to four. Most of the time you will fail in four. Why not hope they fail in three?

EXERCISES ON COMPETITIVE BIDDING (1)

A. The bidding has started:

WEST	NORTH	EAST	SOUTH
1♠	No	2♠	No
No	?		

What should North do now?

1. ♠ 5 3	2. ♠ J 7 3 2	3. ♠ 9 7 5	4. ♠ 4 3	5. ♠ 4 3
♡ A 9 8 2	♡ K Q 8 6 4 2	♡ 6 4	♡ K Q 6 2	♡ K Q 6 2
◇ K 7 4 3	◇ J 9	◇ A 9 7 3	◇ K 9 7 4 3 2	◇ 5
♣ Q 6 3	♣ 4	♣ A Q 7 3	♣ 5	♣ K 9 7 4 3 2

B. The bidding has started:

WEST	NORTH	EAST	SOUTH
1♡	No	2♡	No
No	Dble	No	?

What should South do now?

1. ♠ Q 7	2. ♠ K Q 5 4	3. ♠ A K 4 2	4. ♠ 8 5	5. ♠ 9
♡ K 6 2	♡ J 8 7 2	♡ 7 6 3	♡ Q 7 6 4	♡ K Q 5 2
◇ J 9 7 3 2	◇ 4	◇ Q 8	◇ 4 2	◇ Q J 7 3
♣ K 9 6	♣ J 10 6 3	♣ A 9 6 4	♣ K Q 8 7 2	♣ Q 10 6 2

COMPETITIVE BIDDING: How should the following hands be bid? West is the dealer each time and neither side is vulnerable.

SET 31— WEST	SET 31 — NORTH	SET 31 — EAST	SET 31 — SOUTH
1. ♠ 8 6	1. ♠ K Q 10	1. ♠ A 9 3	1. ♠ J 7 5 4 2
♡ K J 3 2	♡ 10 9 7	♡ Q 8 6 4	♡ A 5
◇ A J 7 4 2	◇ K 9 8	◇ 6 5 3	◇ Q 10
♣ K 7	♣ A 9 6 3	♣ Q 10 4	♣ J 8 5 2
2. ♠ A	2. ♠ K J 6 5 4	2. ♠ 9 8 3	2. ♠ Q 10 7 2
♡ J 10 8 3	♡ A K 6 4	♡ 9 2	♡ Q 7 5
◇ 9 7 6 5 4	◇ J	◇ K Q 8 2	◇ A 10 3
♣ J 10 2	♣ Q 8 7	♣ A K 5 3	♣ 9 6 4
3. ♠ K 5 2	3. ♠ Q 7 4	3. ♠ A J 8	3. ♠ 10 9 6 3
♡ 9 8	♡ A Q 7 3	♡ 6 4 2	♡ K J 10 5
◇ 8 5 3	◇ Q 10 6 2	◇ K J 4	◇ A 9 7
♣ K 9 6 3 2	♣ 10 8	♣ A Q 7 5	♣ J 4
4. ♠ 10 6 3	4. ♠ K 9 8 4	4. ♠ A 2	4. ♠ Q J 7 5
♡ 10 5 4	♡ K 6	♡ 9 8 3	♡ A Q J 7 2
◇ A 8 3 2	◇ 9 7 6	◇ Q J 10 4	◇ K 5
♣ A Q 2	♣ J 10 6 3	♣ K 9 8 4	♣ 7 5
5. ♠ A 6 3	5. ♠ K J 7 2	5. ♠ Q 8 5 4	5. ♠ 10 9
♡ A Q 8 7 3	♡ J	♡ K 6 5 4	♡ 10 9 2
◇ A 7	◇ K 9 6 5 2	◇ 10 4	◇ Q J 8 3
♣ J 8 2	♣ 7 4 3	♣ Q 9 5	♣ A K 10 6
6. ♠ A 6	6. ♠ 10 9 8 4 3	6. ♠ K J 7	6. ♠ Q 5 2
♡ K J 8 5	♡ 3 2	♡ Q 9	♡ A 10 7 6 4
◇ A Q 7 4 2	◇ K 5	◇ J 9 8 3	◇ 10 6
♣ 6 2	♣ A K J 9	♣ 10 7 5 4	♣ Q 8 3
7. ♠ 10 7 4	7. ♠ A K J 3	7. ♠ 8 5	7. ♠ Q 9 6 2
♡ A	♡ Q J 4	♡ 8 7 6 5 3 2	♡ K 10 9
◇ A 9 6 3 2	◇ J 8	◇ K Q 4	◇ 10 7 5
♣ J 9 8 7	♣ K 6 4 3	♣ A 10	♣ Q 5 2

PLAY HANDS ON COMPETITIVE BIDDING (1)
(These hands can be made up by using pages 176-183)

Hand 65: Delayed overcall — 3-over-2 rule

Dealer North : Nil vulnerable

NORTH
♠ 8 6 5 4 3 2
♡ A 7 2
◇ 10
♣ K 3 2

WEST
♠ 1 0 9 7
♡ K J 9 4
◇ A 9 2
♣ J 10 9

EAST
♠ K J
♡ Q 10 8 3
◇ K 7 5 4 3
♣ A 8

SOUTH
♠ A Q
♡ 6 5
◇ Q J 8 6
♣ Q 7 6 5 4

WEST	NORTH	EAST	SOUTH
	No	1◇	No
1♡	No	2♡	No
No	2♠	3♡	All pass

Bidding: With such a poor suit, North should not make a direct overcall of 1♠ and South should not bid 2♣ over 1◇. It would be premature for South to take action over 2♡. South is in the direct seat, not the pass-out seat. North must not sell out to 2♡ (3-over-2 rule). The delayed 2♠ overcall indicates length but not strength in spades. East-West should not sell out to 2♠. With a trump fit, be prepared to push to the three-level. As East has good shape, East should take the push. Note the power of the spade suit in these part-score battles.

Lead: 10 of diamonds. With trump control, a singleton appeals.

Recommended play: 3♡ should be defeated. West wins the ◇10 lead and plays a trump. North rises with ♡A and switches to a spade. South wins, gives North a diamond ruff, wins the next spade and gives North another diamond ruff.

Notes: (1) Even on other leads, 3♡ should fail. On a club lead, the defence can take one club, two spades, one heart and one diamond and accurate defence will also come to five tricks on a spade or a heart lead.
(2) After ◇10 lead, North should rise with ♡A at once as North wants to obtain two ruffs.
(3) East-West are wise to bid to 3♡ as 2♠ can be made. Better to be minus 50 than minus 110.
(4) In 2♠, after the normal heart lead, North ducks, wins the next heart and ruffs a heart. After cashing ♠A, declarer exits with a diamond. Later declarer leads a second round of trumps. If declarer has to tackle clubs, play East for the ace. Lead a low club to the queen and duck the second round.

Hand 66: Delayed double — 3-over-3 rule

Dealer East : N-S vulnerable

NORTH
♠ J 9 8
♡ 8 7 3
◇ A K 7 3
♣ K 5 4

WEST
♠ Q 7 6 2
♡ K Q
◇ 8 4 2
♣ J 10 6 3

EAST
♠ A K 10 4 3
♡ A 9 6 2
◇ Q 6
♣ 9 8

SOUTH
♠ 5
♡ J 10 5 4
◇ J 10 9 5
♣ A Q 7 2

WEST	NORTH	EAST	SOUTH
		1♠	No
2♠	No	No	Dble
No	3◇	3♠	All pass

Bidding: With 7 losers, East should not try for game over 2♠. South should contest the part-score (3-over-2 rule). Short in spades and with support for the other suits, a delayed double is the best choice.

With nine trumps together, East-West should not pass out 3◇. Push on to 3♠ (3-over-3 rule). As East might have only four spades in a 4-3-3-3 hand, West passes the decision to East who takes the push to 3♠. If playing 5-card majors, West should bid 3♠ over the double ('take the push at once'). This would usually shut out North.

Lead: Jack of diamonds. Top of the solid sequence.

Recommended play: North wins with the ◇K and cashes the ◇A. Whether North continues diamonds or switches, the defence can take only two diamonds and two clubs. When declarer comes in, three rounds of trumps are drawn, the ♡K-Q are cashed and declarer later ruffs the heart loser in dummy.

Notes: (1) North-South gained nothing this time by competing over 2♠ but some East-West pairs might give up over 3◇ and some days 3♠ might fail.
(2) South should be prepared to make a delayed double despite the adverse vulnerability. 3◇ can be defeated but it is virtually impossible for East-West to find a penalty double. In 3◇, after ♠A and ♣9 switch, declarer wins with the ♣K, ruffs a spade, comes to hand with a trump and ruffs the third spade. Declarer should lose one spade, one diamond and three hearts.
(3) If East unwisely switches to ♡A after cashing ♠A, 3◇ will succeed.

Hand 67: Delayed 2NT — 3-over-3 rule

Dealer South : E-W vulnerable

NORTH
- ♠ 7 4 3 2
- ♡ A J 9 8 6
- ◇ J 6 2
- ♣ J

WEST
- ♠ A K 9 5
- ♡ 5 3
- ◇ K 9 5 4
- ♣ 7 6 2

EAST
- ♠ J 10
- ♡ 10 7
- ◇ A Q 10 3
- ♣ Q 10 9 5 3

SOUTH
- ♠ Q 8 6
- ♡ K Q 4 2
- ◇ 8 7
- ♣ A K 8 4

WEST	NORTH	EAST	SOUTH
			1NT
No	2♣	No	2♡
No	No	2NT	No
3◇	3♡	All pass	

Bidding: North uses Stayman, planning to sign off in 2♡ over 2◇. When 2♡ comes back to East (3-over-2 rule), even though South opened 1NT, East should contest the part-score despite the vulnerability. You lose *more often* by passing than by competing. The delayed 2NT is a takeout bid for the minors. With an extra trump, North takes the push to 3♡ (3-over-3 rule) but East-West do not compete further (4-over-3 rule).

Lead: Ace of spades. Leading from a suit headed by A-K is usually attractive. You win the trick, see dummy and see partner's signal.

Recommended play: East plays the jack, an encouraging signal. West continues with the king of spades and the 5 of spades. The ♠9 is too risky as it would set up dummy's ♠7 as a winner. East ruffs the third spade and might sensibly switch to the queen of clubs. Declarer wins this and draws trumps, East discarding a club on the second heart. If South continues with a third round of trumps, East can safely discard a diamond. Later declarer loses two diamonds.

Notes: (1) A low diamond lead by West is riskier but would also work. East wins and shifts to the ♠J.
(2) Even though South followed the 3-over-3 rule, 3♡ fails. That is West's reward for not selling out to 2♡, which would have succeeded.
(3) 3◇ would have also failed (two hearts, two clubs and a club ruff). It is quite common for both sides to fail at the three-level. It is important to realise that the 3-over-2, 3-over-3 and 4-over-3 guidelines are not infallible. Their success rate is better than 80% which is excellent but there will still be occasions when following the rules will lead to a loss. Since this will be rare, it is sensible to abide by the rules.

Hand 68: Delayed 2NT — Taking the push at once

Dealer West : Both vulnerable

NORTH
- ♠ K Q J 6
- ♡ K J 8 6
- ◇ A 10
- ♣ J 3 2

WEST
- ♠ A 7 3 2
- ♡ 9
- ◇ Q 9 8 4 3
- ♣ K 8 5

EAST
- ♠ 8 5
- ♡ 10 5 3
- ◇ K J 6 2
- ♣ A Q 7 4

SOUTH
- ♠ 10 9 4
- ♡ A Q 7 4 2
- ◇ 7 5
- ♣ 10 9 6

WEST	NORTH	EAST	SOUTH
No	1♡	No	2♡
No	No	2NT	3♡
No	No	No	

Bidding: Neither East nor West is worth early action. When 2♡ comes back to East, 3-over-2 applies. 2NT shows at least 4-4 in the minors and no interest in the unbid major. South knows that the partnership has 9+ hearts together and so takes the push at once to 3♡ (applying the 3-over-3 rule). West does not compete to 4◇ because of the 4-over-3 rule (even though 4◇ does make this time).

If South passes 2NT, West bids 3◇ and to do well, North-South need to push on to 3♡. East-West should then pass.

Lead: If South bid 3♡ over 2NT, East might well lead the 8 of spades. If West did bid 3◇, the ◇2 would be East's choice.

Notes: (1) On ♠8 lead to West's ace, North should play the queen (to try to fool West in case East's lead was a singleton). If West returns a spade, North wins in dummy, draws trumps and cashes the rest of the spades to discard a diamond on the fourth spade. Making 3♡ is South's reward for 3♡ over 2NT.
(2) If West wins ♠A and shifts to a diamond, it is too late. Declarer wins, draws trumps and continues with the spades for the diamond discard.
(3) If West ducks the first spade, North draws trumps with ♡K, ♡J, ♡Q, followed by the spades.
(4) If West has had the chance to bid 3◇, East would start with the ◇2. West's queen knocks out North's ace and now the defence can come to five tricks. North draws trumps and shifts to the ♠K. West wins and leads a low club (as only one diamond can be cashed, club tricks are needed). East wins, cashes ◇K and a second club. West wins the third club for one down. If West did return a diamond after winning ♠A, East would have to shift to clubs next.

CHAPTER 18
PART-SCORE COMPETITIVE BIDDING (2)

Your side has entered the bidding

(a) You bid but partner did not reply

The decision whether to bid a second time will be influenced by three factors:

(1) Are you stronger than your original action promised?

(2) Have the opponents bid and raised a suit to the two-level?

(3) Are you short in the opposition suit?

If the answer to (1) is YES, you should try to find a second action if the bidding has not gone beyond the two-level.

If the answer to the first question is NO, but the answer to (2) is YES, you should strive to bid again (3-over-2 rule). If the answer to (3) is YES, you should bid again if the bidding is not beyond the two-level. If the answer to all three questions is YES, you should definitely bid on. If the answer to all three questions is NO, you should pass.

Competing on the second round

If your first action was an opening bid, do not repeat the suit if you have no extra length in that suit. If your original bid was an overcall, do not rebid your suit if it is only a 5-card suit. Overcalling and repeating the suit should be a 6-card suit. With a 5-3-3-2 or 5-4-3-1 short in their suit, choose a takeout double. If desperate to bid again but unsuitable for a double and no worthwhile second suit, you may repeat a 5-card suit if the suit quality is 8 for a two-level rebid, 9 for a three-level rebid.

(1)

WEST	NORTH	EAST	SOUTH
1♣	1♡	2♣	No
No	?		

North should generally bid again. The aim of competing in such situations is similar to competing when you have not been in the bidding at all on the first round: *Push them to the three-level and then defend at the three-level* (3-over-2).

If your initial action was a takeout double and the situation indicates you should compete further:

Double again is still for takeout, as partner has not bid yet, and is usually the best second action.

Doubling first and bidding a new suit next shows a good 5+ suit, a strong hand and a one-suiter.

(2)

WEST	NORTH	EAST	SOUTH
1♣	Dble	2♣	No
No	?		

With a normal takeout double, North should double again. If North bids 2♢, 2♡ or 2♠, this would show a good 5+ suit in a one-suiter of 16 points or more.

If you opened 1NT and LHO overcalls, passed back to you:

(3)

WEST	NORTH	EAST	SOUTH
1NT	2♢	No	No
?			

In standard methods, double by a 1NT opener is for penalties. It makes more sense to play these re-opening doubles for takeout since partner has passed. If you do, make sure you have agreed on this with your partner. To double for takeout as a 1NT opener you need a doubleton in their suit.

What if partner passes your 1NT opening and RHO overcalls?

(4)

WEST	NORTH	EAST	SOUTH
1NT	No	No	2♢
?			

Again, standard style is to treat double here as penalties. It is most unlikely that you will have enough to be confident of taking six tricks in defence, although partner figures to have some values. A sound approach for low-level penalty action is to expect a two-trick defeat. Then, if your A-K suit takes only one trick, you still beat their contract. On frequency, prefer to play double in this auction as takeout, with a doubleton in their suit. Again, this requires partnership agreement.

(b) You have bid and partner has replied

In all normal situations you should not sell out at the two-level unless you sense a misfit.

If they have bid and raised a suit to the two-level, keep on bidding (3-over-2).

If your side has bid and raised a suit to the two-level, keep on bidding if they bid above you at the two-level (3-over-2).

(5)

WEST	NORTH	EAST	SOUTH
1♢	1♠	2♢	2♠
No	No	?	

OR

(6)

WEST	NORTH	EAST	SOUTH
1♣	1♡	1♠	2♡
2♠	No	No	?

In both of these auctions, it is unsound for the bidding to be passed out at 2♠. You do *not* require any extra strength to push on to the three-level when you are in the pass-out seat. You simply have to recognise that the situation demands that you compete further. As long as the partnership appreciates this strategy, then bidding in the direct seat to the three-level would show extras. If West in (5) or North in (6) bid over 2♠, this would show better than a minimum opening/overcall.

The Law of Total Tricks

Discovered in the 1950s by Frenchman Jean-René Vernes and popularised in the 1990s by Larry Cohen's book, *To Bid Or Not To Bid*, the Law of Total Tricks is a useful tool in competitive auctions. The law states that on any deal the total number of trumps is usually equal to the total number of tricks. Total trumps = North-South's longest trump fit + East-West's longest trump fit. Total tricks = tricks taken by North-South in their trump fit + tricks taken by East-West in their trump fit.

The Law is the basis of the 3-over-2, 3-over-3 and 4-over-3 rules. If both sides have an 8-card fit, total trumps = 16. If the points are roughly equal, then each side is likely to win eight tricks. Therefore, do not sell out to them at the two-level, since they figure to make their contract. Better to bid to three and go one down than to have them make a part-score: the 3-over-2 rule.

One side has an 8-card fit, the other side has a 9-card fit. Total trumps = 17, so total tricks = 17. If the points are about equal, one side figures to make nine tricks and the other side eight tricks. Therefore, if the bidding has reached the three-level it is sensible to bid above them at the three-level. If your side is making nine tricks, you will make your contract and if their side is the one making nine tricks, you are better off going one down than letting them make their part-score: 3-over-3 rule.

Example Deal

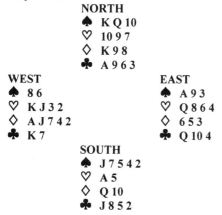

                NORTH
                ♠ K Q 10
                ♡ 10 9 7
                ◇ K 9 8
                ♣ A 9 6 3
    WEST   EAST
    ♠ 8 6   ♠ A 9 3
    ♡ K J 3 2   ♡ Q 8 6 4
    ◇ A J 7 4 2   ◇ 6 5 3
    ♣ K 7   ♣ Q 10 4
                SOUTH
                ♠ J 7 5 4 2
                ♡ A 5
                ◇ Q 10
                ♣ J 8 5 2

This exercise deal from the previous chapter is a good illustration of the Law. North-South have eight spades and East-West have eight hearts. Total trumps = 16. As each side has 20 HCP, each side figures to take eight tricks. Playing in spades, North-South should lose 1 spade, 1 heart, 1 diamond and 2 clubs: eight tricks. In hearts, East-West should lose 1 spade, 1 heart, 2 diamonds and 1 club: eight tricks. Total tricks = 16, so total trumps = total tricks.

You need not know the underlying theory but you do need to know the principles and guidelines for competing which flow from the Law of Total Tricks.

While it is not hard to estimate how many trumps your side has, it is hard to be certain of their combined trump length. If you know your side has nine trumps and they have a trump fit, you can count on 17 total trumps and so 17 total tricks. With the points shared, neither side is likely to make ten tricks. Therefore, compete above them at the three-level but do not push to four: 4-over-3 rule. Many players push too hard here and are unwilling to sell out to the three-level. Experience shows that with only part-score points, the four-level is usually too high. You need 25-26 points to make 4♡ or 4♠ and you need the same to have a decent play for 4♣ or 4◇. Follow the 4-over-3 rule and you will come out in front most of the time. Also, at the four-level, they are much keener to double.

Doubling the opponents for penalties

If you have a trump fit, it is unsound to look for penalties at the one-level or two-level. Prefer to support your partner. The best penalties at a low level come when you are strong in the enemy suit and short in partner's suit, no more than a doubleton, and at least 20 HCP for your side.

If you have a trump fit and the bidding has reached the three-level, you will bid above them at the three-level if your side has nine trumps (3-over-3). However, what if they have bid to the three-level and your side has only eight trumps?

If the points are roughly equal, 20-20, 21-19, 22-18, do not double when your side has a trump fit.

Where the points are so shared, consider it **nobody's hand** and if you do not have the nine trumps needed to bid 3-over-3, simply pass and defend. However, if you have a clear superiority in points, 23-17 or 24-16, it is **your hand**. If unable to bid 3-over-3, double for penalties.

The same applies when they have bid 3-over-your-3. If it is nobody's hand, pass and defend. If it is your hand, double. Do not bid 4-over-3.

Competing after they have opened 1NT and responder removes to a suit at the two-level

(7) WEST	NORTH	EAST	SOUTH
1NT	No	2♡	No
No	?		

Be reluctant to sell out in this type of auction. It is true that they may have a 5-2 fit but most of the time it is a 5-3 or 6-2 fit. With three cards in their suit, you need sound values to bid but if short in their suit a takeout double is often the best action.

(8) WEST	NORTH	EAST	SOUTH
1NT	No	2◇	No
2♡	No	No	?

Where responder's action is a transfer, do not take action in the direct seat (North above should pass 2♡) as responder could still have a strong hand. After two passes, be prepared to compete, using double for takeout and 2NT for the minors.

EXERCISES ON COMPETITIVE BIDDING (2)

A. The bidding has started:

WEST	NORTH	EAST	SOUTH
1♣	1♡	2♣	No
No	?		

What should North do now?

1. ♠ J 4 3 2
   ♡ A Q 6 4 3
   ◊ K 9 8
   ♣ 7

2. ♠ K J 4
   ♡ A K 7 6 2
   ◊ Q J 6
   ♣ 4 2

3. ♠ Q J 9 8
   ♡ K Q J 9 3
   ◊ 4 2
   ♣ J 9

4. ♠ 4 3
   ♡ K Q 9 6 2
   ◊ A K 7 3
   ♣ 5 2

5. ♠ Q 4 3
   ♡ A Q 9 6 2
   ◊ 5
   ♣ A J 10 3

B. The bidding has started:

WEST	NORTH	EAST	SOUTH
1NT	No	2♡*	No
*Transfer	2♠	No	No
			?

What should South do now?

1. ♠ 7
   ♡ K 9 6 2
   ◊ J 9 7 3
   ♣ A Q 9 6

2. ♠ K 9 6 2
   ♡ J 8
   ◊ A J
   ♣ J 10 6 3 2

3. ♠ K 2
   ♡ 7 6
   ◊ Q J 8 4
   ♣ A 10 6 4 3

4. ♠ 8 5
   ♡ A Q 6 4
   ◊ K J 2
   ♣ K 8 5 2

5. ♠ 9 6
   ♡ 8 2
   ◊ A J 3
   ♣ A K J 8 6 3

COMPETITIVE BIDDING : How should the following hands be bid? West is the dealer each time and neither side is vulnerable.

SET 32— WEST	SET 32 — NORTH	SET 32 — EAST	SET 32 — SOUTH
1. ♠ 8 6 4 ♡ K J 7 3 ◊ A K J 4 ♣ K 5	1. ♠ K Q 10 5 2 ♡ 10 6 5 ◊ 9 7 ♣ A 7 3	1. ♠ J 7 ♡ Q 8 2 ◊ Q 6 5 3 ♣ J 8 4 2	1. ♠ A 9 3 ♡ A 9 4 ◊ 10 8 2 ♣ Q 10 9 6
2. ♠ Q 10 7 ♡ 10 9 8 5 3 ◊ 9 7 6 5 ♣ K	2. ♠ K J 6 5 4 ♡ A K 6 4 ◊ J ♣ Q 8 7	2. ♠ 9 8 3 ♡ J 2 ◊ A K Q 8 2 ♣ A 10 3	2. ♠ A 2 ♡ Q 7 ◊ 10 4 3 ♣ J 9 6 5 4 2
3. ♠ K 5 4 ♡ Q J 10 7 3 ◊ 8 3 ♣ 6 3 2	3. ♠ A 2 ♡ 9 8 ◊ Q 10 7 6 2 ♣ A 10 9 8	3. ♠ Q 8 7 ♡ K 6 4 2 ◊ K 5 4 ♣ K Q 7	3. ♠ 10 9 6 3 2 ♡ A 5 ◊ A J 9 ♣ J 5 4
4. ♠ 10 6 2 ♡ A J 10 5 4 ◊ A J 8 2 ♣ 8	4. ♠ K 9 8 4 ♡ 6 3 ◊ K 9 7 ♣ J 10 6 3	4. ♠ A 3 ♡ 9 8 7 2 ◊ Q 10 4 3 ♣ A 9 4	4. ♠ Q J 7 5 ♡ K Q ◊ 6 5 ♣ K Q 7 5 2
5. ♠ A 6 3 ♡ A Q 8 ◊ 10 7 2 ♣ K 8 6 2	5. ♠ K 8 7 4 ♡ 9 7 3 ◊ J 8 5 3 ♣ A 3	5. ♠ J 10 9 5 2 ♡ K 6 4 ◊ A 4 ♣ 9 7 5	5. ♠ Q ♡ J 10 5 2 ◊ K Q 9 6 ♣ Q J 10 4
6. ♠ Q 8 6 4 ♡ J 8 7 ◊ Q J 10 ♣ 8 6 3	6. ♠ 9 2 ♡ Q 10 5 2 ◊ A 9 5 4 2 ♣ A Q	6. ♠ A K J 7 3 ♡ 9 3 ◊ 8 7 ♣ K 10 7 5	6. ♠ 10 5 ♡ A K 6 4 ◊ K 6 3 ♣ J 9 4 2
7. ♠ Q 10 4 3 ♡ A 6 5 ◊ 9 8 4 ♣ K 8 5	7. ♠ J 9 7 ♡ Q 10 2 ◊ 6 3 2 ♣ 10 9 6 4	7. ♠ A K 8 5 2 ♡ 8 7 3 ◊ K Q J ♣ Q 3	7. ♠ 6 ♡ K J 9 4 ◊ A 10 7 5 ♣ A J 7 2

PLAY HANDS ON COMPETITIVE BIDDING (2)
(These hands can be made up by using pages 176-183)

Hand 69: Re-opening double — 3-over-3 rule

Dealer North : N-S vulnerable

NORTH
♠ Q J 5 2
♡ K 8
◇ A Q 8 6 3
♣ Q 8

WEST
♠ 10 9 4
♡ 9 3
◇ J 10 2
♣ A J 6 3 2

EAST
♠ K 7 6
♡ A Q J 6 2
◇ 7
♣ K 7 5 4

SOUTH
♠ A 8 3
♡ 10 7 5 4
◇ K 9 5 4
♣ 10 9

WEST	NORTH	EAST	SOUTH
	1◇	1♡	2◇
No	No	Dble	No
3♣	3◇	All pass	

Bidding: With 5-3 in the majors, overcalling 1♡ is preferable to double when under 16 HCP. East has every reason not to sell out to 2◇: extra values, they have bid and raised their suit to the two-level and East is short in their suit. Double is the best re-opening action. There is no urgency for South to bid to 3◇ over the double. When West bids 3♣, North is in 3-over-3 territory and with an extra trump, North should compete with 3◇. Following 4-over-3, neither East nor West push to 4♣.

Lead: 4 of clubs. East has no attractive lead. As West bid clubs, a club becomes the preferred choice.

Recommended play: West wins with the ♣A and should switch to the ♡9. East wins and cashes the ♣K and a second heart. East should exit with a low heart, not a third club. West ruffs and North overruffs and draws trumps. North loses a spade trick later as long as East covers the ♠Q or ♠J. One down.

Notes: (1) Had East passed 2◇, North-South would score +90.
(2) After winning ♣A, West notes that there is at most one more trick in clubs for the defence. East would have led a heart from A-K-x-x-x and so East is likely to have A-Q-x-x-x or similar. Therefore West should switch to a heart. On the actual deal, the heart switch is not essential.
(3) East-West have done well not to sell out to 2◇ and North-South have done well not to give up at 3♣, which would make ten tricks along normal lines.
(4) East-West have 9 clubs, North-South 9 diamonds. Total trumps 18. East-West make ten tricks in clubs, North-South eight tricks in diamonds. Total tricks 18. Swap over North's ♡K and South's ♠A and both sides make nine tricks. When a finesse works for one side, it loses for the other.

Hand 70: Delayed double — 3-over-3 rule

Dealer East : E-W vulnerable

NORTH
♠ 8 6
♡ A 9 7
◇ K 10 9 4 3 2
♣ 8 2

WEST
♠ A Q J 4 2
♡ 6 4 3
◇ J 8 7
♣ J 10

EAST
♠ K 10 7 5
♡ Q 8
◇ A Q
♣ K 9 6 5 3

SOUTH
♠ 9 3
♡ K J 10 5 2
◇ 6 5
♣ A Q 7 4

WEST	NORTH	EAST	SOUTH
		1♣	1♡
1♠	2♡	2♠	No
No	3◇	No	3♡
No	No	3♠	All pass

Bidding: North is good enough for 2♡ over 1♠ but not strong enough for 2◇, which would indicate 10+ points. South in the direct seat passes 2♠ to indicate a minimum overcall. North does not sell out to 2♠ (3-over-2). North could bid 3♡ but 3◇ is used to suggest an alternative contract. 3◇ indicates good diamonds and minimum heart support. With four hearts, North would choose 3♡. East-West push on to 3♠ (3-over-3).

Lead: Ace of hearts. It is not attractive to lead an ace in a trump contract but opposite an overcall it is safer than usual.

Recommended play: South should discourage the hearts as South wants a club switch. Staring at the ◇K, North can tell the shift should be to clubs. North plays the ♣8, low, queen, jack. South cashes ♡K and ♣A, followed by a third club. West ruffs high, draws trumps and takes the diamond finesse. Nine tricks.

Notes: (1) If West's 1♠ showed 4+ spades, West should take the push to 3♠, but if East-West use the double of 1♡ to show four spades and 1♠ shows five, then East takes the push to 3♠ over 3◇.
(2) After North suggests diamonds, South is quick to revert to hearts.
(3) If left to play in 3♡, South is likely to succeed, either by setting up the diamonds or by ruffing two clubs in dummy. The trump position is favourable for South with the queen doubleton with East.

Hand 71: Re-opening action — When to compete, when to sell out

Dealer South : Both vulnerable

NORTH
- ♠ K J 6 4
- ♡ J 10 6
- ◇ A K Q 10 2
- ♣ J

WEST
- ♠ A Q 9 8 3
- ♡ A Q 7
- ◇ 7
- ♣ A 10 6 5

EAST
- ♠ 2
- ♡ 9 5 2
- ◇ J 5 4 3
- ♣ K 9 4 3 2

SOUTH
- ♠ 10 7 5
- ♡ K 8 4 3
- ◇ 9 8 6
- ♣ Q 8 7

WEST	NORTH	EAST	SOUTH
			No
1♠	2◇	No	No
Dble	No	3♣	No
No	No		

Bidding: When 2◇ comes back to West, a re-opening double is the most flexible action. West has extra strength and is short in the enemy suit, two of the key signs for keeping the bidding open. North should take no further action after 3♣ as East-West are already at the three-level and there is no evidence that North-South have 9+ trumps.

Lead: 8 of diamonds. You need a very strong reason to choose something other than partner's suit.

Recommended play: North wins with the ◇Q and should shift to the ♣J. North should diagnose that the hand is likely to play as a cross-ruff with dummy short in diamonds and East probably short in spades. The best defence against a cross-ruff is trump leads at every opportunity. Declarer can win with the ♣A, play ♠A and ruff a spade, take the heart finesse, ruff a third spade, cross to the ♡A and play the fourth spade. When North follows, East can throw the heart loser. This line yields ten tricks.

Notes: (1) Declarer should play the hand on ruffing lines rather than draw trumps. Declarer could ruff diamonds in dummy and spades in hand and this should also lead to ten tricks.
(2) If North unwisely competes further with 3◇. East-West can exact a heavy penalty. East leads ♠2 to the ace and ruffs the ♠9 return (high card = high suit entry). East shifts to a heart, won by West, and ruffs another spade. A heart to the ace is followed by a fourth spade, ruffed by East with the ◇J. A club to the ace gives the defence seven tricks and +300. Better to sell out to 3♣.

Hand 72: 3-over-2 rule — 3-over-3 rule

Dealer West : Nil vulnerable

NORTH
- ♠ A K 9 8
- ♡ K Q 7 5 3
- ◇ A J
- ♣ J 4

WEST
- ♠ Q
- ♡ A J 10
- ◇ Q 7 6 3
- ♣ K Q 10 3 2

EAST
- ♠ J 10 3
- ♡ 9 6 4
- ◇ K 10 5
- ♣ 9 8 6 5

SOUTH
- ♠ 7 6 5 4 2
- ♡ 8 2
- ◇ 9 8 4 2
- ♣ A 7

WEST	NORTH	EAST	SOUTH
1♣	Dble	No	1♠
No	2♠	No	No
Dble	No	3♣	3♠
No	No	No	

Bidding: North is too strong for an overcall and with both majors, double would be preferable anyway. West is not strong enough to take action over 1♠. North's 2♠ shows 4-card support and about 16-18 points, 5 losers. When South passes, West is in 3-over-2 territory. Double for takeout is the most flexible and East can do little else but 3♣. South knows the partnership has nine trumps and so pushes on to 3♠ (3-over-3 rule).

Lead: King of clubs. Better to lead from a K-Q combination than from split honours or from a suit with just one honour.

Recommended play: Win with the ♣A and lead a heart. West should play low and the king wins. Cash ♠A and lead a low heart from dummy. West wins with the ♡J, cashes the ♣Q and shifts to a low diamond. On the actual layout it works to win the ◇A, cash ♠K and ruff a heart, but playing the ◇J gives declarer easier access to dummy later. East wins and returns, say, a diamond. The ◇A wins, the ♠K is cashed and a heart is ruffed. South makes nine tricks, losing one trick in each suit. If West had started with four hearts, declarer could make nine tricks via a crossruff on the recommended line.

Notes: (1) A bid by West (in the direct seat) over 1♠ would indicate a strong hand after partner was unable to bid at the one-level.
(2) West's later double of 2♠ should be played as competitive for takeout. It is a sensible principle at duplicate that a double after the opponents bid and raise a suit to the two-level is for takeout.
(3) It is not so tough for South to bid 3♠. North went 2♠ opposite possibly no values at all. South has one sure trick with the ace of clubs and an extra trump as well.

CHAPTER 19
DOUBLES

Negative Doubles

All the basic material on negative doubles is in the *Guide To Better Acol Bridge*. There are three areas you should discuss in your regular partnerships.

1. Negative double after a 1♡ overcall

WEST	NORTH	EAST	SOUTH
1♣	1♡	Dble	

versus

WEST	NORTH	EAST	SOUTH
1♣	1♡	1♠	

Many partnerships use the double to show exactly four spades and the 1♠ bid to show 5+ spades. In each case the strength is 6+ points.

Other partnerships prefer to use the 1♠ bid to show 4+ spades and the double to deny four spades. The theory is that we can handle 1♣ : (Pass) : 1♠ as a 4-card suit well enough and 1♣ : (1♢) : 1♠ shows 4+ spades and we can manage that as well, so why do we need 1♣ : (1♡) : 1♠ to show five spades? Why not use the 1♠ bid for 4+ spades as usual and harness the double to deal with the problem hands, the 6-9 point hands with the unbid minor and which cannot bid 1NT because of the lack of a stopper in hearts?

After 1♣ : (1♡) : ? what would you call with these?

♠ 6 3	♠ 6 3 2	♠ 5 4 2
♡ 9 6 2	♡ 9 6 2	♡ 6 3 2
♢ K Q 3 2	♢ K Q 7 3	♢ K 10 8 5 3
♣ K 8 6 3	♣ Q 7 5	♣ A 2

If 1♣ can be a 3-card suit, then raising to 2♣ with only 4-card support is not attractive although it is rarely fatal. On the second and third hands, it would be normal to pass 1♡. Using the double to show 6-9 points without 4 spades would allow you to double on each of the above. It would be reasonable to play this negative double as promising 4+ cards in the unbid minor. This would certainly help competitive action later if fourth player raises to 2♡.

2. Rebids by the opener when fourth player raises the suit overcalled

WEST	NORTH	EAST	SOUTH
1♣	1♠	Dble	2♠
?			

What action should West take with these hands?

(1)	(2)	(3)
♠ 6 4	♠ J 3	♠ 4 2
♡ 9 3	♡ 9 6 4 2	♡ Q J 3 2
♢ K Q 3	♢ K Q	♢ K Q
♣ A K 8 6 3 2	♣ A Q 7 4 2	♣ A K J 9 2

As responder need have no more than 6 points for the double, opener needs about 19 points to bid game. If opener is going to bid at the three-level with 12 points or with 17-18, how can responder ever tell when to push on to game and when to leave it at three? If opener bids 3♣ with (1), what would opener do with the ♡A instead of the ♡9?

If opener bids 3♡ on (2) with a 7-loser, 12-point hand, how can opener describe the superior 6-loser hand (3)?

The recommended solution is that opener should pass 2♠ with a minimum opening without four hearts. On (1) opener should pass. If 2♠ reverts to responder, the 3-over-2 rule (see Chapters 17-18) will ensure that the bidding does not end there. Responder can now support opener's minor with four, bid the other minor with five or double again with other patterns.

A bid by opener should show the 16-18 point 5-6 loser hand (bid 3♡ on hand 3) while double by opener shows four hearts in a minimum hand. This is important so that your side is not cut out of a heart contract by a further spade raise.

3. The negative double as an invitational raise

WEST	NORTH	EAST	SOUTH
1♡	2♢	?	

In standard style, 2♡ is a modest raise and many play that the jump to 3♡ is a limit raise (10-12). The game raise of 4♡ is still used as a pre-emptive raise while bidding the enemy suit covers hands of 13+ points including those with support for opener.

Those who use pre-emptive jump-raises or the Jacoby 2NT do not relish the loss of these bids. However, 2NT is needed here as a natural bid, 10-12 points, their suit stopped, no primary support for opener's major and no 4+ cards in the other major.

To cover the gamut of raises one can play :

2♡ = normal single raise

3♡ and 4♡ = pre-emptive raises

3-their-suit = game-force raise (like the Jacoby 2NT)

Double and support opener at 3-level = limit raise

2NT = natural, 10-12

Double and bid their suit next time = game-force without primary support for opener

Once they have bid, the usefulness of a pre-emptive raise to the three-level is doubtful. One could use 2♡ as 6-9 points and 3-card support, 3♡ as 6-9 points with 4-card support and the rest as above. The jump to the 3-level will have some pre-emptive effect but the hand will include some defence. In addition, jumping to the three-level with 4-card support follows the principles from the Law of Total Tricks.

Responsive doubles

(1) At the two-level

WEST	NORTH	EAST	SOUTH
1♢	Dble	2♢	?

With 6+ points, South is expected to bid and a bid of 2♡ or 2♠ would show 6-9 points and a 4+ suit. What should South do with two 4-card majors?

♠ K 7 5 4	South could bid 2♡ or 2♠ but it
♡ K 5 3 2	is silly to pick one of the majors
♢ 10 5 3	and find you are in a 4-3 fit with
♣ J 8	a 4-4 fit in the other major.

The solution is to use double for takeout, sensible here since a penalty double has little value when they bid and raise a suit to the two-level. South's double after partner has made a takeout double and third player raises opener is called a 'responsive double'. It shows two 4- or 5-card suits of the same rank. At the two-level, 6+ points is the expected strength.

If the suit opened is a major, (1♡) : Double : (2♡) for example, the responsive double shows both minors. The responsive double is valuable in eliminating the guess when the suits are of the same rank and you have four or five cards in each.

The responsive double can also be used with stronger hands:

♠ K 7 5 4	After the same start as above,
♡ K 5 3 2	South would double and raise
♢ 10 5 3	partner's major to the three-level
♣ A 8	as a game invitation.

If West pushes on to 3♢, passed back to South, South would pass with 6-9 points (3-over-3 rule) but with 10-12 points, South should double again.

With 13+ points and both majors, South could start with a double and raise partner's major to game. If West raises to 3♢, South could insist on game and partner choosing the major by bidding 4♢.

The responsive double applies only if third player raises opener's suit. If responder changes suit, double is best played as penalties.

WEST	NORTH	EAST	SOUTH
1♢	Dble	1♠	Dble

South's double is a penalty double. It shows 6+ points and 4+ spades. Exposing a probable psyche is an important use for the double in this context. South may have been planning to bid 1♠ or 2♠ or more. East's spades may be genuine but there are enough larcenous players in the bridge jungle to require a survival kit of penalty doubles here.

(2) At the three-level

WEST	NORTH	EAST	SOUTH
1♢	Dble	3♢	?

South is expected to be a bit stronger to bid a major here and double would still be responsive with equal length in the majors. Expectancy would be an 8-loser hand or just a touch under. Likewise, a bid of 3♡ or 3♠ has game-inviting overtones.

WEST	NORTH	EAST	SOUTH
1♠	Dble	3♠	?

Double by South would show both minors and game-invitational values. Expectancy is at least 4-4 in the minors and about a 7-loser hand.

WEST	NORTH	EAST	SOUTH
1♡	Dble	3♡	?

It is worth discussing this particular sequence in your partnerships. You can treat the double here as above, a responsive double showing both minors and inviting game.

There is a case for treating this auction differently and using 3♠ as purely competing for the part-score with a 5+ spade suit (3-over-3 rule) and to use the double as a game invitation in spades. The 3♠ bid could then be quite weak, as low as 6 points as long as advancer (the partner of the doubler or overcaller) had more than four spades.

My preference is to use the double as responsive with both minors and to bid 3♠ with respectable values, allowing partner to raise to game with better than a minimum double. However, there is merit in the other approach.

(3) At the four-level

WEST	NORTH	EAST	SOUTH
1♢	Dble	4♢	?

If responder has a semblance of sanity, you will have little need for a penalty double. South's double should show both majors and game-inviting values or better. You can hardly be precise here as you have lost so much bidding space.

Where the opposition suit is a major, responder's support may be no more than four trumps. Double as responsive for the minors is still recommended but if partner does not have a great holding in the minors, partner can leave the double in. Advancer should have 10+ HCP for the double. If advancer wants to insist on partner choosing a minor, bid 4NT.

Doubling no-trumps for takeout

WEST	NORTH	EAST	SOUTH
1♠	No	1NT	?

Traditionally the double of 1NT is for penalties but there is little value doubling a 1NT response for penalties. The opponents have about 20 points together and most of the strength sits over the doubler. It is best to play double by South in auctions like the above as a takeout double of the suit opened.

WEST	NORTH	EAST	SOUTH
1♡	Dble	2NT	?

Most play East's 2NT over the double as a good raise of the suit opened. Double by South in this context is best used as a responsive double, showing both minors (and sacrifice possibilities) after a major suit opening and both majors after a minor suit opening. The double should show only competitive values. Bid their suit if stronger.

Competitive doubles

The competitive double is a double (intended for takeout) which occurs later in the auction than a straightforward takeout double or a negative double. Bridge terminology could improve in this area. So many doubles these days are meant for takeout that their description would improve if prefaced by the player making the double. Thus, the traditional takeout double after an opening bid could be a 'defender's double', the negative double would be 'responder's double' and a second round double by opener would naturally be 'opener's double'.

A competitive double occurs generally on the second round of bidding or is a double for takeout by the advancer.

WEST	NORTH	EAST	SOUTH
1♡	2◇	2♡	Dble

This double by advancer is akin to the negative double. It would indicate spades and tolerance for clubs or diamonds as well.

WEST	NORTH	EAST	SOUTH
1♡	1♠	2◇	Dble

It is strange to have a double for takeout when there is only one suit left. However, it is silly to use double for penalties when the suit doubled is forcing. South's double here shows a club suit plus tolerance for spades.

Competitive doubles are common when following the rule of 3-over-2:

WEST	NORTH	EAST	SOUTH
1◇	1♠	Dble	2♠
No	No	Dble	

East's first double is negative, a responder's double. East's second double is competing for the part-score. East is not prepared to sell out to 2♠.

Competitive doubles by opener occur when responder has bid. After a major suit response, the double by opener is used to show 3-card support and so the double is known as a 'support double':

WEST	NORTH	EAST	SOUTH
1◇	No	1♠	2♣
Dble			

Opener's double shows 3-card spade support. The strength might be a minimum opening but it might also be a strong hand. After hearing responder's reply to the double, opener might be intending to bid on to game.

One of the great benefits of the competitive double occurs when the double is not used.

WEST	NORTH	EAST	SOUTH
1◇	No	1♠	2♣
?			

Given that the double shows 3-card support, what would it mean if West bid 2♠? This should show the 4-card raise. The ability to distinguish between 3-card support and 4-card support is essential if the partnership is to compete sensibly when the bidding has reached the three-level.

A rebid by opener of 2◇ would show long diamonds but would also deny three spades (failure to double). A rebid of 2♡ by opener would be a reverse, strong hand with 4 hearts and 5+ diamonds but it would deny three spades (failure to double). *Corollary:* Since opener has denied 3-card support, responder's rebid of the same suit should be a 6+ suit (or an extremely strong 5-card suit).

Opener needs no extra strength to double to show the 3-card support. Pass by opener would show a minimum opening with no attractive descriptive rebid available. The implication is less than 3-card support for partner although opener is allowed to pass with poor 3-card support if the enemy bidding has caused opener to revalue the hand to a sub-minimum opening.

The primary concern of any competitive double is the major suits. Thus, the competitive double focuses first on 3-card support for responder's major and second on any unbid major.

WEST	NORTH	EAST	SOUTH
1♣	No	1◇	1♠
Dble			

Opener's double here would show four hearts, just like a regular negative double or takeout double of 1♠ implies four hearts. This in turn allows responder to bid 1◇ freely over 1♣ with 4 diamonds and 4 hearts. There is no risk that a 4-4 heart fit will be missed since opener has the double available to show the hearts, even with minimum values.

Many duplicate players follow the general principle that *all doubles of a suit at the one- or two-level are for takeout regardless of the preceding auction.* Some add a few restrictions (such as doubles after a redouble are for penalties, doubles after a takeout double has been passed for penalties are also for penalties) but it is quite workable to play all suit doubles at low level are for takeout. This would include doubles of an overcall after partner's 1NT opening.

Playing for penalties

The best low-level penalties arise when you are short in partner's suit and strong in the enemy suit. If a double is stipulated as takeout, then to obtain penalties you pass. Partner is very likely to re-open the bidding with a takeout double of some kind and again you pass this for penalties.

How high should competitive doubles be played?

The more you play competitive doubles, the more you appreciate their value. Most play competitive doubles only at the one- or two-level. Negative doubles are often played to the four-level and responsive doubles to the 4◇ level. Doubles of pre-emptive action are usually played for takeout in the same way that doubles of pre-emptive openings are played for takeout. You are more likely to have a hand short in their pre-empt suit than long in that suit.

EXERCISES ON DOUBLES

A. The bidding has started:

WEST	NORTH	EAST	SOUTH
1◇	1♠	Dble	2♠
?			

What should West do now?

1. ♠ 7 4	2. ♠ 9 6 2	3. ♠ 7 4	4. ♠ 8 5	5. ♠ 6 3
♡ K 6	♡ K 8	♡ K 9 6 2	♡ A J 6 4	♡ Q 2
◇ A J 8 4 3	◇ A J 8 6 3 2	◇ K Q 9 3 2	◇ K J 9 7 3	◇ K Q J 9 5 3
♣ A Q 6 4	♣ K J	♣ A 6	♣ A K	♣ A K J

B. The bidding has started:

WEST	NORTH	EAST	SOUTH
1♡	Dble	2♡	?

What should South do now?

1. ♠ J 4 3 2	2. ♠ J 4	3. ♠ J 9 8	4. ♠ 9 4	5. ♠ 3 2
♡ Q 6	♡ Q 6 3 2	♡ 9 7 4	♡ J 9 8	♡ A 2
◇ K 9 8 7 3	◇ K 9 8 7 3	◇ A K 4 2	◇ A J 7 4	◇ 8 6 5 4 3
♣ 9 7	♣ 4 2	♣ 10 9 5	♣ K 9 5 2	♣ A 10 8 3

C. The bidding has started:

WEST	NORTH	EAST	SOUTH
1◇	No	1♠	2♣
?			

What should West do now?

1. ♠ J 4 3 2	2. ♠ K J 4	3. ♠ J 9 8	4. ♠ 9	5. ♠ 3
♡ A Q 6	♡ A K 7	♡ 9	♡ J 9 8	♡ A 2
◇ K 9 8 7 3	◇ Q J 6 5 2	◇ A K J 7 4 2	◇ A K J 7 4 2	◇ K Q 8 6 5
♣ K	♣ J 2	♣ K 9 5	♣ K 9 5	♣ A 10 8 3 2

COMPETITIVE BIDDING: How should the following hands be bid? West is the dealer each time and neither side is vulnerable.

SET 33— WEST	SET 33 — NORTH	SET 33 — EAST	SET 33 — SOUTH
1. ♠ 8 6	1. ♠ K Q 10 5 2	1. ♠ 9 7 4	1. ♠ A J 3
♡ K J 7 3	♡ 10 6 5	♡ A Q 8 2	♡ 9 4
◇ A J 7 5 4	◇ K 9	◇ 10 6	◇ Q 8 3 2
♣ K 10	♣ A 7 3	♣ Q 8 4 2	♣ J 9 6 5
2. ♠ 10 5 4	2. ♠ K J 6	2. ♠ A Q 9 8 3	2. ♠ 7 2
♡ 9 8 5	♡ A K 6 3	♡ 10 2	♡ Q J 7 4
◇ A Q 7 6 5	◇ J	◇ K 9 8 2	◇ 10 4 3
♣ 5 4	♣ K Q 7 6 2	♣ 10 3	♣ A J 9 8
3. ♠ 7 5 4	3. ♠ K Q J 6 2	3. ♠ A 9 8 3	3. ♠ 10
♡ Q J 10 7	♡ 8 5	♡ A 6 4 3	♡ K 9 2
◇ A J 8 3	◇ K 10 7 6	◇ 4	◇ Q 9 5 2
♣ 6 3	♣ 10 8	♣ A K J 5	♣ Q 9 7 4 2
4. ♠ A 10 6 5	4. ♠ K 9 8	4. ♠ Q 3	4. ♠ J 7 4 2
♡ 9	♡ 10 7 5 3	♡ J 8 2	♡ A K Q 6 4
◇ A 8 7 4 2	◇ K 9	◇ Q J 10 3	◇ 6 5
♣ Q 8 7	♣ J 10 6 2	♣ A 9 4 3	♣ K 5
5. ♠ 10	5. ♠ K 8 6 4	5. ♠ A J 7 5 2	5. ♠ Q 9 3
♡ A Q 8 7 4	♡ J 5 3	♡ 9 2	♡ K 10 6
◇ A 7 2	◇ 10 8 6 4 3	◇ K J 9 5	◇ Q
♣ K J 6 2	♣ 4	♣ 7 5	♣ A Q 10 9 8 3
6. ♠ K 9 2	6. ♠ 8 6	6. ♠ A Q 10 5 4	6. ♠ J 7 3
♡ 2	♡ Q 10 7	♡ 8 6 5 4	♡ A K J 9 3
◇ A K 9 5	◇ 10 8 4 2	◇ 6 3	◇ Q J 7
♣ A Q 10 3 2	♣ 9 6 5 4	♣ J 8	♣ K 7

PLAY HANDS ON DOUBLES
(These hands can be made up by using pages 176-183)

Hand 73: Competitive double — Trump technique

Dealer North : E-W vulnerable

```
                NORTH
             ♠ 7 5 4
             ♡ K J 10 6
             ◇ A 9 8 3
             ♣ 6 3
WEST                      EAST
♠ 10                     ♠ K Q J 6 2
♡ Q 7 2                  ♡ 9 5
◇ Q J 5 2                ◇ K 10 7 6
♣ Q 9 7 4 2              ♣ 10 8
                SOUTH
             ♠ A 9 8 3
             ♡ A 8 4 3
             ◇ 4
             ♣ A K J 5
```

WEST	NORTH	EAST	SOUTH
	No	No	1♣
No	1◇	1♠	Dble
No	2♡	No	4♡
No	No	No	

Bidding: After a 1♣ opening, when you have 4 diamonds and a 4-card major, it is usually best to respond 1◇. East is just strong enough to come in with 1♠ at this vulnerability. After East's 1♠ overcall, South's double shows 4 hearts. There is no additional message in this auction and no promise of 3-card diamond support. The missing major takes priority. When North can bid 2♡, South's hand is worth 19 points, enough to bid game.

Lead: King of spades. The obvious choice.

Recommended play: Take ♠A and start a cross-ruff: ◇A, diamond ruff, ♣A, ♣K, club ruff with the ♡J. If East had the ♡Q, East would almost certainly over-ruff. When the ♡J holds, ruff another diamond and lead another club, ruffing with the ♡10. When the fourth diamond is ruffed in dummy, declarer is home (even if East discarded a diamond on the third club and ruffs in with ♡9, forcing out the ♡A).

Notes: (1) If declarer starts with ♠A, ♡K and runs the ♡J (playing East for the ♡Q), West wins and a third trump leaves declarer at least one trick short.
(2) Cashing the top hearts first could be risky if trumps are 4-1. Leaving the trumps alone and starting on a cross-ruff gives declarer a chance to overruff either opponent.
(3) It would be reasonable for declarer to play a spade at trick 2, since a spade trick can be set up. If East cashes two spades and leads a fourth spade, North can overruff West.

Hand 74: Support double — Trump technique

Dealer East : Both vulnerable

```
                NORTH
             ♠ J 7 3
             ♡ A K Q 9 3
             ◇ Q J 7
             ♣ K 7
WEST                      EAST
♠ A Q 10 5 4            ♠ K 9 2
♡ 8 6 5 4              ♡ 2
◇ 6 3                  ◇ A K 9 5
♣ J 8                  ♣ A Q 10 3 2
                SOUTH
             ♠ 8 6
             ♡ J 10 7
             ◇ 10 8 4 2
             ♣ 9 6 5 4
```

WEST	NORTH	EAST	SOUTH
		1♣	No
1♠	2♡	Dble	No
2♠	No	4♠	All pass

Bidding: It is risky to come into the bidding when both opponents are bidding, but North has enough. East's double shows 3-card support for spades (2♠ would thus show 4-card support). West is content with two spades but with 16 HCP and a singleton in North's suit, East has enough to bid the game.

Lead: Ace of hearts. Clear-cut.

Recommended play: South should signal with the ♡J. This will discourage a heart continuation if North does not have the queen (the ♡J denies the ♡Q) and will tell North it is safe to continue the hearts if North does have the queen. If North shifts to a low diamond, declarer can win, cash ♠K and ♠A, then lead the ♣J to take the club finesse while dummy still has a trump. North covers, and the ace wins. West can draw the last trump and set up an extra club trick to make eleven tricks.

Notes: (1) If North continues with a heart at trick 2, declarer ruffs in dummy. Declarer cannot afford to draw trumps for if the club finesse loses, West could lose a club and three hearts.
(2) On a heart continuation ruffed at trick 2, declarer should play a low club to the jack. North wins but dummy's clubs are set up. If North plays a third heart, dummy ruffs with the 9, the ♠K is cashed followed by ◇A, ◇K, diamond ruff and trumps are drawn. Making eleven tricks.

Hand 75: Penalty pass — Competitive double — Defensive technique

Dealer South : Nil vulnerable

NORTH
- ♠ A J 6 5 2
- ♡ 9 2
- ◇ K J 9 5
- ♣ 7 5

WEST
- ♠ K 8 7 4
- ♡ J 5 3
- ◇ 10 8 6 4 3
- ♣ 4

EAST
- ♠ Q 9 3
- ♡ K 10 6
- ◇ Q
- ♣ A Q 10 9 8 3

SOUTH
- ♠ 10
- ♡ A Q 8 7 4
- ◇ A 7 2
- ♣ K J 6 2

WEST	NORTH	EAST	SOUTH
			1♡
No	1♠	2♣	No
No	Dble	No	No
No			

Bidding: Even though both opponents have bid, East's suit is good enough to justify 2♣. With good trumps and short in partner's suit, South has the right hand type for penalties. South passes and when North re-opens with a competitive double, South passes for penalties. No action by North is as attractive as a double which leaves 2♠, 2♡, 2NT, 2◇ or a penalty pass open. The double gives you the most options and is usually the best action when you have enough to bid but no clear-cut choice.

Lead: 10 of spades. Nothing else suggests itself.

Recommended play: North wins with the ♠A and could give South a spade ruff. North however should switch to the ♡9. If South had ♡A-K, South would have led a heart, and so South's hearts might well be headed by A-Q or K-Q. In either case, South will welcome a heart switch. East ducks and South wins with the ♡Q, cashes the ♡A and leads the ♡8 to give North a ruff. North recognises the ♡8 as a suit-preference signal for spades and returns the ♠2, low card for the low suit, diamonds. After South ruffs the spade, South is in no need of any more ruffs and so South continues with ◇A and another diamond. South comes to two more trump tricks and declarer is held to five tricks. Three down, +500 to North-South.

Notes : (1) North-South can make 4♡, but it is unlikely that they will reach game.
(2) If North wins with the ace of spades and returns a spade at trick 2, it is unlikely that North will come to a heart ruff and declarer might escape for two down.

Hand 76: Bidding after negative double — Hold-up play — Defensive technique — Card combination

Dealer West : N-S vulnerable

NORTH
- ♠ 8 6
- ♡ K J
- ◇ A J 8 4 3
- ♣ A K 7 4

WEST
- ♠ J 7 4
- ♡ Q 10 8 3
- ◇ Q 9 7 6
- ♣ J 8

EAST
- ♠ A Q 10 9 5
- ♡ 6 5 2
- ◇ 5
- ♣ Q 10 9 2

SOUTH
- ♠ K 3 2
- ♡ A 9 7 4
- ◇ K 10 2
- ♣ 6 5 3

WEST	NORTH	EAST	SOUTH
No	1◇	1♠	Dble
2♠	3♣	No	3NT
No	No	No	

Bidding: East has enough to overcall but West's raise is a bit skimpy. If challenged, West would claim the vulnerability made him do it. North's 3♣ denies four hearts and shows about 16-18 points. That is enough to encourage South to take a shot at 3NT. Note South's problem if 3♣ could be a minimum opening or could be 16-18. That is why opener should bid at the three-level in these auctions only with the 16-18 hand (all right, all right, an excellent 15 will do).

Lead: 4 of spades. Any other lead could lead to a divorce.

Recommended play: If East wins with the ace of spades and returns a spade, South should hold off with the king. South wins the third spade and should then lead a club to the ace, followed by a low diamond to the 10. West wins but has no more spades. South comes to nine tricks easily.

Notes: (1) East should not play ♠A at trick 1. The bidding marks South with the ♠K and East can afford to put in the 9. This will discover whether South started with K-J-x (and West perhaps with 7-4-2). It is very hard for South to duck the 9 (East may have Q-J-10-9-x in spades and West A-7-4 and then South would make no spade tricks). If South does duck, East can continue with the ♠Q and if South ducks again to try to block the suit, East will have scored a spectacular triumph.
(2) After South takes the first or second spade, South needs to bring in the diamond suit. The bidding gives no clear-cut indication who has the ◇Q. As dummy's diamond tenace has the 8 as well, it is best to start with ◇K, followed by ◇10. This caters for West holding Q-9-x-x. You cannot deal with Q-9-x-x with East.
(3) If South starts with ◇K and then ◇2 to the jack, West playing low each time, West scores a diamond trick. Because of the ◇8 in dummy, it is vital to lead the ◇10 after the ◇K.

CHAPTER 20
MICHAELS CUE-BIDS

The unusual 2NT overcall showing a weak two-suiter with at least 5-5 in the minors has been around for a long time. It is a useful tool to find a good sacrifice against their major suit games. Used properly, the unusual 2NT fulfils an important role in your duplicate armoury. (For more about the Unusual 2NT, see the *Guide To Better Acol Bridge*.)

It was not long before the question was asked, 'Why do we have a bid only for both minors? Why can't we show other two-suiters, too?' Michaels Cue-bids were devised to answer that question. This is how they work:

(1♣) : 2♣ = 5+ hearts and a 5+ minor
(1♡) : 2♡ = 5+ spades and a 5+ minor
(1◇) : 2◇ = at least 5-5 in the majors
(1♣) : 2♣ = at least 5-5 in the majors

The normal strength is less than an opening hand.

Bidding the enemy suit at once was traditionally used to show a huge hand, one that would have been opened with a game-forcing bid. These bids were used to insist on game whereas a double followed by a new suit or a jump-rebid is not forcing on advancer. Such powerhouse hands are rare and just as weak twos are preferred over strong twos, so the Michaels Two-Suiters have taken over from the game-force cue-bids.

After a minor suit opening, the Michaels Cue shows at least 5-5 in the majors. After their 1◇ opening, you would bid 2◇ with these:

♠ A Q 8 6 3	♠ K Q J 3 2	♠ Q J 7 6 3 2
♡ K 10 8 7 3	♡ J 10 9 7 4 2	♡ J 9 8 6 4 2
◇ 8	◇ 3	◇ 5
♣ 6 4	♣ 9	♣ - - -

After a major suit opening, Michaels shows 5+ cards in the other major and a 5+ minor. These would be suitable for 2♡ Michaels over their 1♡ opening:

♠ Q J 8 6 3	♠ J 10 6 3 2	♠ A J 7 5 4 2
♡ 9	♡ 9	♡ 6 3
◇ K Q 9 3 2	◇ 3	◇ K 10 8 5 2
♣ 6 4	♣ K Q 7 5 4 2	♣ - - -

For a 5-5, the expected strength is 7-11 HCP. For a 6-5 the strength can drop by two points or so, and for a 7-5, 6-6 or freakier, the point count is hardly relevant because of the great playing strength. For a 5-5, you should have at least four honour cards in the two long suits. For a 6-5, three honours will do. The expected playing strength is 6-7 losers for a minimum and 5-6 losers for a maximum.

The aim is not just to find a good sacrifice but also to find your own good major suit games. With a strong fit (4+ cards) in partner's major, advancer needs only three useful tricks to bid game.

Advancer's action opposite major suit Michaels

(a) With a weak hand

With no ambitions for game, advancer should support partner's major if possible. Bid it at the cheapest level or make a jump bid as a pre-empt. With no fit for the major, advancer can bid 3♣. Partner corrects to 3◇ with diamonds.

WEST	NORTH	EAST	SOUTH
1♡	2♡	No	?

If weak, South can bid 2♠ or pre-empt with 3♠. The jump to 4♠ might be pre-emptive but might also be based on game-going values. With a doubleton in spades and a doubleton or worse in one of the minors, it would be prudent to bid 2♠. It is highly likely that partner's minor is opposite your minor suit shortage.

With no fit for spades, South bids 3♣ and North will correct to 3◇ with diamonds. Some play that 3♣ and 3◇ are genuine suits and advancer should use 2NT to ask for partner's minor. This is playable but it is superior to use 2NT as a strong bid to find out more about partner's shape and strength.

(b) With a strong hand

You may bid game in partner's suit or 3NT, bid the enemy suit to ask for a stopper for 3NT or use the 2NT enquiry with sufficient values to invite game or insist on game.

Replies to 2NT after a major suit Michaels

You could play simply 3♣ or 3◇ shows the minor and let advancer take over or you can adopt a more detailed set of replies:

3♣ = minimum, second suit is clubs
3◇ = minimum, second suit is diamonds
3♡ = maximum, second suit is clubs
3♠ = maximum, second suit is diamonds
3NT = 6-5 with 6-major and 5+ clubs
4♣ = 6-5 with 5-major and 6+ clubs
4◇ = 6-5 with 5-major and 6+ diamonds
4♡ = 6-5 with 6-major and 5+ diamonds

Advancer should be able to place the contract after this information. The replies for a 6-5 spill into the four-level as it is unlikely that advancer will want to end in 3NT opposite such freak shape.

Advancer's action opposite minor suit Michaels

With a weak hand, support the major where you hold more cards. With equal length, choose the stronger holding. Jumps to 3-major are pre-emptive.

With a strong hand, bid game or bid the other minor (natural and forcing), bid their suit to ask for a stopper for 3NT or use the 2NT strong inquiry to which opener replies 3♣ (5-5, minimum), 3◇ (5-5, maximum), 3♡ (6 hearts) or 3♠ (6 spades).

Michaels only in the majors

Some play that bidding their major is Michaels but bidding their minor is natural. Given the frequency of artificial club openings and fake diamonds, this is a sensible approach. However, on the basis of frequency and usefulness, you will be better off playing Michaels in all suits. The hands suitable for a natural overcall of their minor can be shown by (1♣) : 3♣ or (1♢) : 3♢ as an intermediate jump or by passing and bidding the minor later if you judge that the hand is not worth the three-level.

Michaels with strong hands

The basic Michaels two-suiter is a weak hand, below 12 HCP. With similar shape and opening points, you can start with an overcall or a double, depending on the suits held and the suit strengths. If you double, you must be strong enough to remove an unwelcome reply to a good 5+ major.

Many pairs play that Michaels can be the usual weak holding or a very strong hand, about 3-4 losers. The strong variety must be good enough that you intend to bid again if third player jumps to game. For example:

WEST	NORTH	EAST	SOUTH
1♡	2♡	4♡	No
No	?		

With the strong variety, North should double with five spades and bid 4♠ with six spades. South can remove to 5♣ ('pass-or-correct': pass with clubs, bid 5♢ with diamonds) with no tolerance for the spades.

WEST	NORTH	EAST	SOUTH
1♠	2♠	4♠	No
No	?		

With the strong hand, North can double or bid 5♣/5♢ with 6-minor or 4NT with six hearts.

How to bid your powerhouse if you play Michaels

To show a strong hand after they open, start with a double. After partner's minimum suit reply:
Bid new suit or raise partner = 16-18, 5 losers
Jump new suit or jump-raise partner = 19+, 4 losers
Bid the enemy suit = very powerful, usually 3 losers or better. Even these powerhouse hands need to be bid conservatively if no trump fit exists and you do not have a self-sufficient suit (Suit Quality 10).

WEST	S	W	N	E	EAST
♠ A K 3	1♢	Dbl	No	1♠	♠ 10 7 5 2
♡ K Q J 8	No	2♢	No	?	♡ 6 3
♢ 6					♢ 8 7 5 4 2
♣ A K Q 3 2					♣ 9 6

After the doubler bids the enemy suit, a sound idea is to have advancer repeat the first suit bid with a hopeless hand (even without 5+ cards in that suit). The doubler is allowed to pass that bid. On the hand above East would bid 2♠ and West can pass this. With reasonable values making game likely, the advancer rebids anything other than the original suit reply. The bidding will then continue to game.

Michaels over weak twos and pre-empts

Some pairs use the Michaels' concept over weak two openings. The big difference is that here the Michaels two-suited bid shows a good hand, a sound opening, around the five-loser mark. It is reasonable to hope for two tricks from partner.

Playing 'Strong Michaels' follows the basic rule of competitive bidding: over their strong bids, your actions are weak; over their weak openings, your actions are strong. See Chapter 22 for details.

The same idea can be applied over pre-empts with (3♣) : 4♣ or (3♢) : 4♢ showing at least 5-5 in the majors with a 5-loser hand or better. (3♡) : 4♡ can show 5+ spades and a 5+ minor but you would not use this over 3♠, since this bypasses 4♡.

Bidding after their Michaels Cue-Bid in a major

Suppose the bidding has gone 1♠ : (2♠). Responder has a choice of these actions :
3♠ = sound raise to the two-level
3♣/3♢ = new suit, natural, forcing
3♡ = their suit, asking for a stopper for 3NT
Double = looking for penalties, the same sort of hand which would redouble after 1♠ : (Double).
2NT = limit raise or stronger. Promises support for opener and 10+ points. Opener may bid, bid a new suit as a trial bid or sign off in 3-major. A new suit beyond 3-major is a cue-bid with slam potential.
4♣ / 4♢ / 4♡ = splinter, as usual over 1♠

If third player doubles partner's Michaels Cue all bids retain their usual meaning and Redouble says, 'Please make the cheapest possible bid and then pass my rebid.' This allows advancer to escape into a long, strong suit.

If third player bids, advancer should pass with a weak hand unless a sacrifice is attractive. Be reluctant to sacrifice with a balanced hand and do not sacrifice with only 3-card support for partner. With a good hand, support partner's major (3-major invites game), double for penalties, bid game or bid 4NT to ask for partner's minor.

Bidding after their Michaels Cue-Bid in a minor

Suppose the bidding hast started 1♢ : (2♢), showing both majors.
3♢ = sound raise to 2♢
4♢ or 5♢ = pre-emptive
3♣ = 6-9 points, long clubs, not forcing
2♡ = 10+ points, game-try or stronger in clubs. May have diamond support as well.
2♠ = 10+ points, game-try or better in diamonds

This approach is similar to bidding over the unusual 2NT where 3♣ = game-try or better in hearts and 3♢ = game-try or better in spades.
3♡/3♠/4♣ = splinter raise, game-force
Double = Looking for penalties, 10+ points
2NT = Natural and limited, both majors stopped
3NT = Natural, with stoppers in both majors

The structure follows analogous paths when the bidding has started 1♣ : (2♣).

EXERCISES ON MICHAELS CUE-BIDS

A. Right hand opponent has opened 1♡. What action would you take, playing Michaels, with these hands?

	1.	2.	3.	4.	5.
♠	A J 4 3 2	K J 10 5 2	J 9 8 6 4 3	A K 4 3 2	K 6 4 3 2
♡	A Q	2	---	2	2
◇	K 9 8 6	Q J 10 6 3	4	K Q J 9 8 4 3	Q 4
♣	7 2	4 2	Q 9 7 6 4 2	---	K 8 5 3 2

B. The bidding has started (1♡) : 2♡ : (No) : to you.   What would you do with these hands?

	1.	2.	3.	4.	5.
♠	7	K 9 6 2	K 9 7 5 4	Q 5	9 6
♡	K 9 6 2	J 8 4 2	7 6 2	A Q 6 4	8 7 5 4 2
◇	J 9 7 3 2	A J	Q J 8 4	A K 4	A K 3 2
♣	A 9 6	A 7 2	3	Q 8 5 2	6 3

C. The bidding has started:

WEST	NORTH	EAST	SOUTH
1♠	2♠	No	2NT
No	?		What should North rebid with these hands?

	1.	2.	3.	4.	5.
♠	7	2	9 7	---	9
♡	K 10 9 6 2	K J 8 7 4 2	K Q J 6 2	A Q 6 4 2	K 7 5 4 2
◇	J 9	7	A J 10 8 4	A 4 3	K Q 9 7 4 3 2
♣	Q J 10 6 4	A J 10 9 2	3	J 10 9 8 5	---

COMPETITIVE BIDDING : How should the following hands be bid? West is the dealer each time and neither side is vulnerable.

	SET 34— WEST	SET 34 — NORTH	SET 34 — EAST	SET 34 — SOUTH
1. ♠ ♡ ◇ ♣	8 6 K J 7 3 2 A K 9 K 10 2	K Q 10 5 2 10 6 5 --- A 9 8 7 3	9 7 Q 8 Q J 6 5 3 Q J 6 4	A J 4 3 A 9 4 10 8 7 4 2 5
2. ♠ ♡ ◇ ♣	A 7 A 8 7 5 J 9 6 9 8 7 4	Q 6 4 2 3 A K 3 Q J 6 5 2	K J 9 8 3 K Q 9 4 2 8 2 10	10 5 J 10 6 Q 10 7 5 4 A K 3
3. ♠ ♡ ◇ ♣	Q Q J 10 7 K 8 4 A K 6 3 2	J 8 7 5 4 A 8 3 2 10 8 7 4	A K K 9 6 5 4 J 10 6 Q J 5	10 9 6 3 2 2 A Q 9 7 5 3 9
4. ♠ ♡ ◇ ♣	J 10 6 2 J 9 4 Q 9 7 2 A 6	A K 9 8 4 3 6 3 8 5 Q 10 3	7 A Q 10 8 5 A K J 10 4 K 4	Q 5 K 7 2 6 3 J 9 8 7 5 2
5. ♠ ♡ ◇ ♣	A 6 3 A K J 10 7 2 K J 6 2	Q J 7 4 2 9 3 K Q J 6 5 3	K 10 9 5 2 A 10 9 7 A 7 5 4	8 Q 8 6 5 4 8 4 3 Q 10 9 8
6. ♠ ♡ ◇ ♣	10 9 7 5 4 2 K Q 8 7 2 6 3	Q J 10 9 5 J 10 9 4 K 9 8 6	K J 8 3 3 A 8 5 3 2 J 7 5	A 6 A 6 4 K Q 7 A Q 10 4 2

PLAY HANDS ON MICHAELS CUE-BIDS
(These hands can be made up by using pages 176-183)

Hand 77: Michaels — Sacrifice — Defensive technique

Dealer North : Both vulnerable

NORTH
- ♠ Q J 5 2
- ♡ 9 8
- ◇ A J 8 6 3
- ♣ 5 2

WEST
- ♠ 9
- ♡ K 10 7
- ◇ K Q 10 9 5
- ♣ A 8 6 4

EAST
- ♠ K 6 3
- ♡ A Q J 6 5 2
- ◇ 7 2
- ♣ K 7

SOUTH
- ♠ A 10 8 7 4
- ♡ 4 3
- ◇ 4
- ♣ Q J 10 9 3

WEST	NORTH	EAST	SOUTH
	No	1♡	2♡
2NT	4♠	Dble	All pass

Bidding: Over South's 2♡, 2NT = 10+ HCP with support for opener. A jump to 4♡ by West would be a shape raise, 2NT is a raise based on strength. This enables your side to gauge whose hand it is. After a shape raise, you may wish to sacrifice, after a strength raise you tend to defend. With only one defensive trick, North should bid 4♠. Opposite seven losers, North brings two tricks and so 4♠ should be no more than two down. With values in spades, East doubles to indicate a desire to defend. West may overrule this with great shape or considerably extra strength.

Lead: 3 of spades or ace of hearts. A trump lead is often best when the opponents are sacrificing.

Recommended play: On a trump lead, North ducks this to the queen, repeats the spade finesse and draws the last trump. The clubs are set up and the defence takes two hearts and two clubs. One down.

Notes: (1) East-West can take 4♠ two down if East can ruff the third club with the ♠K. The defence might achieve this via ♡A lead, encouraged by West. East continues with the 2 of hearts, a suit-preference signal for clubs. If West switches to a low club to the king and a club comes back, East-West can collect 300.
(2) East-West can always make 4♡ but if East-West push on to 5♡, North-South will have a stunning victory if South leads the ♠A and switches to the singleton diamond. North wins and can give South a diamond ruff for one down.
(3) If North-South do not play Michaels and South merely overcalls 1♠, it would be tougher to find 4♠.

Hand 78: Michaels with a strong hand — Shape raise — Sacrifice decision

Dealer East : Nil vulnerable

NORTH
- ♠ Q J 10 6 4
- ♡ 10 9 6 5
- ◇ A
- ♣ J 10 2

WEST
- ♠ 3
- ♡ A Q J 7 2
- ◇ K Q 10 9 7 2
- ♣ A

EAST
- ♠ 8 2
- ♡ 8 4
- ◇ J 8 5
- ♣ K 8 7 5 4 3

SOUTH
- ♠ A K 9 7 5
- ♡ K 3
- ◇ 6 4 3
- ♣ Q 9 6

WEST	NORTH	EAST	SOUTH
		No	1♠
2♠	4♠	No	No
5◇	No	No	No

Bidding: West has only three losers. You can use Michaels with this strength as long as you do not pass out 4-major if they bid it. North has a shape raise and 4♠ shows 4+ trumps, decent shape but fewer than 10 HCP. West is not going to sell out to 4♠ and 5◇ shows 6+ diamonds and 5 hearts. East has no trouble passing but South has a tough problem deciding whether to pass, double or push on to 5♠. The balanced hand suggests not sacrificing and South has no significant defensive tricks against 5◇. Many would pass on the South cards.

Lead: Queen of spades or ace of diamonds.

Recommended play: On the ♠Q lead, South may well overtake and switch to a trump. North wins and may shift to a club or continue spades. West wins, crosses to dummy with a trump and takes the heart finesse. The ♡A is cashed, felling the king, followed by a low heart ruffed in dummy. A club taken by West allows the last trump to be drawn and the hearts are set up. Eleven tricks opposite next to nothing.

Notes: (1) On ◇A lead followed by a spade shift won by South and a second trump, the play follows similar lines. The second trump is won in dummy and then comes heart finesse, ♡A and a heart ruff.
(2) Double by West over 4♠ shows better defensive values while 4NT is used to show 6+ hearts. Then, if not interested in hearts, advancer bids 5♣ and partner will correct to diamonds if necessary.
(3) Given South has no defensive values against 5◇ (perhaps one spade trick but the ♡K looks badly placed), South could choose to sacrifice in 5♠. North's shortage on the bidding is likely to be in diamonds. West would double 5♠ and the defenders can collect four tricks (two hearts and two clubs) for +300 after the ♣A lead, while the ◇K lead would give South the chance to escape for one down.

Hand 79: Michaels over a minor — Sacrifice — Competitive judgement

Dealer South : N-S vulnerable

NORTH
- ♠ Q
- ♡ J 10 9 5
- ◇ J 10 9 4
- ♣ K 9 8 6

WEST
- ♠ 10 9 7 6 4 2
- ♡ K Q 8 7 2
- ◇ 6
- ♣ 3

EAST
- ♠ K J 8 3
- ♡ 3
- ◇ A 8 5 3 2
- ♣ J 7 5

SOUTH
- ♠ A 5
- ♡ A 6 4
- ◇ K Q 7
- ♣ A Q 10 4 2

WEST	NORTH	EAST	SOUTH
			1♣
2♣	3♣	4♠	Dble
No	No	No	

Bidding: West's 2♣ shows at least 5-5 in the majors. You need little strength with a 6-5 pattern. North has little but 3♣ is reasonable. (If the 1♣ opening might be short, Pass is more prudent.) East has the ideal hand to take a shot at game: 4+ support for one of the majors, short in the other major and an outside ace. East bids 4♠ hoping to make and expecting not to be worse than one down. It is hard for South with three aces and 19 points to avoid the double.

Lead: Ace of spades followed by a second spade. A trump lead is often best when your side has the majority of high cards.

Recommended play: East wins the second trump and leads a heart. South grabs the ace of hearts and can take the ace of clubs but that is all for the defence. There is no way to beat 4♠ as the cards lie.

Notes: (1) If South ducks the heart, dummy wins, a low heart is ruffed followed by ◇A, diamond ruff and another low heart ruffed. This sets up dummy's hearts and declarer makes eleven tricks.
(2) If South grabs the ace of hearts and fails to cash the ♣A, East can discard two clubs on the top hearts and set up the fifth heart to discard the third club. This again gives declarer eleven tricks.
(3) Note the efficacy of the Michaels 2♣ bid. Without that, how would East-West manage to find 4♠? You would not want to overcall 1♠ on the West cards. Left alone, North-South would reach 3NT and if West leads a heart, 3NT would be easy.
(4) The winning move for North-South is to sacrifice in 5♣, one down if West collects the diamond ruff but making on a non-diamond lead. It is no easy task for North-South to find 5♣.

Hand 80: Michaels — Penalties — S.O.S. rescue

Dealer West : E-W vulnerable

NORTH
- ♠ Q J 10 6 3
- ♡ K 3
- ◇ K Q 10 9 5
- ♣ 9

WEST
- ♠ 5 4
- ♡ A Q 9 8 5 4
- ◇ A 2
- ♣ K 5 4

EAST
- ♠ A K 9 8 7
- ♡ 10 7
- ◇ J 8 7 6
- ♣ Q 3

SOUTH
- ♠ 2
- ♡ J 6 2
- ◇ 4 3
- ♣ A J 10 8 7 6 2

WEST	NORTH	EAST	SOUTH
1♡	2♡	Dble	Rdble
No	2♠	Dble	3♣
Dble	No	No	No

Bidding: North has a very sound Michaels Cue at favourable vulnerability. East's double is for penalties, showing strength in North's suit(s) and shortage in partner's. It is not hard for South to deduce North's suits. South wants to play in 3♣ but if South bids 3♣, North will correct to diamonds. To play in your own long suit, start with a redouble. This asks partner to make the cheapest possible bid (2♠ here) and then pass your next bid. West does not have a great double of 3♣ but knowing East has 10+ points and a shortage in hearts, the double is reasonable.

Lead: Ace of hearts. Hoping for East to have a singleton heart.

Recommended play: After ♡A and a second heart taken by dummy, declarer leads ♠Q won by East who might switch to a diamond. West takes ◇A and plays the ♡Q, ruffed in dummy and overruffed by East. Declarer loses 1 spade, 1 heart, 1 overruff, 1 diamond and 1 club. One down.

Notes: (1) If East shifts to a trump at trick 4, South plays low and West wins. South now loses one spade, two hearts, one diamond and one club. One down.
(2) One down in 3♣ doubled is as good as South can do. 2♠ doubled or 3◇ doubled would be no better.
(3) East-West can make 3NT as the cards lie but it is very hard to reach that spot.
(4) If East-West end up in some number of hearts, declarer is going to struggle after the lead of the queen of spades. If declarer elects to finesse the queen of hearts, not a far-fetched play by any means, declarer could easily suffer a spade ruff and a club ruff.

CHAPTER 21
INTERFERENCE OVER YOUR 1NT
– THE LEBENSOHL CONVENTION

There are dozens of conventions for bidding after they have opened 1NT. No doubt you have your favourite. For more information about some of the better methods after they open 1NT, see *Bridge Conventions, Defences and Countermeasures*. Here we are concerned with covering as many problems as possible if they interfere over your 1NT opening.

WEST	NORTH	EAST	SOUTH
1NT	2♡	?	

How does your partnership cope in the East seat? The standard treatment here is to play double for penalties, suit bids at the cheapest level not forcing and bid of the enemy suit to replace Stayman.

At duplicate most top pairs prefer to play more sophisticated methods:

(1) Double for takeout

Penalty doubles are great when they come along but most sensible opponents have a strong suit and do not go for large numbers when they come in over your 1NT. Is responder more likely to have length and strength in their suit or a shortage in their suit? On the score of frequency, the takeout double is more valuable.

One of the problems with the standard approach is that there is no game invitational bid to show a missing major. You can bid their suit as Stayman but this is forcing to game. What if responder has:

♠ Q 9 7 2	To bid 2♠ is silly and 2NT can
♡ 9 4	lose the spades. How much easier
◇ K Q 9 3	if responder can double 2♡ for
♣ A 6 4	takeout to show this hand type.

(2) Lebensohl 2NT

This is the preferred approach for many top pairs. A suit bid at the two-level merely competes for the part-score. It is not even invitational (double covers the invitational hands). A change of suit at the three-level is natural and forcing.

The 2NT response is *Lebensohl* and requires the 1NT opener to bid 3♣. Responder may be intending to pass 3♣ with a weak, competitive hand with long clubs. After opener's forced 3♣, a new suit lower ranking than the enemy suit is to play, merely competing for the part-score.

WEST	NORTH	EAST	SOUTH
1NT	2♠	3♡ . . .	

East's 3♡, a new suit at the three-level, is forcing.

WEST	NORTH	EAST	SOUTH
1NT	2♠	2NT	No
3♣	No	3♡ . . .	

East's 3♡, preceded by the Lebensohl 2NT, is not forcing and not even encouraging.

There are four strong actions for responder:

Immediate 3NT response = game points but no stopper in their suit and no 4-card major

Immediate bid of their suit = game points, at least one unbid major (4 cards) but no stopper in their suit

2NT Lebensohl followed by a 3NT rebid after the forced 3♣ puppet = game points, no 4-card major but at least one stopper in their suit

2NT Lebensohl followed by a bid of their suit after the forced 3♣ puppet = game points, at least one 4-card major plus a stopper in their suit

The memory guide here is that the more often you bid no-trumps, the happier you are with no-trumps. Thus, using 2NT Lebensohl and following up with a strong action shows the stopper. Showing a strong hand without 2NT denies the stopper. Other versions exist but this is the popular treatment.

Lebensohl allows responder to play in a part-score at the three-level in a suit lower-ranking than their suit and also allows responder to describe game-going hands with or without a major and with or without at least one stopper in their suit. If responder shows no stopper and opener has no stopper either, it would be prudent to play somewhere other than in 3NT.

WEST	NORTH	EAST	SOUTH
1NT	2♡	2NT	No
3♣	No	3♠ . . .	

What is the distinction between this sequence and responder's bidding 3♠ at once over 2♡? Both sequences must be strong since with a weak hand, East could bid just 2♠. Following the above memory guide, travelling via 2NT shows a stopper in their suit and 5+ spades while the direct 3♠ bid shows 5+ spades but denies a stopper in their suit.

The same would apply to hearts in this auction:

WEST	NORTH	EAST	SOUTH
1NT	2◇	3♡ . . .	

versus

WEST	NORTH	EAST	SOUTH
1NT	2◇	2NT	No
3♣	No	3♡ . . .	

2♡ was available as a weak action merely to compete for the part-score so that both these sequences are strong. In the first, East is showing 5+ hearts but no stopper in the diamonds. In the second, East shows 5+ hearts and at least one stopper in diamonds. Knowing whether responder does or does not have a stopper in the enemy suit must help opener make a sensible decision.

What if their interference is artificial?

Many conventions show a suit other than the suit bid, such as 2♣ showing hearts and another, or 2♦ showing spades and a minor. In this case, the enemy suit is the suit shown, not the suit bid. One consequence is that you have three bids of the enemy suit available, one at the two-level, one at the three-level immediately and one at the three-level after Lebensohl 2NT. The three-level bids have their usual meanings and the two-level bids can be used for takeout with a singleton or void in that suit.

WEST	NORTH	EAST	SOUTH
1NT	2♡*		?

*Showing 5+ spades

(1)	(2)	(3)
♠ 8 6 3	♠ K 3 2	♠ - - -
♡ K 10 8 7	♡ K 10 8 7	♡ J 9 8 6
♦ A Q	♦ A Q	♦ A K Q 3
♣ K Q 4 2	♣ Q 7 5 3	♣ K 8 6 3 2

(1) Bid 3♠ (four hearts but no stopper in spades).
(2) Bid 2NT and over the puppet 3♣, rebid 3♠ (four hearts plus a stopper in spades).
(3) Bid 2♠, game-force with a spade singleton or void.

If their bid shows two suits

WEST	NORTH	EAST	SOUTH
1NT	2♦		?

If 2♦ is used to show both majors, East-West will not be looking to play in a major. Bid 2♡ if short in hearts or 2♠ if short in spades. The jump to 3♡ asks for a stopper in hearts and may have a spade stopper. Opener can bid 3♠ to ask for help there. Responder's 3♠ asks for a spade stopper and shows a heart stopper.

If East bids 2NT and follows up with 3♡ or 3♠, this asks for a stopper in the suit bid and shows a stopper in the other major.

More on the takeout double

WEST	NORTH	EAST	SOUTH
1NT	2♡	Dble	

Where the overcall is 2♡ natural, the takeout double need not have four spades. The double should be based on game-inviting values. With enough for game, three-level action with or without Lebensohl is available.

Opener can bid 2♠ if minimum with four spades (over which responder can bid 2NT or 3-minor without four spades), 2NT if minimum without four spades or 3♡ / 3♠ / 3NT if maximum.

WEST	NORTH	EAST	SOUTH
1NT	2♦	Dble	

Where the overcall is 2♦ natural, the double shows inviting values but need not have a major. Opener can bid at the two-level if minimum and 3-major or 3NT or 3♦ if maximum. If opener's rebid is unsuitable, responder rebids naturally.

WEST	NORTH	EAST	SOUTH
1NT	2♠	Dble	

Over 2♠, double should include four hearts. If minimum, opener needs to know whether 3♡ is safe.

Expert methods

When they interfere over your 1NT, one problem is that your partnership loses transfers. Lebensohl recaptures Stayman on game-going hands and the takeout double does the work of Stayman on game-inviting hands. Would it not be attractive to have transfers as well?

Transfer Lebensohl

It is possible to have transfers by using 2NT or higher bids as Lebensohl combined with transfers.

WEST	NORTH	EAST	SOUTH
1NT	2♠		?

2NT = Lebensohl, requiring opener to bid 3♣. As usual, responder is allowed to pass this. If responder continues, 3♠ and 3NT have the usual Lebensohl meanings, while 3♦ or 3♡ shows that 2NT was a transfer: 3♦ = 5+ clubs, 4 diamonds, enough for game and 3♡ = 5+ clubs, 4 hearts and enough for game.

3♣ = Transfer to diamonds. Opener may super-accept by bidding 3NT or with 3♠ to ask for a spade stopper.

3♦ = Transfer to hearts. Opener may super-accept via 4♡ or 3♠ to ask for a spade stopper.

3♡ = Both minors and slam potential. If responder is 5-4 in the minors, it will be 5 diamonds and 4 clubs since the other way around, responder would bid 2NT and rebid 3♦ over 3♣ (see above).

WEST	NORTH	EAST	SOUTH
1NT	2♡		?

2♠ = Natural, 5+ spades, not forcing

2NT = Lebensohl requiring opener to bid 3♣, as above. If responder continues, 3♡ and 3NT have the usual Lebensohl meanings, while 3♦ or 3♠ shows that 2NT was used as a transfer: 3♦ = 5+ clubs, 4 diamonds and enough for game and 3♠ = 5+ clubs, 4 spades and enough for game.

3♣ = Transfer to diamonds. Super-accepts are allowed as above.

3♦ = Transfer to *spades*. This is necessary as 3♡ is the Lebensohl bid, showing four spades and no stopper in hearts.

3♠ = Both minors and slam potential. If responder is 5-4 in the minors, it will be 5 diamonds and 4 clubs (see above).

The principles are:

2NT requires 3♣ as usual. If responder continues with their suit or 3NT, then 2NT was Lebensohl. If responder continues with a new suit, then 2NT was a transfer, showing 5+ clubs and the new suit.

3♣ is always a transfer to diamonds.

3♦ is always a transfer to the other major.

3-other-major = both minors and slam prospects.

Where a major suit has not been bid, then 3♦ can be used as a transfer to hearts and 3♡ as a transfer to spades, 3♠ as the hand with both minors and slam potential. This method may be needed if their bid has not promised an anchor suit.

(For another excellent method after they bid over your 1NT, see Appendix 5: Rubinsohl.)

EXERCISES ON LEBENSOHL

A. Partner 1NT, right hand opponent 2♡ natural. What action would you take, playing standard Lebensohl?

1. ♠ A J 4 3	2. ♠ A J 5 2	3. ♠ J 4 3	4. ♠ J 4 3	5. ♠ K 6 4 3 2
♡ A Q	♡ 7 5 2	♡ 8 5	♡ A 8	♡ A 8
♢ 8 6 4 3	♢ K 6 4 3	♢ A K 6 2	♢ Q 7 5 3	♢ Q 4
♣ K 5 2	♣ A Q	♣ A Q 5 3	♣ A K 8 4	♣ K J 5 2

B. The bidding has started 1NT : (2♢ overcall, showing spades and a minor) to you.   What do you do now?

1. ♠ 7 5	2. ♠ 2	3. ♠ 5 4	4. ♠ 5 4	5. ♠ 9 6
♡ K 9 6 2	♡ K 9 6 2	♡ Q J 7 6 2	♡ A 7 6 3 2	♡ J 2
♢ K J 2	♢ A K 3	♢ K Q 7 4	♢ A K J 4	♢ K 9 3
♣ A Q J 6	♣ A 8 7 4 2	♣ 3 2	♣ J 2	♣ K J 9 8 4 3

C. WEST : 1NT, NORTH : 2♠ (natural). What should East do with these hands if playing Transfer Lebensohl?

1. ♠ 7	2. ♠ 2	3. ♠ 9	4. ♠ 7	5. ♠ 9
♡ K 10 9 6 2	♡ K Q 8 7 4 2	♡ K Q 6	♡ K Q 6	♡ A 4 2
♢ A Q 9 3	♢ 7 3	♢ A K 10 8	♢ A K 10 8 3	♢ K J 9 7 4 3 2
♣ A J 6	♣ A K 6 2	♣ K Q 8 5 3	♣ K Q 8 5	♣ 6 2

PARTNERSHIP : How should the following hands be bid, playing standard Lebensohl? West is the dealer each time and there is no opposition action other than the bidding shown.

SET 35 — WEST	SET 35 — EAST	SET 36 — WEST	SET 36 — EAST
1. North bids 2♡	1. North bids 2♡	1. North bids 2♡	1. North bids 2♡
♠ 10 9 6 2	♠ A K 5 4	♠ A 9 6	♠ Q 8 5 2
♡ Q 3	♡ 10 6 5	♡ A Q 3	♡ 8 2
♢ K Q J	♢ A 8	♢ Q 9 5	♢ A K 3 2
♣ K Q 10 4	♣ 9 7 3 2	♣ J 10 4 3	♣ K Q 6
2. North bids 2♡	2. North bids 2♡	2. North bids 2♡	2. North bids 2♡
♠ Q 3	♠ K 10 5 2	♠ A K 3	♠ Q 8 5 2
♡ A 9 6 2	♡ 10 4	♡ J 4 3	♡ 8 2
♢ K Q 7 2	♢ A 4 3	♢ K Q 8	♢ A 7 3 2
♣ Q 10 3	♣ K J 7 2	♣ 10 7 4 2	♣ A K Q
3. South bids 2♡	3. South bids 2♡	3. South bids 2♠	3. South bids 2♠
♠ K 3	♠ A J 5	♠ 7 5	♠ A K 3
♡ 4 2	♡ A 6 5	♡ J 10 8 7 4 3	♡ 9 6 2
♢ Q 9 7 6 4 2	♢ J 8 3	♢ 9 5 4	♢ K Q 8
♣ A 6 4	♣ K J 7 3	♣ A K	♣ J 7 4 2
4. South bids 2♡	4. South bids 2♡	4. South bids 2♠	4. South bids 2♠
♠ A K	♠ Q J 5 2	♠ 7 5	♠ 9 8 3
♡ 4 2	♡ A 6 5	♡ J 10 8 7 4 3	♡ A K 6 2
♢ 6 4 2	♢ J 8 3	♢ K Q 4	♢ 9 7
♣ Q 9 7 6 4 2	♣ A J 3	♣ J 5	♣ A K 9 2
5. North bids 2♠	5. North bids 2♠	5. North bids 2♠	5. North bids 2♠
♠ J 5	♠ 9 3	♠ 7 5	♠ J 4 2
♡ Q 6 3 2	♡ A K	♡ A J 3	♡ K Q
♢ Q 8 3	♢ A K 9 7 6 4	♢ 8 5 4	♢ K Q J 3
♣ A K J 7	♣ 6 4 3	♣ A K 6 5 2	♣ Q J 4 3

PLAY HANDS ON LEBENSOHL OVER 1NT
(These hands can be made up by using pages 176-183)

Hand 81: Showing a stopper in their suit — Unblocking technique

Dealer North : Nil vulnerable

NORTH
- ♠ K 9 7 4 3 2
- ♡ - - -
- ◇ 9 8 7 2
- ♣ J 10 8

WEST
- ♠ J 6
- ♡ A 8 5 2
- ◇ 6 3
- ♣ A K 5 4 3

EAST
- ♠ A 10 5
- ♡ 7 6 3
- ◇ A K 4
- ♣ Q 9 7 6

SOUTH
- ♠ Q 8
- ♡ K Q J 10 9 4
- ◇ Q J 10 5
- ♣ 2

WEST	NORTH	EAST	SOUTH
	No	1NT	2♡
2NT	No	3♣	No
3NT	No	No	No

Bidding: North is too weak and has the wrong shape for a weak two opening. West's 2NT forces 3♣ and the 3NT rebid denies four spades and promises at least one stopper in hearts.

Lead: King of hearts. No reason to prefer the ◇Q.

Recommended play: If clubs are 3-1, the club suit is blocked. Declarer should duck the first heart, duck the second heart and duck the third heart. Once East is void in hearts, declarer can discard the blocking club on the ♡A and take 1 spade, 1 heart, 2 diamonds and 5 clubs.

Notes: (1) If East wins the ♡A on the first, second or third round, there are only eight tricks. There is no way to reach the fifth club in dummy.
(2) If South switches to ◇Q after the first or second heart, the ♡A is the entry to dummy later.
(3) If South switches to ◇Q after three rounds of hearts, East wins and cashes ♣Q, ♣K and ♣A. East's last club is discarded on dummy's ♡A and dummy's remaining club winners can now be cashed.

Hand 82: Competing over their overcall — Creating an extra trump trick

Dealer East : N-S vulnerable

NORTH
- ♠ A 3
- ♡ J 3
- ◇ 7 3 2
- ♣ 9 8 6 5 4 3

WEST
- ♠ Q 4
- ♡ 9 8 7 6 4
- ◇ A Q 9 6
- ♣ A Q

EAST
- ♠ 9 8
- ♡ K Q 5 2
- ◇ K J 4
- ♣ K J 10 2

SOUTH
- ♠ K J 10 7 6 5 2
- ♡ A 10
- ◇ 10 8 5
- ♣ 7

WEST	NORTH	EAST	SOUTH
		1NT	2♠
3♡	No	4♡	All pass

Bidding: At unfavourable vulnerability, you require six sure tricks for a two-level overcall and some hope of seven tricks. South has just enough. West's 3♡ shows five hearts and is forcing when playing Lebensohl.

If East-West were playing transfer Lebensohl, West would bid 3◇, East 3♡, West 3♠ to ask for a stopper and East 4♡. South would lead the singleton club. Judging the lead to be very likely a singleton, North should signal with the ♣9, suit preference for spades if South gains the lead in trumps. South would take the ♡A on the first round, lead a spade and receive a club ruff.

Lead: Ace of spades. It is normal to lead partner's suit.

Recommended play: South encourages and wins the second spade. It should be clear to South that if West has 12+ HCP that North cannot hold the ♣A. South therefore leads a third spade, North ruffs with the jack of hearts (uppercut) and South has two trump tricks.

Notes: (1) A club lead would also work but how could North tell? Unless there are clear indications, you should stick to partner's bid suit.
(2) Although the third spade gives declarer a ruff-and-discard, declarer has no useful loser to discard. With no tricks available outside trumps, try for a trump promotion.

Hand 83: Lebensohl sequence to replace Stayman — Declarer and defensive technique

Dealer South : E-W vulnerable

```
                    NORTH
                 ♠ K 8 5 2
                 ♡ 8 3 2
                 ◇ A K J
                 ♣ Q 10 5
 WEST                             EAST
 ♠ 3                              ♠ Q 10 9 6 4
 ♡ Q J 10 7 6 5                   ♡ 9 4
 ◇ Q 10 9 3                       ◇ 7 5 2
 ♣ A 7                            ♣ K 6 4
                    SOUTH
                 ♠ A J 7
                 ♡ A K
                 ◇ 8 6 4
                 ♣ J 9 8 3 2
```

WEST	NORTH	EAST	SOUTH
			1NT
2♡	3♡	No	3NT
No	No	No	

Bidding: A sound overcall over 1NT should have about six playing tricks. The point count is not as important as the playing tricks. North's 3♡ replaces Stayman: it shows four spades and denies a stopper in hearts. South has an easy 3NT rebid.

Lead: Queen of hearts. What else?

Recommended play: Declarer has six top tricks and should tackle the clubs. Even if both finesses worked in spades and diamonds, that is only eight tricks. The best chance is to cross to the king of spades and lead a low club from dummy. East should rise with the ♣K and send back a heart. South wins and if a second club is played, declarer is two down. If instead declarer tried the diamond finesse and the spade finesse that would hold the losses to one down. Although both finesses work this time, the more common result of this line would be three down. It is better for South to hope that East started with only two hearts and both club honours.

Notes: (1) East should reason that if South has ♣ A-J-x-x or longer, the ♣K is doomed anyway. East goes up with the ♣K to preserve partner's hoped for entry to the hearts later. There is almost no risk of colliding with West's ♣A singleton. That would give South six clubs.
(2) If East ducks with the ♣K, South plays the ♣9. It does not help West to duck this, for South plays a second club. Now West's entry is eliminated before the hearts are set up.
(3) Note South's technique in crossing to dummy and leading the first club from there. If South leads the first club from hand, the defence can hardly get it wrong.

Hand 84: Lebensohl sequence to replace Stayman — Deceptive defence

Dealer West : Both vulnerable

```
                    NORTH
                 ♠ Q J 6 2
                 ♡ 5 3 2
                 ◇ A 2
                 ♣ A K 9 7
 WEST                             EAST
 ♠ 10 9 8 5                       ♠ 3
 ♡ A 7 6                          ♡ K Q J 10 9
 ◇ 9 8 5 4 3                      ◇ J 7
 ♣ J                              ♣ 10 8 6 5 4
                    SOUTH
                 ♠ A K 7 4
                 ♡ 8 4
                 ◇ K Q 10 6
                 ♣ Q 3 2
```

WEST	NORTH	EAST	SOUTH
No	1NT	2♡	3♡
No	3♠	No	4♠
No	No	No	

Bidding: If East-West have a method to show a heart-club two-suiter, then East might use it, but the hearts are so good and the clubs so weak, that 2♡ is eminently reasonable. South's 3♡ replaces Stayman and playing Lebensohl, 3♡ shows 4 spades and no stopper in hearts. North bids 3♠ to show a maximum hand with four spades in case South has slam ambitions, but South has no desires beyond reaching game.

Lead: King of hearts. Automatic.

Recommended play: West can see that the defence will take at most two hearts and perhaps the king of clubs with East. West decides to try a little subterfuge in case East has led from a 5-card suit. West overtakes the ♡K with the ace and returns the ♡6. East wins and from the play so far, both East and North think West started with a doubleton heart. When East plays the third heart, almost every declarer would ruff high in dummy. That creates a trump trick for West and holds declarer to ten tricks.

Notes: (1) There is a slight risk that North started with two hearts and the third heart will give North a ruff and discard. Given dummy's minor suit holdings, it is wildly unlikely that such a discard will be of any use to North. If your ruse does work, what a story to tell for weeks afterwards.
(2) Holding North to ten tricks should give East-West a top board.
(3) The alternative line is to take the second heart and switch to the ♣J, hoping East has the ♣K.

CHAPTER 22
DEFENCE AGAINST WEAK TWOS

Against their natural weak two

For defences against multi-twos, see Chapters 23-24.

Over their weak actions your primary aim is to cope with your strong hands. This is quite a task as you have lost the one-level and most of the two-level. There is very little value in showing weak hands over their weak two, and so jump-overcalls are strong, 2NT shows a strong balanced hand and not the unusual 2NT for the minors. Basic strategy is to play partner to provide at least two tricks. Thus, an overcall at the three-level is a 6-loser hand while (2♠) : 4♥ should be a 5-loser hand. If partner provides the expected two tricks, these levels should be safe enough. The recommended approach:

2NT = 16-18 balanced with at least one stopper in their suit. 15 HCP will do with a double stopper.

3NT = 21-22 balanced, at least one stopper in their suit. With 19-20 balanced or 23+, start with a double.

Double = for takeout. Same values as for a double at the one-level. If minimum, the hand must be short in their suit with 4+ cards in the other major.

Suit bid= natural, strong 5+ suit. 2♠ over (2♥) might be a 6-loser or 7-loser hand but a three-level overcall should be 5-6 losers. With 4 losers, the hand is too strong for an overcall. Start with a double. The jump to 3♠ over (2♥) should be a 5-loser hand. If better than this, start by doubling.

Bidding their suit asks for a stopper for 3NT. The usual hand type is a long, strong minor suit, a hand too strong to overcall 3♣ or 3♦. Bidding their suit as Michaels is also an option but being able to show a powerful minor suit hand without going beyond 3NT is more useful. The Michaels option can be covered by:

Jump to 4♣ or 4♦ = 'leaping Michaels', showing 5+ in the minor suit bid and 5+ in the other major. The hand should be a 5-loser hand or better since the bid virtually commits the partnership to game and you should not count on partner for more than two tricks.

With a game-force powerhouse, start with a double and bid their suit on the next round to force to game.

4NT =the 'unusual', with both minors, at least 5-5. The hand should be no worse than a 4-loser hand.

After (2♥ / 2♠) : No : (No) to you, reduce the requirements for 2NT, double and suit bids by 3 points.

After (2♥) : 2NT or (2♠) : 2NT

3♣ = Stayman (some play this as Puppet Stayman, as after a 2NT opening — see Chapter 5, page 35).

3♦ = Transfer to the other major

Their suit = singleton or void in their suit game-force, typically a 4-4-4-1 or 5-4-3-1 with a 5-card minor

3-other-major = at least 5-4 in the minors, forcing to game, slam interest

4♣/4♦ = natural, game force, slam interest

After (2♥) : Double or (2♠) : Double

The standard approach is to bid at the cheapest level with a poor hand and give a jump response with about 10 points or more. The problem here is that you have lost so much bidding space. While it is all right to jump to 3♣/3♦ after (1♥/1♠) : Double, you do not want to jump to 4♣ or 4♦ and so bypass 3NT. Even without that, a three-level reply to the double has a very wide range. After (2♠) : Double : (Pass) : 3♥, how is the doubler expected to judge what to do next if the advancer could have 0, 1, or 2 points or could have as much as a reasonable 7-9 points?

The preferred solution is to harness the Lebensohl concept for this area. In reply to the double:

2NT = Lebensohl, requesting the doubler to bid 3♣. Advancer may be intending to pass 3♣ or bid a suit at the 3-level to show a hand in the 0-6 point range. With a weak hand, advancer will have at best 2 cover cards.

3-level suit bid = around 7-10 points, encouraging but not forcing.

(2♥) : Double : (No) : 3♠ = 7-10 points, 5+ spades.

Bidding 2NT first and then bidding 3♠ over the forced 3♣ shows 7-10 points and only four spades.

3NT = Single stopper in their suit

2NT-followed-by-3NT-over-3♣ = Double stopper

Bid their suit = game force with a singleton or void in their suit

2NT-and-later-bid-their suit = game force, stopper probe but 2+ cards in their suit

If the doubler is very strong, 4 losers or better, decline the 3♣ puppet. Advancer should then bid on with one trick or better. If the doubler bids the enemy suit over 2NT Lebensohl, this shows a 3-loser or better hand. With 19-20 balanced, the doubler should accept the 3♣ puppet. 19-20 balanced has a lot of losers.

Other Lebensohl situations

Because the Lebensohl principle is so valuable, it has been harnessed to other auctions analogous to the reply to a double of a weak two.

WEST	NORTH	EAST	SOUTH
1♠	No	2♠	Double
No	?		

Use 2NT Lebensohl with a weak hand and bid at the three-level with 7-10 points.

After (1♠) : Double : (2♠), however, Lebensohl does not apply as advancer is not obliged to bid at all.

WEST	NORTH	EAST	SOUTH
2♦	No	2♥	Double
No	?		

After a multi-2♦, South's double of the 2♥ reply = a double of a weak 2♥. North's 2NT = Lebensohl.

EXERCISES FOR DEFENDING AGAINST WEAK TWOS

A. The bidding has started with (2♠) on your right. What action would you take with these hands?

1. ♠ K 7 3	2. ♠ K 7 3	3. ♠ 3	4. ♠ 8	5. ♠ 8
♡ A 2	♡ A J	♡ 6	♡ K Q 10 5 2	♡ A K 8 3 2
◇ A K 5 3 2	◇ A K 8 4	◇ K Q J 9 3	◇ A K J 4 3	◇ A K Q
♣ Q 9 3	♣ A J 4 2	♣ A Q J 7 4 3	♣ 9 2	♣ A Q J 5

B. The bidding started (2♡) : Double : (No) to you. What is your reply to the double with these hands?

1. ♠ A Q 8 7 4	2. ♠ A Q 7 4	3. ♠ 7 2	4. ♠ 7 2	5. ♠ K 4
♡ 6 3	♡ 6 4 3	♡ 7 5 3 2	♡ 7 5 3 2	♡ A Q 4
◇ J 8 7 2	◇ J 8 7 5 2	◇ Q J 6 4	◇ Q J 6 4	◇ A J 9 3
♣ 9 5	♣ 2	♣ 7 4 2	♣ A J 2	♣ J 10 3 2

C. The bidding has started (2♠) : Double : (No) : 2NT, (No) back to you, the doubler. What action should you take with these hands, given that 2NT is Lebensohl, requesting 3♣ from you?

1. ♠ 4 3	2. ♠ 7 2	3. ♠ A 4 2	4. ♠ 2	5. ♠ 3
♡ K Q 7 6	♡ A Q J 3 2	♡ Q 6 4	♡ A K 6 4	♡ A Q 3
◇ A K 4 2	◇ A K	◇ A K J 5	◇ K Q J 10	◇ A K J
♣ K 5 2	♣ K Q 9 3	♣ A Q 2	♣ A K Q 2	♣ K Q J 7 4 3

PARTNERSHIP BIDDING: How should these hands be bid? North or South opens as indicated.

SET 37 — WEST	SET 37 — EAST	SET 38 — WEST	SET 38 — EAST
1. North opens 2♡	1. North opens 2♡	1. North opens 2♠	1. North opens 2♠
♠ A Q 7 2	♠ 6 3	♠ 8 7 4 2	♠ 3
♡ 6 4 2	♡ A Q 3	♡ K 2	♡ A Q 3
◇ Q 9 8	◇ A K 6 2	◇ 8 6 5	◇ A K J
♣ 9 8 4	♣ A Q J 3	♣ 10 9 5 2	♣ K Q J 7 4 3
2. South opens 2♣	2. South opens 2♣	2. South opens 2♡	2. South opens 2♡
♠ 6 3	♠ 7 5 4	♠ A Q 6 3	♠ 7 2
♡ A Q 3	♡ K 7 6 4 2	♡ 8 5	♡ Q J 4
◇ A K 6 2	◇ 9 7 3	◇ A 6 4	◇ K Q 9 7 3
♣ A Q J 3	♣ 8 5	♣ K J 3 2	♣ 9 8 7
3. North opens 2♠	3. North opens 2♠	3. North opens 2♡	3. North opens 2♡
♠ 10 7 2	♠ 6 3	♠ 7 2	♠ A Q 6 3
♡ J 10 8 6 4 2	♡ A K	♡ Q J 4	♡ 8 5
◇ 7 4	◇ A K Q 8	◇ K Q 9 7 3	◇ A 6 4
♣ 7 6	♣ A Q J 3 2	♣ 9 8 7	♣ A K 6 2
4. South opens 2♣	4. South opens 2♠	4. North opens 2♡	4. North opens 2♡
♠ A Q 8	♠ 7 5 4	♠ 9 6 5	♠ K Q J 7 3
♡ J 9	♡ K 10 7 4 3	♡ J 7 5	♡ 8
◇ A K 6 2	◇ 9 7	◇ 9 3 2	◇ A K J 6 4
♣ Q J 3 2	♣ A K 5	♣ K 5 4 3	♣ 8 2
5. South opens 2♡	5. South opens 2♡	5. South opens 2♠	5. South opens 2♠
♠ K 3	♠ Q J 8 7 5 2	♠ 7	♠ A K 3 2
♡ A 10 3	♡ 6	♡ A Q 7 5 3	♡ J 6
◇ K 6 4	◇ A Q J	◇ A K 4	◇ Q 9 6 2
♣ K Q J 3 2	♣ 9 7 4	♣ A K J 2	♣ Q 8 5

PLAY HANDS ON DEFENDING AGAINST WEAK TWOS
(These hands can be made up by using pages 176-183)

Hand 85: Game force after their weak two — Trump reduction — Defensive countermeasure

Dealer North : N-S vulnerable

NORTH
- ♠ A K Q 9 8 5
- ♡ 5
- ◇ 10 6 2
- ♣ 9 7 4

WEST
- ♠ 7 6 2
- ♡ J 10 8 6 4 2
- ◇ 7 4
- ♣ Q 8

EAST
- ♠ J 3
- ♡ A K
- ◇ A K Q 8
- ♣ A K J 3 2

SOUTH
- ♠ 10 4
- ♡ Q 9 7 3
- ◇ J 9 5 3
- ♣ 10 6 5

WEST	NORTH	EAST	SOUTH
	2♠	Dble	No
2NT	No	3♠	No
4♡	No	No	No

Bidding: With 25 HCP and better than 3 losers, East has enough to insist on game. With 3♠ as Michaels, huge hands are shown by double first, bid their suit later. West uses Lebensohl 2NT, planning to sign off in 3♡. Over East's 3♠, West has an easy 4♡. East does not know how many hearts West has but there is nothing to suggest that 5♣ or 5◇ will be better. As it happens, 5♣ is easier than 4♡ but for all East knows, West could have a singleton or void in clubs. 5♣ could be hopeless with 4♡ comfortable. After much soul-searching, East passes 4♡.

Lead: Ace of spades. What else?

Recommended play: South plays high-low on the first two spades and North continues with a third spade, ruffed with the king of hearts. South discards a club. The ♡A is cashed, followed by a club to the queen and the jack of hearts, revealing the bad break. South wins and returns a diamond, taken in dummy. West should now fail. West can tempt South by playing ♣A, ♣K but as long as South does not ruff, South will come to an extra trump trick. West can ruff a club and ruff a diamond but is in hand at trick 12.

Notes: (1) If South ducks the ♡J, West can succeed via trump reduction technique: a club to the ace, club ruff, diamond to the ace and club ruff. A diamond to dummy at trick 11 holds South to one trump trick.
(2) The same technique is available if South captures ♡J and exits with a club. Recognising that a trump reduction is West's only hope, South must play a diamond to attack dummy's later entry. This leaves West one entry short. West can reduce the trumps to the same length as South's but dummy has no entry at trick 11.
(3) If North fails to lead a third spade, West has no problem drawing South's trumps.

Hand 86: 2NT over weak two — Transfer by advancer

Dealer East : E-W vulnerable

NORTH
- ♠ Q J 8 7 5 2
- ♡ 6
- ◇ A J 9
- ♣ 9 7 4

WEST
- ♠ A 6
- ♡ 8 4 2
- ◇ 7 6 5 2
- ♣ A 10 8 6

EAST
- ♠ 10 9 4
- ♡ K Q J 10 9 5
- ◇ Q 8 4
- ♣ 2

SOUTH
- ♠ K 3
- ♡ A 7 3
- ◇ K 10 3
- ♣ K Q J 5 3

WEST	NORTH	EAST	SOUTH
		2♡	2NT
No	3◇	No	3♠
No	4♠	All pass	

Bidding: With a 5-3-3-2 and a 5-card minor, it is more attractive to bid no-trumps than the minor provided the hand fits the requirements for the no-trump overcall. North has enough to jump to 4♠ but unless you have a strong reason to be declarer, you should use a transfer sequence. In these auctions, 3◇ is a transfer to the other major. With enough for game and only five spades, North would rebid 3NT over 3♠ but with six spades, North should bid the spade game.

Lead: 4 of hearts. West has no reason to choose another lead.

Recommended play: Win ♡A and lead the king of spades, taken by West. If West exits with a trump or a heart, trumps are drawn and South starts on the clubs. West should hold off with the ace until the third round and then play a heart, ruffed in dummy. Declarer should finesse East for the ◇Q. 11 tricks.

Notes: (1) If West takes the ♣A on the first or second round of clubs, declarer can set up the fifth club and avoid the need to pick the diamond position. Given East has opened with a weak two at unfavourable vulnerability and West has turned up with both black aces, East figures to have the ◇Q.
(2) If West gives East a club ruff after winning ♠A, declarer is held to ten tricks. If West switches to a diamond after taking the ♠A, South has an easy path to 11 tricks.
(3) If North bids 4♠ over 2NT, East might lead the singleton club, which would defeat 4♠. West wins, gives East a club ruff and gives East a second club ruff after taking ♠A. With South declarer, why would West lead a club?

Hand 87: Rejecting the Lebensohl puppet — Counting and card reading

Dealer South : Both vulnerable

NORTH
♠ 9 5
♡ 10 8 6 2
♢ 8 7 5
♣ 10 9 4 3

WEST
♠ 7
♡ A Q 7 5 3
♢ A K 4
♣ A K J 2

EAST
♠ A K 3 2
♡ J 4
♢ Q 9 6 2
♣ Q 8 5

SOUTH
♠ Q J 10 8 6 4
♡ K 9
♢ J 10 3
♣ 7 6

WEST	NORTH	EAST	SOUTH
			2♠
Dble	No	2NT	No
3♡	No	4NT	No
5♣	No	6NT	All pass

Bidding: East was planning to reach 3NT and show two stoppers in spades by using 2NT followed by 3NT next. West is expected to bid 3♣ but West is strong enough to reject the puppet. 3♡ shows 5+ hearts, 19+ points and 4 losers. That spurs East into slam mode. East cannot be sure that slam will be a good bet but it would be timid to play this in just game. 4NT is RKCB setting hearts as trumps and 5♣ shows 0 or 3 key cards, clearly three. With no obvious trump fit, East opts for 6NT.

Lead: Queen of spades. The obvious start.

Recommended play: East wins and leads a low heart, in case South has the king of hearts singleton. The queen wins and a low heart is conceded in order to cater for a 3-3 split. South wins and continues with the jack of spades, taken by East who continues with a club to the ace and the ♡A, with East and South both pitching spades. The clubs are cashed, South discarding spades, followed by the ♢A and ♢K, South dropping the ♢J under the king. East has to decide whether to play for diamonds 3-3 or whether to finesse the 9 of diamonds. After a moment's reflection, East confidently plays a diamond to the queen. 12 tricks.

Notes: (1) If East leads the jack of hearts early, South should cover with the king. If East leads a low heart, South should play low. There is no benefit in rising with king-doubleton in front of dummy's A-Q.
(2) The final diamond play is no guess. South is known to have started with two hearts and two clubs only. South cannot hold more than six spades (North followed twice) and so South began with three diamonds.
(3) At trick 12, when North follows to the 4 of diamonds, declarer knows that North's last card is the 10 of hearts and therefore the remaining diamond must be with South.

Hand 88: Responding to the takeout double — Card reading and trump management

Dealer West : Nil vulnerable

NORTH
♠ K J 9 6 2
♡ J 9 6 5
♢ J
♣ K 6 5

WEST
♠ Q 8 7
♡ A
♢ 9 8 6 5 4
♣ 10 7 3 2

EAST
♠ 5
♡ K Q 10 7 4 3
♢ A 10 2
♣ 9 8 4

SOUTH
♠ A 10 4 3
♡ 8 2
♢ K Q 7 3
♣ A Q J

WEST	NORTH	EAST	SOUTH
No	No	2♡	Dble
No	3♠	No	4♠
No	No	No	

Bidding: South has an obvious double and North's 3♠ shows 5+ spades and around 7-10 points. With only four spades and the same strength, use 2NT Lebensohl and rebid 3♠ over the 3♣ puppet. With 16 HCP and six losers, South is worth a shot at 4♠.

Lead: King of hearts. Nothing else is attractive.

Recommended play: West takes the ♡A perforce and returns a diamond (not a club, obviously). East wins and continues with ♡Q and a third heart. North ruffs with dummy's ace of spades and follows with the 10 of spades, letting it run if West plays low. If necessary, the spade finesse is repeated. 10 tricks.

Notes: (1) If North fails to ruff the third heart or ruffs low, West scores a trump trick. One down.
(2) Given East started with a weak two, the ♠Q is more likely to be with West. It is usually right to play the partner of the pre-emptor for length in the other suits and thus key queens or jacks in those outside suits. After East turns up with 9 HCP (♡K-Q and ♢A), it is even more likely that West has the ♠Q. Therefore, ruff the third heart high and then finesse against West.

CHAPTER 23

THE MULTI-2◇ OPENING

The multi-2◇ opening is the most popular of the multi-openings. In the quest for greater efficiency, players have tried to compress more meanings into fewer bids. Why use two opening bids for the weak twos in the majors when you can get by with just one? This approach enables your system to cover more and more hand types and one measure of a system's value is the number of hands with which it can cope. Most who play a multi-2◇ use it to cover:
(a) a weak two in hearts, *OR* (b) a weak two in spades, *OR* (c) a number of strong hand types.

Some do use it differently but the above is the most common structure. A typical multi-2◇:
Weak two in hearts *OR* **Weak two in spades** *OR*
21-22 points balanced *OR*
9-10 playing tricks in clubs (Acol Two type) *OR*
9-10 playing tricks in diamonds (Acol Two type).

This frees the 2♡ / 2♠ / 2NT openings for other purposes. Some use only the weak options for the multi-2◇ and there are countless varieties for the strong possibilities.

RESPONDING TO 2◇

2♡ = 'Pass or correct': Pass with hearts. If not, opener bids 2♠ (weak two in spades), 2NT (the strong balanced option) or bids at the three-level to show other strong options (e.g., 3♣ = 9-10 playing tricks in clubs, 3◇ = the same in diamonds).

If opener removes to 2♠, the bidding proceeds as after a weak 2♠ opening (see Chapter 9). If opener removes to 2NT, bidding proceeds as though the opening bid was 2NT (see Chapter 4). Bidding, if any, after other strong options is natural.

2♠ = 'Pass or correct': To play if opener has the weak two in spades. 2♠ is used when responder has an excellent fit for hearts (good shape and 3+ support) but is not so good in spades. 2♠ operates as a game invitation in hearts. Opener passes with the weak two in spades. With the weak two in hearts, opener bids 3♡ if minimum and 4♡ if maximum. Other rebids (e.g., 2NT, 3♣, 3◇) show the strong options.

3♡ / 3♠ / 4♡ = pre-emptive in the major suit bid. Opener passes if holding that major. If not, bid the other major or make a natural strong rebid. Responder will be prepared for the strong rebid.

3♣ / 3◇ = Natural, strong responses. Opener rebids naturally (jump to 4-Major with a Suit Quality of 10).

2NT = Strong inquiry. This is used for hands which are worth game or a game invitation opposite a weak two. 2NT is normally based on a strong opening hand (13+ points) and more than three quick tricks.

If opener has a strong option opposite the 2NT reply, there should be sufficient values for a slam. The three-level replies are used for the weak two types.
Scheme A for opener's rebids:
3NT = A-K-Q-x-x-x in the major suit. Responder will usually be able to tell which major is held. If not, bid 4♡ and opener will bid 4♠ with spades.
3♠ = Spades, minimum points, only one top honour
3♡ = Hearts, minimum points, only one top honour
3◇ = Spades, better than the 3♠ reply, so either minimum with two top honours *or* maximum points
3♣ = Hearts, better than the 3♡ reply, so either minimum with two top honours *or* maximum points
4♡ / 4♠ = Maximum weak twos with a SQ of 10
4NT = The strong balanced option. You can use 5♣ Stayman and transfers but there is little room to explore. Responder usually bids either 6NT or 7NT.
4♣ / 4◇ = Other strong options. A new suit by responder is best played as a cue-bid with opener's suit as trumps.

Over 3♠ or 3♡, responder should be able to place the contract. Over 3♣ or 3◇, responder can 'relay', that is, inquire further by making the cheapest bid (3◇ over 3♣ or 3♡ over 3◇). Opener then rebids:
1st step = minimum points, two top honours. As this is opener's major, responder can pass at the 3-level.
2nd step = maximum points, two top honours
3rd step = maximum points, one top honour

This scheme gives responder as much information as can be obtained by the Ogust 2NT enquiry in response to a natural weak two. The Multi-2◇ thus will not lag behind a natural weak two.

If responder is contemplating 3NT and one top honour in opener's suit is enough, responder will know that with opener's first reply. If responder needs two honours, responder uses the 'relay'.

If responder does not use the 'relay', bidding opener's major is a sign-off (even at the three-level) and so are other game bids. Bidding the other major below game is natural and forcing (responder had no chance earlier to bid the other major without risking a pass), while a minor suit rebid is best used as a cue-bid with opener's major as trumps.
Scheme B: Different rebids after the 2NT inquiry
3♣ = Minimum with hearts
3◇ = Minimum with spades
3♡ = Maximum with *spades*
3♠ = Maximum with *hearts*
Advantage: Responder can always become declarer and so the opponents know very little about the hidden hand. The 3♡ and 3♠ replies commit the partnership to game. Over the 3♣ or 3◇ reply, the 'relay' rebid is available or responder can sign off.

What if they double partner's 2◇ opening?

Any bid by responder has its usual meaning.

Pass = 5+ diamonds. Opener passes, bids the major or shows the relevant strong option.

Redouble = 'Bid 2♡ and then pass my next bid.' This allows responder to escape into a long, strong suit. Opener will bid 2♡ with either weak two, show the strong option (leave the redouble in with a strong hand in diamonds!), or bid 2♠ with a weak two in spades *and* a suit quality of 10.

What if they bid over partner's 2◇ opening?

If they bid 2♡ or 2♠, double is for takeout. Partner will be pleased to leave it in with six in their suit. 2NT and suit bids have their normal meaning.

If they bid 2NT, double is for penalties. A bid of a major suit invites game. Minor suit bids are natural and forcing.

If they bid at the three-level or higher, double is for takeout and 'Pass or correct' applies to a major suit bid.

Defending against the multi-2◇

It is tough defending against any multi opening if the opening does not promise a specific suit (no 'anchor suit'). This is because both partners lack a cue-bid of the enemy suit to show a strong hand.

The 'no anchor suit' feature also makes multi-twos unpopular with administrators. You may find that you are not permitted to use multi-twos at your local club and perhaps not even in events below national championship level. This is unfortunate since it is attractive to be able to show so many weak hand types. Often you can make a game with less than half the high card strength and you may also be able to locate a profitable sacrifice.

This is the recommended defence to a multi-2◇ :
Double = 16+ points, any shape except for the 2NT and 3NT bids, and the jump-overcall.
2NT = 19-21 balanced   **3NT** = 22-24 balanced
Suit bids = natural, good suit but below 16 HCP, a strong 5-card major and a good opening at the two-level, a strong suit and 6-losers at the three-level.
Jump-suit = 6+ suit, Suit Quality 9+, 5-loser hand.

Otherwise pass and wait for responder to bid. If responder makes a weak bid in a major, double is best used for takeout. In fourth seat, treat the action by RHO as though that is their opening.

WEST	NORTH	EAST	SOUTH
2◇	No	2♡	?

South should treat the position as though there has been a weak 2♡ opening on the right. It would be wrong to pass with a strong hand (unless you are very strong in hearts). The bidding could end at 2♡.

In reply to the double of 2◇:

2♡ = artificial negative, 0-7 points. All others = 8+ points and forcing to game. Further bidding is natural. Jump-rebids by opener after a 2♡ negative are very strong but not forcing.

How to use your 2♣ opening if you are using the other twos as multis or weak twos

The strong options in the multi-2◇ opening should be very closely defined. As a result, most of your very strong hands will still start with a 2♣ opening. Benjamin Twos work well because they provide two strong opening bids to distinguish the game force hands from those just below that strength. It is possible to retain much of this benefit even if opening 2♣ on all or almost all the strong hands.

Use the 2♣ opening to show a game-going hand (either 23+ HCP or 10+ tricks) or a hand of 8½-9½ playing tricks with a 6+ suit, usually a one-suiter hand with 19+ points. You will need to dovetail the content of the 2♣ opening with the strong options for the multi-2◇. There is no point in having an overlap. For example, if the multi-2◇ includes a long strong minor with 9-10 playing tricks, then 2♣ might include the minor one-suiters just below this strength, perhaps 8-8½ playing tricks, 19+ points or the equivalent.

Responses to 2♣

2◇ = Artificial negative, 0-7 points.
Others = natural, game forcing, 8+ points. Suit responses are 5+ suits in principle.
2NT = natural positive reply, balanced hand.
7 points is borderline. With 7 HCP made up of an ace and a king, give a positive reply. Do the same with 7 HCP including a suit headed by the A-Q. These are 1½ quick tricks, which make slam a fair bet opposite a game force.

After a positive reply, if opener bids game sooner or later, this shows the 8½-9½ trick hand and slam bidding is responder's responsibility.

After 2♣ : 2◇, opener's rebids are :

2♡ = *artificial*, 23+ HCP or 10+ playing tricks
2♠ = Natural game force, 5+ spades
2NT = strong, balanced (21-22 or 23-24, whatever range is not covered elsewhere). Continue as though the opening bid had been a natural 2NT.
3♣ / 3◇ / 3♡ / 3♠ = 8½-9 playing tricks
4♣ / 4◇ / 4♡ / 4♠ = 9½-10 playing tricks
3NT = Long, solid minor, 9 playing tricks, stoppers in at least two other suits

Thus opener's two-level suit rebids are stronger than the three-level and four-level one-suiter rebids.

After 2♣ : 2◇, 2♡

2♠ = artificial, second negative, 0-4 points
Other replies are natural with 5-7 points.

After 2♣ : 2◇, 2♡ : 2♠, opener's rebids are:

Suit bids = natural and forcing to game. Open 2♣ + rebid 2♡ + suit rebid = game force.
2NT = 25+ balanced. Forcing to game. Continue as though the opening had been a natural 2NT so that:
     3♣ = simple or 5-card major Stayman
     3◇ / 3♡ = transfers, and so on
     4NT = slam invitation   **5NT** = 'Pick a slam'

EXERCISES FOR THE MULTI-2◊ (weak two in either major, 23-24 balanced or 9-10 tricks in a minor)

A. Partner has opened 2◊. What is your response with each of these hands?

	1.		2.		3.		4.		5.
♠	A 7 3	♠	K Q 7 6 2	♠	3	♠	A J 7	♠	8
♡	8 2	♡	- - -	♡	Q 9 3	♡	9 2	♡	7 2
◊	K Q 7 5 3 2	◊	K Q	◊	A K 9 4 3	◊	A Q J 4	◊	Q 9 8 6 5 3 2
♣	7 6	♣	A K J 8 4 2	♣	K Q 4 2	♣	K Q 9 2	♣	J 9 4

B. The bidding has started 2◊ : 2NT. What is opener's rebid with these hands?

	1.		2.		3.		4.		5.
♠	4 3	♠	6 2	♠	A K 8 7 4 2	♠	A K Q 8 7 2	♠	K Q J 10 4 2
♡	K Q 10 7 6 3	♡	K J 10 4 3 2	♡	9 6 4	♡	6 4	♡	7
◊	J 6 4	◊	8 4	◊	8	◊	9 2	◊	K 5 3
♣	6 2	♣	K 8 4	♣	Q J 2	♣	7 4 2	♣	7 4 2

C. RHO has opened 2◊, multi. What action would you take with these hands?

	1.		2.		3.		4.		5.
♠	A Q 8 3	♠	J 8 5	♠	A 6	♠	A 5	♠	K 3 2
♡	K 9	♡	K Q 2	♡	K Q J 9	♡	K Q J 7 4 3	♡	8
◊	Q J 8	◊	A K 7	◊	7 4	◊	A K	◊	Q J 9 8 6 3
♣	A J 4 2	♣	A K 3 2	♣	K 10 4 3 2	♣	8 4 2	♣	A Q 7

COMPETITIVE BIDDING : How should the following hands be bid? West is the dealer each time and neither side is vulnerable.

	SET 39— WEST		SET 39 — NORTH		SET 39 — EAST		SET 39 — SOUTH
1. ♠	J 8	1. ♠	A K 10 7 5 2	1. ♠	9 4	1. ♠	Q 6 3
♡	J 7 5 3	♡	10 6	♡	K Q 8 2	♡	A 9 4
◊	K J 10	◊	9 4	◊	Q 7 6 5	◊	A 8 3 2
♣	K J 3 2	♣	8 7 6	♣	Q 10 4	♣	A 9 5
2. ♠	K 7	2. ♠	A J 6 5 4	2. ♠	9 8	2. ♠	Q 10 3 2
♡	A 10 9 8 5 3	♡	6 4	♡	K Q J 2	♡	7
◊	Q 7 6 5	◊	J 10	◊	2	◊	A K 9 8 4 3
♣	2	♣	Q 9 8 6	♣	A 10 7 5 4 3	♣	K J
3. ♠	5 2	3. ♠	Q 7 6 4 3	3. ♠	A 8	3. ♠	K J 10 9
♡	Q J 10 7 3 2	♡	A 8 5	♡	K 6 4	♡	9
◊	8 3	◊	Q 10 6	◊	9 7 5 4	◊	A K J 2
♣	A 3 2	♣	Q 9	♣	J 8 7 4	♣	K 10 6 5
4. ♠	A Q 10 7 6 2	4. ♠	9 8	4. ♠	K 5 3	4. ♠	J 4
♡	10 6 5	♡	A 9 8 7 4 3	♡	J	♡	K Q 2
◊	K 2	◊	J 9	◊	A Q 10 5 4	◊	8 7 6 3
♣	8 3	♣	J 10 6	♣	K 9 4 2	♣	A Q 7 5
5. ♠	A Q 6 3 2	5. ♠	4	5. ♠	K 8 5	5. ♠	J 10 9 7
♡	7 2	♡	K Q J 9 8 3	♡	A 6 4	♡	10 5
◊	7 2	◊	J 8 5 3	◊	A K 10 4	◊	Q 9 6
♣	K 8 6 2	♣	9 3	♣	Q J 7	♣	A 10 5 4
6. ♠	8 6 4	6. ♠	9 2	6. ♠	K J 7 3	6. ♠	A Q 10 5
♡	A J 8 7 6 3	♡	K Q 10 5 2	♡	9	♡	4
◊	Q J 10	◊	A 9 5	◊	8 7 4	◊	K 6 3 2
♣	3	♣	10 7 4	♣	K 8 6 5 2	♣	A Q J 9

PLAY HANDS ON THE MULTI-2◇ OPENING

(These hands can be made up by using pages 176-183)

Hand 89: Responding to a multi-2◇ — Action by fourth player — Playing for penalties

Dealer North : E-W vulnerable

NORTH
- ♠ 8 6 4
- ♡ A J 8 7 6 3
- ◇ Q J 10
- ♣ 3

WEST
- ♠ A Q 10 5
- ♡ 4
- ◇ K 6 3 2
- ♣ A Q J 9

EAST
- ♠ 9 2
- ♡ K Q 10 5 2
- ◇ A 9 5
- ♣ 10 7 4

SOUTH
- ♠ K J 7 3
- ♡ 9
- ◇ 8 7 4
- ♣ K 8 6 5 2

WEST	NORTH	EAST	SOUTH
	2◇	No	2♡
Dble	No	No	No

Bidding: South bids 2♡ ('pass-or-correct') and West doubles for takeout. (If West's majors were reversed, West would pass. With a weak two in spades, North would correct 2♡ to 2♠ and West could double that for takeout.) North's pass confirms the weak two in hearts and East's pass confirms that North-South are in deep trouble. Leave the double in when you are strong in trumps, particularly sitting over the long suit, and your side has at least half the HCP. It is true that passing could miss a game (here East-West make 3NT easily) but game may not be on and perhaps you can do even better by defending.

Lead: 2 of diamonds. Second choice, the 4 of hearts.

Recommended play: East wins with the ace and shifts to the 9 of spades, jack from South and queen from West who shifts to the 4 of hearts. If declarer ducks this, East wins with the 10 and returns the 2 of spades, low from dummy, 10 from West who cashes the ace of spades on which East discards the 9 of diamonds (top from a remaining doubleton). Next comes the king of diamonds and the ◇3, ruffed by East who switches to clubs. The defence takes three spades, two diamonds and a diamond ruff, three hearts and one club. That leaves North five down, +1100 to East-West, adequate compensation for the missed 3NT.

Notes: (1) South is better off to rise with the ♡A and lead a second diamond. Now East has no convenient entry to lead a second spade. West wins and exits with a diamond but now North-South escape for 'only' –800.
(2) South would like to run from 2♡ doubled but there is nowhere to go. If South does attempt a rescue, East-West double everything thereafter for penalties.
(3) On an initial trump lead, ducked in dummy, East wins, shifts to a spade and the play proceeds as before.

Hand 90: Competing against the multi — Card-reading to avoid a fatal mistake

Dealer East : Both vulnerable

NORTH
- ♠ 9 3
- ♡ A K Q J 9 8
- ◇ A 3
- ♣ A 8 2

WEST
- ♠ - - -
- ♡ 6 5 2
- ◇ Q J 9 8 5 2
- ♣ K J 9 7

EAST
- ♠ K Q J 10 6 4
- ♡ 3
- ◇ 7 6 4
- ♣ Q 10 4

SOUTH
- ♠ A 8 7 5 2
- ♡ 10 7 4
- ◇ K 10
- ♣ 6 5 3

WEST	NORTH	EAST	SOUTH
		2◇	No
2♡	4♡	All pass	

Bidding: West fears the worst upon hearing 2◇. If someone doubles after East corrects to spades, it is not easy to judge whether to play there or run. With a good 5-5, you might start an S.O.S. redouble sequence. As it happens, diamonds plays better than spades but this need not be so. It would not be silly for West to pass the 2◇ opening.

North knows that East's suit is spades. Rather than waste time and give the opponents more space, North hopes for two tricks from partner and jumps straight to 4♡. As West has given a weak reply, it is not too much to expect South to produce two tricks. Any decent partner would.

Lead: King of spades. All your leads should be this easy.

Recommended play: What a good fellow South is. There are the two tricks needed. Careful, do not squander one of those tricks. Declarer should play low in dummy and low again on the next spade. The third spade is ruffed by North who draws trumps, crosses to the ◇K and discards a loser on the ♠A.

Notes: (1) It is not easy to avoid the instinctive play of the ♠A at trick 1. You need to be conscious that East has a weak two in spades and therefore six spades. Add the five in dummy and your two and that leaves West with a void. If you play the ♠A, West ruffs and your ten easy tricks have been telescoped into nine. If you fell for this trap, they may soon be calling you 'the magician': you make tricks disappear.
(2) It is not easy for North-South to find the highest scoring spot of 3NT.
(3) If declarer does play the ♠A at trick 1 and West ruffs, West should return a trump or the ◇Q. A club switch works but on other layouts, it might help declarer take an extra finesse with dummy very short of entries.

Hand 91: Inviting game — High level takeout double — Opening lead — Defensive technique

Dealer South : Nil vulnerable

NORTH
♠ 9 8
♡ K Q J 2
◇ 2
♣ A 10 7 5 4 3

WEST
♠ A J 6 5 4
♡ 6 4
◇ Q 10
♣ Q 9 8 6

EAST
♠ Q 10 3 2
♡ 7
◇ A K 9 8 4 3
♣ K 2

SOUTH
♠ K 7
♡ A 10 9 8 5 3
◇ J 7 6 5
♣ J

WEST	NORTH	EAST	SOUTH
			2◇
No	2♠	No	4♡
No	No	Dble	No
4♠	No	No	No

Bidding: North's 2♠ is to play opposite a weak two in spades and invites game opposite a weak two in hearts. South has a maximum weak 2♡ and so bids 4♡ (3♡ would be a minimum). East is awkwardly placed over 2♠. Double would be takeout of spades and East is happy to defend a spade contract. East's double of 4♡ is logically for takeout since South has shown six hearts and North's 2♠ = a strong fit for hearts. With no attractive suit, West may leave the double in. Here 4♠ is sensible.

Lead: Ace of clubs.

Recommended play: North continues with the *ten* of clubs at trick 2 and South ruffs. Recognising the 10 as a suit preference for hearts, South leads a low heart (the 9 is a good card, saying you do not want hearts returned). North overtakes with the jack and leads a third club. Dummy ruffs high, but South overruffs. One down after an exceptionally fine defence.

Notes: (1) Even if East-West fail, they have done well as 4♡ is unbeatable. The defence can take one diamond and two spades but South can comfortably set up the club suit, using dummy's trumps as entries.
(2) If North does not find the winning lead, North would be better off sacrificing in 5♡. Say North leads the king of hearts. The best South can do is overtake and switch to the ♣J. North takes the ace and gives South a club ruff but that is the end of the North-South defence. On the ◇2 lead, West should win in hand and play as safely as possible for ten tricks via ♠A and another spade. West should recognise that 4♠ is an excellent contract for East-West and making an overtrick is less important than ensuring the contract.
(3) The ♣A lead is not far-fetched if North elects to defend. South is unlikely to have more than one defensive trick. Therefore, ruffs are needed to defeat the contract. After leading the ♣A North can decide whether to continue clubs or try for a diamond ruff.

Hand 92: Delayed competitive action — Playing for penalties

Dealer West : N-S vulnerable

NORTH
♠ 7 5 3
♡ A K Q 9 5 3
◇ 9 8 4
♣ 2

WEST
♠ Q 4
♡ J 8 4 2
◇ 7 6 5
♣ K 8 5 3

EAST
♠ K 9 8 6
♡ 7 6
◇ K Q J
♣ A 9 7 4

SOUTH
♠ A J 10 2
♡ 10
◇ A 10 3 2
♣ Q J 10 6

WEST	NORTH	EAST	SOUTH
No	2◇	No	2♡
No	No	Dble	No
2NT	No	3♣	Dble
No	No	No	

Bidding: East is too weak to take action at once over 2◇ and South is too weak to do more than 2♡. After North passes to confirm a weak two in hearts, most tournament players would compete with a takeout double. This shows modest values because of East's failure to double 2◇ (to show 16+ points). South waits in ambush and West bids 2NT Lebensohl. 3♣ at once by West would show a maximum passed hand, as East can have up to 15 HCP. When East bids 3♣ as required, South lowers the boom.

Lead: 10 of hearts. Try not to smile as you see dummy.

Recommended play: North should overtake and cash a second heart. The defence will come to one spade, two hearts, one diamond and two clubs for two down, +300.

Notes: (1) Note how Lebensohl can be used even in these belated auctions. Lebensohl has a fringe benefit when advancer intends to pass 3♣. It follows the principle 'If you are in deep trouble, let partner be declarer!'
(2) East should not be deflected from competing in future in auctions such as these just because of an occasional rotten result. To be a successful pairs player, you have to compete, you have to be pushy. With that kind of approach, you are bound to stumble and hurt yourself from time to time.

CHAPTER 24
OTHER MULTI-TWO OPENINGS

2♡ / 2♠ / 2NT openings when using a Multi-2◇

If the multi-2◇ includes the weak twos in the majors, the question arises 'What do the 2♡ and 2♠ openings now mean?', and if 2◇ also includes the balanced 21-22 hand, what does 2NT now mean?

Some use 2♡ and 2♠ to show strong natural openings just short of game-force values. Most prefer to use the freed bids to show weak two-suiter hand types. This is a common approach :

2♡ = Hearts and another suit
2♠ = Spades and a minor suit
2NT = Both minors

The pattern should be 5-5 at least and the strength should be about 6-10 HCP, below opening values. The above combination covers all two-suiters.

Over 2♡ or 2♠, responder may pass or raise the major pre-emptively. With no tolerance for opener's first suit, bid the next available suit. Opener will pass if holding that suit or show the second suit held. A suit bid other than the cheapest suit is strong and forcing. With other strong hands, you can use the 2NT relay. Opener then bids the second suit. With a maximum 6-5, opener shows the 6-card suit (rebid the major or bid the second suit at the four-level).

The RCO 2♡, 2♠ and 2NT openings

These show weak 2-suiters, 6-10 HCP and at least a 5-5 pattern. RCO stands for Rank-Colour-Odd.

2♡ = **R**ank. Same rank. Major suits or minors. For example, open 2♡ with:

♠ K Q 10 4 2	*or*	♠ 8 3
♡ Q J 9 6 4		♡ 3
◇ 9 2		◇ K 10 8 7 4
♣ 5		♣ A J 10 6 3

2♠ = **C**olour. Same colour. Red suits or blacks. For example, open 2♠ with:

♠ A Q J 7 5	*or*	♠ 8 3
♡ 6		♡ Q 9 7 4 3 2
◇ 9 4		◇ K J 7 6 3
♣ J 10 7 5 2		♣ - - -

2NT = **O**dd. Two suits of different colour and different rank, so spades + diamonds *or* hearts + clubs. Memory guide: **NT = N**on-**T**ouching. For example, open 2NT with:

♠ A 10 7 6 2	*or*	♠ 8
♡ 5		♡ Q J 10 7 4
◇ K J 10 7 4		◇ 4
♣ 6 3		♣ K J 10 9 7 2

A useful memory guide for the RCO order is **R**esponder **C**an **O**perate. At adverse vulnerability, it is prudent to be maximum or have a 6-5.

The CRASH Convention

CRASH is similar to RCO Twos except that 2♡ is colour (C), 2♠ is rank (RA) and the SH for opening 2NT is the abbreviation for *sh*ape, referring to the pointed suits, spades-diamonds, or the rounded suits, hearts-clubs. There is little difference between the methods. RCOs have a slight advantage in opening 2♡ with both majors, while with CRASH, the opening bid with both majors is 2♠. Holding both majors gives you a competitive edge. Silly to give this advantage away, isn't it? Using RCO, you can often stop at the two-level after a 2♡ opening. Playing CRASH, you usually have to reach the three-level to locate your major suit fit. This tilts the scale in favour of RCO Twos.

Responding to RCO 2♡ or 2♠ with a weak hand

Pass = you know which suits partner has and prefer the suit partner has bid. If you have five cards in one possible combination and eight in the other, the odds are strong that partner has the two-suiter where you hold five cards. If you are 4-9 in the combinations, it is very, very likely that partner has the combination opposite your four.

Otherwise bid a suit where you have 3+ cards. Usually choose your cheapest option. Any suit bid is P/C, 'pass-or-correct'.

With a 4+ fit with a suit in each combination, you may wish to pre-empt. Jump replies to 3♠, 4♣ or 4◇ are pre-emptive and are P/C, 'pass-or-correct'. Any jump to game in a suit is also P/C. To play in your own suit, use the 2NT inquiry and bid game in your suit after opener's reply.

Responding to 2♡ or 2♠ with a strong hand

If strong enough to invite game or force to game, bid 2NT. This asks for opener's suits and strength. Opener bids the cheaper suit if minimum and the higher suit if maximum.

After 2♡ : 2NT relay, opener rebids :

3♣ = minors and minimum
3◇ = minors and maximum
3♡ = majors and minimum
3♠ = majors and maximum

After 2♠ : 2NT relay, opener rebids :

3♣ = black suits and minimum
3◇ = red suits and minimum
3♡ = red suits and maximum
3♠ = black suits and maximum

Replies at the 4-level show a maximum with 6+ cards in the suit bid.

Responding to 2NT with a weak hand

Bid a suit, pass-or-correct, but 3♣ is not available as that is the strong relay. If you figure partner has hearts and clubs and you prefer clubs, you cannot escape below 4♣ if you bid. With a very weak hand, it may be better to pass 2NT and if they double 2NT, you can later escape to 3♣. Pass 2NT also if weak with very long diamonds and you figure opener has hearts and clubs. Maybe you can escape into your diamonds later.

Responding to 2NT with a strong hand

Over 2NT the strong relay is 3♣, again asking for opener's suits and range. Opener rebids:

3♦ = diamonds + spades and minimum
3♡ = hearts + clubs and minimum
3♠ = diamonds + spades and maximum
3NT = hearts + clubs and maximum

Replies at the four-level show a 6-5 pattern with six cards in the suit bid and a maximum.

Responder's action after opener's reply to the relay (2NT over 2♡ / 2♠ or 3♣ over 2NT)

After a minimum reply, responder can pass or bid opener's other suit as a sign-off. Other bids below game are forcing. Game bids are to play.

After a maximum reply, game bids are to play and suit bids below game are all forcing.

Responder often wants to set a trump suit early in order to use RKCB. This can be achieved by responder bidding 4♣ or 4♦ after opener's reply to the relay. 4♣ or 4♦ sets the minor suit bid if that is one of opener's suits. If not, 4♣ / 4♦ sets opener's major suit. In the case of both majors with opener, 4♣ sets hearts and 4♦ sets spades. For example:

WEST	EAST	Over 3♣/3♦, 4♣/4♦ sets the
2♡	2NT	minor suit bid. Over 3♡/3♠, 4♣
?		sets hearts and 4♦ sets spades.

If responder wants to sign off over 3♣, responder can pass or convert to 3♦.

WEST	EAST	Over 3♣/3♠, 4♣ sets clubs
2♠	2NT	and 4♦ sets spades. Over
?		3♦/3♠, 4♣ sets hearts, 4♦ sets diamonds.

If responder wants to sign off after a minimum reply, responder can do so at the three-level.

WEST	EAST	Over 3♦/3♠, 4♣ sets spades
2NT	3♣	and 4♦ sets diamonds. Over 3♡,
?		4♦ sets hearts, 4NT sets clubs.

4♣ is needed as a sign-off over 3♡ and so 4NT is necessary to set clubs. Over 3NT (maximum with hearts and clubs), 4♣ sets clubs, 4♦ sets hearts.

Action if they bid over your RCO opening

1. They double 2♡ or 2♠

Pass = pass-or-correct: 'If this is one of your suits, this is where I wish to play.'
Suit bids = pass-or-correct.
2NT = Strong relay as usual.

Redouble = 'Please make the cheapest bid and pass my next bid.' This allows responder to escape into a long suit with no fit for either of opener's suits.

If the double is passed back to opener, pass if holding the suit doubled. If not, opener can show extra shape: Redouble = extra length in the distant suit. Bidding the cheaper suit shows equal length or longer in the cheaper suit. Other bids show the fragment with a 5-5-3-0. For example:

W	N	E	S	Rdble	= longer diamonds
2♡	Dble	No	No	2♠	= 3-0-5-5 pattern
?			3♣	= equal or clubs longer	

2. They double your 2NT opening

Suit bids are still pass-or-correct except for 3♣, which is still the strong relay. Responder's pass of 2NT doubled = a preference for clubs over hearts. 3♣ is not available as a rescue since 3♣ is the artificial relay. Responder's redouble asks opener to bid 3♣ and pass responder's next bid.

If the double is passed back to opener, opener redoubles to show extra length in the distant suit and bids the cheaper suit with equal length in the suits or with greater length in the cheaper suit.

3. They bid a suit over your RCO opening

Double = takeout at the two-level or three-level and shows game-inviting values or better. It is possible to play the double for penalties but experience has shown that using the double for takeout is more effective. Opener can of course leave the double in with 5+ cards in the suit bid. Doubles at the four-level or higher are penalties.
Suit bids = pass-or-correct, but showing decent strength. Suits bids below game show game-inviting values and if maximum, opener should bid game.
Bidding the enemy suit = force to game and asks opener to bid the cheaper suit held. If opener has their suit, bid the other suit held.

Defending against RCO Twos

Use the same basic defensive approach as against the multi-2♦ (see Chapter 23) :
Double = 16+ points, any shape except for the 2NT and 3NT bids
2NT = 19-21 balanced
3NT = 22-24 balanced
Suit bids = natural, good suit but below 16 HCP

The negative reply to a double of 2♠ or 2NT is 3♣. If strong in the suit doubled, you may leave the double in. If you have no clear-cut action, it is often best to pass and wait for the suits to be clarified before entering the fray. It is no fun to come into the bidding and land in one of opener's 5-card suits.

Pass and later double at the 2-level or 3-level is takeout but less than 16 HCP.

In fourth position treat any weak action by RHO as their opening bid. If the bidding starts, multi on your left : No : No to you, double = 12+ HCP.

EXERCISES FOR RCO TWOS

A. Partner has opened 2♠, RCO. What action should you take as responder with neither side vulnerable?

1. ♠ 9 7	2. ♠ K 7 6 4 2	3. ♠ J 9 8 4 2	4. ♠ J 9 7 2	5. ♠ 8 6 2
♡ A 8 2	♡ 6	♡ K 9 6 3	♡ 2	♡ A 9 8 2
◇ Q 7 5 3	◇ A 8 4 3	◇ A 4 3	◇ Q J 4 3 2	◇ K Q 8 5 2
♣ K 7 6 3	♣ 9 8 4	♣ 2	♣ K Q 2	♣ 4

B. You opened 2NT (RCO) and partner has responded 3♣, relay. What is your rebid with these hands?

1. ♠ A J 9 8 4	2. ♠ K J 10 7 4	3. ♠ 2	4. ♠ 4	5. ♠ 3
♡ 6	♡ 7 2	♡ K Q J 4 2	♡ A Q J 7 3	♡ A K 7 3 2
◇ Q J 7 5 2	◇ K Q J 8 3	◇ 9 5	◇ 10 8	◇ 5
♣ 9 3	♣ 9	♣ J 10 8 7 4	♣ Q J 10 9 2	♣ Q J 10 7 4 2

C. RHO has opened 2♡ RCO (majors or minors). What action would you take with neither side vulnerable?

1. ♠ A J 4 3 2	2. ♠ 7 5	3. ♠ K J 4 2	4. ♠ A 9 2	5. ♠ A K 8 3
♡ K 3	♡ 6	♡ Q J 6 4	♡ 6	♡ Q 7 4 3
◇ K 6 4 2	◇ A 9 8 4	◇ A J 8	◇ A K Q 2	◇ 8
♣ 6 2	♣ A K J 8 4 2	♣ A K	♣ A J 7 4 2	♣ A J 3 2

COMPETITIVE BIDDING : How should the following hands be bid? West is the dealer each time and neither side is vulnerable. Both sides are playing R.C.O. two-suited openings.

SET 40 — WEST	SET 40 — NORTH	SET 40 — EAST	SET 40 — SOUTH
1. ♠ A J 8	1. ♠ K 10 7 5 3	1. ♠ 4	1. ♠ Q 9 6 2
♡ J 7 5 3	♡ 10 6 4 2	♡ Q 8	♡ A K 9
◇ K 10	◇ 9 4	◇ Q J 7 6 5	◇ A 8 3 2
♣ J 9 3 2	♣ A 5	♣ K Q 10 8 4	♣ 7 6
2. ♠ Q 7	2. ♠ K J 6 5 4	2. ♠ A 9 8	2. ♠ 10 3 2
♡ A 10 9 8	♡ 6 3	♡ K Q J 2	♡ 7 5 4
◇ K 7 6 5	◇ 10	◇ Q J 9 4	◇ A 8 3 2
♣ 7 4 2	♣ K Q 10 8 6	♣ A J	♣ 9 5 3
3. ♠ 6	3. ♠ K 9 5 4 3	3. ♠ A Q 8 7 2	3. ♠ J 10
♡ 7	♡ A Q 10	♡ J 4	♡ K 9 8 6 5 3 2
◇ A Q 10 9 5	◇ 6 2	◇ J 8 7 4 3	◇ K
♣ Q 10 9 6 4 2	♣ A 7 3	♣ J	♣ K 8 5
4. ♠ 9 7 2	4. ♠ - - -	4. ♠ A K 4	4. ♠ Q J 10 8 6 5 3
♡ J 10 9 6 5	♡ 4 3	♡ A 7	♡ K Q 8 2
◇ K 2	◇ Q 10 9 5 3	◇ A 8 6 4	◇ J 7
♣ A 8 3	♣ K J 7 6 5 2	♣ Q 10 9 4	♣ - - -
5. ♠ A J 10 9 5	5. ♠ K Q	5. ♠ 8 3	5. ♠ 7 6 4 2
♡ 7	♡ Q 9 8 5 3	♡ K J	♡ A 10 6 4 2
◇ Q J 9 8 3 2	◇ 7 6	◇ K 10 5 4	◇ A
♣ 6	♣ A Q J 8	♣ K 10 9 5 4	♣ 7 3 2
6. ♠ 7 2	6. ♠ Q J 10 6 5	6. ♠ A K 8	6. ♠ 9 4 3
♡ K 8 3 2	♡ 9	♡ A Q J 5 4	♡ 10 7 6
◇ K 9 6 5	◇ Q J 10 8 4 3	◇ 7	◇ A 2
♣ A 9 4	♣ 5	♣ K Q 8 3	♣ J 10 7 6 2

PLAY HANDS ON RCO TWOS
(These hands can be made up by using pages 176-183)

Hand 93: Competitive bidding — Card reading

Dealer North : Both vulnerable

NORTH
- ♠ A J 8
- ♡ J 7 5 3
- ◇ K 7
- ♣ J 8 3 2

WEST
- ♠ Q 9 6 2
- ♡ A K 9
- ◇ A 8 3 2
- ♣ 7 6

EAST
- ♠ K 10 7 5 3
- ♡ 10 6 4 2
- ◇ 9 4
- ♣ A 5

SOUTH
- ♠ 4
- ♡ Q 8
- ◇ Q J 10 6 5
- ♣ K Q 10 9 4

WEST	NORTH	EAST	SOUTH
	No	No	2♡
No	3♣	No	No
Dble	No	3♠	All pass

Bidding: South's 2♡ = majors or minors. RCOs are not for the faint-hearted. West is too weak for immediate action. North bids 3♣, the desired contract opposite the minors and prepared to reach 3♡ opposite the majors. If weaker, North might bid 2♠, false preference. South's pass confirms the minors and West should compete even though vulnerable. Treat the position as though the bidding had started 3♣ : No : No. If you would re-open then, you should re-open now. East is content with 3♠ since West's pass over 2♡ showed 15 points or less.

Lead: King of clubs.

Recommended play: East wins with the ace of clubs and leads a spade to the queen. North wins and returns a club, won by South who shifts to a diamond. Declarer takes the ace and leads a spade to the 10. The last trump is drawn and declarer loses one trick in each suit.

Notes: (1) North-South would make 3♣ if allowed to play there. You will not always be right to compete on the West cards but passing is likely to be the losing action more often than not. North is a passed hand and South has made a weak opening. As partner is bound to have some values, West's double is not so heroic.
(2) If South leads the ◇Q, the defence must shift to clubs urgently lest declarer set up the ♡10 for a club pitch.
(3) As South is 5-5 in the minors, spades are likely to be 3-1 with South having the singleton. There is slight extra confirmation from the opening lead. If South had two spades and one heart, South might have led the singleton heart. The failure to lead a heart carries a suggestion that South has one spade, two hearts.

Hand 94: Pre-emptive response — Competitive decisions

Dealer East : Nil vulnerable

NORTH
- ♠ J 10
- ♡ K 9 8 6 5 3 2
- ◇ K
- ♣ K 8 5

WEST
- ♠ A Q 8 7 2
- ♡ J 4
- ◇ J 8 7 4 3
- ♣ J

EAST
- ♠ 6
- ♡ 7
- ◇ A Q 10 9 5
- ♣ Q 10 9 6 4 2

SOUTH
- ♠ K 9 5 4 3
- ♡ A Q 10
- ◇ 6 2
- ♣ A 7 3

WEST	NORTH	EAST	SOUTH
		2♡	No
4♠	No	5♣	No
5◇	No	No	No

Bidding: East's 2♡ = majors or minors. It is dangerous for South to bid in the direct position on these modest values. West can tell there is a ten-card fit in spades or diamonds and so jumps to 4♠ pre-emptively. On a good day 4♠ may make and if East-West have the majors, North-South have a mighty club fit. East's 5♣ says, 'I have the minors' and West corrects to 5◇. West expects 5◇ to fail but knows it should be a good sacrifice against their heart contract.

Lead: 6 of hearts. East has both minors and West has shown good spades. That leaves only hearts.

Recommended play: South takes the ace and might switch to a spade (in case West has the ♡K and North the ♠A). West wins and leads the jack of clubs. North should allow this to go to South, otherwise South will be exposed to a ruffing finesse later. West later ruffs a club, leads a diamond (North's singleton king is a delight), draws trumps and ruffs out the clubs. Making 11 tricks.

Notes: (1) North-South do very well in hearts but how should they enter the auction? To bid at once over 2♡ on the South hand is very risky. Over 4♠, 5♡ by North could be one of the great debacles of all time if East does have the majors. South might well double 5♣ and now North can bid 5♡ because East has the minors, West's 4♠ implies weak hearts and South's double shows some values.
(2) 4♡ is unbeatable and the defence has to be careful defending 5♡. If East leads the spade singleton and West cashes two spades, a third spade will allow 5♡ to make. East should signal violently for a diamond shift (in case North has K-x in diamonds) or, at teams, ruff the second spade and cash the ◇A.

Hand 95: Competitive bidding — Slam play technique

Dealer South : N-S vulnerable

NORTH
- ♠ A K 8
- ♡ A Q J 10 5
- ◇ 7
- ♣ K Q 8 3

WEST
- ♠ Q J 10 6 5
- ♡ 9
- ◇ A J 10 8 4 3
- ♣ 5

EAST
- ♠ 9 4 3
- ♡ 7 6 4
- ◇ Q 2
- ♣ J 10 7 6 2

SOUTH
- ♠ 7 2
- ♡ K 8 3 2
- ◇ K 9 6 5
- ♣ A 9 4

WEST	NORTH	EAST	SOUTH
			No
2NT	Dble	No	No
3◇	Dble	3♠	4♡
No	4NT	No	5♡
No	6♡	All pass	

Bidding: West's 2NT = spades-diamonds *OR* hearts-clubs. North's double shows a very strong hand. There is no urgency for East to bid here and the same applies to South. West's 3◇ = spades-diamonds with diamonds longer or equal length. (With spades longer, use redouble to show extra length in the further suit. East bids 3♣ and West's 3◇ then = 6+ spades and 5 diamonds.) North's double of 3◇ = takeout and East corrects to 3♠. South ventures 4♡ and that spurs North on to slam. As South should have at most two spades, North needs only two other losers covered.

Lead: Queen of spades. Leading the singleton club or the ◇A are both reasonable gambles.

Recommended play: Win with the ♠A and draw two rounds of trumps with ♡A, ♡Q. When West shows out, leave the last trump out and lead dummy's singleton diamond. When East plays low, West is sure to have the ace, so duck the diamond to West. Win West's exit, cash ♠K and ruff the spade loser in hand. Continue with ♣A, ♣K, ♣Q (East who has the last trump is known to have club length) and ruff dummy's fourth club. Ruff a diamond high and draw the last trump.

Notes: (1) It would be no surprise if North-South did not reach this good slam, especially after West opens.
(2) If declarer draws three rounds of trumps early, declarer will not be able to ruff both a spade and a club.
(3) At the vulnerability, North-South should bid game or slam rather than take the penalties in 3♠ doubled.
(4) East-West should not sacrifice over 6♡ since they do not have a great trump fit, perhaps 6♡ will fail and minus 800 will be a bad board anyway, as many pairs will not reach this slam.

Hand 96: Competitive bidding — Opening lead inferences from the auction

Dealer West : E-W vulnerable

NORTH
- ♠ Q 7
- ♡ A 10 9 8
- ◇ K 7 6
- ♣ 7 4 3 2

WEST
- ♠ K J 10 6 5
- ♡ 6 4 3
- ◇ ---
- ♣ K Q 10 8 6

EAST
- ♠ 8 4 2
- ♡ 7 5
- ◇ 10 8 5 4 3 2
- ♣ A 5

SOUTH
- ♠ A 9 3
- ♡ K Q J 2
- ◇ A Q J 9
- ♣ J 9

WEST	NORTH	EAST	SOUTH
2♠	No	No!	Dble
No	2NT	No	3♣
No	3♡	No	4♡
No	No	No	

Bidding: 2♠ = red suits *OR* black suits. It takes some courage to pass on the East cards but with eight red cards and five black cards, the odds are strong that West has the black suits. With a weak hand, East does not want to be at the three-level with such skimpy support. Playing RCOs can be a test of courage.

South doubles and West's pass confirms the black suits. North's 2NT shows values (the negative reply to a double of 2♠ or 2NT is 3♣). South bids 3♣ Stayman, planning to end in 3NT or 4♡.

Lead: 2 of diamonds. The reasons follow later.

Recommended play: West ruffs the lead, plays a low club to East's ace and receives another diamond ruff. The ♣K is cashed and declarer is one down.

Notes: (1) As North-South have used a Stayman sequence it is very likely that they have a 4-4 fit in hearts. If so, West must have three hearts and therefore West's shape will be 5-3-0-5. Expecting West to ruff the first diamond, East leads the *two* of diamonds as a suit preference signal for a club return in case that is not obvious after dummy appears.
(2) 2♠ East-West would make comfortably, but 3♠ is touch and go.
(3) If East leads a spade, declarer should place West with the ♠K and go up with the ♠A, draw trumps and make 10 tricks. The risk of a diamond ruff is low but the chances are tiny that East is leading from the ♠K.
(4) If East leads the ♣A, West needs to signal that a diamond switch is needed. On a discouraging signal, East might simply switch to a spade. The ♣Q on the ace might be enough to jolt East into the right action.

APPENDIX 1
DEFENDING AGAINST THEIR SYSTEMS

It is not the province of this book to cover every convention or everything that you may encounter in your tournaments. For more details on conventions, how to defend against them and how to counter their defences, it is worth consulting *Bridge Conventions, Defences and Countermeasures*.

There are a number of systems and conventions which you are likely to meet quite often. It is important that you are ready and prepared to deal with them.

Defence against strong 1♣ openings

The most common of these is Precision, which enjoyed considerable popularity during the '70s but is now somewhat on the wane. The basic Precision approach is:

1♣ = 16+ points, any shape
1♡/1♠ = 11-15 points, 5+ major
2♣ = 11-15 points, 5+ clubs
1NT = 13-15 balanced
1♢ = 11-15, all opening hands not covered by the above opening bids.

There are many strong 1♣ systems. One modern version is Moscito, which resembles Precision but the common openings show 10-14 points rather than 11-15 and 4-card major suit openings are permitted. The Moscito net-work:

1♣ = 15+ points, any shape
1♡/1♠ = 10-14 points, 4+ major. The bid of one major denies the other major.
1NT = 10-14, both majors
2♣ = 10-14 points, 5+ clubs
1♢ = 10-14, no 4-card major

The Achilles heel of the strong 1♣ systems is the 1♣ opening. As this merely advertises strength and reveals no suits yet, this is the moment of greatest danger for them. When they open 1♣, your side is unlikely to have game and so your aim should be to damage their auction as far as possible. The following approach works well:

Bid with bad hands, pass with good hands.

It is safe to pass with a decent hand since the 1♣ opening is forcing and you will have an opportunity to bid on the next round if you wish. Therefore, pass on all hands with 13+ HCP and good 12s. If you take action on the next round, partner will know you have 13 points or more.

If the responder to 1♣ bids the 1♢ negative, treat opener's rebid as their opening bid and take action accordingly. In other words, if opener rebids 1NT, use your normal defence to a 1NT opening. If opener rebids 1♡ or 1♠, bid as though they had opened 1♡ or 1♠.

If responder to 1♣ gives a positive response, this is usually forcing to game in their methods. Now you would do well to keep out of the auction. If they have game values and you have 13+ HCP, partner must have very little. You are wise to stay quiet and let them bid to their destination. You ought to be defending and with your strength sitting over the strong opener, your prospects in defence figure to be favourable. In addition, by not bidding, you will have given declarer no inkling of the location of the missing high card strength.

Action with weak hands

Jump bids = pre-empts at the three-level, weak jump-overcall single-suiters at the two-level. Suit Quality of 9 at the three-level and 8 at the two-level is advisable.

2NT = a freak two-suiter, any 6-5 or wilder shape. Lesser shapes are shown with a double or via an overcall at a lower level (see below). Over 2NT, advancer should bid the cheapest tolerable suit. Partner may pass or raise or remove to the cheapest suit held. All bidding is natural.

Suit bids = the suit bid and the next suit along:
(1♣) : 1♢ = diamonds + hearts
(1♣) : 1♡ = hearts + spades
(1♣) : 1♠ = spades + clubs
(1♣) : 2♣ = clubs + diamonds

Double = the suit doubled and its non-touching mate:
(1♣) : Double = clubs + hearts

No-trumps = the other pair of non-touching suits:
(1♣) : 1NT = diamonds + spades

5-5 or 5-4 patterns are sensible but at favourable vulnerability or after partner has passed, two 4-card suits are acceptable, particularly with a 4-4-4-1. With a 4-4-4-1, show the two stronger suits or if your hand is quite weak, choose the cheapest bid to show your suits. Suppose North opens (1♣) strong.

What should East do, nil vulnerable, with:

	(1)	(2)	(3)
♠	A Q 7 2	Q 8 6 3	8 7 6 3
♡	9 6 4 2	J 9 6 4	Q 9 6 4
♢	K Q 9 7	K J 7 2	K 9 7 4 2
♣	9	8	- - -

With (1), bid 1NT to show spades and diamonds, your good suits. This is likely to work better than 1♢ (diamonds + hearts) or 1♡ (hearts + spades). With (2), if you wish to come in, bid 1♢. It would be all right to bid 1♡ but not 1NT, which commits you to the two-level while either of the others lets you out at the one-level. With (3), you want to show your longest suit, the diamonds, and 1♢ is better than 1NT, again because it lets you out at a cheaper level if partner does not have decent support for you.

Advancer's job is to push the bidding as high as discretion allows. Raise to the two-level with 4-card support and jump to the three-level with 5-card support. Bidding a suit other than partner's shown suits is natural and not forcing, and also very risky if the suit is not strong.

With some ambitions for game, advancer bids 1NT after a one-level bid and 2NT after a two-level bid. In reply, partner bids clubs with a minimum hand while any other bid is natural and shows the upper range, around 9-11 points.

It is particularly important to interfere quickly if the opponents are playing relay methods. A simple overcall will usually not disrupt their relays. A jump overcall will. If partner shows a two-suiter at the one-level, this will not hamper them but if you can raise the bidding to the two-level or three-level, you will have jammed their relays and they will have to start a natural auction at a high level.

These disruptive methods are so effective that you should adopt them also after (1♣) : No : (1♦) : ? and against strong 2♣ and 2♦ openings. Over 2♣, your actions are the same as over 1♣ except that everything is one level higher. Naturally, you will need more shape to come in at this higher level and it is vital to keep an eye on the vulnerability, too.

Over 2♦, jumps to 3♥ or higher are pre-empts, bids at the two-level show the suit bid and the next suit along, while 3♣ = clubs + diamonds and 3♦ = diamonds + hearts. Double of 2♦ = diamonds + spades (the suit bid and the non-touching suit), while 2NT = clubs + hearts (the other non-touchers).

Once you are used to this approach, you will want to use this interference also against pairs that use game-force relay responses. For example, suppose they bid (1♥ natural) : (1♠ artificial game-force reply). As they have shown the values for game, your aim is to disrupt, disrupt, disrupt. No matter what game-force relay they use, you adopt the same structure: Jump bids are weak one-suiters, a suit overcall shows the suit bid and the next suit along, double = the suit bid + the non-touching suit and no-trumps shows the other non-touching suits. Thus, after their (1♥ : 1♠ game-force relay), for example:

2♣ = clubs + diamonds
2♦ = diamonds + hearts
2♥ = hearts + spades
2♠ = spades + clubs
Double = spades + diamonds
1NT = hearts + clubs, the other non-touching suits.

Jumps to 3♣ or higher are weak one-suiters and 2NT is the 6-5 or freakier hand.

If you can push the bidding up by more than three steps you will usually be able to wipe out their relay methods or make them far less effective as the bidding drags them too high. You will find that this approach provides a lot of action. It is not only fun but also highly effective.

Defence against the Unusual 2NT

After 1♥ : (2NT) or 1♠ : (2NT), a simple defence would be:

Double is looking for penalties, 3-partner's-major is a sound raise but not forcing, 3-other-major is natural and forcing, while bidding 3-minor asks for a stopper in the suit bid in a quest for 3NT.

You will no doubt be interested in something more sophisticated and also more effective:

Double = Looking for penalties. Responder needs about 10 HCP or more, a strong 4+ holding in at least one of their minors and a shortage in opener's major. If advancer removes to 3-minor, opener should double if strong in that minor. Otherwise, opener should pass in case responder is able to double this minor for penalties. (The double of 2NT is similar to responder's redouble in:

WEST	NORTH	EAST	SOUTH
1♠	Dble	Rdble ...	

East's redouble seeking penalties should have 10+ HCP, a shortage in opener's suit and strong holdings in at least two of the unbid suits.)

3-opener's-major = natural, weaker than a normal limit raise but respectable, 8-9 HCP or a good 6-7.

4-opener's-major = natural, pre-emptive, exactly the same as 1♥ : 4♥ or 1♠ : 4♠. Not a strong bid. This will help opener decide whether to double or whether to bid on if they sacrifice in 5-minor.

3-other-major = strong 6+ suit, 6-9 HCP, denies support for opener's major, not forcing.

3♣ = 10+ HCP, game-invitation or better in hearts. If the opening bid was 1♠, the 3♣ response may yet have spade support.

3♦ = 10+ HCP, game invitation or better in spades. If the opening bid was 1♥, the 3♦ response denies heart support. With heart support and spades as well, start with the 3♣ response.

After 3♣ or 3♦, if opener bids 3-major as an intended sign-off, responder passes only with the 10-11 point minimum. With more, responder should bid on to game or higher. If responder has shown support for opener's major, a bid of 4-minor by either partner is a cue-bid while 3NT is best used as RKCB based on opener's major.

Over the 3♣ reply, 3♦ by opener is a waiting bid. Responder can then bid 3♥, non-forcing, or 3♠ non-forcing if the opening bid was 1♠, but any other bid by responder is forcing to game. Again 4-minor would be a cue-bid and 3NT RKCB.

4♣ or 4♦ over 2NT = standard splinter raise of opener's major. See Chapter 6 on splinters.

4NT = RKCB with opener's major as trumps. It would be cheaper, of course, to bid 3♣ or 3♦ and perhaps use 3NT as RKCB later but the opponents are not always so co-operative. Responder may well be concerned about a pre-emptive leap of 5♣ or 5♦ shutting out the key card asking-mechanism.

Coping with interference to RKCB 3NT or 4NT

If they bid over your RKCB enquiry, you can play DOPI. In the basic version Double = 0, Pass = 1, but playing RKCB, we can do better. For example:

WEST	NORTH	EAST	SOUTH
1♠	2NT	4NT	5♦
?			

Pass = 0 or 3 key cards
Double = 1 key card
5♡ = 2 key cards, no trump queen
5♠ = 2 key cards plus the trump queen
5NT = 4 key cards, no trump queen
6♣ = 4 key cards plus the trump queen. If four key cards are not enough for the slam, partner's reason for bidding 4NT should make interesting listening.

Over the pass, double by partner says, 'Pass if you have 0 key cards, bid on with 3.' This allows the partnership to collect penalties when the lack of key cards may make even the five-level dangerous. When bidding on, Step 1 = no trump queen, and Step 2 shows the trump queen.

After the double, showing one key card, partner can pass if that makes slam unappealing and the five-level risky. A bid by partner here, or after the pass showing 0 or 3 key cards, will have its usual meaning (trump queen ask, king ask, etc.).

Slam Sacrifice Doubles

With the proliferation of weak two-suited openings and two-suited overcalls (such as the Michaels Cue-Bid), you will often find that your side has an excellent trump fit. What if the opponents bid to a slam? It may be clear to you that a sacrifice will cost relatively little because of your good trump fit, but it would still be silly to sacrifice if their slam is likely to fail. It is no great triumph to be down only 300 if you could have been +100.

If their slam is very likely to make, be prepared to sacrifice if you have a great trump fit and your hands are not balanced. Sacrifices on balanced hands are usually too expensive. If you have a good chance to beat their slam, do not take a sacrifice.

The problem is, how can you tell? When your side is clearly the sacrificing side, you have established an excellent trump fit and the opponents have bid to six or seven, slam sacrifice doubles work like this:

Against a small slam:

The player in the direct seat should—
Double with 2 defensive tricks. That ends the bidding.
Pass = 0 or 1 defensive trick.

When the pass reverts to partner:
Pass with 2 defensive tricks.
Sacrifice with no defensive trick as partner has at most one defensive trick.
Double = 1 defensive trick. After this double, partner will pass if also holding 1 defensive trick (each partner has one trick) and will sacrifice if holding no defensive trick.

Against a grand slam:

Double in the direct seat with one trick. Partner must pass if you double. With no defence or merely potential for a trick, pass. After the pass, partner should pass with one reasonably certain trick or better, double with potential for one trick and sacrifice with no hope for a trick. If partner has doubled in the pass-out seat, you should leave the double in if you also have potential for a trick and sacrifice with no vestige of a trick in defence. If you have potential for a trick and partner's double indicates potential for a trick, there is sufficient chance of defeating the grand slam to reject the sacrifice. If only one of you has potential for a trick, the odds favour sacrificing.

The tough aspect is recognising what is likely to be a defensive trick or what has potential for a trick. You will not always be right but having some method to avoid silly sacrifices is better than having no method at all.

The 3NT, 4♣ and 4♦ Openings

In standard methods, the 4♣ and 4♦ openings are pre-empts based on one playing trick better than a 3♣ or 3♦ opening. The 3NT opening is often played as the Gambling 3NT: a solid 7+ minor and little else. The Gambling 3NT is out of favour with top players because defending against it is relatively simple (lead an ace).

There are other useful approaches for these opening pre-empts. One is the Namyats Convention :
4♣ = a strong 4♡ pre-empt
4♦ = a strong 4♠ pre-empt
The hand should contain exactly eight playing tricks. The major suit should be solid, or a one-loser suit (SQ 10) with an ace outside as compensation. It follows that an opening bid of 4♡ or 4♠ will not be as strong, either in playing tricks or in suit strength.

The 3NT Pre-empt

If playing Namyats or something similar, the 3NT is commonly used as a multi: a pre-empt of 4♣ or 4♦. Opener's suit need not be solid.

Defending against Namyats

Against 4♣ or 4♦:
Bid their suit = strong takeout with 0-1 cards in their suit.
Double = takeout but weaker than bidding their suit.
4NT = strong two-suiter in the minors
Against their 3NT opening
Double = strong hand. Suggests doubling them for penalties if they run to 4-minor.
4♣ = takeout for the majors with no preference or preference for hearts
4♦ = also takeout for the majors, but with definite preference for spades
4♡ or 4♠ = natural, to play.
Pass and double their run to 4♣ or 4♦ = takeout double but weaker than immediate action

APPENDIX 2
ACTION AFTER OPENER'S 1NT REBID

Chapter 2 covers the current, popular approach to responder's rebids after opener has rebid 1NT. In brief, a two-level suit rebid other than 2♣ is weak unless it is a higher-ranking suit than responder's first suit. For example, 1◇ : 1♡, 1NT : 2◇ is weak, asking to be passed, as is 1♣ : 1◇, 1NT : 2◇.

Transfers after a 1NT opening have become popular because they expand your bidding vocabulary. Bids which used to have one meaning have given way to bids with multi-meanings. Where 1NT : 2◇ was once a weakness takeout, 1NT : 2◇ as a transfer allows responder to sign off in 2♡, invite game with five or six hearts, force to game with a two-suiter, and so on. A single purpose response has been revitalized to carry out many functions.

The same can be done after opener's 1NT rebid. The main function of the 2♣ Checkback is to deal with responder's game-invitation hands. It does so by inquiring about opener's range and major suit holdings. However, instead of asking about opener's hand, and thus revealing unnecessary information to the opponents, the same (and more) can be achieved by using the 2♣ rebid as a 'puppet' to 2◇.

A 'puppet' is a bid that conveys no information and asks no questions. It is an instruction to partner: 'Please make the cheapest possible bid.' After the 1NT rebid, responder's 2♣ says, 'Please bid 2◇.'

The first benefit comes when responder wishes to sign off in diamonds. Opener bids 2◇ and responder passes. This eliminates the need for a weakness 2◇ rebid, which can then be harnessed for other ends.

If responder does not pass 2◇, any rebid is game-inviting. For example:

1♣ : 1♡ 1NT : 2♡	The 2♡ rebid is a sign-off.
1♣ : 1♡ 1NT : 2♣ 2◇ : 2♡	The 2♡ rebid after 2♣, 2◇ shows a hand worth a game-invitation with five hearts.
1♣ : 1♠ 1NT : 2♡	The 2♡ rebid asks opener to pass or give preference to 2♠.
1♣ : 1♠ 1NT : 2♣ 2◇ : 2♡	The 2♡ rebid after 2♣, 2◇ shows a hand worth a game-invitation with five spades and four hearts.
1♣ : 1♠ 1NT : 2♣ 2♡ . . .	If using 2♣ Checkback to invite game with five spades, opener may reveal a 4-card heart holding in which responder has no interest.
1♣ : 1♠ 1NT : 2♣ 2◇ : 2♠	When using 2♣ puppet, responder discloses only relevant information. Opener's heart length is not revealed.

Bidding structure after opener's 1NT rebid

2♣ = Puppet to 2◇

2◇ = Artificial, forcing to game

2♡ = A weak rebid if the initial response was 1♡ or 1♠. Forcing to game after a 1◇ response. The sequence will be 1♣ : 1◇, 1NT : 2♡. See below.

2♠ = A weak rebid if the initial response was 1♠. Forcing to game after a 1◇ or 1♡ response. This is known as responder's reverse. See below.

2NT = Puppet to 3♣. Used to sign off in clubs or to show other hand types. See later.

Jumps to the three-level = forcing to game with a highly distributional hand. If it is a new suit, the shape will be at least 5-5. If it is a rebid of responder's suit, it will be at least a 6-card suit.

The 2◇ force to game is used on hands that are not highly distributional and normally not for three-suiters. Responder's reverse forced to game with a three-suiter. These hands are hard to show otherwise.

Responder's reverse

1♣ : 1◇ 1NT : 2♡	Responder's rebid in these auctions is forcing to game and promises a three-suiter. Opener should normally rebid 2NT over which responder will show the third suit held (and hence the short suit). Opener can then judge whether 3NT will be safe.
1♣ : 1◇ 1NT : 2♠	
1♣ : 1♡ 1NT : 2♠	

♠ A K 7 2
♡ - - -
◇ Q J 9 7 2
♣ K J 5 4

After 1♣ : 1◇, 1NT, responder needs to be able to show the heart shortage. Responder's reverse does it: 1♣ : 1◇, 1NT : 2♠, 2NT : 3♣.

In this auction, responder could also be 4-1-4-4.

♠ A K 7 2
♡ K 9 6 4
◇ A J 6 3
♣ 4

1♣ : 1◇, 1NT : 2♡, 2NT : 3♠ reveals the club shortage. Responder would use the same sequence if holding a 4-4-5-0.

Responder cannot use the reverse auction when the 5-card suit is spades or with a 0-5-4-4 pattern.

♠ A J 7 3 2
♡ K Q 4 2
◇ Q J 6 2
♣ - - -

After 1♣ : 1♠, 1NT or 1◇ : 1♠, 1NT, responder should continue with 2◇, the artificial game force, to find the best spot.

♠ 8
♡ A Q 4 2
◇ K J 6 2
♣ Q J 3 2

After 1◇ : 1♡, 1NT, responder should also continue with 2◇, the artificial game force.

Responder's rebids after the 2♣ puppet to 2◇

Pass = Responder wants to play in 2◇.

2♡ = Invitational with hearts.

2♠ = Invitational with spades.

2NT = Inviting 3NT. Responder has no extra length in the majors to be revealed.

3♣ / 3◇ = Inviting game, length in the minor bid.

3♡ / 3♠ = Stronger invitation than 2♡ / 2♠. Perhaps a 5-5 hand, perhaps a 6-card suit, depending on the sequence.

3NT = Game interest only and a 5-3-3-2 pattern. Opener is asked to choose 3NT or 4-Major. With a 4-3-3-3 pattern, 3NT is usually the better choice.

WEST	W	E	EAST
♠ Q 3 2	1♣	1♠	♠ A K 7 5 4
♡ A K 7	1NT	2♣	♡ 8 4 2
◇ A 5 2	2◇	3NT	◇ 9 7 6
♣ K 9 5 4	No		♣ A 3

If the spades are 3-2, you have ten tricks in 4♠. However, the same ten tricks are available in 3NT. If spades are 4-1 (about a 1-in-4 chance), 4♠ will usually fail but you still make 3NT.

WEST	W	E	EAST
♠ Q 3 2	1♣	1♠	♠ A K 7 5 4
♡ A K 7	1NT	2♣	♡ 8 4 2
◇ A 5	2◇	3NT	◇ 9 7 6
♣ K 9 5 4 2	4♠	No	♣ A 3

With 3-card support for responder's major and an outside doubleton, opener should support the major. Here there are ten tricks in 3NT if spades break normally but if so, you will usually make at least eleven tricks in 4♠.

After responder's rebid after the puppet to 2◇

Bidding is natural. Opener passes if minimum with support for the suit mentioned, raises if maximum with support, bids no-trumps or else something suitable.

Bidding after the 2◇ game-force rebid over 1NT

Bidding is natural. Opener shows the cheapest relevant feature. For example:

1◇ : 1♠	Opener now bids 2NT if 4-3-3-3.
1NT : 2◇	Otherwise bid 2♡ with four hearts,
?	2♠ with 3-card support or, with no feature in either major, bid 3♣ or 3◇ as appropriate.

Note the use of the 2◇ bid in this auction. It is not a sign-off. To play in 2◇, responder would have used the 2♣ puppet, forcing opener to bid 2◇, which responder would then pass. A jump to 3◇ by responder after 1NT would have shown at least five spades and five diamonds and enough values to insist on game.

Bidding after the 2NT puppet to 3♣

Since 2♣ is artificial after the 1NT rebid, there is a need to be able to play in a club part-score. This can be achieved via the puppet to 3♣.

WEST	W	E	EAST
♠ K Q	1◇	1♠	♠ J 7 5 4
♡ A 7 2	1NT	2NT	♡ 8 4
◇ A K 9 8 2	3♣	No	◇ 6
♣ 9 6 5			♣ K J 8 4 3 2

The best chance for the maximum plus score for East-West is in clubs at the lowest possible level. With 2♣ not available, the given auction reaches the best spot possible. The same applies here:

WEST	W	E	EAST
♠ A K 2	1♣	1♠	♠ J 7 5 4
♡ K J 2	1NT	2NT	♡ Q 4 3
◇ A 8 4	3♣	No	◇ 3
♣ 10 9 6 5			♣ Q J 7 4 2

Responder can also use the 2NT puppet for other purposes. This is a useful structure after 3♣ is bid:
New suit = singleton or void in the suit bid and 6+ cards in responder's suit, i.e., a splinter.
3NT = A-K-Q-x-x-x and no short suit, offering opener the choice of 3NT or 4-major. With instant winners, choose 3NT. With aces to knock out or finesses to take, 4-major will usually be better.
Repeat responder's suit = 6+ suit with two of the top three honours and no short suit outside.

WEST	W	E	EAST
♠ K J 2	1◇	1♠	♠ A Q 7 5 4 3
♡ A 7 5	1NT	2NT	♡ K 4
◇ A 9 6 2	3♣	3♠	◇ 8 5
♣ A 4 3	3NT	No	♣ 7 6 2

There are ten tricks in spades but also ten in 3NT. It makes sense at pairs to play in 3NT.

WEST	W	E	EAST
♠ K 8 2	1◇	1♠	♠ A Q 7 5 4 3
♡ J 7 5	1NT	2NT	♡ K 4
◇ K Q J 4	3♣	3♠	◇ 8 5
♣ A Q 3	4♠	No	♣ 7 6 2

Even if the spade suit is running, 3NT may fail. You will usually score better in 4♠.

WEST	W	E	EAST
♠ K J 2	1◇	1♠	♠ A Q 7 5 4 3
♡ J 7 5	1NT	2NT	♡ 4
◇ K Q J 6 2	3♣	3♡	◇ A 8 5
♣ A 4	4♣	4◇	♣ K 6 2
	4NT	5♠	
	6♠	No	

3♡ = short hearts; 4♣ and 4◇ = cues, 4NT RKCB.

Exercises

(a) Using 2♣ puppet instead of 2♣ Checkback, do Exercise A and Partnership Bidding on page 17.

(b) How should the bidding go on hands 5-8, pages 18-19? *Answers to (a) and (b) on page 173.*

APPENDIX 3
BID BETTER AFTER YOUR SIDE OPENS 1NT

Unless you are serious about wanting to win and eager to do better than before, do not bother continuing with this appendix.

Traditional methods stay with us because we are too complacent to change. Even if we are keen, our partners often cannot be bothered to try something new, something that needs a little learning. Bidding after a 1NT opening is by and large simple and straightforward. However, with just a bit of effort we can do things better than current methods. This is the recommended structure for responder:

1NT : ?

2♣ = Puppet to 2♦. Opener is asked to bid 2♦. A 'puppet' bid requires partner to make the bid requested and await further information. The puppet does not ask a question (unlike Stayman which asks for a major suit) and does not show anything (unlike a transfer which shows 5+ cards in a given suit).

2♦ = Transfer to hearts

2♡ = Transfer to spades

2♠ = Asking bid. Range inquiry: 'Are you maximum or minimum?'

2NT = Transfer to clubs

3♣ / 3♦ / 3♡ / 3♠ = Splinters. These show a singleton or void in the next suit. Thus 3♣ = short in diamonds, 3♦ = heart shortage, 3♡ = spade shortage and 3♠ = short in clubs.

Bidding after the 2♣ puppet to 2♦

1NT : 2♣
2♦ : No   Responder wants to play in 2♦.

Playing standard transfers, the partnership cannot stop in 2♦. Using 2♣ puppet, you can.

WEST	W	E	EAST
♠ A Q J 2	1NT	2♣	♠ K 5 3
♡ A 7 2	2♦	No	♡ K 8 6
♦ J 7 4			♦ Q 10 8 6 3
♣ J 6 3			♣ 8 4

If you pass 1NT, this is highly likely to fail, while 2♦ should make comfortably and may make nine tricks some days. Even if clubs are 4-4 and 1NT does succeed, you achieve a better score in 2♦. It is likely that the opponents can make 3♣ but they have yet to find that spot. The same phenomenon is in evidence on this deal, which arose in a national championship:

Dealer West : Both vulnerable

```
              NORTH
              ♠ A J 9 7
              ♡ 10 9 7 5
              ♦ K
              ♣ J 10 9 8
WEST                        EAST
♠ 8 4 2                     ♠ K Q 10 3
♡ A J 6 3                   ♡ 8
♦ A 5 4 3                   ♦ 10 9 8 7 2
♣ K 3                       ♣ 6 5 2
              SOUTH
              ♠ 6 5
              ♡ K Q 4 2
              ♦ Q J 6
              ♣ A Q 7 4
```

Standard auction:

WEST	NORTH	EAST	SOUTH
1NT	No	No	No

(1) East is too weak to take action and playing transfers you transfer to a minor with a very weak hand only with a 6+ suit.

Against 1NT, North would lead the ♣J. As long as the defence takes a heart trick, declarer loses 3 clubs, 2 diamonds, a spade and a heart. One down. The puppet auction is much better:

WEST	NORTH	EAST	SOUTH
1NT	No	2♣	No
2♦	No	No	No

Against 2♦, North would also lead the ♣J. West wins the second club and ducks a diamond. North wins and plays another club, ruffed by West who cashes the ♦A. Declarer makes nine tricks since the defence can take no more than 1 spade, 2 diamonds and a club. +110 in 2♦ is better than −100 in 1NT.

North-South might make 2♡ and South might compete when 2♦ is passed to South. If so, West should push to 3♦ (despite the strong holding in hearts) because of the 4-card support for diamonds. North-South have the choice of passing 3♦, which makes, or pushing on to 3♡ which will fail. Notice how the 2♣ puppet allows East-West to win the part-score battle.

1NT : 2♣
2♦ : 2♡   Responder has hearts and the values to invite game. With support and a minimum, opener can pass and stop at a low level. With support and a maximum, opener raises. Without support and a minimum hand, opener can bid 2♠ (four spades) or 2NT (denies four spades). Without support and a maximum, opener can bid 3♠ (four spades) or 3NT (denies four spades).

WEST	W	E	EAST
♠ Q 7	1NT	2♣	♠ K J 4
♡ K Q 7 6	2♢	2♡	♡ J 8 4 3
♢ K 6 3	No		♢ A Q J 7
♣ Q J 3 2			♣ 7 5

On a normal day this will make nine tricks but any slight deviation (trumps 4-1, three rounds of clubs leading to a trump promotion or a singleton diamond lead) might limit you to eight tricks. A 'standard' auction might go 1NT : 2♣, 2♡ : 3♡ : No. An enthusiastic East might jump to 4♡, which has no hope. A realistic East would be content with 3♡, which West should pass, but this could be too high. Using Stayman to invite game also invites disaster when the three-level is too high. It is much better to be able to invite game and stop at the two-level when opener has a minimum.

1NT : 2♣

2♢ : 2♠ Responder has spades and the values to invite game. With support and a minimum, opener can pass and stop at a low level. With support and a maximum, opener raises. Without support opener can bid 2NT (minimum) or 3NT (maximum).

WEST	W	E	EAST
♠ A J 9 5	1NT	2♣	♠ K Q 7 2
♡ 8 7 2	2♢	2♠	♡ K J 3
♢ A 9 2	No		♢ K 6 5 3
♣ Q J 7			♣ 8 4

The standard auction again reaches the three-level via 1NT : 2♣ : 2♠, 3♠ : No. Again 4♠ has no play. It would be no great surprise to lose two hearts, a diamond and two clubs for one down. On a particularly unlucky day (doubleton heart lead) even 2♠ could fail. Clearly, if you are not going to reach game, 2♠ is considerably safer than 3♠.

1NT : 2♣

2♢ : 3♣ or 3♢ Responder has 6+ cards in the minor suit bid and the values to invite game. With a maximum, opener should head for 3NT and may do so even with a minimum and a good fit for the minor.

WEST	W	E	EAST
♠ A 5	1NT	2♣	♠ 9 7 2
♡ J 9 8 4	2♢	3♣	♡ 7 3
♢ A 9 3 2	3NT	No	♢ K 6
♣ K 5 2			♣ A Q 9 7 6 4

Standard methods generally do not provide a path to invite game with a long minor. The above is an easy route to 3NT which will make nine tricks almost all the time. Note that 3NT would still be a great spot if East held no more than:

♠ 9 7   ♡ 7 3   ♢ 8 6   ♣ A Q 9 7 6 4 3

Principle 1: *1NT : 2♣ puppet to 2♢ followed by a suit bid at the cheapest level is natural and invites game.* Opener rebids according to strength and fit.

Suppose partner opens 1NT (12-14). How would you plan the bidding with these cards:

♠ Q J 8 6
♡ A K 2
♢ A 8 4
♣ J 6 2

Part of you wants to bid 3NT because of the terrible shape for suit play. If you bid 3NT you will be a hero if opener holds:

(a)   ♠ A K 4 3
       ♡ Q J 3
       ♢ K 6 3
       ♣ 9 8 5

Even though there is a 4-4 spade fit, 4♠ will fail almost all the time with four losers in the minors. Before you pat yourself on the back for your fine decision to bid 3NT, consider how you would feel to be in 3NT if opener has these cards:

(b)   ♠ A K 4 3
       ♡ Q J 3
       ♢ K 6 3 2
       ♣ 9 8

This time 4♠ is much better. Even if they do not cash five or more clubs at once and you make nine tricks in 3NT, you will score badly. Those in 4♠ will be making ten tricks.

If you have to guess which way to go, it is better to look for the major fit. If opener has four spades, there are six patterns which include a doubleton, and thus a ruffing value, and only one 4-3-3-3 pattern. However, wouldn't it be better to avoid the guess and to find the best spot time and time again?

What do you need to know? If opener has a 4-3-3-3, 3NT will be right almost every time. If opener has four spades and a doubleton, 4♠ will usually be right. How do you find out? Just ask opener, 'Excuse me, do you have a doubleton?' That is exactly what 1NT : 2♣, 2♢ : 2NT means!

1NT : 2♣

2♢ : 2NT This is forcing to game and responder is asking about opener's hand pattern.

Opener's replies:

3♢ = 4-3-3-3. 3♢ = dreadful, dull, dismal.

3♣ = doubleton somewhere. After 3♣, responder bids 3♢ to ask, 'Do you have a 4-card major?'

The above hands would be bid:

(a)	Opener	Responder	(b)	Opener	Responder
	1NT	2♣		1NT	2♣
	2♢	2NT		2♢	2NT
	3♢	3NT		3♣	3♢
	No			3♠	4♠
				No	

The 1NT : 2♣, 2♦ : 2NT shape inquiry

Opener rebids:

3♣ = doubleton somewhere. Not a 4-3-3-3 and no 5-card major.
3♦ = any 4-3-3-3
3♥ or 3♠ = 5-card major

1NT : 2♣
2♦ : 2NT
3♣ : ?   Responder bids 3♦ to ask for a 4-card major or bids 3♥ / 3♠ to show a 5-card major. (In addition, 4♣ or 4♦ by responder, without using 3♦ or after using 3♦, shows a 4-card minor and is looking for a 4-4 fit.)

1NT : 2♣
2♦ : 2NT
3♦ : ?   Responder bids 3♥ or 3♠ to show four cards in that major, looking for a 4-4 fit.

WEST	W	E	EAST
♠ A K 4 3	1NT	2♣	♠ Q J 8 6
♥ Q J 3	2♦	2NT	♥ A K 2
♦ K 6 3	3♦	3♠	♦ A 8 5 4
♣ 9 8 5	4♠	No	♣ J 6

Even though opener is 4-3-3-3, responder has a ruffing value and wants to be in 4♠ if a 4-4 fit exists.

Responder would use the 2NT rebid on any hand looking for game or slam and seeking a 4-4 fit. You should also use this path with a 5-card major and a 5-3-3-2 pattern Even though you may have an 8-card or 9-card major suit fit, a 5-3-3-2 opposite a 4-3-3-3 will make the same number of tricks in no-trumps as in the suit contract most of the time. If that number is nine, clearly 3NT is best but even if the number is ten, those in 3NT will score best. For example:

Dealer North : Nil vulnerable

       NORTH
       ♠ J 7 2
       ♥ J 10 2
       ♦ A K J 3
       ♣ K 7 4

WEST	EAST
♠ Q 6	♠ K 10 9
♥ 9 6 5	♥ A K 4 3
♦ 10 7 5 4 2	♦ 9 6
♣ 8 6 2	♣ J 10 9 5

       SOUTH
       ♠ A 8 5 4 3
       ♥ Q 8 7
       ♦ Q 8
       ♣ A Q 3

Standard transfer auction:

WEST	NORTH	EAST	SOUTH
	1NT	No	2♥
No	2♠	No	3NT
No	4♠	All pass	

The transfer followed by 3NT offers the choice between 4♠ and 3NT. While North might wish to pass 3NT, this is usually unsound with 3-card support as South could be short in hearts or clubs. You can see that 4♠ is a terrible spot with two hearts and two spades to lose. It would be a lucky day when 4♠ makes, even though trumps are 3-2, yet 3NT cannot be defeated (and is likely to make even when spades are 4-1).

Because a 5-3-3-2 facing a 4-3-3-3 plays well in no-trumps, responder does well to inquire about opener's shape. This is a much better sequence:

WEST	NORTH	EAST	SOUTH
	1NT	No	2♣
No	2♦	No	2NT
No	3♦	No	3NT
No	No	No	

This deal from the final of the 1992 Women's Teams Olympiad carries a similar message:

Dealer West : Nil vulnerable

       NORTH
       ♠ A Q 7 5
       ♥ A K 6
       ♦ 6 4 2
       ♣ Q 7 6

WEST	EAST
♠ J 9	♠ 10 6
♥ Q 5 4	♥ J 7 3 2
♦ 7 3	♦ Q J 10 9 8 5
♣ A K 10 9 5 3	♣ 2

       SOUTH
       ♠ K 8 4 3 2
       ♥ 10 9 8
       ♦ A K
       ♣ J 8 4

Austria reached 4♠ without interference:

WEST	NORTH	EAST	SOUTH
	1NT*	No	2♥
No	2♠	No	3NT
No	4♠	All pass	

*15-17

The ♣A, ♣K and a club ruff quickly put paid to 4♠. The above puppet auction to 3NT would have been more successful Let the opponents bemoan their ill-fortune while you enjoy your plus score in 3NT.

Principle 2: *The 2♣ puppet followed by 2NT is forcing to game and asks about opener's shape.*

Other puppet sequences

1NT : 2♣
2♦ : 3♥ or 3♠   Forcing to game. Responder has 5+ diamonds and four cards in the major suit bid. (The 2♣ has been used here as a transfer.)

1NT : 2♣
2♦ : 3NT   Slam invitation. Responder has five diamonds in a 5-3-3-2 pattern and is inviting slam.

The 1NT : 2◇ and 2♡ transfers

If you choose the 1NT : 2♣ puppet to invite a major-suit game only when you have a 4-card major and are looking for a 4-4 major fit, you need not change any of your structure for transfers to a major. However, there is a strong case for using the puppet invitation when holding a 5-card major as well.

When the invitation is rejected, the transfer sequence takes you to the three-level in an auction such as 1NT : 2◇, 2♡ : 2NT, 3♡ : No. By contrast the puppet auction can stop lower: 1NT : 2♣, 2◇ : 2♡. Consider this deal from a national championship:

Dealer North : Nil vulnerable

```
              NORTH
              ♠ Q J 9 5
              ♡ J 8 5 3
              ◇ Q J
              ♣ A Q 8
WEST                        EAST
♠ A 2                       ♠ K 10 7 4
♡ K 7 6                     ♡ Q
◇ 10 9 8 6 5               ◇ A 4 3 2
♣ 6 4 2                     ♣ 9 7 5 3
              SOUTH
              ♠ 8 6 3
              ♡ A 10 9 4 2
              ◇ K 7
              ♣ K J 10
```

Standard transfer auction:

WEST	NORTH	EAST	SOUTH
	1NT	No	2◇
No	2♡	No	2NT
No	3♡	All pass	

Even if the spade lead is not found, West will switch to the ♠A when in with the ♡K on the second round of trumps. The third-round spade ruff will hold declarer to eight tricks. Those in 3♡ will rue being too high. Not those who play puppet:

WEST	NORTH	EAST	SOUTH
	1NT	No	2♣
No	2◇	No	2♡
No	No	No	

After 1NT : 2♣, 2◇ : 2♡

When responder can have a 5-card major for this sequence, opener passes with a minimum and 3-card or 4-card heart support. With a maximum, opener raises to 3♡ with 3 trumps (responder rebids 3NT with only four hearts) and to 4♡ with 4 trumps. The same approach applies after 1NT : 2♣, 2◇ : 2♠. To cater for responder having both majors:
  Use 1NT : 2♣, 2◇ : 2♡ if invitational with five hearts and four spades.
  Use 1NT : 2◇, 2♡ : 2♠, *non-forcing*, if invitational with 4-4 or 5-5 in the majors or with five spades and four hearts.

WEST	W	E	EAST
♠ A K 4 3	1NT	2◇	♠ Q J 8 6
♡ Q J 3	2♡	2♠	♡ A 7 5 2
◇ K 6 3	No		◇ 9 8 5
♣ 9 8 5			♣ K Q

A Stayman auction might reach 4♠ but even 3♠ could be too high. One could lose one heart, three diamonds and a club without raising an eyebrow. The above auction keeps you at a safe level.

After 1NT : 2◇, 2♡ : 2♠

Pass with a minimum and three or four spades
3♠ = maximum with three spades and not four hearts
4♠ = maximum with four spades
3♡ = minimum with four hearts
4♡ = maximum with four hearts

Without support for either major, opener will bid 2NT (minimum) or 3NT (maximum).

The puppet approach will sometimes leave you in 2♡ or 2♠ in a 4-3 fit. That may be a challenge but it will usually be a safer spot than 2NT, which is the contract that Stayman would reach. Witness:

WEST	W	E	EAST
♠ Q 10 4	1NT	2◇	♠ A K J 5
♡ Q 6 4	2♡	2♠	♡ K J 3 2
◇ J 9 7	No		◇ 6 3
♣ A K J 2			♣ 9 7 5

Where would you rather be, in 2♠ or in 2NT? Declarer should be able to make 2♠ easily and an overtrick for +140 would not be uncommon. By contrast the 1NT : 2♣, 2◇ : 2NT auction will see you fail via the diamond suit more often than not.

WEST	W	E	EAST
♠ 10 6	1NT	2◇	♠ A 9 5 4 2
♡ Q 8 4	2♡	2♠	♡ K J 7 6 2
◇ K 9 7 6	2NT	3♡	◇ Q 3
♣ A K 6 4	No		♣ 5

West's 2NT denies three spades and so East removes to 3♡, as West should have three cards in one of the majors. It would be tough to make 4♡. A trump lead would beat it and the normal 4-2 spade split would almost certainly spell defeat.

How do you force to game with 5-4 majors?

1NT : 2♡, 2♠ : 3♡ = game-force with 5+ spades and 4+ hearts. Now 3♠ = strong preference, 4♠ = weak preference, 4♡ = weak preference and 4♣ or 4◇ cue-bid = strong preference for hearts.

1NT : 2◇, 2♡ : 3♠ = game-force with 4 spades and 5+ hearts. Now 4♠ = weak preference, 4♡ = weak preference, 4♣ = strong hand with heart support and 4◇ = strong hand with spade support.

If the game-invitational hand with a 5-card major is shown using either the 1NT : 2♣ puppet auction or 1NT : 2◇, 2♡ : 2♠ then the transfer followed by 2NT has become vacant. It can be used profitably.

1NT : 2◇, 2♡ : 2NT or 1NT : 2♡, 2♠ : 2NT

Such a sequence shows 5+ cards in the major suit and exactly four cards in one of the minors. This would be a typical holding:

♠ A J 8 7 3   ♡ 6   ◇ A K 6   ♣ Q 7 5 4

You cannot tell the best spot. If partner has 3+ spades, then 4♠ figures to be best but what if opener has a doubleton spade? Many pairs would bid 1NT : 2♡, 2♠ : 3NT and play it there. It is not attractive to introduce the clubs and look for 5♣. To introduce a minor also carries a mild inference of slam interest and you do not want to suggest that.

If opener has a doubleton spade, the problem hinges on whether the hearts are well stopped. Most partnerships do not have the methods to discover the information vital to judge the right spot. Using the 2NT rebid to force to game can do the job.

Opener's rebids after 2NT

3♣ = 'I have a doubleton in your major. What is your short suit?'

3◇ = 'I have support for your major. Are you looking for slam?'

After 3♣, responder bids the short suit. If the short suit is clubs, responder rebids the major suit shown. If responder has a 5-4-2-2 pattern, bid 3NT with no slam interest or 4♣ / 4◇ (the 4-card minor held) with slam interest. After the short suit is revealed, opener can judge whether 3NT is safe enough (with a double stopper in responder's short suit, 3NT is a reasonable move). If too weak in the short suit, opener can bid 4-major to play the 5-2 fit (Q-x or better doubleton support is recommended) or bid 4♣ or 4◇ to seek the minor suit game.

WEST	W	E	EAST
♠ 6 2	1NT	2♡	♠ A J 8 7 3
♡ Q 8 4	2♠	2NT	♡ 6
◇ Q J 5 2	3♣	3♡	◇ A K 6
♣ A K 9 3	4♣	5♣	♣ Q 7 5 4
	No		

3♣ = doubleton spade. 3♡ = heart shortage. 4♣ = offer to play clubs. 5♣ = 4 clubs and not very good spades. With strong spades (3-4 honours), responder would bid 4♠ over 4♣. For example:

WEST	W	E	EAST
♠ 6 2	1NT	2♡	♠ A K J 10 4
♡ Q 6 4	2♠	2NT	♡ 7
◇ K J 7	3♣	3♡	◇ A 9 6 3
♣ A Q 8 5 3	4♣	4♠	♣ J 7 2
	No		

3♣ = doubleton spade. 3♡ = heart shortage. 4♣ = offer to play clubs. 4♠ = very strong spades.

After 4♣, responder's 4◇ bid would say, 'My minor is diamonds and my spades are not great.'

WEST	W	E	EAST
♠ K 5	1NT	2♡	♠ A Q 8 6 3
♡ J 6 3	2♠	2NT	♡ 7 4
◇ A 6 3 2	3♣	3NT	◇ K Q 7 4
♣ A J 4 2	4♠	No	♣ Q 8

3NT = 5-2-4-2 or 5-2-2-4 and no slam interest. 3NT may succeed but 4♠ has better chances.

Where opener's rebid is 3◇ (showing support for responder's major), responder bids 4-major with no slam interest. That is the most common situation and it gives the opening leader no information about the minor suit in dummy.

With slam interest after 3◇, responder shows the minor suit artificially: 3♡ = clubs, 3♠ = diamonds. Opener can now bid 4-major with a poor fit, 4-minor with a double fit and cue-bid with a strong fit.

Opener's other rebids after 2NT

3-agreed major = Support for the major, strong hand with no minor suit interest

4-agreed major = Support for the major, minimum hand and no minor suit interest

3-other-major = doubleton in responder's major, five cards in the bid major

WEST	W	E	EAST
♠ K 5	1NT	2♡	♠ A 9 6 4 2
♡ Q 6 5 3 2	2♠	2NT	♡ A J 4
◇ A Q 2	3♡	4♡	◇ K J 6 4
♣ Q 9 4	No		♣ 8

If you do not open 1NT with a 5-card major, this situation will not arise but if you are among the growing number who see the benefits in including the 5-3-3-2 pattern with a 5-major in the 1NT opening, these auctions and the 1NT : 2♣, 2◇ : 2NT shape inquiry can discover the 5-3 major fits.

Since the transfer-then-2NT auction shows 5-major and 4-minor, forcing to game, another benefit is that transfer to major and then 3-minor promises at least a 5-5 pattern. This is a much better base for exploring slam potential than when the 3-minor can be based on a 4-card suit or a longer suit.

After responder's 3-minor showing the 5-5, opener would show major suit support as first priority. With a doubleton in responder's major, opener can bid 3NT with the missing suits well held, bid a new suit at the 3-level to show strength there in a stopper quest for 3NT or support the minor.

WEST	W	E	EAST
♠ K 5	1NT	2♡	♠ A Q 6 4 2
♡ A 5 4	2♠	3♣	♡ 7
◇ A 7 6 2	4♣	...	◇ K 5
♣ Q 9 6 3			♣ K J 8 4 2

If using the suggestions on page 77, East could now bid 4◇ RKCB and finish in 6♣. Note that 6♣ might be making easily when 3NT is failing.

The 1NT : 2♠ auction

The 2♠ response starts off as a simple question: 'Are you maximum or minimum?' Opener bids 2NT if minimum, 3♣ if maximum. If that is the information needed for game, responder can pass 2NT or bid 3NT over 3♣. If the information was for a slam, responder bids 3NT over 2NT or 6NT / 7NT over 3♣. If some more fine tuning is needed for slam, responder can bid 4NT over 2NT or over 3♣. You can see that while a natural 1NT : 2NT invitation has a single purpose, the 1NT : 2♠ range finder can be used for game or slam auctions.

There is a worthwhile additional use. After the 2NT or 3♣ reply, responder can introduce a suit bid below game. This shows a one-suited hand, a 6+ suit and slam interest. A big advantage here is that responder has already discovered opener's range. With poor support, 10-x or worse, opener makes the cheapest possible bid. With good support, J-x or better, opener shows key cards by steps. With a good suit, such as A-Q-10-x-x-x or K-Q-10-x-x-x, responder will be pleased to learn of J-x support.

1NT : 2♠
2NT : 3♦ (strong 1-suiter in diamonds)
?

Opener bids 3♥ with poor support for diamonds. With decent support, 3♠ = 0 or 3 key cards, 3NT = 1 key card (4 key cards are not possible for a weak 1NT), 4♣ = 2 key cards, no trump queen, and 4♦ = 2 key cards + the trump queen. Over 3♥, poor support, responder can sign off in game or make the cheapest bid (3♠) to ask for key cards anyway.

If responder bids 3♥ to set the trump suit and opener bids 3♠, poor support, 3NT asks for key cards anyway. It is not a sign-off. Where opener's reply to 2♠ was 3♣, responder has to bid 4♣ to set clubs as trumps. The same principles then apply: 4♦ = weak support, 4♥ / 4♠ / 4NT / 5♣ are key cards replies with good support.

The 1NT : 2NT auction

The 2NT response is a transfer to clubs. It is used to sign off in 3♣ or to seek the best game or to invite slam. These are the sequences:

1NT : 2NT
3♣ : ?

Pass = sign-off, weak with 6+ clubs
3♦ = game-force with both minors, at least 5-4. The diamonds may be longer than the clubs.
3♥ or 3♠ = game-force with 5+ clubs and four cards in the major suit bid.
3NT = Slam invitation with 5 clubs and a 5-3-3-2.

Over 3♥ or 3♠, a new suit is a cue-bid, supporting responder's major. After the 3♦ reply, opener can bid 3NT with both majors well held, 3♥ or 3♠ as a stopper bid or support either minor at the 4-level.

The 1NT : 3-level splinters

One of the toughest problems in standard methods is responder with game values and a short suit. If a major suit trump fit is found, well and good, but if not, responder usually has to resort to guesswork. The trouble is that responder usually does the asking instead of the showing. With a short suit, it is best to tell opener where the short suit lies and let opener judge whether 3NT will be safe. For example:

WEST	W	E	EAST
♠ Q 9	1NT	2♣	♠ A J 8 7
♥ A Q J	2♦	3NT	♥ 6
♦ J 5 2	No		♦ K 8 7 3
♣ K 9 6 3 2			♣ A Q J 4

A simple Stayman auction might go that way and the best contract of 3NT is reached. This is more by good fortune than fine bidding. The two hands might just as easily be:

WEST		EAST
♠ Q 9		♠ A J 8 7
♥ J 5 2		♥ 6
♦ A Q J		♦ K 8 7 3
♣ K 9 6 3 2		♣ A Q J 4

Now 3NT will probably fail, with 5♣ the best spot and 6♣ better than 3NT. Indeed, 6♣ would be an excellent contract if opener held:

♠ K 2   ♥ J 5 2   ♦ A Q 2   ♣ K 9 6 3 2

Since responder can show a powerful one-suiter after starting 1NT : 2♠, the jumps to the 3-level can be harnessed for a better purpose as splinters. This is the recommended approach:

1NT : 3♣ = short in diamonds

1NT : 3♦ = short in hearts

1NT : 3♥ = short in spades

1NT : 3♠ = short in clubs

By bidding the suit below the short suit, responder prevents a lead-directing double and gives opener more space to describe the values held. Opener will bid 3NT with the short suit well held. If not, opener can bid the short suit with a maximum 1NT and at most one point wasted in the short suit. Any other suit bid shows a 4+ suit and a minimum 1NT, possibly with some wasted strength in the short suit. If opener bids a suit below 3NT and responder rebids 3NT, this denies 4-card support for opener and does not show any high card values in the short suit. Opener can judge what to do next.

1NT : 3♣
? Opener can bid 3♥ or 3♠ with a 4-card suit, 3NT with no major and diamonds stopped, or 4♣ as the last choice.

For more information on the bidding in this appendix, see *Bid Better, Much Better After Opening 1NT*.

APPENDIX 4
THE JACOBY 2NT TWO-STEP

Chapter 8 included the Jacoby 2NT response to a major suit opening. Jacoby 2NT is an excellent addition to your system since it can locate a shortage in opener's hand and that can help responder judge slam potential.

Opener's rebids after 1♡ : 2NT or 1♠ : 2NT

Playing standard Jacoby, opener has these options:

New suit at the 3-level = singleton or void in the suit bid

4♣ / 4♢ = strong second suit (at least two of the top three honours in a 5-card or longer suit). This takes priority over showing a short suit.

3NT = extra strength, no extra length, no shortage

4-agreed major = minimum opening, 11-13 points

3-agreed-major = extra length, extra strength, no short suit

Fine though it is, Standard Jacoby does have some drawbacks. When opener shows a singleton, it may tip off the defenders to avoid that lead. When no singleton is shown, the defenders also have possibly vital information. When a slam is in the offing, the risk may be worth taking but when the end result is just game, you have gained nothing by using the Jacoby structure. Indeed the Jacoby rebid may allow the opponents to find the killing defence. The less information you give them the better.

Another drawback occurs when opener's rebid is 4-major to show a minimum hand with no shortage. If responder is very strong, the bidding is at a high level to explore slam possibilities further.

These drawbacks can be eliminated by adopting the 'Jacoby Two-Step'. This does everything that standard Jacoby can do and much more. The crux is opener's 3♣ rebid shows any minimum opening without a void and without a strong second suit. Other rebids, except for 3♢, show a strong opening.

Jacoby Two-Step:

3♣ = any minimum hand with no good second suit, no void

3♢ = any strength, a good second suit or a void somewhere. With freak shape, fit is more important than strength.

All the other rebids promise a strong opening:

4♣ / 4♢ / 3-other-major = singleton in the suit bid

3-agreed-major = extra strength, no shortage (may be 5-4-2-2 with a modest second suit or a 6-3-2-2)

3NT = extra strength, but no extra length. If playing a 12-14 1NT this would indicate a 4-card suit and 17-19 points. If playing 5-card majors, it would show a 5-3-3-2 pattern. With 15-16 points and just a 4-card suit, opener rebids 3♣. With a balanced hand 15-16 is a minimum.

4NT = Blackwood

Bidding after the 3♣ rebid

After 3♣ minimum, responder with no slam interest should jump to 4-major. Thus the opponents do not know whether opener has a singleton or a balanced hand. Responder can also rebid 3NT over 3♣ with a 4-3-3-3 pattern. Opener can pass 3NT when that seems the best spot.

If 3♣ has not dampened responder's ardour for slam, responder bids 3♢ to ask about shape. Opener then bids as above from 3♡ onwards to show the same patterns (singleton or extra length, and so on). 1♣ or 1♢ : 2NT, 3♣ : 3♢, 3NT = 15-16 points with a 4-card suit if playing a weak no-trump. Over 3♡, a new suit bid other than 3♢ would be a cue-bid and sets a slam auction in motion.

Bidding after the 3♢ rebid

After 3♢ (good second suit or void somewhere), responder bids 3♡ for clarification:

3♠ says, 'I have a void.' 3NT asks where it is and 4♣ or 4♢ shows the void in the suit bid. 4♡ = void in the other major. Playing standard Jacoby, opener cannot differentiate between a singleton and a void.

4♣ or 4♢ shows a second 5+ suit, headed by at least K-Q. 4♡ shows such a suit in the other major.

3NT = 'My pattern is 5-4-2-2 with a good second suit, at least K-Q-x-x.' With a 5-4-3-1 or 6-4-2-1 shape, prefer to show the shortage first. 4♣ asks and opener shows the second suit. After 1♠ : 2NT, 3♢ : 3♡, 3NT : 4♣, opener bids 4♢ or 4♡ to show the second suit there and 4♠ if the second suit is clubs. After 1♡ : 2NT, 3♢ : 3♡, 3NT : 4♣, opener bids 4♣ if 5=2=4=2 and 4♡ if the second suit is clubs. With a 5-4-2-2 and a good second suit, bid 3♢ only if better than a minimum opening. With a void or a 5-5 shape, you can bid 3♢ with minimum values.

Example hands

WEST	EAST	WEST	EAST
♠ A J 7 5 2	♠ K Q 4 3	1♠	2NT
♡ A Q 9 5 2	♡ K J 7	3◇	3♡
◇ 6	◇ A 8 4	4♡	4NT
♣ 4 3	♣ A 7 5	5♡	7♠
		No	

3◇ = void or good second suit. 3♡ asked which it is and 4♡ showed a strong second suit in hearts, K-Q-x-x-x or better. Once West shows two key cards, East knows enough to bid the grand slam. The hearts should provide the discards from East's hand for the minor suit where West has two or three cards. The grand slam should be reached whether playing Standard Jacoby or Jacoby 2NT Two-Step. (With Standard Jacoby West rebids 4♡ over 2NT.)

WEST	EAST	WEST	EAST
♠ A Q 7 5 2	♠ K J 3	1♡	2NT
♡ A Q 9 6 4 2	♡ K J 10 7	3◇	3♡
◇ ---	◇ Q 10 4	4♡	5♣
♣ 4 3	♣ A 9 7	5◇	5NT
		6♡	7♡
		No	

3◇ = void or good second suit. 3♡ asked which it is and 4♡ showed a strong second suit in the other major. The good second suit is shown ahead of showing a singleton or a void. Concerned about diamond control, East cue-bids 5♣ to show first-round control there and West's 5◇ shows first-round diamond control. East asks about West's trump holding with 5NT and 6♡ shows two of the top three honours (in a simple method where 6♣ = 0, 6◇ = 1, 6♡ = 2 and bid seven with all three).

After 5♣, West would bid 5♡ with two losing diamonds and 6♡ with second round diamond control.

Playing Standard Jacoby there is no provision to show the good 5-card spade suit with a 6-5 pattern.

WEST	EAST	WEST	EAST
♠ 9 4	♠ A 7 3	1♡	2NT
♡ A J 8 6 3	♡ K Q 7 5 4	3◇	3♡
◇ A 2	◇ K 6 4	3NT	4♣
♣ A Q 5 3	♣ K J	4♡	4NT
		5♣	7♡
		No	

3◇ = void or good second suit. 3♡ asked which it is and 3NT = strong opening and a 5-4-2-2 pattern with the second suit at least K-Q-x-x. 4♣ asks for the second suit and 4♡ says it is clubs. 4NT is RKCB and 5♣ = 0 or 3 key cards, obviously 3. East can tell the spade losers will vanish on opener's clubs and has an easy 7♡ bid.

Most pairs would find 6♡ but few would be able to judge to bid the grand slam. Standard Jacoby has no provision for showing a strong 4-card second suit.

WEST	EAST	WEST	EAST
♠ A J 7 4	♠ K 3	1◇	2NT
♡ A Q 7 6 5 3	♡ K 9 8 2	3◇	3♡
◇ ---	◇ Q 8 7 4	3♠	3NT
♣ 9 6 3	♣ K Q J	4◇	4NT
		5♣	6♡
		No	

3◇ = void or good second suit. 3♡ asked which, 3♠ = void, 3NT = where? 4◇ = diamonds, 4NT = RKCB, 5♠ = two key cards plus the ♡Q.

This is an excellent slam to reach with minimum values, thanks to the facility within Jacoby 2NT Two-Step for opener to show a void below game-level. Playing Standard Jacoby, West would bid 3◇ over 2NT. This could be a singleton or a void. East may well now bid 4♡ as an attempted sign-off. Would West bid on? Swap East's minor suit holdings and the five-level could prove too high.

Being able to distinguish between voids and singletons can be essential. With A-x-x opposite a singleton, responder has fine values but the ace may be virtually wasted if facing a void.

WEST	EAST	WEST	EAST
♠ 2	♠ K 9 3	1♡	2NT
♡ A Q 9 7 4	♡ K J 10 5	3♠	4♣
◇ A Q 7	◇ K 10 4 2	4◇	4♡
♣ K 8 6 2	♣ A 9	4NT	5♡
		6♡	No

3♠ = singleton and a strong opening ('strong' will usually be 15+ HCP). Although the ♠K is wasted, East can afford a courtesy 4♣ cue-bid as West has shown a good hand. West's sign-off over 4◇ indicates no extra values but, fortified by the 4♣ cue-bid, West has enough to head for slam.

Playing Standard Jacoby, East would sign off in 4♡ after the 3♠ bid, as West has not showed any extra values. West might still push on with 4NT but it could be an error to make another move if East began with, say:

♠ K Q   ♡ 8 6 5 3   ◇ J 8 3 2   ♣ A Q J

With this hand, responder should sign off even after opener's 3♠ singleton bid showing extras.

WEST	EAST	WEST	EAST
♠ 9	♠ A K Q	1♡	2NT
♡ A J 8 6 3	♡ K Q 7 4	3♣	4♡
◇ K Q J	◇ 7 6 5	No	
♣ Q 6 4 2	♣ 8 7 3		

3♣ = any minimum other than those with a void or a strong second 5+ suit. East cannot see any slam prospects and signs off in game. West figures to make 4♡ on a major suit lead. Ignorant of West's shape, North might lead a spade. Playing Standard Jacoby West bids 3♠ over 2NT and now a spade lead is far less likely.

EXERCISES ON JACOBY 2NT TWO-STEP

A. The bidding has started 1♥ : 2NT (Jacoby Two-Step). What should opener rebid with these hands?

1.	♠ A 6	2.	♠ A 6	3.	♠ A 6	4.	♠ 2	5.	♠ A 7 3 2
	♥ K Q J 5 3		♥ K Q J 5 3		♥ K Q J 5 3		♥ K Q J 5 3		♥ K Q J 5 3
	♦ Q 5		♦ A 5		♦ 7 5		♦ 7 5 2		♦ Q J 8 4
	♣ J 7 6 4		♣ Q J 8 5		♣ A Q J 3		♣ A Q J 3		♣ - - -

B. 1♥ : 2NT (Jacoby Two-Step), 3♣ by opener, 3♦ from responder. What should opener bid now?

1.	♠ A 6	2.	♠ 2	3.	♠ A 9 8 6	4.	♠ J 8 2	5.	♠ K J 7
	♥ K Q J 5 3		♥ K Q J 5 3		♥ K Q 3 2		♥ Q J 7 4 3 2		♥ K Q 8 2
	♦ Q 5		♦ 7 5 2		♦ A 2		♦ A K		♦ 3
	♣ J 7 6 4		♣ A Q J 3		♣ Q 8 3		♣ Q 4		♣ K 8 6 4 2

C. 1♥ : 2NT (Jacoby Two-Step), 3♦ by opener, 3♥ from responder. What should opener bid now?

1.	♠ A 7 3 2	2.	♠ A 6	3.	♠ A Q 7 3 2	4.	♠ 8 7	5.	♠ - - -
	♥ K Q J 5 3		♥ K Q J 5 3		♥ J 9 7 5 3 2		♥ A K 7 3 2		♥ A Q 8 7 2
	♦ Q J 8 4		♦ 7 5		♦ A		♦ K Q 8 4 2		♦ A K 4
	♣ - - -		♣ A Q J 3		♣ Q		♣ 9		♣ 9 8 6 3 2

D. Playing Jacoby 2NT Two-Step, how should the bidding go on Hands 29-32, pages 54-55?

PARTNERSHIP BIDDING: How should the following hands be bid? West is the dealer each time.

SET 41 — WEST	SET 41 — EAST	SET 42 — WEST	SET 42 — EAST
1. ♠ A Q 8 7 4	1. ♠ K J 9 3 2	1. ♠ A 9 7 4 2	1. ♠ K Q 8 6 3
♥ K 7 5 2	♥ Q 8 6	♥ K Q 3	♥ A J
♦ A 6	♦ K Q	♦ K 8 4 3	♦ A 5 2
♣ 9 4	♣ K 7 5	♣ 5	♣ 8 7 4
2. ♠ K 8 6	2. ♠ 7 5 3	2. ♠ A J 7 4 2	2. ♠ K Q 8 6
♥ A 9 7 3 2	♥ K Q J 8	♥ K Q 3	♥ 8 7 4 2
♦ K Q 7 2	♦ A 6	♦ K 8 4 3	♦ A 5 2
♣ 3	♣ A Q J 7	♣ 5	♣ A J
3. ♠ 6	3. ♠ 7 5 3	3. ♠ A K 7 4 3 2	3. ♠ Q 9 8 6
♥ A 9 7 3 2	♥ K Q J 8	♥ 9 6	♥ A K Q J
♦ K Q 7 2	♦ A 6	♦ A K	♦ 9 7 5
♣ K 8 6	♣ A Q J 7	♣ K 8 5	♣ A 6
4. ♠ A Q J 9	4. ♠ K 5	4. ♠ J	4. ♠ A 7 6 2
♥ K J 10 6 2	♥ Q 9 8 5 3	♥ Q 8 4 3 2	♥ A K 9 6 5
♦ - - -	♦ A K 9 6	♦ Q 7	♦ A 6
♣ K 8 5 2	♣ A 4	♣ A K J 7 4	♣ Q 9
5. ♠ A K 8 5 3	5. ♠ Q 9 6 4	5. ♠ 4	5. ♠ A 7 6
♥ K Q 8 2	♥ A J 6 3	♥ Q 8 4 3 2	♥ A K 9 6 5
♦ 7 3	♦ A K 2	♦ K 7	♦ A 3
♣ A 8	♣ 5 4	♣ A K 8 7 4	♣ Q J 3
6. ♠ A K 9 5 2	6. ♠ Q J 8 7 3	6. ♠ Q 8 5 4 2	6. ♠ A K J 7 3
♥ 7	♥ K Q 4	♥ J	♥ A K 6
♦ A 9 6 2	♦ K 4 3	♦ A K 9 4 3	♦ 8 2
♣ A 8 7	♣ Q 5	♣ A 5	♣ K 8 2

APPENDIX 5
RUBINSOHL

Chapter 21 covers the Lebensohl Convention to cope with interference over your side's 1NT opening. Lebensohl is a very popular method but a different approach with major benefits is highly effective. It appeared in an article by Bruce Neill (Australia) in *The Bridge World*, May 1983. His ideas were based on articles by Jeff Rubens (USA) and so the method was called 'Rubensohl'. *The Official Encyclopedia of Bridge* notes that a similar idea to replace 'Lebensohl' had been devised much earlier by Ira Rubin (USA). Accordingly, the name 'Rubinsohl' has been adopted.

How Rubinsohl works

After interference at the two-level the basic approach looks like this:

2NT = transfer to clubs
3♣ = transfer to diamonds
3♦ = transfer to hearts
3♥ = transfer to spades
3♠ = no 4-major, no stopper (always)
3NT = natural, always includes stopper
Exception: *Bidding the suit below their suit = Stayman and promises at least one major.*

For example:

WEST	NORTH	EAST	SOUTH
1NT	2♠*		

* Natural overcall

If East wants to take action:

2NT = transfer to clubs, 5+ clubs
3♣ = transfer to diamonds, 5+ diamonds
3♦ = transfer to hearts, 5+ hearts
3♥ = Stayman, shows exactly four hearts
3♠ = denies four hearts, denies a spade stopper
3NT = denies four hearts, promises a spade stopper

Advantages of Rubinsohl

1. You can compete by transferring to any suit.

2. You can transfer to a major and rebid 3NT (5-card major) or raise the major (6+ suit).

3. You can transfer to a minor and then show a 4-card major.

4. Bidding the suit below their suit = Stayman (shows a 4-card major). It allows opener to play in the major or *to bid the enemy suit to deny a stopper.*

5. Transfer to a suit followed by 3NT shows a stopper in their suit.

6. Transfer to a suit followed by a bid of their suit denies a stopper.

7. The 3♠ (no major, no stopper) and 3NT bids always mean the same.

Other principles which work well in conjunction with Rubinsohl are:

Suit bid at 2-level = natural, not forcing
Double = takeout, shows the values to invite game

Another example:

WEST	NORTH	EAST	SOUTH
1NT	2♥*	?	

* Natural overcall

If East wants to take action:

2♠ = natural, not forcing
2NT = transfer, 5+ clubs
3♣ = transfer, 5+ diamonds
3♦ = suit below their suit and so shows four spades. Opener can now bid spades (3♠ strong, 4♠ weak), 3NT without four spades and hearts stopped or 3♥ without four spades to ask for a heart stopper.
3♥ = transfer, 5+ spades
3♠ = no 4 spades, no stopper in hearts
3NT = no 4 spades, promises a stopper in hearts
Double = for takeout, does not promise four spades. Opener can bid 2♠ if minimum, 3♠ if maximum, when holding four spades. Responder will support with four spades or remove to no-trumps otherwise. When not holding four spades, opener can bid 2NT, 3♣ or 3♦ if minimum, or 3NT (stopper) / 3♥ (no stopper) if maximum.

Where their overcall refers to another suit, the above structure from 2NT applies.

Bidding the shown suit at the two-level shows a singleton or void in their suit and a 3-suiter type.

WEST	NORTH	EAST	SOUTH
1NT	2♦*	?	

*Spades and another

Now 2♥ = natural, not forcing, 2♠ = 3-suiter with singleton or void spade, bids from 2NT onwards are as above, with 3♥ (suit below their known suit) as Stayman, while Double shows invitational values.

Where their overcall shows two suits

If one suit is unknown, play as above regarding the known suit. If both suits are known, (e.g., 2♥ showing both majors), *transfer to either suit shows a stopper in that suit.* If neither suit known, play full Rubinsohl and double for takeout = Stayman.

Where their overcall is 2♣, play 'System On'.

Double of 2♣ replaces your own 2♣ response (Stayman or Puppet), while all other responses have their normal meaning. If they double 1NT to show a 1-suiter, again play 'System On': ignore the double.

Example auctions

If playing Rubinsohl, how should the bidding continue on these hands?

Hand 81 (from page 121)

WEST	EAST
♠ A 10 5	♠ J 6
♥ 7 6 3	♥ A 8 5 2
♦ A K 4	♦ 6 3
♣ Q 9 7 6	♣ A K 5 4 3

WEST	NORTH	EAST	SOUTH
1NT	2♥	. . .	

Hand 82 (from page 121)

WEST	EAST
♠ 9 8	♠ Q 4
♥ K Q 5 2	♥ 9 8 7 6 4
♦ K J 4	♦ A Q 9 6
♣ K J 10 2	♣ A Q

WEST	NORTH	EAST	SOUTH
1NT	2♠	. . .	

Hand 83 (from page 122)

WEST	EAST
♠ A J 7	♠ K 8 5 2
♥ A K	♥ 8 3 2
♦ 8 6 4	♦ A K J
♣ J 9 8 3 2	♣ Q 10 5

WEST	NORTH	EAST	SOUTH
1NT	2♥	. . .	

Hand 84 (from page 122)

WEST	EAST
♠ Q J 6 2	♠ A K 7 4
♥ 5 3 2	♥ 8 4
♦ A 2	♦ K Q 10 6
♣ A K 9 7	♣ Q 3 2

WEST	NORTH	EAST	SOUTH
1NT	2♥	. . .	

Answers:

Hand 81:

WEST	NORTH	EAST	SOUTH
1NT	2♥	3NT (1)	All pass

(1) 3NT shows a stopper in hearts and denies four spades. Do not show the clubs.

Hand 82:

WEST	NORTH	EAST	SOUTH
1NT	2♠	3◊ (1)	No
3♥	No	3♠ (2)	No
4♥	No	No	No

(1) 3◊ = transfer to hearts
(2) Bidding their suit denies a stopper in that suit.

Hand 83:

WEST	NORTH	EAST	SOUTH
1NT	2♥	3◊ (1)	No
3NT (2)	No	No	No

(1) Bidding the suit below their suit = Stayman and is forcing to game. East is showing four spades.
(2) 3NT shows a stopper in hearts and denies four spades. With no stopper in hearts, West bids 3♥.

Hand 84:

WEST	NORTH	EAST	SOUTH
1NT	2♥	3◊ (1)	No
3♠ (2)	No	4♠	All pass

(1) 3◊ = Stayman, shows four spades
(2) Maximum hand with four spades, in case East has slam interest. 4♠ would show a weaker hand. As there is no tangible benefit for West to play the hand, West could bid 4♣ over 3◊ as a cue-bid with spade support. East would still sign off in 4♠.

Other examples:

WEST	EAST
♠ A 4 2	♠ 9 3
♥ K 7	♥ A Q J 8 6
♦ K 6 5 4	♦ A 8 3
♣ K 8 6 3	♣ Q J 2

WEST	NORTH	EAST	SOUTH
1NT	2♣	3◊ (1)	No
3♥	No	3♠ (2)	No
4♥ (3)	No	No	No

(1) 3◊ = transfer to hearts
(2) 3♠ = no stopper in spades
(3) 4♥ = prepared to play in the 5-2 fit. It could be right to bid 3NT as West but unless there are nine running tricks, there is a danger that the spades come in for North-South before declarer can set up the extra tricks needed. On the actual layout if North has the ♣A, which is highly likely, 3NT figures to fail while 4♥ has excellent chances. (If West had bid 4♣ or 4◊ rather than 4♥, East should bid 4♥.)

WEST	EAST
♠ K 4	♠ 9 3
♥ A 7 3	♥ K J 8 6 4 2
♦ A Q 6 3	♦ K 2
♣ 8 5 4 2	♣ K Q J

WEST	NORTH	EAST	SOUTH
1NT	2♣	3◊ (1)	No
3♥	No	4♥	All pass

(1) 3◊ = transfer to hearts

Played by West, 4♥ has better prospects than if played by East. If East is declarer it would not be a surprise to lose two spades, one heart and one club.

Exercises: Playing Rubinsohl, give answers for:
(a) Exercises A, B and C on page 120
(b) Partnership Bidding Practice, page 120

(Answers on page 175)

ANSWERS TO EXERCISES AND QUIZZES

Page   **Answers and Comments**

12   **A.** 1. 2♡   2. 2♡. If opener can find 3♡ or 3♠, you can bid the game.   3. 2♠
      4. 2◇   5. 2♠
   B. 1. 4♠   2. 3♡   3. 3♠. Shows five spades. The suit quality of the spades is irrelevant.
   4. 3♣. Slam in clubs is possible.   5. 3♡
   C. 1. 2NT. Expectancy is 15-18 balanced.   2. 2NT   3. 3NT. 19-20 balanced. Denies five hearts
and denies four spades.   4. 2NT. Strong enough for 3NT but this could inhibit responder from
showing 3-card heart support. If responder bids 3NT, raise to 4NT to show the extra values.
   5. 2NT. Enough for 3NT but that could miss the spade fit. Bid 2NT and raise 3NT to 4NT.

Bidding Set 1

1. W	E	2. W	E	3. W	E	4. W	E	5. W	E	6. W	E
1♣	1♡	No	1♣	1◇	1♠	No	1◇	1◇	1♠	1◇	1♠
1NT	2◇	1♠	1NT	2♣	2◇	1♠	1NT	1NT	2♡	1NT	2♡
2♡	No	2♠	No	No		2◇	No	2♠	No	3♠	4♠
										No	

It is worth rebidding these hands to see what would happen if the bidding starts 1X: 1Y, 2NT (17-18).
#3: If West rebid 1NT, this would not be the crime of the century. East would still revert to 2◇.
#5: West is maximum and has good cards for the majors. However, the shape is poor (no ruffing value) and
the K-Q holdings in the minors make it less attractive (although partner has no singleton this time).
#6: This West hand is at least one trick better than #5. Here West has two winners in the minors and three in
the majors, while in #5, West had two *useful* minor winners and only two winners in the majors. In addition,
West in #6 has ruffing potential with the doubleton heart.

Bidding Set 2

1. W	E	2. W	E	3. W	E	4. W	E	5. W	E	6. W	E
No	1◇	1♣	1♠	1♠	2♣	1♠	2♣	1♠	2♣	1♡	2♣
1♠	2NT	2NT	3♡	3NT	No	2NT	3♠	2NT	3NT	2NT	3♠
3♠	4♠	4♣	4♡			4◇	4♠	4NT	6NT	4♡	4NT
No		No		*3NT = 19-20*		No		No		5♠	6♠
		4♣ = cue-bid				*4◇ = cue-bid*		*4NT = 19-20*		No	
										4♡ = cue-bid	

How would these hands bid if opener has to rebid 3NT to show 19 points?
When opener cue-bids or bids 4NT over 3NT, opener is usually showing the 19-20 hand.

17   **A.** 1. 2♣, checkback   2. 3♣, game-force   3. 3♡. Game-force with 5-5 in the majors.
   4. 2NT. Forcing 3♣ and intending to rebid 3♡ as a game-force with only four hearts.
   5. 2NT. Forcing 3♣ and intending to rebid 3NT to show a 4-4-4-1 or 5-4-4-0 short in opener's suit.
   B. 1. 3♠. Denies three hearts. Shows strength in spades and concern about clubs for 3NT.
   2. 2◇. Artificial to show 15 points or a very bad 16.   3. 2♡. 16 points with three hearts.
   4. 3◇. 17-18 points with five diamonds. Does not deny three hearts.   5. 3♡. 17-18 with three hearts.
   C. 1. 3♠. Game-force with exactly five spades.   2. 3♡. Game-force with five spades - four hearts.
   3. 3◇. Game-force with 5+ diamonds (see page 16).   4. 3NT. Three-suiter short in opener's suit.   5. No bid

Bidding Set 3

1. W	E	2. W	E	3. W	E	4. W	E	5. W	E	6. W	E
1♣	1♠	No	1◇	No	1◇	1◇	1♠	No	1◇	1♣	1♠
1NT	2♣	1♠	1NT	1♡	1NT	1NT	2♣	1♡	1NT	1NT	2♣
2◇	2♡	2♣	3♠	2NT	3♣	3♡	4♡	2♣	2◇	2◇	2♡
No		3NT	No	No		No		No		No	
		3♠ = 17-18		*2NT forces 3♣*		*3♡ = 17-18*		*2◇ = 15 points*			

#3: How would you manage to sign off in clubs in standard methods?
#4: Without four hearts, East should rebid 3♠ with five spades.
#5: West has 16 points but a poor 16 with unsupported honours in the majors. 4♡ is not a good contract.

Bidding Set 4

1. W	E	2. W	E	3. W	E	4. W	E	5. W	E	6. W	E
1♣	1♥	1♣	1♥	1♥	1♠	1♣	1♠	No	1♣	No	1♣
1NT	2♠	1NT	3♥	1NT	3♥	1NT	2NT	1◇	1NT	1◇	1NT
4♥	No	3NT	No	3♠	4♠	3♣	3♠	2NT	3♣	2NT	3♣
2♠ = game-force		3♥ = six hearts		No		4♠	No	3NT	No	3NT	4♣
		3NT = 1 heart		3♥ = 3 hearts		2NT forces 3♣				No	

#2: The bidding could start 1♣: 1♥, 2◇ . . . but the 1NT rebid is not terrible when the diamonds are so weak.

#5 and #6: West's sequence shows a three-suiter short in opener's suit.

24   **A.**   1. 2◇. Transfer to hearts and planning to pass 2♥. Any 5-card major is acceptable.

2. 2♥. Transfer to spades.   3. 2♠. Transfer to clubs.   4. 2♣, Stayman. This hand is too good to sign off in diamonds via a transfer. There are reasonable chances for game opposite a maximum 1NT even if opener does not have the ◇Q. 2♣ followed by 2NT invites game but note that in this approach 2♣ does not promises a major and this needs to be alerted to the opponents.

5. 2♣, Stayman. Do not transfer to a minor with invitational values. Transfer to a minor to sign off or with slam prospects.

B.   1. 2♥   2. 2♥. You are not allowed to reject the transfer.   3. 2♥. The hand is maximum but the flat shape argues against a 3♥ super-accept.   4. 3♥. This has all three important features: excellent support, maximum points and a doubleton.   5. 2♠. Shows a super-accept for hearts and four spades as well. If partner is prepared to be in 2♥ opposite a minimum with two hearts, then it should not be so terrible to be in 3♥ with three hearts and a maximum.

C.   1. 3NT. Maximum but without support for hearts.   2. 3♥. Great support for hearts but the shape is terrible and the unsupported honours all combine to make this a minimum opening. You therefore reject the game invitation.   3. 4♥. Maximum with three hearts.   4. Pass. Minimum with only two hearts.

5. 4♥. Only 13 points but everything is good for hearts: 4-card support, doubleton and aces are undervalued in the standard point count. Three aces is closer to 13 points than 12.

Bidding Set 5

1. W	E	2. W	E	3. W	E	4. W	E	5. W	E	6. W	E
1NT	2◇	1NT	2♥	No	1NT	No	1NT	1NT	2♥	1NT	2◇
2♥	No	2♠	2NT	2◇	2♥	2♥	3♠	3♠	4♠	2♥	2NT
		3♠	No	2NT	4♥	No		No		4♥	No
				No							

#2: East has a good hand but with the poor spades, 2NT is enough. With 3-card support, West chooses 3♠.

#3: You might open an unbalanced 11-count but an 11-point 5-3-3-2 should pass in first or second seat.

#4: Treat the super-accept as equivalent to 15-16 points. You cannot blame West for passing but 4♠ could make (diamond lead to the ace) and if West's red suits were reversed, 4♠ is excellent. Tough game, bridge, but it illustrates the power of the 6-4 shape when partner has good support for the 6-card suit.

#5: Note the value of the super-accept. East might well pass 2♠.

Bidding Set 6

1. W	E	2. W	E	3. W	E	4. W	E	5. W	E	6. W	E
1NT	2♠*	No	1NT	1NT	2NT	1NT	2♣	No	1NT	1NT	2♥
3♣	No	2NT	3◇	3♣	3NT	2♠	2NT	2◇	2NT	2♠	3♠
*Transfer to clubs		No		No		No		3NT	No	4♠	No

#1: West is maximum and has a top club but for a super-accept of a minor you want primary values, aces and kings, which make nine tricks in 3NT feasible opposite six tricks in responder's minor.

#2: East has the primary values and is maximum but has no help for responder's minor.

#3: With the primary values and the top honour in diamonds, West gives a super-accept. East figures the diamonds should now play for six tricks and if partner's outside values are primary, 3NT should be a fair bet.

#4: East has invitational values and so uses 2♣ followed by 2NT to invite game.

#5: East's 2NT shows a 4-3-3-3 and 14 points made up of aces and kings (the queen in partner's major and three aces outside would also make it suitable for 2NT). Such hands may play better in 3NT.

#6: East's 3♠ shows six spades and invitational values.

31 **A.** 1. 2♠. Transfer to clubs, to be followed by 3♥, game-force. 2. 2♣. Too weak for a transfer sequence. Use Stayman and play in hearts or no-trumps. 3. 3NT. Risky but that is what the pairs game is all about. The hand is not worth slam and to transfer to clubs and then show the diamonds would suggest slam possibilities. You might then miss the best spot of 3NT.
4. 3♥. This shows a single-suiter, 5+ hearts with slam aspirations.
5. 4♥. Because of the tenaces in spades and diamonds.
B. 1. 4♥ 2. 4♦. Cue-bid showing support for hearts, a maximum 1NT, the ♦A and no ace of clubs.
3. 4♠. Weak preference. 4. 3NT. No support for either major. 5. 3♠. Strong preference.
C. 1. 4♣. With the weak spades, you must show the club support, as responder has slam hopes.
2. 4♥. Very little in partner's suits and poor shape. Therefore reject the cue-bid of 3♠. 3. 3NT
4. 3♠. Cue in support of hearts. 5. 3NT. Despite the clubs because all the strength is in the unbid suits.

Bidding Set 7											
1. W	**E**	**2. W**	**E**	**3. W**	**E**	**4. W**	**E**	**5. W**	**E**	**6. W**	**E**
1NT	2♥	1NT	2♦	1NT	2NT	1NT	3NT	1NT	2♦	1NT	2♥
2♠	3NT	2♥	4♥	3♦	3♠	No		2♥	3NT	2♠	3♥
4♠	No	No		3NT	No			No		4♠	No

#1: 4♠ should score more than 3NT.
#4: Not enough for a slam and therefore do not transfer with length in the minors. Have a go at 3NT.
#6: 4♠ is weak preference: bad shape, poor values.

Bidding Set 8											
1. W	**E**	**2. W**	**E**	**3. W**	**E**	**4. W**	**E**	**5. W**	**E**	**6. W**	**E**
1NT	2♦	1NT	3NT	1NT	2♥	1NT	2♦	1NT	2♥	1NT	2♥
2♥	2♠	No		2♠	3♦	2♥	3♣	2♠	3♣	2♠	3♣
4♠	No			3♠	4♦	3♦	6♣	4♠	No	3♦	3♥
				5♣	6♠	No				3♠	4NT
				No						5♥	7♣
										No	

#1: West does not have enough for a super-accept. Choose the 4-4 fit to try for maximum tricks.
#2: With a long minor and game values only, do not transfer to the minor. Just bid 3NT.
#3: 3♠ shows strong preference, 4♦ = cue-bid, 5♣ = cue-bid.
#4: 3♦ = cue-bid in support of clubs. This also denies 3-card support for hearts. Once East receives the club support and there cannot be two aces missing, the small slam should be a good chance. East can work out that West would not have enough to make the grand slam worthwhile.
#5: 4♠ = weak preference. Despite the 4-card support for spades and East's slam hopes, West gives the weaker raise, because so few of West's values are in the black suits and West has no ruffing potential.
#6: 3♦ = cue-bid in support of clubs and denies three spades. 3♥ = cue-bid and 3♠ = cue-bid. Normally 3♠ would be expected to show the ace of spades but it is all right to cue-bid the king in partner's long suit. If partner has the ace, partner knows the cue-bid shows the king. If partner lacks the ace, partner still expects to lose a trick in the long suit.

36 **A.** 1. 3♣, Stayman. 2. 3♦, transfer to hearts. Follow up with 3NT. 3. 3♦. Follow up with 3♠.
4. 3♠ to show 5 spades - 4 hearts, or Stayman and rebid 3♠ over 3♦. 5. 3♥ and pass 3♠.
B. 1. 4♥ 2. 4♥ 3. 3NT. Shows four spades and game hopes only. 4. 3♠. Shows four spades and slam values (otherwise would have bid 3NT). 5. 4NT. Heading for 7♥ or 6NT.
C. 1. 3NT. All the strength is in the minors. 2. 4♥ 3. 4♣. Cue-bid in support of spades. Prefer the 4-4 fit to the 5-4 fit at pairs. 4. 4♦. Cue-bid in support of spades. 5. 4♦

Bidding Set 9											
1. W	**E**	**2. W**	**E**	**3. W**	**E**	**4. W**	**E**	**5. W**	**E**	**6. W**	**E**
No	2NT	2NT	3♦	2NT	3♦	No	2NT	No	2NT	2NT	3♥
3♥	3♠	3♥	No	4♥	No	3♥	3♠	3♦	3♥	3♠	3NT
4♠	No			*East would pass*		4♠*	No	3NT	No	4♠	No
Note how badly				*3♥. Note how*		**Too good*				*With 3-card*	
3NT plays.				*good 4♥ is.*		*to pass 3♠.*				*support, choose*	
										the major game.	

#1 and #4: It would be timid to pass 3♠.
#3: After a transfer over 2NT, opener should super-accept with 4-card support and an outside doubleton.

Bidding Set 10											
1. W	E	2. W	E	3. W	E	4. W	E	5. W	E	6. W	E
2NT	3♣	2NT	3♣	No	2NT	No	2NT	2NT	3♠	No	2NT
3♠	4♠	3♡	3NT	3◇	3♡	3◇	3♡	4♡	No	3♡	3♠
No		4♠	No	3♠	3NT	3♠	4♡	*or*		4♡*	4♠
					No	4NT	5♣	2NT	3♣	No	
						No		3♡	4♡	*Shows 5-5 in*	
								No		*the majors.*	

#1: 4♠ is much better than 3NT. After 1NT or 2NT, you must aim for a 4-4 major fit first and foremost.

#2: East's sequence shows four spades but no interest in slam. This allows opener to play any game contract.

#3: West has shown five hearts and four spades and East has support for neither major.

#4: West is definitely worth a slam try once opener supports one of the majors.

#5: Bid 2NT: 3♠ if using that response to show precisely 5 spades and 4 hearts. If not, travel via 3♣.

#6: Responder could not afford to bid 4♡ with only a 4-card suit. There might not be an 8-card fit in either major. Bidding game in a new suit is taken as showing at least a 5-card suit.

42 **A.** 1. 4♡. Too weak for a splinter.   2. 4♣. Splinter raise, short in clubs.   3. 3♠. Splinter
4. 2♣. Do not make an immediate splinter with only 3-card support.   5. 4◇. Splinter
B. 1. 4♠. Minimum hand and now the ♣Q is wasted.   2. 4NT. Even though the clubs are wasted, you are very strong elsewhere. Opposite 3 key cards, slam should be a good bet.   3. 4◇. Cue-bid to show slam interest.   4. 4♠. The club holding is terrible opposite a singleton or void.   5. 4♠. The club shortage is wasted. Singleton opposite a singleton means no ruffing values there in either hand.
C. 1. 3♣. Natural and forcing.   2. 4♣. Just strong enough for the 4♣ delayed splinter.
3. 3♠. Delayed splinter, short in spades and 3-card heart support.   4. 3♠. Delayed splinter. Great slam prospects opposite just three aces or ♡A-Q-x-x-x-x and ♣A.   5. 4♡. Too weak to splinter.

Bidding Set 11											
1. W	E	2. W	E	3. W	E	4. W	E	5. W	E	6. W	E
1♠	4♣	1♠	4♣	1◇	1♡	1◇	1♡	1♣	1♠	1♣	1♠
4NT	5♡	4♠	No	4♣	4NT	4♣	4♡	2NT	3NT	4♠	4NT
6♠	No	*West's clubs are*		5♡	6♡	No		4♠	No	5♡	6♠
West's clubs are		*awful opposite*		No		*East has*		*2NT = 19-20*		No	
ideal for slam.		*a singleton.*		*4♣ = splinter*		*terrible clubs.*		*game-force*		*4♠ = 4-2-2-5*	

#1: Although opener has just a minimum opening, the club holding is perfect. Opposite a singleton or a void, West has no club losers and only five losers outside. As East's splinter shows the high card values for a game raise, opener can expect 4+ cover cards from responder. That reduces West's losers from 5 to 1. Basic cover card expectancy is 7-9 points = 2 cover cards, 10-12 points = 3, 13-15 points = 4, and so on.

#3: Even though East has only minimum high card values, the club holding is ideal. East has five losers outside the clubs and West's strong rebid makes it very likely that West will be able to cover those five losers. Slam should be a good bet as long as two aces are not missing.

#4: This East hand is much worse than the East in #3. The ♣K is probably useless and having only four trumps is a drawback. Slam on a 4-4 fit usually requires 30+ HCP.

#5: With the 19-20 HCP balanced hand, opener can rebid with a jump to 2NT here to force to game and show the strength and shape of the hand. When responder bids 3NT or a new suit, opener can then show the spade support.

#6: The jump to 4♠ should be a 5-4-2-2 pattern: not 4-4-3-2 or 4-3-3-3 (rebid with a jump to 2NT) and no singleton or void because of the failure to splinter. A different but sensible approach is to play that opener's jump raise to game in responder's major is a weak, distributional hand (sort of a gambling game raise by opener). With a full value raise to game, use the 2NT jump rebid for the flattish hands including the 5-4-2-2s (and revert to responder's major next round) or give a splinter raise with a shapely hand and 4-card support.

Bidding Set 12											
1. W	**E**	**2. W**	**E**	**3. W**	**E**	**4. W**	**E**	**5. W**	**E**	**6. W**	**E**
1♥	4♥	1♣	1♠	1♣	1♠	1♠	2♥	1♠	2♥	2♣	2♦
No		2♣	3♥	2♣	2♥	4♣	4♦	4♣	5♣	2♠	4♣
East is too weak		4♦	4NT	4♦	4NT	5NT	6♦	5♥	No	7♠	No
for a splinter,		5♥	6♣	5♥	6♥	7♥	No	*4♣ = splinter*		*2♣ = game-*	
which should be		*3♥ = splinter*		No		*4♣ = splinter*		*5♣ = cue-bid*		*force*	
10 or more HCP.		*4♦ = cue-bid*		*4♦ = splinter*		*4♦ = cue-bid*		*5♥ = sign off*		*2♦ = negative*	
						5NT = trump ask				*4♣ = splinter*	

#2: As 2♥ by East would be forcing, it is sensible to harness the jump to 3♥ as a splinter raise of clubs.

#3: Even though West has a minimum opening, it costs nothing to show the splinter support for hearts. With spades and diamonds reversed, West would jump to 4♥ over 2♥.

#4: Once East can cue-bid 4♦, West figures that the spades should dispose of any extra diamond losers in the East hand. The remaining problem is whether East has the ace of hearts. 4NT would not solve that question, since a 5♥ reply to show two aces leaves West wondering which other ace East holds. The 5NT trump ask is covered in Chapter 15.

#5: East's cue-bid of 5♣ does not encourage West at all since with a void opposite, the ace is of little value. West's sign off also focuses on diamonds and as East has no diamond control either, a poor slam is avoided.

#6: Once East has shown the weakness of the hand with the negative reply, East can freely splinter next round.

47 **A.** 1. Pass. No worthwhile suit.   2. 1♥. Strong suit.   3. 2♠. A weak two in third seat is all right with a strong 5-card suit.   4. 1♦. Otherwise pass.   5. 1♠. Not 1NT.

    B. 1. 1♣. HCP + spade length = 16, therefore open.   2. Pass. HCP + spade length = 13.   3. 2♥. 4th seat weak two = 8-12 points.   4. 3♣. Otherwise pass.   5. 4♠. To avoid a competitive auction.

    C. 1. Open 1♥ and raise 1♠ to 2♠. Over 2♣ or 2♦, rebid 2♥.   2. Open 1NT. Otherwise, open 1♥ and rebid 2♣ or 2♦ over 1♠.   3. Open 1♥. Over 1♠, jump to 2NT to show shape and strength, but support spades next round. Over 2♣ or 2♦, rebid 2NT (forcing), not 3NT, which could lose the spade suit.

    4. Open 1♥. Over 1♠, rebid 2NT (19-20, game-force). Over 2♣ or 2♦, rebid 2NT (15+, forcing). To jump to 3NT could miss a 5-3 heart fit.   5. Open 1♥. Over 1♠, rebid 2NT (19-20, game-force). Over 2♣ or 2♦, rebid 3NT showing 19-20 points and denying 5 hearts and denying 4-4 in the majors.

Bidding Set 13											
1. W	**E**	**2. W**	**E**	**3. W**	**E**	**4. W**	**E**	**5. W**	**E**	**6. W**	**E**
No	1♥	No	1♠	No	1♥	1♥	2♣	1♥	1♠	1♥	2♣
2♣	2♦	2♠	No	4♥	No	2NT	3♠	2♠	No	2NT	3♥
2♥	No	*With 9 losers,*		*If worth 4♥, bid*		4♦	4♠	*or open 1NT on*		4NT	5♦
2♣ = Drury		*prefer 2♠ to 2♣*		*it even after 3rd*		4NT	5♦	*the West cards.*		5NT	6♥
		Drury (8 losers)		*seat opener.*		6♠	No			6NT	No

#1: East might have opened 2♥.   #2: In third seat, you are usually better to open a strong 4-card suit than 1NT which can easily be doubled for penalties.   #4: After East's early bidding, West has enough to push on to slam despite East's attempted sign off.   #6: Once West receives the delayed heart support, West has slam prospects, particularly with the club fit. Once West locates all the kings, West should choose 6NT rather than 6♥.

Bidding Set 14											
1. W	**E**	**2. W**	**E**	**3. W**	**E**	**4. W**	**E**	**5. W**	**E**	**6. W**	**E**
No	1♦	No	2♠?	No	1♠	No	1♠	1♥	2♣	1♠	2♣
No		No		2♣	2♥	2♥	No	4♥	4NT	2NT	3NT
East's 1♦ gives		*East is in the*		3♥	4♥			5♦	5NT	4NT	6NT
West the best		*best position*		No				6♥	6NT	No	
lead.		*for a psyche.*		*2♣ = Drury*				No		*4NT = 19-20,*	
								4♥ = SQ 10		*balanced*	

#1 & #2: North-South obviously will be bidding on but this as high as East-West should go.

#3: Note how Drury leads you to the superior 4-4 heart fit while No: 1♠, 3♠ would land you in 4♠ which will play one trick worse most of the time.

#5: West's rebid with a jump to 4♥ shows a self-sufficient suit (Suit Quality 10 or better). Having located one ace and two kings, East judges that 6NT should play as well as 6♥. If there are two heart losers, that would be fatal in 6♥ but perhaps not in 6NT. At pairs, 5NT asking for kings is often used to probe for a good 6NT.

53   A.   1. 3♡. Limit hand with 6 respectable hearts.   2. 4♡. Suit Quality 10.   3. 3NT
   4. 2♠. Fourth-suit in case partner has 3-card heart support.   5. 2♠. Too strong for 3♡ (not forcing)
   but the hearts are not good enough for 4♡. Bid 2♠ fourth-suit and rebid 3♡ forcing.
   B.   1. 3♡ (but 3♠ if playing Bergen, 2♣ in Power)   2. 2♣ or 2♢ as the start of a delayed game
   raise but isn't 2NT Jacoby more attractive? (Bid 2♢ in Power as a game-force.)   3.   4♡   in   any
   approach
   4. No bid (but 3♡ is available if playing pre-emptive raises). Not enough for 4♡.   5. 3♠, splinter.
   C.   1. 3♢. Shows the singleton diamond.   2. 3♢. Singleton diamond. May be weak or strong.
   3. 4♢. Shows strong suit, K-Q-x-x-x or better.   4. 4♠. Weak 5-3-3-2/5-4-2-2.   5. 3NT. 16+ HCP.

Bidding Set 15					
1. W E	**2. W E**	**3. W E**	**4. W E**	**5. W E**	**6. W E**
1♢ 1♡	1♡ 1♠	1♣ 1♢	1♣ 1♢	1♣ 1♢	No 1♠
2♣ 2♠	2♣ 2♢	1♡ 1♠	1♡ 2♠	1♡ 2♠	2♣ 2♢
3♡ 4♡	2NT 3♠	2♠ No	2NT 3NT	3♢ 5♢	2♡ No
No	4♢ 4NT	*1♠ = natural*	No	No	*2♣ = Drury but*
2♠ = 4th suit	5♡ 6♠	*and forcing*	*2♠ = 4th suit*	*2♠ = 4th suit*	*not promising*
	2♢ = 4th suit		*forcing, denies*		*spade support*
	4♢ = cue-bid		*four spades*		

#1: It would be premature and misguided to rebid 3NT over 2♣.

#2: After using fourth-suit, East's 3♠ is forcing to game. Without spade support, West would rebid 3NT. West has already denied 3-card spade support by bidding 2NT over 2♢. West's 4♢ shows maximum values within the context of the auction and a doubleton spade. West upgrades the hand because of the queen of spades. With a rag doubleton in spades, West would simply raise to 4♠.

#3 and #4: After 1♣: 1♢, 1♡ responder's 1♠ is natural, 4+ spades and forcing. 2♠ is used as fourth-suit and denies four spades.

#5: West's 3♢ shows 3-card diamond support and denies a spade stopper. West's 3♢ is not forcing and opposite minimum values, East is not worth a slam try. As West has at most two spades and East has nothing in spades, this is the time to forego 3NT.

#6: West's sequence shows four hearts only (failure to respond 2♡ at once). East should pass with three or four hearts. With two hearts or fewer, East should not pass 2♡.

Bidding Set 16					
1. W E	**2. W E**	**3. W E**	**4. W E**	**5. W E**	**6. W E**
1♠ 2NT	1♠ 2NT	1♠ 2NT	1♡ 2NT	1♡ 2NT	1♠ 2NT
3♣ 4NT	3♣ 4♠	3NT 4♠	4♣ 7♡	4♣ 4NT	4♠ No
5♢ 6♠	No	4NT 5♡	No	5♢ 5NT	*4♠ = minimum*
No	*East is minimum*	6♠ No	*4♣ = 5+ clubs,*	6♡ 7NT	*and no short*
2NT = Jacoby	*and the club*	*3NT = 16+*	*at least two top*	*East can count*	*suit*
3♣ = short suit	*holding is poor.*	*4♠ = sign off*	*honours*	*thirteen tricks.*	

#1: Jacoby is for opener what a splinter raise is for responder. Just as it is valuable for responder to reveal a short suit, so locating a short suit with opener can be vital in appraising slam chances. East could not be happier after finding opener has a singleton or void in clubs. With only four losers outside clubs, even a minimum opening should supply enough winners to cover four losers.

#2: Opposite a singleton, a doubleton can only eliminate one extra loser. You then need extra high card values to bid on to slam.

#3: East has a minimum 2NT and signs off despite opener's strong rebid. Opener is allowed to bid on despite the sign off and here West has ample to try for slam. Facing 13+ points, opener can expect responder to provide four cover cards and West has just five losers. West could also use a cue-bidding sequence over 4♠. West 5♣, East: 5♢, West: 5♠ indicating worry about hearts, East: 6♠. (See Chapter 14.)

#4: As East is staring at the ♣Q, East knows that West's 4♣ must be no worse than A-K-x-x-x. West's clubs should provide whatever discards East needs. Unable to locate the ♣J, East should not attempt 7NT.

#5: This time East has ♣Q-J-x opposite the promised ♣A-K-x-x-x. That should bring in five club tricks. Counting five tricks in hearts and the outside aces gives East twelve tricks. When 5NT locates an extra king with opener, East can take a sensible shot at 7NT. Playing teams, East would settle for 7♡ which is a touch safer.

#6: West's 4♠ shows a minimum opening with no short suit. The pattern will be 5-3-3-2 or 5-4-2-2.
While it is a triumph to reach good slams, it is just as much a triumph to avoid silly slams.

58 **A.** 1. 2♥. Maximum weak two. 2. 1♠. Too strong for a weak two. 3. No bid. Hearts too weak for 2♥.
4. No bid. Do not open a weak two with four cards in the other major. 5. 2♠.
B. 1. 4♥. With four trumps and a singleton, you should bid game opposite a weak two regardless of strength, either to make or as a sacrifice. 2. No bid. You need better than three winners to try for game. With an extra heart, a pre-emptive raise to 3♥ would be acceptable. 3. No bid. With a misfit, pass below 16 HCP. 4. 2NT. You have more than three winners. Bid game opposite a maximum and sign off in 3♥ opposite a minimum. 5. 2NT. Bid 3NT opposite a maximum and 3♥ opposite a minimum. Opener will reply 4♥ with Suit Quality 10.
C. 1. 3♦. Minimum with two top spade honours. 2. 3NT. A-K-Q-x-x-x.
3. 3♥. Maximum points but only one top spade. 4. 3♣. Minimum and only one top spade honour.
5. 3♠. Maximum with two top honours in spades.

Bidding Set 17											
1. W	**E**	**2. W**	**E**	**3. W**	**E**	**4. W**	**E**	**5. W**	**E**	**6. W**	**E**
2♥	2NT	No	2♥	2♠	4♠	2♠	4♠	No	2♠	2♥	2NT
3♠	4♥	No		No		No		4♠	No	3♣	3♥
No				*With 4 trumps*		*East should*		2♠ *is OK in*		No	
Treat 8 HCP and				*and a singleton,*		*consider a*		*third seat on a*		3♣ = *minimum*	
three cover cards				*bid game.*		*4NT or 3♥*		*strong 5-card*		*and bad suit. 3♥*	
as maximum.						*psyche.*		*suit.*		*may be too high.*	

#4: East can tell that the opponents have at least 25 HCP (East has 5 and West has at most 10) and that the opponents have at least eight hearts (West should not have four hearts with a 2♠ opening) and eight diamonds (as West should not have five diamonds as well as six spades). The missing spades will be 1-1 or 2-0 and so East can tell that the opponents can make a game for sure and possibly slam. This is no time to be timid. 4♠ is the very least that East should do, at any vulnerability. As the opponents have game on, East-West will lose little in a spade sacrifice, East could well try some bluff manoeuvre. Bidding 3♥ (natural and forcing) may steal their suit. If doubled, you can always run back to spades. 4NT asking for aces is a pretence of slam values. Partner is bound to have insufficient aces and so you will sign off in 5♠. Only at adverse vulnerability would it be likely to cost you to reach 5♠ doubled. Against less gullible opponents, a 2NT reply showing game invitational values or better is a more subtle psyche. You need to judge what your opponents will swallow.

Bidding Set 18											
1. W	**E**	**2. W**	**E**	**3. W**	**E**	**4. W**	**E**	**5. W**	**E**	**6. W**	**E**
2♥	No	2♥	3NT	2♥	3NT	2♠	2NT	2♠	2NT	2♠	2NT
East hopes N-S		No		4♥	No	3♠	4♠	3♦	3NT	3NT	4♠
will bid and East		*West would bid*		*With worse*		*With 3½+*		*East can count*		*Prefer the major*	
can double for		*4♥ with a Suit*		*hearts, West*		*tricks, try*		*nine tricks but*		*if you need to set*	
penalties.		*Quality of 10.*		*would pass 3NT.*		*for game.*		*not ten.*		*up tricks.*	

#4: Opposite a minimum, East would sign off in 3♠. Remove West's ♣K and 3♠ is perhaps too high.
#5: One of the great boons of the 2NT Ogust structure is to be able to locate the top honours in opener's major and thus judge when 3NT is the best contract despite the good major suit fit.
#6: When you need to take a finesse, or you need to establish winners by knocking out an ace, and thus losing the lead, it is preferable to play in the major suit game and not 3NT. If East-West play in 3NT on #6, a heart lead or a club lead may not defeat the contract but may well hold declarer to nine tricks. That would result in a very poor board as ten tricks in spades are virtually certain.

63 **A.** 1. 1♥. Rebid 3♥. With 5-6 losers, you can afford a 1-opening. You need two tricks from partner for game and with that, partner will respond to your 1-opening. 2. 2♣. 9 playing tricks and 16 HCP.
3. 1♥. Longest suit is too weak for 2♣. 4. 2♣. Too many HCP for 1♠. 5. 2♣, and rebid 3♣.
B. 1. 2♦, but you will certainly bid on the next round. 2. 2♠. 8+ points and 5+ spades.
3. 2NT. 8+ points and no 5+ suit. 4. 3♦ 5. 2♠. The least of evils.
C. 1. 3♥. Shows 6+ hearts and nine playing tricks exactly. 3NT would be an acceptable gamble.
2. 3NT. Nine playing tricks and a solid 6+ minor. You should be prepared to risk the heart position.
3. 3♣. 4. 2NT. Shows 23-24 points balanced, not forcing.
5. 2♠. The spades are not good enough or long enough for a jump to 3♠.

Bidding Set 19											
1. W	E	**2. W**	E	**3. W**	E	**4. W**	E	**5. W**	E	**6. W**	E
2♣	2◇	2♣	2◇	No	2♣	No	2♣	No	2♣	2♣	2◇
3♡	No	3♡	4♡	2◇	3♠	2◇	3♠	2◇	3NT	2♡	4♣
3♡ = 9 playing		No		No		4♠	No	No		4◇	4♠
tricks.		East has potential		3♠ = 9 playing		West has one		3NT is a sensible		6♡	No
		for one trick.		tricks.		sure trick.		gamble.		4♣ = splinter	

#1 and #2: One of the great advantages of the Benjamin 2♣ opening is how it allows opener to describe the playing strength so accurately (9 tricks here) and as a consequence, responder is able to bid game on the slightest values, as in #2.

#6: Note again how the weak hand splinter enables the partnership to bid a slam on low HCP total.

Bidding Set 20											
1. W	E	**2. W**	E	**3. W**	E	**4. W**	E	**5. W**	E	**6. W**	E
2♣	2♠	No	2♣	2♣	2♡	No	2♣	2♣	3♣	No	2♣
3♣	3♠	2♡	2♠	2♠	4♠	2♠	3◇	3♡	4NT	2◇	2NT
4♠	4NT	2NT	3NT	No		4◇	4NT	5♡	5NT	3♣	3♠
5♡	5♠	No		4♠ is weaker		5♡	6◇	6♡	6NT	4NT	5♠
No				than 3♠ here.		5♡		Worth the risk.		6♠	No

#1: Although 5♠ may fail, it would be conservative for East not to try for a slam. Give West the ♠A instead of the ◇K-Q and 6♠ is a great contract. Even ♡A instead of ◇K-Q gives 6♠ very good chances.

#2: When there is no trump fit, slam needs the full high card values.

#3: The responsibility for slam bidding after a 2♣ opening usually falls on responder's shoulder. 3♠ here by East would be a stronger raise and suggest hopes for slam.

#4: East should have about nine playing tricks and as West has two aces and ruffing potential in hearts and clubs, it is not hard for West to envisage slam possibilities. That is why West raises to 4◇.

#5: Although it is not appealing to ask for aces with no control in two unbid suits, East has no better choice over 3♡. In addition, as West has a strong hand and at most five points in hearts, it is very likely that West will have the controls needed in spades and diamonds. Note the use of 5NT for kings, even though an ace is missing, to investigate the prospects for 6NT. This occurs quite often enough at pairs.

#6: After 3♣ Stayman, West sees slam prospects opposite 23-24 points balanced when East shows four spades and denies four hearts.

67   **A.** 1. 2♡. Artificial negative, 0-7 points, any shape.   2. 2♡. Nice hand but still a negative.
        3. 3◇. Natural positive reply.   4. 2NT. 8+ points, no 5-card suit.   5. 3♣. Least of evils.
        B. 1. 2♠. Natural, and game-forcing.   2. 4♡. Suit Quality 10 and only just under three losers.
        3. 3♠. Sets spades as trumps and asks partner to cue-bid any ace.
        4. 2NT. 25-27 balanced, forcing to game.   5. 3NT. Balanced hand, 28-30 points.
        C. 1. 3♡. 5+ hearts, 0-7 points. 2♡ was artificial.   2. 3♠. Stronger than 4♠. Promises an ace or a king (or a singleton or void if only three trumps are held).   3. 4◇. Splinter. Shows 4+ trumps and a singleton or void in diamonds.   4. 4♠. Spade support but poor hand.   5. 2NT. No spade support, no 5+ suit.

Bidding Set 21											
1. W	E	**2. W**	E	**3. W**	E	**4. W**	E	**5. W**	E	**6. W**	E
2◇	2♡	No	2◇	2◇	2♡	No	2◇	No	2◇	2◇	2♡
2NT	3♣	2♡	2♠	4♠	No	2♡	2♠	2♡	2NT	2♠	3♡
3♠	4♠	2NT	3♡	West has three		4♣	4NT	3♣	3♡	5♡	No
3♣ = Stayman		4♡	No	losers, East less		5◇	7♠	4♡	No	5♡ asks for	
				than 1½ tricks.		4♣ = splinter		3♣ = Stayman		good trumps.	

#1 : 4♠ is a much better spot than 3NT. What kills no-trumps is not the lack of stoppers but short suits. Here the doubleton heart opposite the doubleton heart spells probable doom for 3NT.

#3 : While slam is possible, it is usually poor odds where the 2◇ opener has three clearcut losers and partner gave a negative response, denying 1½ quick tricks. Such slams are generally 50% at best.

#4 : This is an impressive grand slam to reach. Aren't splinters marvellous when they crop up?

#6 : Even opposite these miserable trumps 6♡ could make. Opposite ♡K-x-x-x-x-x, 6♡ would be excellent.

Bidding Set 22											
1. W	**E**	**2. W**	**E**	**3. W**	**E**	**4. W**	**E**	**5. W**	**E**	**6. W**	**E**
No	2◇	2◇	3♣	2◇	2NT	No	2◇	2◇	2♡	No	2◇
2NT	3NT	3♡	4♡	3♣	3♡	2♡	2♠	3NT	6NT	3♡	3♠
6NT	No	4NT	5♡	3NT	7NT	2NT	3♡	No		3NT	6NT
3NT = balanced		5NT	6◇	No		4♡	4NT	*The 3NT rebid*		*Opposite a*	
25-27, no major.		7NT	No	*3NT = 25-27*		5◇	7♡	*shows 28-30,*		*positive, East*	
				balanced with		No		*balanced.*		*has enough for*	
				four spades.						*6NT.*	

#1: Where opener has 25+ balanced and responder shows 8+, opener should pass the decision to responder when opener is minimum. Opener's strategy is to show the 25-27 balanced by bidding 3NT and leaving the decision for a small slam or a grand slam to responder.

#2: Note the vital pairs strategy of checking for kings to determine whether 7NT is there.

#3: West's 3♣ Stayman followed by 3NT shows 25-27 points. East knows the partnership has 37+ points.

#4: East has a one-loser hand and needs to find only the ♡A to bid the grand slam after the heart fit is found. East must not try 7NT here as the spade suit may not produce five tricks in no-trumps.

#5: A 2NT rebid by West would show 25-27 HCP and a balanced hand. The 3NT rebid shows 28-30 points balanced and leaves further action to responder. Here East has an easy 6NT rebid. Note that even with West's great strength, 3NT could fail opposite a yarborough.

#6: East can tell from the points West has shown that 6NT should be a reasonable prospect.

72   **A.**   1. 5♡. 2 key cards, no ♡Q.   2. 5♠. 2 key cards plus the ♡Q.   3. 5♣. 0 or 3 key cards.
     4. 5♣. 0 or 3 key cards. Says nothing about the trump queen. 5. 6♣. 5 key cards + the trump queen.
    B.   1. No bid. Two aces are missing.   2. No bid. You are missing two aces or one ace + the ◇K.
     3. 6◇. You are missing one ace. It is a little risky, but you could bid 5NT and settle in 6NT if partner owns up to the king of hearts.   4. 5♡, asking for the trump queen. If partner has 3+ diamond support and shows the trump queen, bid 7NT.   5. 7NT. Partner has the ◇K. What more do you need?

Bid Set 23															
(1)		**(2)**		**(3)**		**(4)**		**(5)**		**(6)**		**(7)**		**(8)**	
W	**E**	**W**	**E**	**W**	**E**	**W**	**E**	**W**	**E**	**W**	**E**	**W**	**E**	**W**	**E**
2◇	2♡	2◇	2♡	No	2◇	No	2◇	1♡	2NT	1♡	2NT	1♣	1♠	1♣	1♠
2♠	3♠	2♠	3♠	3♣	3♠	3♣	3♠	3♣	4♡	3♣	4♡	3♠	4NT	3♠	4NT
4NT	5♣	4NT	5◇	4♠	4NT	4♠	4NT	4NT	5♡	4NT	5♣	5♣	6♠	5◇	7♠
5♠	No	6♠	No	5◇	6♠	5♡	7NT	No		6♡	No	5♣ = 0 or 3		5◇ = 1 or 4	
								2NT= Jacoby		*2NT= Jacoby*		*key cards*		*key cards*	

Note in each case how RKCB helps you solve the slam problems while simple Blackwood would not.

#1 and #2: East has the same shape, the same points, the same high cards, but in #1, slam is a poor bet while in #2, the king in the right place makes slam virtually laydown.

#3 and #4: This time West has the same shape, same points, same high cards. In #3, the wrong black king keeps East-West down to the small slam while in #4, the right black king means 7NT is secure.

#5 and #6: Again the right king gives you the slam, the wrong king makes slam a terrible prospect.

#7 and #8: Locating the trump king means a grand slam on #8 but just a small slam on #7.

Bid Set 24															
(1)		**(2)**		**(3)**		**(4)**		**(5)**		**(6)**		**(7)**		**(8)**	
W	**E**	**W**	**E**	**W**	**E**	**W**	**E**	**W**	**E**	**W**	**E**	**W**	**E**	**W**	**E**
1♣	1♡	1♣	1♡	1♠	2◇	1♠	2◇	1◇	1♠	1◇	1♠	2◇	2♡	2◇	2♡
2♡	4NT	2♡	4NT	2♡	4♠	2♡	4♠	3♠	4NT	3♠	4NT	3♡	4♡	3♡	4♡
5♡	6♡	5♠	7♡	4NT	5◇	4NT	5◇	5♣	5◇	5♣	5◇	4NT	5◇	4NT	5◇
5♡ = 2 key		5♠ = 2 key		5♡	5♠	5♡	5NT	5♡	6♠	5♠	7♠	5♠	5NT	5♠	6♣
cards, no ♡Q		*cards + ♡Q*		No		6♠	No	5♡ = no		5♠ shows		6♡	No	7♡	No
								♠Q		♠Q					

Note in each case how locating the trump queen or finding it is missing solves your slam decisions.

#3 and #4: East's sequence implies just 3-card spade support. After finding East with one ace, West gives up on slam when the ♠Q is missing and bids slam when East has the ♠Q on #4.

#7 and #8: 5♠ asks for the trump queen in each case. In #7, 5NT says 'No' and in #8, 6♣ says 'Yes'.

78 **A.** 1. 6◇. West's 6♣ asks for the club holding, excluding the ace of clubs. 6◇ says, 'No ♣K, no ♣Q'. 2. 6♠. Shows ♣K but no ♣Q. 3. 6◇. No ♣K, no ♣Q. 4. 6♡. ♣Q but no ♣K. 5. 6NT. ♣K + ♣Q.

B. **(a)** 1. 5NT. With 3 key cards, keep bidding and show or deny the trump queen next. 5NT shows 3 key cards and the trump queen. 2. No bid. After a sign-off, bid on only with the higher number of key cards. 3. 5♠. Shows 3 key cards but no trump queen. 4. 5♠ 5. 5NT. 3 key cards plus the trump queen. If showing kings simultaneously, bid 6♣ (see page 83).

(b) 1. 6♣. No outside king. 2. 6♡. Two kings. 3. 6♣. 4. 6◇. One outside king. 5. 6◇

Bid Set 25							
(1)	**(2)**	**(3)**	**(4)**	**(5)**	**(6)**	**(7)**	**(8)**
W E	W E	W E	W E	W E	W E	W E	W E
1♡ 4◇	1♡ 4◇	1♡ 4♣	1♡ 4♣	1♣ 1♡	1♣ 1♡	1♣ 1◇	1♠ 2♣
4NT 5♡	4NT 5♠	4NT 5♣	4NT 5♣	3♡ 3NT	3♡ 3NT	3♣ 4♣	4♣ 4♠
No	6♡ No	5♡ 5♠	5♡ 5NT	4◇ 4♡	4◇ 4♡	4♡ 7NT	5♣ No
	With 10	6♡ No	7♡ No	No	4♠ 6♡	*4♣ set clubs*	*4♠ = 1 or 4*
	trumps, show	*5♠ = no*		*3NT= RKCB*	*4♠ = no*	*4♡ = 0 or 3*	*key cards*
	the trump Q.	*♡Q*			*♡Q*	*key cards*	

#1 and #2: With nine trumps missing queen and jack, the chance of no loser is around 40%. With ten trumps, the odds improve to almost 80%. Therefore if you know that the partnership holds ten trumps you can show the trump queen in your RKCB answer structure.

#3 and #4: West signs off in 5♡ in case East has 0 key cards. In #3, East bids 5♠ to show 3 key cards but no ♡Q. In #4, 5NT shows 3 key cards plus the ♡Q because at least ten trumps are held in the partnership.

#5: Using 3NT as RKCB saves you being possibly too high in 5♡.

#6: East signs off in 4♡ in case West has 0 key cards. 4♠ = 3 key cards plus the trump queen.

#7 and #8: Raising the minor to the four-level is used as setting the trump suit and invoking RKCB at the same time. Partner is allowed to ask for key cards or show the key cards held. Over 4♣, 4◇ = RKCB ask and 4♡/4♠/4NT/5♣ are the standard RKCB replies.

Bid Set 26							
(1)	**(2)**	**(3)**	**(4)**	**(5)**	**(6)**	**(7)**	**(8)**
W E	W E	W E	W E	W E	W E	W E	W E
No 2◇	1♠ 4NT	No 2◇	1♠ 2NT	1♠ 2NT	1◇ 1♠	1◇ 1♡	2◇ 3♣
2NT 3♠	5♠ 5NT	2♡ 2♠	3♣ 3NT	3♣ 3NT	3♠ 3NT	3♠ 3NT	4♣ 4♠
4♠ 4NT	6◇ 7NT	3♠ 3NT	4♣ 4♡	4♣ 4◇	4♠ 4NT	4♠ 4NT	4NT 5◇
5◇ 5♡	No	4♣ 4NT	5♣ 7♠	4♠ 5◇	5◇ 6♣	5♡ 7♡	5♡ 6♣
5NT 6♡	*6◇ = 1 king*	5♡ 6NT	No	4♠ 5♡	6♡ 7NT	No	7NT No
6NT 7NT		No	*2NT = Jacoby*	6♣ 7♠	*5◇ = 1 king*	*3♠ = splinter*	*4♠ = 1 or 4*
		5♡ =	*3NT = RKCB*	*3NT=RKCB*	*6♡ = ♣Q*	*5♡ = 2 kings*	*key cards*
6NT = ♡Q		*2 kings*	*5♣ = ♡K*	*4♠ = ♠Q*	*6♣ = ♡K*		*5◇ = ♣Q*
				6♣ = ♡K			*6♣ = ♡K*

#1: West's 4♠ shows spade support but no ace (failure to cue-bid). East locates the ♠K and ♠Q and follows up with an ask for the ♡Q. When West admits to this as well, East can count thirteen tricks.

#2: After 5♠, East can count twelve top tricks. 7♠ is safe but East checks on kings and can bid 7NT when West shows one king.

#3: East knows an ace is missing but when West shows two kings, 6NT must be as safe as 6♠.

#4: After opener's reply to the Jacoby 2NT, either partner can use 3NT as RKCB. 4♠ showed 0 or 3 key cards, clearly three since West is known to have a singleton club. 4♡ was a Control Ask in hearts and when West showed the ♡K, East could see the grand slam.

#5: Similar to #4 but East also has to find the trump queen. 4◇ asked for the ♠Q and 4♠ said 'Yes, I have it.'

#6: East asks with 3NT and finds two key cards plus the trump queen. 4NT asks for kings and West shows one. Then 6♣ is a Control Ask in clubs and when West shows the ♣Q, East can count thirteen top tricks.

#7: After a minor suit opening and a splinter, it is sensible to retain 3NT as natural but after a 3♠ splinter agreeing hearts, 3NT is better employed as RKCB. As West is likely to have diamond length for this sequence, East would make a Control Ask in 6◇ if West had shown only one king and bid seven only if West had ◇K.

#8: After the minor suit raise to the four-level, East gives RKCB answers (but 4◇ would still be RKCB ask), 4NT asks for the trump queen and 5♡ is a Control Ask in hearts. West can count thirteen tricks.

83   **A.**   1. 3♠. You have the values for slam but need to find club control.   2. 4♣. Spade control needed.
3. 3NT RKCB. You have no void and you do have first or second-round control in every suit. That makes it attractive to ask rather than to cue-bid.   4. 3NT RKCB.   5. 4◇. You need to locate control in both black suits.

B.   1. 5♥. No ace to cue.   2. 5◇. Shows the ace of diamonds. If partner then bids 5♥, pass. Spade control is missing.   3. 5◇, and follow with 5♠ over 5♥.   4. 5◇. You need a strong reason not to cue-bid when a cue-bid below the trump suit is available and partner has started cue-bidding. West could have: ♠ 3 ♥ A K 9 5 3 ◇ K 5 ♣ A K 6 3 2.   5. 6♥. You have ◇A and second-round spade control.

Bid Set 27															
(1)		(2)		(3)		(4)		(5)		(6)		(7)		(8)	
W	E	W	E	W	E	W	E	W	E	W	E	W	E	W	E
2◇	2♥	2◇	2♥	2◇	2♥	No	2◇	No	2◇	No	2◇	1◇	1♠	1♣	1♠
2♠	3♠	2♠	3♠	2♠	3♠	2♥	2♠	2♥	2♠	3♥	3♠	1NT	3♣	3♠	4◇*
4♣*	4◇*	4♣*	4♥*	4♣*	4♠	4♣**	4♥*	3♠	4♣*	4♠	5♣*	3♠	4♣*	5♣*	5◇*
7♠	No	6♠	No	6♠	No	5◇*	7♠	4◇*	4♥*	5◇*	5♥*	4◇*	4NT	5♠	No
*Cue-bids						No		4♠	6♠	6♣*	7♠	5◇	6♠		
						**Splinter		No		No		No			

#1, #2 and #3: West's challenge is to find out whether East has an ace and whether it is the ◇A. If East has it, West can bid seven; if not, six will have to do.

#4, #5 and #6: Here East needs to find controls in two suits: the ace of diamonds and second-round club control with West. If West has both, East can bid the grand slam.

#7: After locating diamond control, responder can sensibly switch over to RKCB.

#8: West's 5♣ denied first-round heart control and 5♠ denied second-round heart control, so East passes.

Bid Set 28															
(1)		(2)		(3)		(4)		(5)		(6)		(7)		(8)	
W	E	W	E	W	E	W	E	W	E	W	E	W	E	W	E
1◇	1♠	1♠	4◇**	1♠	4♣**	1♠	4♣**	1♠	4♣**	1♠	2♥	1♠	2♥	1♠	2♥
1NT	3♥	4♥*	4♠	4NT	5♠	4◇*	4♥*	4◇*	5♣*	3♥	4◇*	3♥	4◇*	3♥	4◇*
3♠	4♣*	No		6♠	No	4NT	5◇	7♠	No	4♥	No	5♣*	5◇*	4♠*	4NT
4◇*	4♥*	4♠ = no ace				6♠	No			4♥ = no		5♥	No	5♣	5NT
5♣*	5◇*	to cue, no								ace to cue				6♣	6♥
5♥*	7♠	void in ◇s												No	
*Cue-bids		**Splinter													

#1: It is very tough to find the key major suit jacks which make 7NT a good bet.

#2: East's 4♠ tells West that the partner is missing the ♣A and has a diamond loser as well. It is risky to reach the five-level with these cards.

#3: Opener's hand is much better suited to asking with 4NT than cue-bidding.

#4: West cue-bids 4◇ to see whether East can cue-bid 4♥. Then when East shows one key card in reply to 4NT, West knows that it is the ace of hearts and not the ace of clubs.

#5: When East cue-bids the club void and simultaneously denies the ♥A, East must have virtually all the cards held to justify the 4♣ splinter.

#7: West's 5♣ denies first-round spade control and 5♥ indicates that the problem is in spades. You might make 6♥ (if they do not lead a spade) by taking the club finesse, but you should take no pride in it.

#8: After locating control in spades, East can switch to 4NT RKCB.

88   **A.**   1. 4♣. Cue-bid showing spade support and a maximum 1NT.   2. 4♠. Spade support but weak.
3. 4♣   4. 4♠. No ace to cue-bid. You must not go beyond 4♠ in standard methods, but if 3♠ shows a slam-going one-suiter, you should bid 4NT with this hand.   5.   3NT. Denies spade support.

B.   1. 6◇. One top honour.   2. 6♣. No top trump.   3. 6♥. Two top honours.   4. 6♥
5. 6♠. Three top honours . . . or you could simply bid the grand slam.

Bid Set 29

(1)		(2)		(3)		(4)		(5)		(6)		(7)		(8)	
W	E	W	E	W	E	W	E	W	E	W	E	W	E	W	E
No	2♣	1♠	4♣**	No	2♦	No	2♦	1♠	2NT	1♠	4♣**	1♠	4♣**	1♠	4♣**
2NT	3♠	4♦*	4♥*	2♠	3♠	2♠	3♠	3♣	4♣*	4♦*	4♥*	4♦*	4♥*	4♦*	4♠
4♦*	4♥*	4NT	5♠	4♣*	4NT	4♦	4NT	4♦*	5♣**	4NT	5♥	4NT	5♠	5♣*	5♥*
5♦*	6♣*	5NT	6♥	5♦	6♠	5♥	7♠	5♥*	5NT	6♠	No	5NT	6♦	6♠	No
6♦*	7♠	7♠	No	No		No		6♥	7♠	♠Q missing		7♠	No		
No		**Splinter						6♥ = two							
*Cue-bids								top trumps							

#1: 4♦ shows spade support and the ♦A. As East should have about nine winners, West is worth the cue-bid with three winners. The hand is a rare example of being able to show third round control (6♦). Usually cue-bidding is concerned only with first and second-round controls (because you run out of bidding space).

#2: West knows from East's 5♠ bid that East has 5+ trumps (as 5♠ showed, in theory, the trump queen). Therefore West knows East will have enough trumps to take care of all the club losers.

#3: After West's 4♣ cue and 5♥ two key cards, East can tell that either the ♦A or the ♠A is missing.

#4: East can tell that West has the ♦A and the ♠A as 4♦ denied the ace of clubs.

#5: The bidding could start 1♠: 3♣, 3♥: 3♠, 4♦ cue: 5♣ cue, 5♥ cue: 5NT, 6♥: 7♠.

#6: West starts a cue-bidding sequence to locate control in hearts. When East shows the ace of hearts, West reverts to 4NT RKCB. On finding that the queen of trumps is missing, West settles for the small slam.

#7: If East had bid 6♣ in reply to 5NT to show no king outside spades, West could still ask for the ♦Q with 6♦ over 6♣ and bid the grand slam if East has the ♦Q.

#8: 4♠ said 'no ace to cue' and now West should be worried about the hearts. When East bids 5♥ to show second-round control in hearts, West is prepared to take a shot at six. At the very worst the slam will be on a finesse, given East should have around 12 HCP or more for the splinter.

Bid Set 30

(1)		(2)		(3)		(4)		(5)		(6)		(7)		(8)	
W	E	W	E	W	E	W	E	W	E	W	E	W	E	W	E
1♣	1♠	1♣	1♠	1♣	1♥	1♥	4♣**	1♠	4NT	2♦	2♥	1♥	4♦**	1♥	2♦
4♦**	4♥*	4♦**	4♥*	4♦**	4NT	4♦*	4NT	5♠	6♣	2♠	3♠	4♣*	4NT	4♣**	5♣*
5NT	6♦	5NT	6♣	5♣	6♥	5♣	5♠	No		4♣*	4♠	5♣	5♦	5♥*	5NT
7♠	No	6♠	No	No		6♦	7♥			5♦*	5♥*	5♠	7♥	6♥	7♦
*Cue-bids		6♣ = no				No				6♠	No	No		No	
**Splinter		top spade				6♦ = ♠K									

#1: After East cue-bids ♥A, West figures that East's heart losers can be discarded on the clubs once they are established. 5NT asks for trump honours and 6♦ = 1. 4NT would not help as East could have the ♦A and the ♥A for the 5♥ reply.

#2: When East denies the ♠A by bidding 6♣, West has to be content with the small slam.

#3: East has no cue-bid but is too strong to give up in game. In such a case take your chances on the unguarded suit and make the RKCB ask.

#4: East has a good hand with which to ask after West encourages slam with the 4♦ cue. As West has cue-bid an ace already, the 5♣ reply must be three key cards. 5♠ was a Control Ask in spades.

#5: East could splinter but the hand is so strong that East may as well ask, planning to bid 7♠ if West can produce three aces.

#6: 3♠ shows support plus at least one control somewhere. 4♠ = no ace and 5♥ = second-round control. Whether the second-round heart control is the king (probably, because of the failure to splinter) or a singleton, West has found out that the small slam is a good contract and that a heart lead does not pose a threat.

#7: Once East hears spade control, East can take charge of the auction. 5♦ asks for the trump queen.

#8: East cannot cue-bid 4♥ over 4♣. That would be taken as an offer to play in 4♥. West's 5♥ is a cue beyond five of the trump suit and so promises first-round control in spades as well. With second-round spade control, West would have jumped to 6♦ over 5♣. With the ♥K to help establish West's hearts, East figures a grand slam should be a good bet if no top trump is missing.

93 **A.(a)** 1. 2♠ via a transfer is reasonable but you might choose to pass. 2. Invite 3NT.
3. Invite 3NT. 4. Use a Stayman sequence and invite game. 5. Bid 3NT and take your chances.
(b) 1. Transfer to 2♠. This will be safer than 1NT most of the time. 2. Bid 3NT. 3. Bid 3NT. The vulnerable game can be bid on the smell of an oil rag. 4. Bid 2♣ Stayman and rebid 4♥ over 2♥, and 2NT over any other reply. 5. Transfer to 3♣ and then bid 3♦, forcing to game. You do not mind reaching 5-minor at teams.
B. 1. Bid 2♣ at teams. At pairs you can gamble on the pass. 2. At teams bid 4♠, the safer game. At pairs, choose 4♥, which may score an extra trick some of the time. 3. Double at teams and at pairs. Do not sell out when they bid and raise a suit to the two-level (see Chapter 17).
4. At teams you should bid 2♦, the safer part-score. At pairs, you might well pass 1NT. If you bid 2♦, the opponents are very likely to compete in hearts. They are less likely to compete at teams.
5. At teams you might bid 2♣ not vulnerable but if vulnerable, bid 3♣ and insist on game. At pairs, prefer 2NT despite the weakness in spades. At pairs you live by the sword . . . 6. At teams you should pass at any vulnerability. Game is unlikely, partner is a passed hand and your diamonds are not so great. At pairs you should risk the overcall. 7. At teams overcall 2♦ or pass. At pairs, use the unusual 2NT if not vulnerable. If vulnerable, a 2♦ overcall will do. 8. At teams bid 7♥. Partner figures to have something like ♠ A x x x x ♥ K Q x x ♦ K x ♣ A x. Even if spades are 4-1, you will be able to set up the fifth spade for your thirteenth trick. At pairs, try 7NT. Partner might have the ♠J and the spades will be 3-2 most of the time. 9. Partner has shown ♠ A-Q-x-x-x and ♣ A-K-x-x-x. At pairs, bid 7NT. At teams, bid the safer 7♠ (in case the clubs are 5-1). 10. Pass at teams and at pairs and at any vulnerability. At teams vulnerable, partner has already fudged the extra point with the invitation. The inviter bids with one point less, not the acceptor.

99 **A.** 1. Double 2. 3♥. Partner should have one spade at most and so is likely to have some hearts. 3. 2NT. Shows 4-4 in the minors, denies 4 hearts. 4. Double. If partner bids 3♣, you have an easy removal to 3♦. 5. Bid 3♣. You would like to double but you cannot afford 4♣ over 3♦.
B. 1. 3♦ 2. 2♠ 3. 2♠. Do not give a jump response to a delayed double. If you do, partner will soon stop competing. 4. 3♣ 5. 2NT. Shows both minors in reply to a delayed double. Do not consider passing the double, even for a second.

Bidding Set 31				2.	WEST	NORTH	EAST	SOUTH
1.	**WEST**	**NORTH**	**EAST**	**SOUTH**		No	1♠	No	2♠
	1♦	No	1♥	No		No	No	2NT	No
	2♥	No	No	2♠		3♦	3♠	All pass	
	3♥	No	No	No					

#1: South is far too weak to come in on the first-round but the delayed overcall is mandatory.
#2: North has the extra trump and so competes to 3♠.

3.	WEST	NORTH	EAST	SOUTH	4.	WEST	NORTH	EAST	SOUTH
	No	No	1♣	No		No	No	No	1♥
	2♣	No	No	Dble		No	1♠	No	2♠
	No	2♥	3♣	All pass		No	No	2NT	No
						3♦	No	No	No

#3: There is a strong case for West bidding 3♣ at once over the double. If West does not, East must. You cannot afford to sell out at the two-level when your side has a trump fit or when their side has a trump fit.
#4: East's 2NT shows both minors. As North-South have only eight spades, they allow the opponents to play at the three-level.

5.	WEST	NORTH	EAST	SOUTH	6.	WEST	NORTH	EAST	SOUTH
	1♥	No	2♥	No		1♦	No	2♦	No
	No	Dble	No	2NT		No	Dble	No	2♥
	3♥	No	No	No		Dble	2♠	Dble	No
						3♦	No	No	No

#5: East's 2NT in reply to the delayed double shows both minors. If West passed, North would bid 3♦. As West intends to bid 3♥ after North's minor suit reply, West is better advised to bid 3♥ immediately over 2NT.
#6: As East can have no more than three spades, West decides that discretion is the better part of valour. In fact, 2♠ should be a comfortable make.

7.	WEST	NORTH	EAST	SOUTH
	No	1♣	No	1♠
	No	2♠	No	No
	2NT	No	3♢	All pass

104 A. 1. Double   2. Double   3. Double. If partner bids 2♢, remove this to 2♡ to offer partner the choice between hearts and spades.   4. 2♢. You do not want to double and hear 2♠.
5. No bid. With length and strength in the enemy suit, pass and defend. Pity partner did not double 2♣ for takeout. You would have left the double in.
B. 1. Double   2. No. Length and strength in their suit.   3. 2NT. Takeout for the minors.
4. Double. The meek shall inherit the earth (but what if they don't want it?), but they lose at pairs.
5. 3♣. You were happy to pass and defend no-trumps. You have far less defence against spades.

Bidding Set 32									
1.	WEST	NORTH	EAST	SOUTH	2.	WEST	NORTH	EAST	SOUTH
	1♢	1♠	2♢	2♠		No	1♠	2♢	No
	No	No	3♢	All pass		No	Dble	No	3♣
						3♢	No	No	No

#1: As North-South have only eight spades, they let the opponents have the three-level. Both 3♢ and 3♠ should fail by one trick.
#2: West has already shown a poor hand by passing East's overcall. The 3♢ bid shows the diamond length. Top defence can take 3♢ two down.

3.	WEST	NORTH	EAST	SOUTH	4.	WEST	NORTH	EAST	SOUTH
	No	No	1NT	No		No	No	No	1♣
	2♢	No	2♡	No		1♡	Dble	2♢	2♠
	No	2NT	No	3♢		No	No	3♡	All pass
	No	No	3♡	All pass					

#3: Courage is needed to compete after a 1NT opening. East-West do well to compete to 3♡ since 3♢ should be comfortable for North-South who are most unlikely to double 3♡.

5.	WEST	NORTH	EAST	SOUTH	6.	WEST	NORTH	EAST	SOUTH
	1NT	No	2♡	No		No	1♢	1♠	Dble
	2♠	No	No	Dble		No*	2♡	No	3♡
	No	3♢	All pass			No	No	No	

*With such poor shape and no obvious trick in defence, West should pass rather than bid 2♠.

7.	WEST	NORTH	EAST	SOUTH
	No	No	1♠	Dble
	2♠*	No	No	Dble
	No	3♣	3♠	All pass

*With the flat shape and nine losers, West is not quite worth an immediate jump to 3♠.

110 A. 1. No bid. Too weak to bid at the three-level.   2. No bid. Too weak for 3♢.   3. Double. In this auction, the double shows four hearts in a minimum hand.   4. 3♡. Four hearts and 16-18 points.
5. 3♢. Expectancy is six diamonds and 16-18 points (like 1♢ : 1♡, 3♢).
B. 1. 2♠. Too good to pass.   2. 3♢   3. 3♢. The only lead you want.   4. Double. Shows 4-4 in the minors and 6+ points.   5. Double. 3♢ would be reasonable but double can hardly land you in the wrong minor suit, while 3♢ might be the inferior spot.
C. 1. 2♠. Shows a minimum opening and four spades.   2. Double. Shows three spades, strength undisclosed.   3. Double   4. 2♢. Denies three spades.   5. No bid. Hoping partner will be able to re-open with a competitive (takeout) double which you will also pass.

Bidding Set 33

1.	WEST	NORTH	EAST	SOUTH
	1♦	1♠	Dble	2♠
	Dble	No	3♥	All pass

2.	WEST	NORTH	EAST	SOUTH
	No	1♣	1♠	Dble
	2♠	3♥	No	4♥
	No	No	No	

#1: West's double shows four hearts but only a minimum opening.
#2: North's 3♥ shows four hearts but a hand in the 16-18 range.

3.	WEST	NORTH	EAST	SOUTH
	No	No	1♣	No
	1♦	1♠	Dble	No
	2♥	No	4♥	All pass

East's double shows 4 hearts. South should spot the misfit and stay out of the bidding.

4.	WEST	NORTH	EAST	SOUTH
	No	No	No	1♥
	Dble	2♥	Dble	2♠
	No	3♥	All pass	

East's double is responsive, both minors. 2♠ by South is a long suit game-try.

5.	WEST	NORTH	EAST	SOUTH
	1♥	No	1♠	2♣
	No	No	Dble	No
	No	No		

West passes 2♣ for penalties and wishes can come true, as East re-opens with a double.

6.	WEST	NORTH	EAST	SOUTH
	1♣	No	1♠	2♥
	Dble	No	2♠	No
	4♠	No	No	No

*West's double showed 3 spades exactly.

115 A. 1. Bid 1♠. 2. 2♥. Michaels. 3. 2♥. With extreme shape, the point count is irrelevant. 4. Bid 2♦, and bid 4♠ over their 4♥. You could use Michaels 2♥ but if they bid 4♥ passed back to you, you are going to bid 5♦ rather than 4♠. It is wildly unlikely that 2♦ will be passed out. 5. Bid 2♥ at favourable vulnerability. Otherwise, pass. The suits are too poor.
B. 1. 3♣. Partner will bid 3♦ with diamonds. 2. 4♠, likely to make. 3. 4♠, a sacrifice but might even make on a very lucky day. 4. 2NT. Game is likely, probably in 3NT. 5. Bid 2♠. Partner is highly likely to have spades and clubs.
C. 1. 3♣. Minimum with clubs. 2. 3NT. Shows 6 hearts and 5 clubs. 3. 3♠. Maximum with diamonds. 4. 3♥. Maximum with clubs. 5. 4♦. 6+ diamonds and 5 hearts.

Bidding Set 34

1.	WEST	NORTH	EAST	SOUTH
	1♥	2♥	No	4♠
	No	No	No	

2.	WEST	NORTH	EAST	SOUTH
	No	1♣	2♣	2♠
	4♥	No	No	No

2♠ = 10+ points with 5+ diamonds

3.	WEST	NORTH	EAST	SOUTH
	1♣	No	1♥	2♥
	3♥	4♠	Dble	All pass

Michaels can also be used over the response. 4♥ cannot be defeated and neither can 4♠. It is hard for East-West with 29 HCP not to double 4♠.

4.	WEST	NORTH	EAST	SOUTH
	No	2♠	4♦	No
	4♥	No	No	No

The jump to 4♦ is Michaels, showing 5+ diamonds and 5+ hearts in a strong hand.

5.	WEST	NORTH	EAST	SOUTH
	1♥	2♥	Dble	3♣
	Dble	3♦	Dble	All pass

East's double of 2♥ tells opener that penalties are the order of the day.

6.	WEST	NORTH	EAST	SOUTH
	No	No	No	1♣
	2♣	3♣	4♠	Dble
	No	No	No	

You have to feel sorry for South, opening with 19 HCP and East-West reach an unbeatable game.

120 A. 1. 2NT and follow up with 3♡ to show 4 spades and hearts stopped.   2. Bid 3♡ at once, to show four spades and no stopper in hearts.   3. 3NT. Enough points for game but no 4 spades and no stopper in hearts.   4. 2NT and follow up with 3NT to promise a stopper in hearts. 5. 2NT and follow up with 3♠ to show five spades and a stopper in hearts.

B. 1. 3♣. Shows four hearts and no spade stopper.   2. 2♠. Game values with a singleton or a void in spades.   3. 2♡. Merely competing for the part-score.   4. 3♡. Natural and forcing. If playing transfer Lebensohl, bid 3◇.   5. 2NT and pass the forced 3♣ ('puppet').

C. 1. 3◇. Transfer to hearts. Follow up with 3♠ over 3♡ to express concern about the spades. 2. 3◇ and follow up with 4♡.   3. Bid 2NT and continue with 3◇ over 3♣. This shows the values for game with 5+ clubs and 4 diamonds. If partner bids 3♡, you should raise to 4♡ to complete the picture of your hand.   4. 3♡. This is artificial and shows both minors with at least 5 diamonds and interest in slam. With 5+ hearts, responder would use the 3◇ transfer (see #1 and #2). 5. 3♣, transfer to diamonds. Competing for the part-score.

Bidding Set 35				
(1)	**(2)**	**(3)**	**(4)**	**(5)**
WEST EAST	WEST EAST	WEST EAST	WEST EAST	WEST EAST
1NT (2♡) Dble	1NT (2♡) Dble	No 1NT (2♡)	No 1NT (2♡)	1NT (2♠) 3NT
2♠ No	2NT No	2NT 3♣	2NT 3♣	4♣ 5◇
East's double is for	*East's double is for*	3◇ No	No	No
takeout.	*takeout.*			*3NT = no spade*
				stopper

#1: East's double is for takeout but does not guarantee four spades. West's 2♠ shows four spades and minimum points. Without spade support, East would rebid 2NT or 3-minor. If West had maximum points, West could bid 3♠, 3NT or 3♡.

#3: 2NT Lebensohl forced East to bid 3♣. West's 3◇ then showed long diamonds but no interest in game. With game invitational values, West would double and remove a minimum bid from East to 3◇. The sequence chosen shows enough to compete for the part-score but not enough to invite game.

#5: If East has no spade stopper, then West sees little value in staying in 3NT. Note how the opposition interference helps East-West. Had North kept quiet, East would have responded 3NT none the wiser about the flaw in the spade department. West's 4♣ is not forcing and East takes a sensible shot at 5◇. If West has no stopper in spades, West's high cards should be useful in hearts, diamonds and clubs.

Bidding Set 36				
(1)	**(2)**	**(3)**	**(4)**	**(5)**
WEST EAST	WEST EAST	WEST EAST	WEST EAST	WEST EAST
1NT (2♡) 3♡	1NT (2♡) 3♡	No 1NT (2♠)	No 1NT (2♠)	1NT (2♠) 3NT
3NT No	4♠ No	2NT 3♣	2NT 3♣	4♣ No
	4♠ is a practical	3♡ No	3♡ 4♡	
	shot at game.			

#1: East's 3♡ shows four spades and denies a stopper in hearts. West has no rebid problem.

#2: With no stopper in hearts either, West shuns 3NT. A 4-3 major suit game is no thing of joy but is the most practical move here. If East had the jack of spades as well, 4♠ would be an excellent game. On the actual cards, it will need a fair slice of luck. 3♡ is forcing to game so there is no chance of stopping in 3♠ (which would in fact show four spades and maximum values, suitable for slam if responder is interested).

#3: West does not have much but it is silly to sell out to 2♠. The sequence chosen indicates merely a desire to compete for the part-score. It denies the values to invite game. Such strength is shown by a double. Add a king to the West hand and West would start with a double and remove a minimum bid to 3♡ and a maximum bid to 4♡.

#4: Even though West's action is merely competing for the part-score, opener should raise to game with all three ingredients required for a super-accept: 3+ support, maximum points and an outside doubleton.

#5: East's 3NT shows the values for game with no stopper in spades and no four hearts. With no spade stopper opposite, West does not fancy 3NT and bids 4♣, not forcing. With no aces and only two kings, East can tell to let the bidding stop in 4♣. With maximum values, West could jump to 5♣ over 3NT or bid 4♠ to show 4-4 in the minors and a maximum.

124 A. 1. 2NT. Much better than 3♢.   2. Double. Too strong for 2NT. If partner bids 2NT Lebensohl, bid 3♣ but over any other action you have enough for 3NT.   3. 4NT. This shows both minors, at least 5-5 and a 4-loser hand or better. While 4NT does entail some risk, other actions could easily see you missing game or not finding your best trump fit.   4. 3♠. Michaels cue-bid but a good hand after a weak two. You are showing 5+ hearts and a 5+ minor in a 5-loser hand or better. After a pre-empt, play partner to provide two tricks for you, and therefore deduct two losers from your own loser count to estimate the playing potential of the partnership hands. On the other side of the table, partner should not be impressed until holding more than two tricks for you.   5. Double. If partner bids 2NT Lebensohl, bid 3♠ to force to game. If partner bids 3♣ or 3♡, you have slam potential. Over 3♢ from partner, you can bid 3♡, forcing after partner has shown some values.

B. 1. 3♠. Shows five spades and around eight losers, not forcing.   2. 2NT and follow up with 3♠ to show the same values as in #1 but with only four spades. If you have 9 or 10 losers, 2♠ is enough. 3. 2NT and follow up with 3♢ over 3♣ to show a rotten hand with 4+ diamonds. 4. 3♢. By not using the 2NT route to 3♢ you are showing 4+ diamonds and about 7-10 points. 5. 2NT followed by 3NT over the 3♣ puppet. This sequence shows the values for 3NT with a double stopper in hearts. With similar values and only one stopper, bid 3NT at once.

C. 1. 3♣, as requested. No justification for any other action. If partner continues with 3♢ or 3♡, pass. If partner continues with 3♠ asking for a spade stopper, rebid 4♢.   2. 3♡. With a 4-loser hand, you are strong enough to reject the 3♣ puppet. 3♡ shows 5+ hearts and a 4-loser hand, asking partner to try for game with one trick or better. Opposite ♡K-x-x and ♣J-x-x-x you would be happy enough to reach 4♡ but if you bid 3♣, that is where you might play.   3. Bid 3♣. Although you have a very strong hand, you do have six losers. Opposite a very weak hand, game is not likely.   4. 3♠. This shows game values in a 3-loser hand or better.   5. 4♣. Shows excellent clubs in a 3-4 loser hand.

Bidding Set 37									
(1)		**(2)**		**(3)**		**(4)**		**(5)**	
WEST	**EAST**	**WEST**	**EAST**	**WEST**	**EAST**	**WEST**	**EAST**	**WEST**	**EAST**
(2♡)	Dble	(2♠) Dble	2NT	(2♠)	Dble	(2♠) 2NT	3♢	(2♡) 2NT	3♢
2♠	2NT	3♣	3♡	2NT	3♠	3♡	3NT	3♠	4♠
3NT	No	No		4♡	No	No		No	

#1: Although West has eight points, West has too many losers to push the bidding to 3♠ (via 2NT Lebensohl). 2♠ will be quite enough if partner cannot bid any higher. East's 2NT rebid shows 19-20 points, balanced. With 16-18, East would have bid 2NT at once.

#2: You may miss game occasionally by passing it out in 3♡ but most of the time 3♡ will be quite high enough. On the actual cards 4♡ is a terrible spot and East has five hearts (might have only four) and has a useful king (the hearts could be jack high or even worse). If West had the same values and four hearts, it would not be a terrible thing to take a gamble (perhaps a gambol?) at 4♡. If that goes wrong, be quick to apologise and ward off any post-mortem.

#3: No one promised you that your decisions will always be easy. East will not enjoy the 4♡ development but what else should East do over 2NT? With 23 HCP and only three losers. East must make the strongest move to reach game. East will be fearful about passing 4♡ (on a bad day West might have only four hearts) but to remove it to 5♣ is a sheer guess. 5♣ could be hopeless with 4♡ laydown. If you are going to guess, you may as well pass 4♡. Choose the guess that will give you the highest scoring result.

#4: West's 2NT shows a balanced 16-18 and spades stopped. 3♢ is a transfer to hearts, the unbid major, and 3NT offers West the choice between 3NT and 4♡.

#5: East's 3♢ is a transfer to *spades*. It makes no sense to transfer to hearts, opener's 6-card major, so after (weak two): 2NT, advancer's 3♢ bid is always the transfer to the other major. As you can transfer to the other major, you do not need a bid of 3♠ here as a natural bid. Use it as a slam try with both minors. After a transfer, partner should jump to game in advancer's major with the three super-accept ingredients: 3+ trumps, maximum values and an outside doubleton. Here West has a simple accept and East has enough to bid 4♠ with six spades and ten points.

Bidding Set 38									
(1)		**(2)**		**(3)**		**(4)**		**(5)**	
WEST	**EAST**	**WEST**	**EAST**	**WEST**	**EAST**	**WEST**	**EAST**	**WEST**	**EAST**
(2♠)	Dble	(2♥)	Dble 3♦	(2♥)	Dble	(2♥)	3♥	(2♠)	Dble 2NT
2NT	4♣	No		3♦	3♥	3♠	No	3♥	4NT
5♣	No			3NT	No			5♣	6NT
								No	

#1: With a four loser hand, East is too strong to overcall just 3♣. Start with a double and follow up with 3♠ over a 3♦ or 3♥ bid showing some values. Over 2NT, East should jump to 4♣ to show the excellent clubs and the 4-loser hand. It is true that you may miss 3NT some days but you cannot cater for everything. To rebid 3♠ over 2NT shows a better hand than this. 4♣ can be dropped, while 3♠ commits you to game. With four losers and a long minor that is not warranted. West makes a sensible decision to take a shot at 5♣ as the West hand is better than it might be. West has four clubs and need not have any. West has a probable winner with the king of hearts and potential for a ruff because of the doubleton. On the actual East-West cards, 5♣ is an excellent game.

#2: East's 3♦ shows respectable values, about 7-10 points, but it is not forcing, of course. West has no reason to push higher.

#3: The bidding starts as in #2 but this time East has enough points to make a game try. One consequence of playing Lebensohl is that you lose the natural 2NT reply to the double. That is a flaw but it is a trade-off against the benefits that flow from advancer being able to express hand strengths more accurately. Most top pairs are prepared to forego the natural 2NT reply in exchange for the Lebensohl benefits. East's 3♥ asks for a stopper in hearts and with a stopper, West bids 3NT. With no stopper in hearts, West would continue with 3♠ (3-card suit, Q-x-x or better, as 3♦ already denied four spades), 4♣ with 4+ clubs or 4♦ with extra length there and no other suit to bid. Over 3♥, West could jump to game if at the top of the range or bid 4♥ to ask partner to pick a game.

#4: 3♥ was Michaels, showing 5+ spades, a 5+ minor and a 5-loser hand or better. West would bid game with 2+ tricks so 3♠ shows a very weak hand. As East has nothing to spare, East should certainly pass. East would need a 4-loser hand to justify going to 4♠.

#5: With 4 losers, West is too strong for 3♥. Start with a double and bid the hearts next time. East bids 2NT en route to 3NT to show two stoppers in spades. West naturally thinks East has a poor hand and is looking to sign off after the 3♣ puppet. With 4 losers, West is strong enough to reject the puppet and 3♥ shows 5+ hearts and a 4-loser hand. Opposite that sort of strength, East is worth a move towards slam. If West has only four losers, East should be able to cover most of them. The jack of hearts may also be helpful in setting up extra tricks there. 4NT is RKCB setting hearts as trumps but East is intending to end in 6NT unless two key cards are missing (if so, bail out in 5♥).

129 **A.** 1. 2♥. Catering for a weak two in hearts.   2. 3♣. Forcing. Over partner's likely 3♥, bid 3♠, still forcing and follow up with 4♠ over 3NT or 4♣. If partner jumps to 4♥ over 3♣ to show Suit Quality 10, you should pass.   3. 2♠. To play opposite the probable weak two in spades. However, if partner has a weak two in hearts, you want to be in game.   4. 2NT. If partner bids 3♥, weak suit and minimum hand you should pass. If partner bids 3♣, relay with 3♦ and pass if opener bids 3♥ to show a minimum. After any other reply, you are worth game.   5. No bid. A calculated gamble but even if partner has a strong hand, game is unlikely to make.

B. 1. 3♣. Weak two in hearts. Although minimum, you have two top honours in hearts. 3♥ would show a minimum weak 2♥ with only one top honour in hearts.   2. 3♥. Speak of the devil.

3. 3♦. Showing a weak 2♠ which is maximum or which has two top honours in spades.

4. 3NT. This shows A-K-Q-x-x-x in either major. If responder is not sure which major, responder bids 4♥ and opener corrects to 4♠ with spades.   5. 4♠. Shows a maximum weak 2♠ with a suit quality of 10. Such a suit is playable opposite a singleton or a void.

C. 1. Double. Over a natural weak two, you would bid 2NT to show 16-18. Over a multi-two, where their suit is unknown, it is better to use 2NT for 19-21 balanced and double with the 16-18 balanced. If partner bids 2♥, the negative reply, you will hunt for the best part-score (here bid 2♠ over 2♥, even with just a 4-card suit). Without four spades you would rebid 2NT, if balanced, over 2♥.

2. 2NT, 19-21 balanced.   3. 2♥. Shows a sound overcall but below 16 HCP (failure to double).

4. Jump to 3♥ to show a strong 6+ suit (Suit Quality of 9+) and a 5-loser hand.

5. 3♦. An overcall at the three-level should show a decent suit and about a 6-loser hand.

	Bidding Set 39								
1.	**WEST**	**NORTH**	**EAST**	**SOUTH**	**2.**	**WEST**	**NORTH**	**EAST**	**SOUTH**
	No	2♢	No	2NT		2♢	No	2♠	No
	No	3♢	No	3♡		4♡	No	No	No
	No	3♠	No	3NT					
	No	No	No						

#1: With better than three winners, South is worth a try for game. Opposite a minimum weak 2♡, South would stop in 3♡. North's 3♢ shows spades and not the worst possible hand. 3♡ asks for further information and 3♠ shows minimum points with two top honours in spades. South knows North must have ♠A-K-x-x-x-x and virtually nothing else (since North has 6-8 HCP only). South can see nine tricks in spades and also nine tricks in 3NT. Guess what South should choose?

#2: East must not bid 2♡ which could be passed out. With game prospects opposite a weak two in hearts but not opposite a weak two in spades, bid 2♠. Partner will pass with spades, bid 3♡ with a weak 2♡ minimum and 4♡ with a weak 2♡ maximum. North-South have a good spade fit but how should North-South enter the bidding? South could bid 3♢ but West will still bid 4♡. What then for North-South? Further competitive bidding on this deal is discussed on page 131, Hand 91.

3.	**WEST**	**NORTH**	**EAST**	**SOUTH**	**4.**	**WEST**	**NORTH**	**EAST**	**SOUTH**
	2♢	No	2♡	Dble		2♢	No	2♡	No
	No	3♠	No	4♠		2♠	No	2NT	No
	No	No	No			3♠	No	4♠	All pass

#3: Treat the reply to a multi-2♢ as their opening. South therefore treats East's 2♡ as a weak 2♡ opening and doubles. You do not need 16+ points here, just what you would need to double a regular weak 2♡ opening (since responder has revealed a relatively weak hand). West's pass confirms a weak two in hearts. North replies to the double as though replying to a double of a 2♡ opening (see Chapter 22). 3♠ shows five spades and game-inviting values. 2NT in reply to the double would be Lebensohl here.

#4: East bids 2♡, expecting West to have a weak two in hearts. When West shows a weak two in spades, East has definite game prospects. 2NT over 2♠ is now regular Ogust (see Chapter 9) and 3♠ shows a maximum with two top honours in spades. Neither North nor South is worth any bid.

5.	**WEST**	**NORTH**	**EAST**	**SOUTH**	**6.**	**WEST**	**NORTH**	**EAST**	**SOUTH**
	No	2♢	Dble	2♡		2♢	No	2♡	Dble
	2♠	No	2NT	No		No	No	No	
	3♠	No	4♠	All pass					

#5: East's double shows 16+ points, any shape. South usually takes the same action over the double as over a pass by East. No bid by South would show 5+ diamonds and allow North to leave it in 2♢ with support. Redouble by South would say, 'Make the cheapest bid and pass my next bid. My suit is better than yours'. With a weak hand, West would pass 2♡ and leave further action to South. 2♠ = 4+ spades, 8+ HCP and is forcing to game. 2NT and 3♠ are natural rebids.

#6: East makes the normal 2♡ pass-or-correct reply and South doubles 2♡ for takeout. West passes to show a weak two in hearts and North passes for pleasure. You can imagine East's thoughts: 'Partner opens a lousy weak two and I have to suffer as declarer in this hopeless mess.' 2♡ doubled should be a massacre. It would have been unfortunate timing for North to make a frisky 2♡ overcall.

134 A. 1. 3♣. To play opposite the black two-suiter. With the red suits, partner will bid 3♢. At teams you should definitely pass 3♢. At pairs, passing 3♢ is also a good move although bidding 3♡ is attractive. The problem is that the opponents have an excellent spade fit and you do not want them to find it. If you bid 3♡, you give them one extra chance to enter the auction. Pass 3♢ and only one opponent has the opportunity to back in. If left in 3♢, you should score very well, whether you make it or not.

2. 3♢. To play opposite the red two-suiter. You would be delighted if partner revealed the black suits.

3. 4♡. Prepared to play in 4♡ opposite the red two-suiter and even happier to hear partner correct to 4♠ with a black two-suiter.   4. 4♢. Prepared to play 4♢ opposite the reds and good enough black suit values to welcome a correction to 4♠.   5. No bid. It's dollars to doughnuts that partner has the black suits, so stop at the lowest level with this semi-misfit. No need to drag yourself into the three-level. If it turns out that partner actually has the red suits, everyone will have a hearty laugh, the opponents as they wipe partner out and your side as you chalk up a top because they have missed 4♠. Even if partner were to go eight down, you are in front if they can make 4♠.

134 B. 1. 3♢. Minimum with spades-diamonds. 2. 3♠. Maximum with spades-diamonds.
3. 3♡. Minimum with hearts-clubs. 4. 3NT. Maximum with hearts-clubs.
5. 4♣. Maximum with six clubs.

C. 1. No bid. To bid 2♠ here is fraught with danger. Opener could easily have 5 spades and 5 hearts.
2. 3♣. Now it is overwhelmingly likely that opener has the majors.
3. 2NT. Shows 19-21 balanced. With 16-18 balanced, start with a double.
4. Double. Showing 16+ HCP and any shape, other than those suitable for a 2NT or 3NT bid.
5. Pass. If opener reveals the minors, you can then double for takeout.

Bidding Set 40								
1.	**WEST**	**NORTH**	**EAST**	**SOUTH**	**2.**	**WEST**	**NORTH**	**EAST**	**SOUTH**
	No	No	2♡	No		No	2♠	2NT	No
	3♣	No	No	Dble		3♣	No	3♡	No
	No	3♠	All pass			4♡	No	No	No

#1: 2♡ = majors or minors. West bids 3♣, pass-or-correct, intending to play in 3♡ if East has the majors. East's pass confirms the minors. It is asking a lot to expect South to bid with a balanced hand opposite a passed partner but in these auctions, it is vital to compete if short in their suit. South should treat this position as though LHO had opened 3♣: Pass: Pass. If you would bid in that auction, you should bid here as well. Therefore South should double 3♣ for takeout (much more efficient than penalty doubles in these auctions). One plus is that partner knows you have below 16 HCP (failure to double 2♢). That is why North will not get too excited and will not look to bid more than 3♠.

#2: 2♠ = red suits or black suits. 2NT = 19-21 balanced and 3♣ = Stayman.

3.	**WEST**	**NORTH**	**EAST**	**SOUTH**	**4.**	**WEST**	**NORTH**	**EAST**	**SOUTH**
	2♡	No	4♠	No		No	2♡	Dble	Rdble
	5♣	No	5♢	All pass		No	2♠	No	No
						Dble	No	2NT	No
						3NT	No	No	No

#3: 2♡ = majors or minors. With a 5-card fit for each of opener's possible combinations, responder should pre-empt to the four-level. East's 4♠ = 'Pass with the majors, bid on with the minors.' West corrects to 5♣ and East converts to 5♢. East expects 5♢ to fail (on a lucky day it might make) but it should be a good sacrifice against the probable heart game for North-South. On the actual cards, North-South can make 4♡ but how should they enter the bidding? For further discussion, see Deal 94.

#4: 2♡ = majors or minors. Double = 16+, any shape. South has little doubt about the rank of opener's suits ('very rank' would be South's thoughts). South wants to play in 2♠ but if South bids 2♠, North will naturally correct to the minors. That would push South up to 3♠, not a rosy prospect on the known misfit. That is the function of the redouble, to allow responder to escape into his own long suit. Redouble says, 'Make the cheapest bid possible and then pass my next bid.' West is happy to pass for the moment and North dutifully bids 2♠ despite the void. It is important for partner to have faith. Hope and charity are also useful attributes. East has said it all with the 16+ double and the bidding reverts to West who tries a competitive double. This is not ideal but what else can West do? West can hardly pass with 8 HCP opposite partner's 16+. North must still have faith and not run or redouble for rescue. East could leave the double in and 2♠ would be beaten. If East bids 2NT, West should raise to 3NT. With three spades and modest hearts it would not be wise to suggest a heart contract in the face of the obvious North-South misfit.

5.	**WEST**	**NORTH**	**EAST**	**SOUTH**	**6.**	**WEST**	**NORTH**	**EAST**	**SOUTH**
	2NT	No	3♢	No		No	2NT	Dble	No
	No	Dble	No	4♡		No	3♢	Dble	3♠
	No	No	No			4♡	No	4NT	No
						5♡	No	6♡	All pass

#5: 2NT = non-touching suits. 3♢ = Pass-or-correct. West's pass confirms diamonds-spades. North has enough for a takeout double showing the other two suits and South is worth 4♡. East might consider a sacrifice (5♢ is only two down) but with secondary values in clubs and hearts, pass is recommended. Perhaps 4♡ will fail.

#6: 2NT = odd suits. Dble = 16+. There is no urgency for South or West to bid yet. 3♢ = diamonds-spades and East's double = takeout of diamonds. South corrects to 3♠ and West is worth 4♡. That is enough to galvanise East into slam mode. 4NT = RKCB with hearts set as trumps.

141   Answers to exercises from Appendix 2

(a) Page 17: A. 1. 2♣ : 2◇, 2♡   2. 2◇, artificial game-force.   3. 3♡, game-force with 5-5 in the majors.   4. 2◇, game-force. 5. 2◇, game-force.

Bidding Set 3, using the 2♣ puppet to 2◇ (Appendix 2)

1. W	E	2. W	E	3. W	E	4. W	E	5. W	E	6. W	E
1♣	1♠	No	1◇	No	1◇	1◇	1♠	No	1◇	1♣	1♠
1NT	2♣	1♠	1NT	1♡	1NT	1NT	2♣	1♡	1NT	1NT	2♣
2◇	2♡	2♣	2◇	2NT	3♣	2◇	2♡	2♣	2◇	2◇	2♡
No		2NT	3NT	No		4♡	No	3◇	No	No	
		No		*2NT forces 3♣*							

Bidding Set 4, using the 2♣ puppet to 2◇ and the 2◇ artificial game force rebid (Appendix 2)

1. W	E	2. W	E	3. W	E	4. W	E	5. W	E	6. W	E
1♣	1♡	1♣	1♡	1♡	1♠	1♣	1♠	No	1♣	No	1♣
1NT	2◇	1NT	2◇	1NT	2◇	1NT	2◇	1◇	1NT	1◇	1NT
2NT	4♡	3♣	3♡	2NT	4♠	2♠	4♠	2♡	2NT	2♡	2NT
No		3NT	No	No		No		3♠	3NT	3♠	4♠
2◇ = game-force		*3♣ denies 3 hearts*		*2NT = 3-4-3-3*		*2♠ shows three*		No		No	
2NT = 3-3-3-4		*3♡ = six hearts*		*The ◇x-x makes*		*spades and a*		*West has shown a*		*West has shown a*	
		3NT = 1 heart		*East choose 4♠.*		*doubleton outside.*		*4-4-4-1 / 4-4-5-0.*		*4-4-4-1 / 4-4-5-0.*	

#3: East chooses a 2◇ rebid after 1NT, rather than 2♣, 2◇ : 3NT to show the 5-3-3-2, to discover whether West has five hearts. After West shows the 3-4-3-3, East could opt for 3NT but the two rag diamonds point to 4♠.

141   (b). Example auctions for hands 5-8, pages 18-19, if using the 2♣ puppet or 2◇ game-force after opener's 1NT rebid.

Hand 5				Hand 6				Hand 7				Hand 8			
W	N	E	S	W	N	E	S	W	N	E	S	W	N	E	S
	1◇	No	1♡			1♣	No				1◇	1♣	No	1♠	No
No	1NT	No	2♣	1♠	No	1NT	No	No	1♠	No	1NT	1NT	No	2♣	No
No	2◇	No	3♡	2♣	No	2◇	No	No	2◇	No	2♠	2◇	No	2NT	No
No	4♡	All pass		2♠	No	3NT	End	No	4♠	All pass		3NT	No	No	No
2♣ = puppet, forcing				*2♣ = puppet*				*2◇ = artificial game-force*				*2♣ = puppet*			
opener to bid 2◇.				*2♠ invites game with five*				*2♠ = three spades and not*				*2NT invites game in 3NT.*			
3♡ invites game with six				*spades.*				*a 4-3-3-3 pattern.*				*Note: Opener's heart suit is*			
hearts.												*not revealed.*			

150   Answers to exercises from Appendix 4

A. 1. 3♣ (minimum opening, no void, no strong second suit)   2. 3♡ (extra length in hearts and a strong opening). If playing 5-card majors, opener would rebid 3NT, extra strength but no extra length.
3. 3◇. Strong second suit or a void somewhere. When the strong second suit is a 4-card suit, opener should not have a minimum opening.   4. 3♣ (minimum hand; the strong club suit does not warrant a 3◇ rebid with a minimum opening; the spade singleton would be shown only with a strong opening)
5. 3◇ (void or good second suit; there is no minimum strength requirement for the 3◇ rebid when opener has a void)

B. 1. 3♡ (extra length if playing 4-card suits; if playing 5-card suits, rebid 3NT: no extra length)
2. 3♠ (showing a singleton in spades) 3. 3NT (playing a weak 1NT, the 3NT rebid shows 15-16 points balanced with only four hearts)   4. 3♡ (extra length in hearts)   5. 4◇ (singleton diamond)

C. 1. 3♠ (I have a void somewhere; 3NT will ask for the void and 4♣ will say it is in clubs)
2. 3NT (I have a strong 4-card suit in a 5-4-2-2 pattern; 4♣ asks for the suit and 4♡ says it is in clubs)
3. 4♡ (Shows a strong 5-card holding in the other major, at least K-Q-x-x-x. Since the opening was 1♡, responder can deduce that opener is at least 5 spades – 6 hearts)
4. 4◇ (strong second 5-card suit in diamonds)
5. 3♠ (void somewhere; 3NT = 'Where is it?' 4♡ = void in spades)

Exercise D: Bidding for hands 29-32, pages 54-55 (Appendix 4, page 150)

Hand 29				Hand 30				Hand 31				Hand 32			
W	**N**	**E**	**S**	**W**	**N**	**E**	**S**	**W**	**N**	**E**	**S**	**W**	**N**	**E**	**S**
	1♥	1♠	2NT			1♠	No				1♥	1♥	No	2NT	No
No	3♣	No	3◇	2NT	No	3♠	No	No	2NT	No	3♣	3♣	No	3◇	No
No	3♥	No	4♥	4♠	No	No	No	No	3◇	No	4♣	3♥	No	4♥	No
No	No	No						No	4NT	No	5♥	No	No		
								No	6♥	All pass					

#29: 2NT is still Jacoby after 1♥ : (1♠). 3♣ = minimum opening. South might sign off in 4♥ at that point. Just in case opener has a singleton spade, South inquires with 3◇ and 3♥ = no short suit but extra length in hearts. South has no further interest.

#30: 3♠ = extra spade length and a strong opening hand. With an absolute minimum, West signs off in 4♠ and as East is also minimum for the 3♠ bid, East leaves it there.

#31: 3♣ shows a minimum and North might give up in game at that point. However, it is worth making one more effort in case opener has a singleton club. 3◇ asks and 4♣ confirms the club singleton. With an ideal holding opposite the singleton, North should look for slam. 4NT = RKCB and 5♥ = two key cards, no ♥Q.

#32: 3♣ shows a minimum. Just in case opener has a singleton club, East inquires. 3♥ denies a short suit and so East settles in 4♥.

Bidding Set 41 (Appendix 4, page 150)

1. W	E	2. W	E	3. W	E	4. W	E	5. W	E	6. W	E
1♠	2NT	1♥	2NT	1♥	2NT	1♥	2NT	1♠	2NT	1♠	2NT
3♣	4♠	3♣	3◇	3♣	3◇	3◇	3♥	3◇	3♥	3♥	4♠
No		4♣	4♥	3♠	4NT	3♠	3NT	3NT	4♣	No	
3♣ = minimum		No		5◇	6♥	4◇	4NT	4♥	4NT		
				No		5♥	6♥	5♣	7♥		
						No		No			

#1: Opposite any minimum, East has no slam ambitions.

#2: When West shows a club singleton, reducing the value of East's club holding, East gives up on slam.

#3: 3♠ shows a singleton spade, music to East's ears. Opposite as little as ♥A, ◇K, ♣K, slam should be a strong chance.

#4: 3◇ = void or a second strong suit. 3♥ asks, 3♠ = a void somewhere. 3NT asks and 4◇ shows the void. Even though East has potentially wasted strength in diamonds, slam should still be a good chance opposite even a minimum opening which includes two key cards. As it is, 6♥ is a great slam

#5: 3◇ = void or good second suit. 3♥ asks, 3NT = strong 4-card suit. 4♣ asks and 4♥ = second suit is hearts. West is now known to be 5-4-2-2 with K-Q-x-x in hearts. 4NT = RKCB for spades, 5♣ = 0 or 3, obviously three on the bidding. East can see that the club loser can be discarded on the fifth round of spades and so chooses 7♥. Played in spades or no-trumps, twelve tricks will normally be the limit. The grand slam in hearts is excellent and will succeed almost all of the time even if hearts split 4-1.

#6: 3♥ = singleton heart and a strong opening (15+ HCP). The singleton heart takes away much of the value in the East hand and so East signs off. With a good or medium hand, East could bid 3♠ or make a cue-bid. West has nothing to spare, despite the good controls, and trusts partner's negative assessment. On an unlucky day, 5♠ could be too high.

Bidding Set 42 (Appendix 4, page 150)

1. W	E	2. W	E	3. W	E	4. W	E	5. W	E	6. W	E
1♠	2NT	1♠	2NT	1♠	2NT	1♡	2NT	1♡	2NT	1♠	2NT
3♣	3♦	3♣	3♦	3♠	4♣	3♦	3♡	3♦	3♡	3♦	3♡
4♣	4NT	4♣	4♠	4♦	4NT	4♣	7♡	4♣	4NT	4♦	4NT
5♦	6♠	No		5♣	5NT	No		5♦	5NT	5♠	5NT
No				6♡	7NT			6♡	7NT	6♦	7♠
3♣ = *minimum*				No				No		No	

#1: 4♣ = singleton club. That is what East had hoped to hear.

#2: This time the singleton club is not good news opposite the doubleton.

#3: 3♠ = extra length, extra strength. 4♣ / 4♦ = cue-bids. 4NT RKCB, 5♣ = 0 or 3. 5NT = all key cards are held and asking for king. 6♡ = two kings. East can count thirteen tricks and bids 7NT, not 7♠.

#4: 3♦ = void or strong second suit. 4♣ = strong 5+ clubs. 7♡ is a mild gamble but a reasonable shot.

#5: 4♣ = strong second suit is clubs. After locating one ace and two kings opposite, East can reasonably count thirteen tricks via five hearts, five clubs, two aces and one king.

#6: 4♦ = strong 5+ diamonds. 4NT RKCB, 5♠ = two key cards + the ♠Q. East knows there are no losers outside diamonds and when 5NT locates the missing king, there should be no losers at all.

152 Answers to exercises from Appendix 5

(a) Page 120: A. 1. 3♦ (Stayman)   2. 3♦ (Stayman)   3. 3♠ (no 4 spades, no heart stopper)
   4. 3NT (no 4 spades, hearts stopped)   5. 3♡ (transfer to spades)

B. 1. 3♡ (bid below their known suit = Stayman; 3♡ shows four hearts and is forcing to game)
   2. 2♠ (shows a singleton or void in their suit and a 3-suiter hand-type)
   3. 2♡ (natural, not forcing)   4. 3♦ (transfer to hearts). Follow up with 3♠, no spade stopper.
   5. 2NT (transfer to clubs, competing for the part-score).

C. 1. 3♦ (transfer to hearts). Continue with 3♠.   2. 3♦ (transfer to 3♡). Continue with 4♡.
   3. 2NT (transfer to clubs). Continue with 3♦ to force to game and showing both minors.
   4. 2NT. Follow the same path as in #3. The ambiguity in minor suit lengths cannot be avoided.
   5. 3♣ (transfer to diamonds, competing for the part-score)

(b) Bidding Set 35 when playing Rubinsohl (Appendix 5)

(1)		(2)		(3)		(4)		(5)	
WEST	EAST	WEST	EAST	WEST	EAST	WEST	EAST	WEST	EAST
1NT (2♡)	Dble	1NT (2♡)	Dble	No	1NT (2♡)	No	1NT (2♡)	1NT (2♠)	3♠
2♠	No	2NT	No	3♣	3♦	2NT	3♣	4♣	5♦
East's double is for		*East's double is for*		No		No		No	
takeout.		*takeout.*		3♣ = *transfer to ♦s*		2NT = *transfer to ♣s*		3♠ = *no four hearts,*	
								no spade stopper	

Bidding Set 36 when playing Rubinsohl (Appendix 5)

(1)		(2)		(3)		(4)		(5)	
WEST	EAST	WEST	EAST	WEST	EAST	WEST	EAST	WEST	EAST
1NT (2♡)	3♦	1NT (2♡)	3♦	No	1NT (2♠)	No	1NT (2♠)	1NT (2♠)	3♠
3NT	No	3♡	4♦	3♦	3♡	3♦	4♡	4♣	No
3♦ =*Stayman*		4♠	No*	No		No			
		*see below		3♦ =*transfer to ♡s*		3♦ =*transfer to ♡s*			

#2: 3♦ = Stayman. 3♡ = no four spades, no stopper in hearts. 4♦ = second suit. 4♠ = a sensible shot at the most likely game.

#4: Even though West's 3♦ transfer to hearts may be merely contesting the part-score, opener should jump to 4♡ with all three ingredients for a super-accept: 3+ support, maximum points and an outside doubleton.

#5: 3♠ = no spade stopper, no four hearts. With no spade stopper either, West bids 4♣ to show four or five clubs. East can tell to let the bidding stop in 4♣. If opener has no spade stopper there are two losers there and with 12-14 points, opener cannot have ♡A, ♦A and ♣A-K to make 5♣ a good bet. It is highly probable that East-West have three losers on top.

PLAY HANDS FOR NORTH

(After each hand, the dealer is given, followed by the vulnerability, e.g., S/E-W means Dealer South, East-West vulnerable.)

1 N/Nil	2 E/N-S	3 S/E-W	4 W/Both	5 N/N-S	6 E/E-W
♠10 9 5 4	♠J 7 4	♠8 4	♠A 7 5 3	♠A K 3	♠J 10 8 4
♡J 8 5	♡Q 10 5	♡A 10 7 6	♡A 8 4 2	♡10 3	♡A 10 5 4
◇8 3	◇10 6 3	◇Q J 5	◇K 3	◇A Q 8 6 2	◇9 8
♣A 10 5 2	♣K Q 10 9	♣A K 7 6	♣A K J	♣A 5 4	♣J 9 2

7 S/Both	8 W/Nil	9 N/E-W	10 E/Both	11 S/Nil	12 W/N-S
♠A K J 9 6	♠K 7	♠Q 3	♠A 8 4	♠J 10 9	♠K 10 8 3
♡8 6 2	♡9 7 5 3	♡J 9 6 4	♡A K 10 9 7	♡10 8 7 4	♡Q 10 3
◇5	◇K 8 3	◇A K Q 8	◇10 9 3 2	◇K 9 8	◇J 10 8 7
♣Q J 3 2	♣8 7 4 3	♣9 7 6	♣5	♣A Q 5	♣Q J

13 N/Both	14 E/Nil	15 S/N-S	16 W/E-W	17 N/Nil	18 E/N-S
♠A K 7 6	♠A 9 2	♠K 7 6 4	♠10 9 2	♠A 2	♠9 6 4
♡K 8 6 2	♡K 9 4	♡10 9 5	♡A K Q 3	♡A 7 5 4	♡10 5
◇Q 7 2	◇J 10 9 6	◇A 7 2	◇9 5 3	◇A 8 4 3	◇Q J 10 8 7
♣9 6	♣J 6 5	♣10 7 4	♣A 9 3	♣A K Q	♣Q 5 4

19 S/E-W	20 W/Both	21 N/N-S	22 E/E-W	23 S/Both	24 W/Nil
♠K 10 9 6 3	♠J 10 8 4 3	♠9 7 6 4	♠K Q 7 3	♠A 10 9 6	♠A K Q J 8 2
♡Q 8 7 2	♡- - -	♡- - -	♡K 7 3	♡- - -	♡K Q 3
◇9 5	◇10 7 6 4	◇A 9 8 7 3	◇A 8 6 4 2	◇10 7 6 4 3	◇- - -
♣7 4	♣Q 7 5 2	♣A 10 9 5	♣3	♣J 7 5 4	♣A Q 7 2

25 N/E-W	26 E/Both	27 S/Nil	28 W/Both	29 N/Both	30 E/Nil
♠K 7 6 4	♠A J 10 7 5	♠A K J 9	♠K J 4 2	♠10 8	♠A 6
♡A Q	♡A 10 2	♡6 5	♡9 5 3	♡Q J 8 5 4	♡6 5 3 2
◇10 7 5	◇10 8 3	◇8 7 3	◇A 9 6	◇A 10 6	◇A 9 7 5 3
♣Q 10 8 3	♣A J	♣Q 8 4 3	♣J 8 6	♣A J 10	♣Q 2

31 S/N-S	32 W/E-W	33 N/Nil	34 E/N-S	35 S/E-W	36 W/Both
♠A 2	♠10 9 7 2	♠6	♠5 3	♠7 4	♠J 10 8
♡A Q 7 4	♡8 4	♡A K J 9 8 3	♡6 5 4 2	♡J 10 9 8	♡A 9 8
◇K 7 2	◇9 8 4	◇J 10	◇K Q 10	◇K Q 9	◇A Q 10
♣9 7 6 2	♣K J 9 5	♣7 4 3 2	♣J 9 6 5	♣K J 6 5	♣10 7 5 4

37 N/N-S	38 E/E-W	39 S/Both	40 W/Both	41 N/E-W	42 E/Both
♠K Q 9 8	♠10 6 5 4	♠J 5 4	♠8 7 6 5	♠2	♠Q 10 7 5
♡10	♡8 6 3	♡K Q J 6 4 2	♡K 3	♡K Q	♡10 9
◇Q 9 3 2	◇5 3	◇Q 3	◇K Q 10 9	◇A Q J 9 8 6	◇10 9 8 6 5 3
♣K 7 6 4	♣J 8 6 4	♣J 2	♣8 7 3	♣A K Q J	♣5

43 S/Nil	44 W/N-S	45 N/Both	46 E/Nil	47 S/N-S	48 W/E-W
♠Q 10 5 3	♠J 9 5 4 3	♠K Q 10 6 3	♠J 8 7 5	♠10 8 5 2	♠A K Q 9 5 4
♡J 9 8 6 4	♡- - -	♡A J 8 7	♡- - -	♡10 9 7 2	♡A J 9 5
◇6 2	◇10 9 8 5 4	◇K 6 4	◇K Q 5 3	◇Q 10 3	◇A 4
♣10 8	♣K J 9	♣8	♣J 7 6 4 2	♣J 8	♣2

PLAY HANDS FOR NORTH

(After each hand, the dealer is given, followed by the vulnerability, e.g., W/Both means Dealer West, both sides vulnerable.)

49 N/Nil
♠ K 7 5 4 2
♥ A K 5 2
♦ A K Q
♣ A

50 E/N-S
♠ 8 7 2
♥ 10 9 8 7
♦ K J 9 6
♣ 10 2

51 S/E-W
♠ A 7 6 4
♥ 4
♦ K Q 8
♣ A 8 6 3 2

52 W/Both
♠ Q 9 5 4 3
♥ 9 8 5 3 2
♦ K Q 8
♣ - - -

53 N/N-S
♠ K 5 3
♥ K 8 4
♦ A K Q 8
♣ 5 4 3

54 E/E-W
♠ A Q 10 6 3
♥ 7 6 2
♦ A K Q
♣ J 8

55 S/Both
♠ 9 7 4
♥ - - -
♦ K 8 7 4
♣ K 7 5 4 3 2

56 W/N-S
♠ 10 9 2
♥ 8 7 6 5 4
♦ K J 10
♣ 5 2

57 N/E-W
♠ A 9 8 7
♥ A 8 2
♦ - - -
♣ K Q 10 7 6 2

58 E/Both
♠ 9 8 7 2
♥ Q J 10 6 3 2
♦ 6
♣ 4 2

59 S/Nil
♠ A K Q 10 5
♥ 9 8 2
♦ 10 2
♣ A K Q

60 W/Nil
♠ 8 4
♥ Q 10 5
♦ 10 6 2
♣ 10 9 8 5 4

61 N/Both
♠ A 8 6
♥ A K J
♦ J 10 9 5 4
♣ 8 3

62 E/Nil
♠ 8 6 4 3
♥ 4
♦ 10 9 8 7 3
♣ 8 3 2

63 S/N-S
♠ 9 4 3
♥ Q 8 5 2
♦ A 7 6
♣ A K 8

64 W/E-W
♠ J 10 8 5
♥ 9
♦ 9 8 2
♣ 10 9 5 4 3

65 N/Nil
♠ 8 6 5 4 3 2
♥ A 7 2
♦ 10
♣ K 3 2

66 E/N-S
♠ J 9 8
♥ 8 7 3
♦ A K 7 3
♣ K 5 4

67 S/E-W
♠ 7 4 3 2
♥ A J 9 8 6
♦ J 6 2
♣ J

68 W/Both
♠ K Q J 6
♥ K J 8 6
♦ A 10
♣ J 3 2

69 N/N-S
♠ Q J 5 2
♥ K 8
♦ A J 8 6 3
♣ Q 8

70 E/E-W
♠ 8 6
♥ A 9 7
♦ K 10 9 4 3 2
♣ 8 2
♠ ♥ ♦ ♣

71 S/Both
♠ K J 6 4
♥ J 10 6
♦ A K Q 10 2
♣ J

72 W/Nil
♠ A K 9 8
♥ K Q 7 5 3
♦ A J
♣ J 4

73 N/E-W
♠ 7 5 4
♥ K J 10 6
♦ A 9 8 3
♣ 6 3

74 E/Both
♠ J 7 3
♥ A K Q 9 3
♦ Q J 7
♣ K 7

75 S/Nil
♠ A J 6 5 2
♥ 9 2
♦ K J 9 5
♣ 7 5

76 W/N-S
♠ 8 6
♥ K J
♦ A J 8 4 3
♣ A K 7 4

77 N/Both
♠ Q J 5 2
♥ 9 8
♦ A J 8 6 3
♣ 5 2

78 E/Nil
♠ Q J 10 6 4
♥ 10 9 6 5
♦ A
♣ J 10 2

79 S/N-S
♠ Q
♥ J 10 9 5
♦ J 10 9 4
♣ K 9 8 6

80 W/E-W
♠ Q J 10 6 3
♥ K 3
♦ K Q 10 9 5
♣ 9

81 N/Nil
♠ K 9 7 4 3 2
♥ - - -
♦ 9 8 7 2
♣ J 10 8

82 E/N-S
♠ A 3
♥ J 3
♦ 7 3 2
♣ 9 8 6 5 4 3

83 S/E-W
♠ K 8 5 2
♥ 8 3 2
♦ A K J
♣ Q 10 5

84 W/Both
♠ Q J 6 2
♥ 5 3 2
♦ A 2
♣ A K 9 7

85 N/N-S
♠ A K Q 9 8 5
♥ 5
♦ 10 6 2
♣ 9 7 4

86 E/E-W
♠ Q J 8 7 5 2
♥ 6
♦ A J 9
♣ 9 7 4

87 S/Both
♠ 9 5
♥ 10 8 6 2
♦ 8 7 5
♣ 10 9 4 3

88 W/Nil
♠ K J 9 6 2
♥ J 9 6 5
♦ J
♣ K 6 5

89 N/E-W
♠ 8 6 4
♥ A J 8 7 6 3
♦ Q J 10
♣ 3

90 E/Both
♠ 9 3
♥ A K Q J 9 8
♦ A 3
♣ A 8 2

91 S/Nil
♠ 9 8
♥ K Q J 2
♦ 2
♣ A 10 7 5 4 3

92 W/N-S
♠ 7 5 3
♥ A K Q 9 5 3
♦ 9 8 4
♣ 2

93 N/Both
♠ A J 8
♥ J 7 5 3
♦ K 7
♣ J 8 3 2

94 E/Nil
♠ J 10
♥ K 9 8 6 5 3 2
♦ K
♣ K 8 5

95 S/N-S
♠ A K 8
♥ A Q J 10 5
♦ 7
♣ K Q 8 3

96 W/E-W
♠ Q 7
♥ A 10 9 8
♦ K 7 6
♣ 7 4 3 2

PLAY HANDS FOR EAST

(After each hand, the dealer is given, followed by the vulnerability, e.g., S/E-W means Dealer South, East-West vulnerable.)

1 N/Nil	2 E/N-S	3 S/E-W	4 W/Both	5 N/N-S	6 E/E-W
♠ A Q	♠ A Q 6	♠ 10 6 5	♠ 10 9	♠ J 10 6 5 2	♠ 7 5
♡ A Q 10 6	♡ A 9 7 2	♡ J 4	♡ K 10 6	♡ Q	♡ Q J 8
◇ K J 7 5	◇ K Q 5 2	◇ 6 4 2	◇ Q J 7 4	◇ 10 7 5	◇ A J 6 3
♣ J 8 3	♣ A 7	♣ J 10 9 3 2	♣ 7 5 3 2	♣ K 10 6 3	♣ A K Q 4

7 S/Both	8 W/Nil	9 N/E-W	10 E/Both	11 S/Nil	12 W/N-S
♠ Q 8 5	♠ J 9 6 2	♠ J 10 8	♠ J 7 6	♠ A 5 3 2	♠ 9 5 4
♡ K Q J 7	♡ A K 10	♡ A K 5	♡ 6 3 2	♡ K Q J 6	♡ 7
◇ J 9 3	◇ 7 6 2	◇ 10 9	◇ K J 5	◇ A 2	◇ K Q 9 5 3 2
♣ 9 6 4	♣ 9 6 2	♣ K Q 4 3 2	♣ 10 7 3 2	♣ 10 7 6	♣ A 7 2

13 N/Both	14 E/Nil	15 S/N-S	16 W/E-W	17 N/Nil	18 E/N-S
♠ 10 3	♠ Q 8 7 4	♠ A Q J 10 9 5	♠ 8 7	♠ Q 9	♠ K J 8 3
♡ 9 7	♡ Q 6 5	♡ K	♡ 10 9 5 4	♡ K Q 9 8	♡ K 7 6 4 2
◇ A J 10 6 3	◇ 7 4 2	◇ 9 6 4	◇ A 8 2	◇ Q 9 6 5 2	◇ 3 2
♣ J 4 3 2	♣ A K Q	♣ K Q 5	♣ Q J 10 2	♣ J 5	♣ 8 3

19 S/E-W	20 W/Both	21 N/N-S	22 E/E-W	23 S/Both	24 W/Nil
♠ J 8 5	♠ 9 7 6	♠ K 5 2	♠ 5 2	♠ 5	♠ 9 7 6
♡ J 10 9 6 4	♡ J 10 9 5 4 3	♡ A J 7 6 4	♡ J 9 8 4	♡ Q 8 3	♡ - - -
◇ K 2	◇ 8 2	◇ Q J 4 2	◇ J 10	◇ K Q 5 2	◇ Q J 10 7 4 2
♣ 10 9 5	♣ 10 6	♣ Q	♣ A K 10 5 4	♣ A K 9 3 2	♣ K J 10 5

25 N/E-W	26 E/Both	27 S/Nil	28 W/Both	29 N/Both	30 E/Nil
♠ 8	♠ 6 2	♠ 6 5 4	♠ 10 8 7	♠ A K J 5 2	♠ K Q 10 9 7
♡ 10 8 6 4	♡ K J 8 5 4	♡ A K 10 9 7	♡ A Q 8	♡ 10 6 2	♡ A Q
◇ Q 9 2	◇ J 7 6 2	◇ A 9 2	◇ 8 5 3	◇ 8 4	◇ 6 4
♣ A K J 9 4	♣ 9 2	♣ K 9	♣ A 9 7 2	♣ Q 9 6	♣ A 7 5 4

31 S/N-S	32 W/E-W	33 N/Nil	34 E/N-S	35 S/E-W	36 W/Both
♠ 8 6 5 4	♠ A 4	♠ K J 9 7	♠ A Q J 10 6 4	♠ 9 8 2	♠ Q 9 6 4
♡ 8 6 5	♡ A J 7 2	♡ 7 5 2	♡ Q 9	♡ Q 5 3	♡ K
◇ Q 9	◇ A K 10 7	◇ K Q 9 2	◇ 7 5 4	◇ A 6 4	◇ 8 7 5 4
♣ K J 8 3	♣ 8 7 4	♣ J 6	♣ 3 2	♣ A Q 7 4	♣ Q J 9 8

37 N/N-S	38 E/E-W	39 S/Both	40 W/Both	41 N/E-W	42 E/Both
♠ A 4 2	♠ A 9	♠ K 10 9	♠ J	♠ K Q 9	♠ 8
♡ A K Q 9 8 7 3	♡ Q J 10 7 5	♡ A 10 9	♡ 9 5 4 2	♡ J 10 9 8 3	♡ A K Q J 2
◇ A 4	◇ 10 6	◇ J 10 9 5 2	◇ 7 6 3	◇ 7	◇ A Q J
♣ Q	♣ Q 10 9 2	♣ 6 5	♣ A K Q J 5	♣ 8 7 4 2	♣ K Q J 2

43 S/Nil	44 W/N-S	45 N/Both	46 E/Nil	47 S/N-S	48 W/E-W
♠ 7 4	♠ 2	♠ J 8 7 5	♠ A K Q 6 4 2	♠ A J 9 6 4	♠ J 10 7 3
♡ 10 3	♡ J 7 6 5 4	♡ 9 4 3 2	♡ A 9 5 4 3	♡ 4	♡ - - -
◇ A K J	◇ A 7 3	◇ Q J 10	◇ A	◇ K 5	◇ 9 8 6 5 2
♣ 7 6 5 4 2	♣ 8 7 6 2	♣ J 3	♣ 8	♣ A K Q 5 2	♣ Q 7 6 5

PLAY HANDS FOR EAST

(After each hand, the dealer is given, followed by the vulnerability, e.g., W/Both means Dealer West, both sides vulnerable.)

49 N/Nil	50 E/N-S	51 S/E-W	52 W/Both	53 N/N-S	54 E/E-W
♠ 6	♠ A 4 3	♠ 3	♠ A J 7	♠ 1 0 9 8	♠ J 8 7 5
♡ Q 9 8 6	♡ A K Q 6 2	♡ 1 0 8 7 5	♡ J 1 0	♡ 1 0 9 7 6 5 2	♡ A K 8 3
◇ J 1 0 9 2	◇ 2	◇ 1 0 9 5 4	◇ A J	◇ 9 5	◇ 1 0 9 4 3 2
♣ Q 1 0 5 3	♣ Q 8 6 3	♣ J 1 0 7 5	♣ K Q 1 0 9 5 2	♣ 7 2	♣ - - -

55 S/Both	56 W/N-S	57 N/E-W	58 E/Both	59 S/Nil	60 W/Nil
♠ J 1 0 6 3 2	♠ K Q J 7 6 4	♠ 4 3 2	♠ A 1 0 6	♠ J 8 7 3	♠ K Q 9 7 5
♡ K 9 5 4	♡ 3	♡ K 1 0 7 5	♡ K 8 7	♡ Q J 1 0	♡ A 6
◇ A Q J 3	◇ A 7 6 5 3	◇ A 9 6 5 3	◇ J 1 0 5	◇ 9 7 5	◇ 3
♣ - - -	♣ A	♣ 5	♣ K Q 7 3	♣ J 9 4	♣ A Q 7 6 3

61 N/Both	62 E/Nil	63 S/N-S	64 W/E-W	65 N/Nil	66 E/N-S
♠ K 7 3 2	♠ Q 1 0 9 2	♠ 8 7 5 2	♠ K Q 2	♠ K J	♠ A K 1 0 4 3
♡ 1 0 8 7 4 3	♡ K J 7 3	♡ 1 0 3	♡ A J 8 6 4 3	♡ Q 1 0 8 3	♡ A 9 6 2
◇ A K 8	◇ K 4 2	◇ Q 1 0 5 3	◇ A 7	◇ K 7 5 4 3	◇ Q 6
♣ 9	♣ Q 5	♣ 7 5 2	♣ J 2	♣ A 8	♣ 9 8

67 S/E-W	68 W/Both	69 N/N-S	70 E/E-W	71 S/Both	72 W/Nil
♠ J 1 0	♠ 8 5	♠ K 7 6	♠ K 1 0 7 5	♠ 2	♠ J 1 0 3
♡ 1 0 7	♡ 1 0 5 3	♡ A Q J 6 2	♡ Q 8	♡ 9 5 2	♡ 9 6 4
◇ A Q 1 0 3	◇ K J 6 2	◇ 7	◇ A Q	◇ J 5 4 3	◇ K 1 0 5
♣ Q 1 0 9 5 3	♣ A Q 7 4	♣ K 7 5 4	♣ K 9 6 5 3	♣ K 9 4 3 2	♣ 9 8 6 5

73 N/E-W	74 E/Both	75 S/Nil	76 W/N-S	77 N/Both	78 E/Nil
♠ K Q J 6 2	♠ K 9 2	♠ Q 9 3	♠ A Q 1 0 9 5	♠ K 6 3	♠ 8 2
♡ 9 5	♡ 2	♡ K 1 0 6	♡ 6 5 2	♡ A Q J 6 5 2	♡ 8 4
◇ K 1 0 7 6	◇ A K 9 5	◇ Q	◇ 5	◇ 7 2	◇ J 8 5
♣ 1 0 8	♣ A Q 1 0 3 2	♣ A Q 1 0 9 8 3	♣ Q 1 0 9 2	♣ K 7	♣ K 8 7 5 4 3

79 S/N-S	80 W/E-W	81 N/Nil	82 E/N-S	83 S/E-W	84 W/Both
♠ K J 8 3	♠ A K 9 8 7	♠ A 1 0 5	♠ 9 8	♠ Q 1 0 9 6 4	♠ 3
♡ 3	♡ 1 0 7	♡ 7 6 3	♡ K Q 5 2	♡ 9 4	♡ K Q J 1 0 9
◇ A 8 5 3 2	◇ J 8 7 6	◇ A K 4	◇ K J 4	◇ 7 5 2	◇ J 7
♣ J 7 5	♣ Q 3	♣ Q 9 7 6	♣ K J 1 0 2	♣ K 6 4	♣ 1 0 8 6 5 4

85 N/N-S	86 E/E-W	87 S/Both	88 W/Nil	89 N/E-W	90 E/Both
♠ J 3	♠ 1 0 9 4	♠ A K 3 2	♠ 5	♠ 9 2	♠ K Q J 1 0 6 4
♡ A K	♡ K Q J 1 0 9 5	♡ J 4	♡ K Q 1 0 7 4 3	♡ K Q 1 0 5 2	♡ 3
◇ A K Q 8	◇ Q 8 4	◇ Q 9 6 2	◇ A 1 0 2	◇ A 9 5	◇ 7 6 4
♣ A K J 3 2	♣ 2	♣ Q 8 5	♣ 9 8 4	♣ 1 0 7 4	♣ Q 1 0 4

91 S/Nil	92 W/N-S	93 N/Both	94 E/Nil	95 S/N-S	96 W/E-W
♠ Q 1 0 3 2	♠ K 9 8 6	♠ K 1 0 7 5 3	♠ 6	♠ 9 4 3	♠ 8 4 2
♡ 7	♡ 7 6	♡ 1 0 6 4 2	♡ 7	♡ 7 6 4	♡ 7 5
◇ A K 9 8 4 3	◇ K Q J	◇ 9 4	◇ A Q 1 0 9 5	◇ Q 2	◇ 1 0 8 5 4 3 2
♣ K 2	♣ A 9 7 4	♣ A 5	♣ Q 1 0 9 6 4 2	♣ J 1 0 7 6 2	♣ A 5

PLAY HANDS FOR SOUTH

(After each hand, the dealer is given, followed by the vulnerability, e.g., S/E-W means Dealer South, East-West vulnerable.)

1 N/Nil
♠ J 7 3
♡ K 9 4 3
♢ Q 10 4
♣ K Q 7

2 E/N-S
♠ 9 8
♡ J 4
♢ A J 9 7
♣ J 8 5 4 2

3 S/E-W
♠ A Q J
♡ K Q 8 5
♢ A K 8 3
♣ 5 4

4 W/Both
♠ 8 6 4 2
♡ 9 5
♢ A 9 8 6
♣ Q 10 9

5 N/N-S
♠ 9 8 4
♡ A J 9 6 4 2
♢ K
♣ 9 7 2

6 E/E-W
♠ 9 3
♡ K 9 6 3
♢ K Q 5
♣ 10 8 7 3

7 S/Both
♠ 10 4 3
♡ A 9 3
♢ A 8 7 4 2
♣ A K

8 W/Nil
♠ A Q 10 5
♡ J 2
♢ Q 10 9 5 4
♣ 10 5

9 N/E-W
♠ K 7 6 5 4 2
♡ 8 7 3
♢ 5
♣ A 8 5

10 E/Both
♠ 9 5 3 2
♡ Q J 5
♢ A 8
♣ A Q J 6

11 S/Nil
♠ K Q 8
♡ A 9 5 3 2
♢ J 10 6 3
♣ 9

12 W/N-S
♠ J 6 2
♡ K J 8 6 2
♢ - - -
♣ K 10 9 6 4

13 N/Both
♠ Q J 5 4 2
♡ A Q J 3
♢ 8 4
♣ A 7

14 E/Nil
♠ K 10 6 5
♡ J 10 7 3 2
♢ 8
♣ 10 7 3

15 S/N-S
♠ - - -
♡ J 8 7 6 2
♢ Q J 10 3
♣ 9 8 3 2

16 W/E-W
♠ K Q J 4 3
♡ 7
♢ K Q J 10
♣ 7 6 5

17 N/Nil
♠ J 8 6 5 4 3
♡ 6 3 2
♢ 10 7
♣ 9 4

18 E/N-S
♠ 10 7
♡ 8 3
♢ K 9 6 5
♣ A 10 9 7 2

19 S/E-W
♠ A 7
♡ A K 3
♢ Q J 4 3
♣ A K J 2

20 W/Both
♠ A 5 2
♡ Q 8 7
♢ 9 5 3
♣ A K J 4

21 N/N-S
♠ Q J 10
♡ Q 10 3
♢ K 10 5
♣ 8 6 4 3

22 E/E-W
♠ A J 10 8 4
♡ A 6
♢ K 3
♣ J 8 7 2

23 S/Both
♠ K Q 8 7 4
♡ J 7 4 2
♢ J 9
♣ Q 10

24 W/Nil
♠ 10 5 4 3
♡ A 7 4 2
♢ 9 8 5 3
♣ 4

25 N/E-W
♠ A J 10 5 3
♡ K J 7
♢ K 4
♣ 7 6 2

26 E/Both
♠ K Q 8 4
♡ 6
♢ 9 5 4
♣ K Q 10 8 5

27 S/Nil
♠ Q 10 3
♡ 8 4 3
♢ Q J 4
♣ J 7 6 2

28 W/Both
♠ A Q 6 5
♡ 6 4
♢ K Q 7 2
♣ 10 4 3

29 N/Both
♠ 9 4 3
♡ A K 9 3
♢ K J 9 3
♣ K 5

30 E/Nil
♠ 4
♡ J 10 9 7 4
♢ Q 10 8
♣ 9 8 6 3

31 S/N-S
♠ K Q 3
♡ K J 10 9 3
♢ A 5 4 3
♣ 4

32 W/E-W
♠ K 8 5 3
♡ 10 3
♢ 6 5 3 2
♣ A 6 3

33 N/Nil
♠ A 8 5 4 3 2
♡ Q 10
♢ A 8
♣ A 8 5

34 E/N-S
♠ 8 7
♡ A K 8 7 3
♢ 9 8 6 3
♣ K 4

35 S/E-W
♠ Q J
♡ A K 6
♢ 10 8 5 3
♣ 10 8 3 2

36 W/Both
♠ 5 3
♡ Q J 10 6 3 2
♢ K J 3
♣ K 2

37 N/N-S
♠ J 10 6 5 3
♡ J 5
♢ K J 6
♣ A 10 5

38 E/E-W
♠ J 3
♡ A 9
♢ A K Q J 7 2
♣ A K 3

39 S/Both
♠ 8 3
♡ 8 7
♢ A K
♣ A K Q 9 8 7 4

40 W/Both
♠ Q 10 9 4 2
♡ 6
♢ 5 4 2
♣ 10 9 4 2

41 N/E-W
♠ J 6 5 4 3
♡ 7 5 4 2
♢ 10 4 3
♣ 6

42 E/Both
♠ 9 6 4 3
♡ 8 7 6 5 4
♢ K 7
♣ A 4

43 S/Nil
♠ A K J 6
♡ A
♢ Q 5 3
♣ A K Q J 3

44 W/N-S
♠ 10
♡ 10 8 2
♢ K Q J 6
♣ Q 10 5 4 3

45 N/Both
♠ A 9 4 2
♡ 6
♢ A 7
♣ A K Q 9 6 5

46 E/Nil
♠ 10 9
♡ Q 10 8
♢ J 9 8 6 4
♣ K 10 5

47 S/N-S
♠ - - -
♡ K Q 8 6 5 3
♢ 9 7 4
♣ 10 9 7 6

48 W/E-W
♠ 2
♡ K 6 4 3 2
♢ Q 10 7
♣ A K 9 3

PLAY HANDS FOR SOUTH

(After each hand, the dealer is given, followed by the vulnerability, e.g., W/Both means Dealer West, both sides vulnerable.)

49 N/Nil
♠ A J 8 3
♥ 7 4 3
♦ 6 5 3
♣ K 8 7

50 E/N-S
♠ J 10 9 6
♥ - - -
♦ Q 10 7 4 3
♣ J 9 5 4

51 S/E-W
♠ K 9 8 5 2
♥ A K Q 6 2
♦ 3
♣ K 9

52 W/Both
♠ K 10 8 6 2
♥ 7
♦ 6 5 3
♣ J 8 4 3

53 N/N-S
♠ A Q J 6 2
♥ J
♦ 6 4 2
♣ A K 8 6

54 E/E-W
♠ K 9 4 2
♥ Q J 5
♦ 7
♣ A K Q 9 6

55 S/Both
♠ - - -
♥ J 10 7 3
♦ 10 9 6 5 2
♣ A Q 10 8

56 W/N-S
♠ 8
♥ Q J 10 9 2
♦ 9 8
♣ K 7 6 4 3

57 N/E-W
♠ K Q J 6 5
♥ Q 9
♦ J 8 7 2
♣ A 9

58 E/Both
♠ K J 5 3
♥ A 9 5
♦ 4 2
♣ J 10 9 5

59 S/Nil
♠ 9 6 4 2
♥ A K 3
♦ A K 4
♣ 8 3 2

60 W/Nil
♠ 10 6 3
♥ J 9 8 7 4
♦ K Q 9 7 4
♣ - - -

61 N/Both
♠ Q 5
♥ 6 2
♦ 7 3 2
♣ A K Q 7 4 2

62 E/Nil
♠ K 7 5
♥ Q 10 8 2
♦ J 5
♣ J 10 9 4

63 S/N-S
♠ A Q 10
♥ A K J 7 6
♦ K 9
♣ Q 4 3

64 W/E-W
♠ 7
♥ 10 7 5
♦ Q J 10 5 3
♣ K Q 7 6

65 N/Nil
♠ A Q
♥ 6 5
♦ Q J 8 6
♣ Q 7 6 5 4

66 E/N-S
♠ 5
♥ J 10 5 4
♦ J 10 9 5
♣ A Q 7 2

67 S/E-W
♠ Q 8 6
♥ K Q 4 2
♦ 8 7
♣ A K 8 4

68 W/Both
♠ 10 9 4
♥ A Q 7 4 2
♦ 7 5
♣ 10 9 6

69 N/N-S
♠ A 8 3
♥ 10 7 5 4
♦ K Q 9 4
♣ 10 9

70 E/E-W
♠ 9 3
♥ K J 10 5 2
♦ 6 5
♣ A Q 7 4

71 S/Both
♠ 10 7 5
♥ K 8 4 3
♦ 9 8 6
♣ Q 8 7

72 W/Nil
♠ 7 6 5 4 2
♥ 8 2
♦ 9 8 4 2
♣ A 7

73 N/E-W
♠ A 9 8 3
♥ A 8 4 3
♦ 4
♣ A K J 5

74 E/Both
♠ 8 6
♥ J 10 7
♦ 10 8 4 2
♣ 9 6 5 4

75 S/Nil
♠ 10
♥ A Q 8 7 4
♦ A 7 2
♣ K J 6 2

76 W/N-S
♠ K 3 2
♥ A 9 7 4
♦ K 10 2
♣ 6 5 3

77 N/Both
♠ A 10 8 7 4
♥ 4 3
♦ 4
♣ Q J 10 9 3

78 E/Nil
♠ A K 9 7 5
♥ K 3
♦ 6 4 3
♣ Q 9 6

79 S/N-S
♠ A 5
♥ A 6 4
♦ K Q 7
♣ A Q 10 4 2

80 W/E-W
♠ 2
♥ J 6 2
♦ 4 3
♣ A J 10 8 7 6 2

81 N/Nil
♠ Q 8
♥ K Q J 10 9 4
♦ Q J 10 5
♣ 2

82 E/N-S
♠ K J 10 7 6 5 2
♥ A 10
♦ 10 8 5
♣ 7

83 S/E-W
♠ A J 7
♥ A K
♦ 8 6 4
♣ J 9 8 3 2

84 W/Both
♠ A K 7 4
♥ 8 4
♦ K Q 10 6
♣ Q 3 2

85 N/N-S
♠ 10 4
♥ Q 9 7 3
♦ J 9 5 3
♣ 10 6 5

86 E/E-W
♠ K 3
♥ A 7 3
♦ K 10 3
♣ K Q J 5 3

87 S/Both
♠ Q J 10 8 6 4
♥ K 9
♦ J 10 3
♣ 7 6

88 W/Nil
♠ A 10 4 3
♥ 8 2
♦ K Q 7 3
♣ A Q J

89 N/E-W
♠ K J 7 3
♥ 9
♦ 8 7 4
♣ K 8 6 5 2

90 E/Both
♠ A 8 7 5 2
♥ 10 7 4
♦ K 10
♣ 6 5 3

91 S/Nil
♠ K 7
♥ A 10 9 8 5 3
♦ J 7 6 5
♣ J

92 W/N-S
♠ A J 10 2
♥ 10
♦ A 10 3 2
♣ Q J 10 6

93 N/Both
♠ 4
♥ Q 8
♦ Q J 10 6 5
♣ K Q 10 9 4

94 E/Nil
♠ K 9 5 4 3
♥ A Q 10
♦ 6 2
♣ A 7 3

95 S/N-S
♠ 7 2
♥ K 8 3 2
♦ K 9 6 5
♣ A 9 4

96 W/E-W
♠ A 9 3
♥ K Q J 2
♦ A Q J 9
♣ J 9

PLAY HANDS FOR WEST

(After each hand, the dealer is given, followed by the vulnerability, e.g., S/E-W means Dealer South, East-West vulnerable.)

1 N/Nil
♠K 8 6 2
♥7 2
♦A 9 6 2
♣9 6 4

2 E/N-S
♠K 10 5 3 2
♥K 8 6 3
♦8 4
♣6 3

3 S/E-W
♠K 9 7 3 2
♥9 3 2
♦10 9 7
♣Q 8

4 W/Both
♠K Q J
♥Q J 7 3
♦10 5 2
♣8 6 4

5 N/N-S
♠Q 7
♥K 8 7 5
♦J 9 4 3
♣Q J 8

6 E/E-W
♠A K Q 6 2
♥7 2
♦10 7 4 2
♣6 5

7 S/Both
8 7 2
♥10 5 4
♦K Q 10 6
♣10 8 7 5

8 W/Nil
♠8 4 3
♥Q 8 6 4
♦A J
♣A K Q J

9 N/E-W
♠A 9
♥Q 10 2
♦J 7 6 4 3 2
♣J 10

10 E/Both
♠K Q 10
♥8 4
♦Q 7 6 4
♣K 9 8 4

11 S/Nil
♠7 6 4
♥- - -
♦Q 7 5 4
♣K J 8 4 3 2

12 W/N-S
♠A Q 7
♥A 9 5 4
♦A 6 4
♣8 5 3

13 N/Both
♠9 8
♥10 5 4
♦K 9 5
♣K Q 10 8 5

14 E/Nil
♠J 3
♥A 8
♦A K Q 5 3
♣9 8 4 2

15 S/N-S
♠8 3 2
♥A Q 4 3
♦K 8 5
♣A J 6

16 W/E-W
♠A 6 5
♥J 8 6 2
♦7 6 4
♣K 8 4

17 N/Nil
♠K 10 7
♥J 10
♦K J
♣10 8 7 6 3 2

18 E/N-S
♠A Q 5 2
♥A Q J 9
♦A 4
♣K J 6

19 S/E-W
♠Q 4 2
♥5
♦A 10 8 7 6
♣Q 8 6 3

20 W/Both
♠K Q
♥A K 6 2
♦A K Q J
♣9 8 3

21 N/N-S
♠A 8 3
♥K 9 8 5 2
♦6
♣K J 7 2

22 E/E-W
♠9 6
♥Q 10 5 2
♦Q 9 7 5
♣Q 9 6

23 S/Both
♠J 3 2
♥A K 10 9 6 5
♦A 8
♣8 6

24 W/Nil
♠- - -
♥J 10 9 8 6 5
♦A K 6
♣9 8 6 3

25 N/E-W
♠Q 9 2
♥9 5 3 2
♦A J 8 6 3
♣5

26 E/Both
♠9 3
♥Q 9 7 3
♦A K Q
♣7 6 4 3

27 S/Nil
♠8 7 2
♥Q J 2
♦K 10 6 5
♣A 10 5

28 W/Both
♠9 3
♥K J 10 7 2
♦J 10 4
♣K Q 5

29 N/Both
♠Q 7 6
♥7
♦Q 7 5 2
♣8 7 4 3 2

30 E/Nil
♠J 8 5 3 2
♥K 8
♦K J 2
♣K J 10

31 S/N-S
♠J 10 9 7
♥2
♦J 10 8 6
♣A Q 10 5

32 W/E-W
♠Q J 6
♥K Q 9 6 5
♦Q J
♣Q 10 2

33 N/Nil
♠Q 10
♥6 4
♦7 6 5 4 3
♣K Q 10 9

34 E/N-S
♠K 9 2
♥J 10
♦A J 2
♣A Q 10 8 7

35 S/E-W
♠A K 10 6 5 3
♥7 4 2
♦J 7 2
♣9

36 W/Both
♠A K 7 2
♥7 5 4
♦9 6 2
♣A 6 3

37 N/N-S
♠7
♥6 4 2
♦10 8 7 5
♣J 9 8 3 2

38 E/E-W
♠K Q 8 7 2
♥K 4 2
♦9 8 4
♣7 5

39 S/Both
♠A Q 7 6 2
♥5 3
♦8 7 6 4
♣10 3

40 W/Both
♠A K 3
♥A Q J 10 8 7
♦A J 8
♣6

41 N/E-W
♠A 10 8 7
♥A 6
♦K 5 2
♣10 9 5 3

42 E/Both
♠A K J 2
♥3
♦4 2
♣10 9 8 7 6 3

43 S/Nil
♠9 8 2
♥K Q 7 5 2
♦10 9 8 7 4
♣- - -

44 W/N-S
♠A K Q 8 7 6
♥A K Q 9 3
♦2
♣A

45 N/Both
♠- - -
♥K Q 10 5
♦9 8 5 3 2
♣10 7 4 2

46 E/Nil
♠3
♥K J 7 6 2
♦10 7 2
♣A Q 9 3

47 S/N-S
♠K Q 7 3
♥A J
♦A J 8 6 2
♣4 3

48 W/E-W
♠8 6
♥Q 10 8 7
♦K J 3
♣J 10 8 4

PLAY HANDS FOR WEST

(After each hand, the dealer is given, followed by the vulnerability, e.g., W/Both means Dealer West, both sides vulnerable.)

49 N/Nil	**50 E/N-S**	**51 S/E-W**	**52 W/Both**	**53 N/N-S**	**54 E/E-W**
♠ Q 10 9	♠ K Q 5	♠ Q J 10	♠ - - -	♠ 7 4	♠ - - -
♥ J 10	♥ J 5 4 3	♥ J 9 3	♥ A K Q 6 4	♥ A Q 3	♥ 10 9 4
♦ 8 7 4	♦ A 8 5	♦ A J 7 6 2	♦ 10 9 7 4 2	♦ J 10 7 3	♦ J 8 6 5
♣ J 9 6 4 2	♣ A K 7	♣ Q 4	♣ A 7 6	♣ Q J 10 9	♣ 10 7 5 4 3 2

55 S/Both	**56 W/N-S**	**57 N/E-W**	**58 E/Both**	**59 S/Nil**	**60 W/Nil**
♠ A K Q 8 5	♠ A 5 3	♠ 10	♠ Q 4	♠ - - -	♠ A J 2
♥ A Q 8 6 2	♥ A K	♥ J 6 4 3	♥ 4	♥ 7 6 5 4	♥ K 3 2
♦ - - -	♦ Q 4 2	♦ K Q 10 4	♦ A K Q 9 8 7 3	♦ Q J 8 6 3	♦ A J 8 5
♣ J 9 6	♣ Q J 10 9 8	♣ J 8 4 3	♣ A 8 6	♣ 10 7 6 5	♣ K J 2

61 N/Both	**62 E/Nil**	**63 S/N-S**	**64 W/E-W**	**65 N/Nil**	**66 E/N-S**
♠ J 10 9 4	♠ A J	♠ K J 6	♠ A 9 6 4 3	♠ 10 9 7	♠ Q 7 6 2
♥ Q 9 5	♥ A 9 6 5	♥ 9 4	♥ K Q 2	♥ K J 9 4	♥ K Q
♦ Q 6	♦ A Q 6	♦ J 8 4 2	♦ K 6 4	♦ A 9 2	♦ 8 4 2
♣ J 10 6 5	♣ A K 7 6	♣ J 10 9 6	♣ A 8	♣ J 10 9	♣ J 10 6 3

67 S/E-W	**68 W/Both**	**69 N/N-S**	**70 E/E-W**	**71 S/Both**	**72 W/Nil**
♠ A K 9 5	♠ A 7 3 2	♠ 10 9 4	♠ A Q J 4 2	♠ A Q 9 8 3	♠ Q
♥ 5 3	♥ 9	♥ 9 3	♥ 6 4 3	♥ A Q 7	♥ A J 10
♦ K 9 5 4	♦ Q 9 8 4 3	♦ 10 5 2	♦ J 8 7	♦ 7	♦ Q 7 6 3
♣ 7 6 2	♣ K 8 5	♣ A J 6 3 2	♣ J 10	♣ A 10 6 5	♣ K Q 10 3 2

73 N/E-W	**74 E/Both**	**75 S/Nil**	**76 W/N-S**	**77 N/Both**	**78 E/Nil**
♠ 10	♠ A Q 10 5 4	♠ K 8 7 4	♠ J 7 4	♠ 9	♠ 3
♥ Q 7 2	♥ 8 6 5 4	♥ J 5 3	♥ Q 10 8 3	♥ K 10 7	♥ A Q J 7 2
♦ Q J 5 2	♦ 6 3	♦ 10 8 6 4 3	♦ Q 9 7 6	♦ K Q 10 9 5	♦ K Q 10 9 7 2
♣ Q 9 7 4 2	♣ J 8	♣ 4	♣ J 8	♣ A 8 6 4	♣ A

79 S/N-S	**80 W/E-W**	**81 N/Nil**	**82 E/N-S**	**83 S/E-W**	**84 W/Both**
♠ 10 9 7 6 4 2	♠ 5 4	♠ J 6	♠ Q 4	♠ 3	♠ 10 9 8 5
♥ K Q 8 7 2	♥ A Q 9 8 5 4	♥ A 8 5 2	♥ 9 8 7 6 4	♥ Q J 10 7 6 5	♥ A 7 6
♦ 6	♦ A 2	♦ 6 3	♦ A Q 9 6	♦ Q 10 9 3	♦ 9 8 5 4 3
♣ 3	♣ K 5 4	♣ A K 5 4 3	♣ A Q	♣ A 7	♣ J

85 N/N-S	**86 E/E-W**	**87 S/Both**	**88 W/Nil**	**89 N/E-W**	**90 E/Both**
♠ 7 6 2	♠ A 6	♠ 7	♠ Q 8 7	♠ A Q 10 5	♠ - - -
♥ J 10 8 6 4 2	♥ 8 4 2	♥ A Q 7 5 3	♥ A	♥ 4	♥ 6 5 2
♦ 7 4	♦ 7 6 5 2	♦ A K 4	♦ 9 8 6 5 4	♦ K 6 3 2	♦ Q J 9 8 5 2
♣ Q 8	♣ A 10 8 6	♣ A K J 2	♣ 10 7 3 2	♣ A Q J 9	♣ K J 9 7

91 S/Nil	**92 W/N-S**	**93 N/Both**	**94 E/Nil**	**95 S/N-S**	**96 W/E-W**
♠ A J 6 5 4	♠ Q 4	♠ Q 9 6 2	♠ A Q 8 7 2	♠ Q J 10 6 5	♠ K J 10 6 5
♥ 6 4	♥ J 8 4 2	♥ A K 9	♥ J 4	♥ 9	♥ 6 4 3
♦ Q 10	♦ 7 6 5	♦ A 8 3 2	♦ J 8 7 4 3	♦ A J 10 8 4 3	♦ - - -
♣ Q 9 8 6	♣ K 8 5 3	♣ 7 6	♣ J	♣ 5	♣ K Q 10 8 6

WHERE TO FROM HERE?

You have come this far and you want to go further. What should you do?

1. Your partner: Find a partner whose company you enjoy and who is as keen and as ambitious as you are. There is no future if one partner is eager to work and practise and try new material and the other is happy playing the same methods that were in vogue thirty years ago. By all means enjoy a social game with social partners but if you want to do better, find an enthusiastic partner.

2. Your tournaments: Play in as tough company as you can. The harder the games, the more you will meet the methods and style that are needed for winning. Pay attention to what happens when you play against the top players. Note how they compete constantly and the actions they take. The more pleasant experts will not mind if you ask them questions about their decisions. The secure experts will even acknowledge that their decision may have been a mistake. (The theory goes that no expert ever makes a mistake: they take a 'wrong view'.)

Whether it is a club championship or a national tournament, always go over the boards after the session. Study in particular the boards on which you did badly. Never let animosity enter your *post mortems*. The aim should be to fix the mistake, not fix the blame. Both partners should approach these discussions in the spirit of 'How could we have done better? Could I have helped you more?' and not 'You botched that one, didn't you?'

3. Your bidding system: Whatever system and conventions you and partner play, make sure you know them thoroughly and that you and partner play them the same way.

4. Your practice sessions: A serious partnership puts in considerable time in bidding practice sessions normally involving just the two partners. The Bidding Challenge features in various magazines are a good source of material, although some of these focus on trap hands rather than the regular routine hands which you need to handle well.

For slam bidding practice, remove twenty low cards (10 or lower) randomly from the pack. That leaves 32 cards, which are shuffled and 13 are dealt to each partner. Do not look at the 6 cards left over. With so many high cards around, you will have game, small slam or grand slam decisions every hand. Write your auction down and each partner should describe the other's hand after the auction is over. If a misunderstanding has occurred, this is a golden opportunity to sort out the problem.

For slam, game and part-score practice, remove only 13 low cards and deal three hands of 13 cards each. Bid two of these and when finished, retain the stronger of these two and bid the third hand with this hand. This allows you to see two sets of possible problems for each of the stronger hands.

For minor suit practice, remove 13 low major suit cards and vice versa for major suit bidding practice.

5. Your behaviour at the table: This should always be impeccable. The game is tough enough without the added pressure of a critical, bickering partner. If you have such partners, get rid of them. If divorce is out of the question, arrange some other partner for your spouse.

It is best not to have any *post mortem* discussions at the table. Reserve these for later when passions have cooled. The less said during the session, the better. Do not try to teach partner at the table and never rebuke or criticise partner. You may well find later that you were the one in the wrong.

Always maintain your composure and have a bright and cheerful disposition. It is in your best interests to be supportive of partner. No one else is on your side and a happy, confident partner will play better. Isn't that what you want?

6. Your personal habits: You need to find the conditions under which you perform best. Most people play better without the effect of alcohol in the bloodstream. Try to have at least an hour's break after a solid meal before the next session. Playing on a full stomach often leads to drowsiness and careless mistakes. Sleep and fitness are also important factors for producing your best efforts.

Suggestions for further reading:
This selection is totally biased, but the following are worth reading if you have not already done so:
The Modern Losing Trick Count
50 Winning Duplicate Tips
Bid Better, Much Better After Opening 1NT
The Power of Shape
When To Bid, When To Pass
Bridge Conventions, Defences and Countermeasures
Bridge Conventions For You
Guide To Better Card Play
100 Winning Bridge Tips
Guide To Better Acol Bridge
Power Acol

My favourite authors are Kelsey, Kantar and Lawrence. You will hardly go wrong with any of their books. There are many bridge magazines around. Subscribe to as many as you can afford.

Well worth studying are the annual world championship books, an excellent source of material on the methods and styles of the world's top players.